DEVELOPING CUSTOM
DELPHI
Components

DEVELOPING CUSTOM
DELPHI
Components

Ray Konopka

 CORIOLIS GROUP BOOKS

Publisher	Keith Weiskamp
Editor	Jeff Duntemann
Cover Design	Anthony Stock
Interior Design	Bradley O. Grannis and Michelle Stroup
Production	Michelle Stroup and Cindy Tellone
Proofreader	Diane Green Cook

Trademarks: Microsoft is a trademark and Windows is a registered trademark of Microsoft Corporation. All other brand names and product names included in this book are trademarks, registered trademarks, or trade names of their respective holders.

Distributed to the book trade by IDG Books Worldwide, Inc.

Library of Congress Cataloging-in-Publication Data

Konopka, Ray
    Developing Custom Delphi Components / by Ray Konopka
        p. cm.
    Includes Index
    ISBN 1-883577-47-0: $39.99

Printed in the United States of America

10 9 8 7 6 5 4 3 2 1

CONTENTS

Chapter 2 Delphi's Object Model 19

Chapter 3 Properties 45

Chapter 4   Exception Handling in Delphi   69

Part 2   The Delphi Component Architecture   89

Chapter 5   Component Anatomy 101   91

Chapter 6   The Visual Component Library   111

Chapter 7   An Overview of the Component Building Process 141

Chapter 8   Enhancing an Existing Component   165

Part 3   Developing Components   197

Chapter 9   Graphical Components   199

Chapter 10   Custom Components from Scratch   251

Chapter 11   Dialogs and Nonvisual Components   313

Chapter 14   Property Editors and Component Editors   415

Introduction

Living half a mile from Borland's Scotts Valley headquarters was a lot of fun. I'd be walking down Hidden Drive with Mr. Byte when Philippe Kahn would jog around the bend, and Mr. Byte would bound off after his fellow Frenchman, yapping amiably until he realized that I (and my pocket full of Milk Bone) was no longer in easy begging range.

But the best part, I think, was getting to know Anders Hejlsberg, the man who wrote Turbo Pascal, Borland Pascal, and most recently, Delphi. (In fairness, I have to add that many other brilliant people like Chuck Jazdzewski have contributed heavily to recent Borland Pascal products, but Anders is their Chief Scientist and still codes the innermost heart of the compilers.) Anders, Gary Whizin, and Zack Urlocker manage the Delphi effort, and they and several other members of the Delphi team met with me for a summit at the Borland International Conference in August 1995. We spoke of many things, but after a while it came down the question of the single greatest contribution Delphi had made to programming. Gary Whizin answered immediately: "Components are objects. Case closed."

In the Delphi world, the spotlight tends to shine on other areas. Certainly, Delphi is by any measure I respect the single most productive software development package in the world today. Things really don't get any better than this—and hold the Swedish Bikini Team, thank you. Zip-zip-zip and your project is done. What could be more important than sheer speed?

Just possibly (even if it's a far tougher thing to appreciate) sheer elegance.

Elegance as I understand it is the harmonious unity of form and function, of medium and message. You can sculpt a copy of Michaelangelo's *David* out of shredded soda bottles, but the medium will definitely clash with the message. Computers have been built out of radio tubes—and there was a decade or two when that was the only way—but radio tubes are analog devices that can express digital logic only with a great deal of persuasion.

Our wobbling steps toward true software components echo this conflict at every turn. Say "software component" today, and many people reflexively reply, "VBX." Yet VBXs were never intended to be software components, or anything but custom scroll bars and push buttons for Visual Basic. A VBX is, in fact, a sort of chocolate-coated manhole cover, an odd mix of clashing elements that have been glued together with little or no thought as to any higher plan. They are tiny naked pieces of Visual Basic, dressed up in little snowsuits to enable them to survive in the outside world. They have function—if you're careful—but no *form*.

At the other end of the computational universe we have the rarefied world of the object theorists, who have been claiming for almost thirty years that objects would solve all of our programming problems, if we would only let them. The problem with objects as the computer scientists know them is that they're all message and no medium. They don't bend at the knee to any computing platform or any particular compiler, all in the interest of, well, something or other that never made much sense to me.

Object classes are much like schematic diagrams for an electronic logic circuit, like an OR gate or a NAND gate. They describe completely what the logic gate is and what it must do. You can "compile" such a schematic diagram by casting it in silicon, and what you get are teeny weeny pieces of silicon the size of a Sen-Sen, each of which is a fully realized NAND gate...but what do they plug into? How do you *use* them?

You can't. As NAND gates made of silicon, they are utterly useless...*until* you package them in a carrier with a standard pinout. Then, shazam! You have an integrated circuit that plugs into a set of common assumptions about logic, voltage levels, and physical circuit layouts that everybody understands and accepts. Lo and behold, you have the building blocks of which our digital civilization is made.

My point is that objects by themselves are completely useless without a standard context into which they can "plug." The real brilliance of Microsoft's VBX idea lay in the standard "plug board"—Visual Basic—into which VBXs could be inserted and used. The VBXs themselves are nothing special; in fact, they're rather random and hard to figure out. They must be written in rather arcane C/C++, so that the people who need and use them most (and who understand Visual Basic the best) have no hope of ever creating their own. That they've pretty much taken over the software components world is a testament to the power of a standard backplane for software components.

Delphi is such a backplane, in all the same ways that Visual Basic is. Delphi's big difference is that its backplane accepts objects, real objects—with all of the advantages that object-oriented programming brings to the table. You can customize a Delphi component—called a VCL, for the Visual Component Library—by inheriting an existing component and tweaking a couple of properties or methods. The two components are not twice as big as one alone—they share whatever code they have in common—nor is writing two twice as much work as writing one. Plus, component objects exist in a hierarchy, making them and their relationships to one another easier to understand, and thus easier to extend and build on.

Component building is definitely "advanced Delphi," but as I've always held, anything can be explained, given enough patience and skill on the part of the explainer. Ray Konopka is one very skilled explainer, and I am proud to have "discovered" him in the pages of *PC TECHNIQUES*, which is about to be reborn as *Visual Developer Magazine*. Ray's explorations of Delphi components can be seen on an ongoing basis in his "Delphi by Design" column. If you start here, and learn Object Pascal and component building from square one, you'll never get lost in your own code or anybody else's. Build it once, make it right, and use it forever—that's the component builder's motto.

Good luck, and go for it!

Jeff Duntemann KG7JF
Coriolis Group Books
Scottsdale, Arizona
November 1995

Acknowledgments

This book would not have been possible without the help and support I received from many people. First, I would like to thank Jeff Duntemann for giving me my start in professional writing. Jeff has been both an editor and a mentor for me over the past few years, and his encouragement led to this book.

I would also like to express my appreciation to Keith Weiskamp for giving me the opportunity to write this book. In addition, the entire Coriolis Group staff needs to be commended for doing such a great job in putting this book together.

Special thanks is given to Bob Ainsbury and Dan Heflin who committed a significant portion of their time to provide valuable feedback during the writing of this book. And of course, I cannot forget to thank the people over at Borland—for without Delphi, these pages would be empty.

Many people offered their support while I was writing this book, and I could not possibly name them all. However, one person does stand out. I would not have made it through this process without the support and encouragement from my lovely wife, Elizabeth.

To my lovely wife, Elizabeth

Part 1

Component Basics

Chapter 1

The Component Advantage

The Component Advantage

Don't reinvent the wheel. Create a wheel that, when necessary, reinvents itself—then use that wheel forever.

Most visual software development tools are based on selecting controls and dropping them onto a form. This is certainly powerful, but an application can only be viewed in terms of the controls that are currently available to the developer. Even though most tools allow broadening this view by adding new controls, they do not encourage *expanding* it. This is because very few visual development environments provide the means to create brand new custom controls. And even if custom controls can be created, the process is often lengthy and requires advanced Windows programming techniques (including brain-basher languages like C++) using a separate development tool.

Borland's Delphi is different. Delphi supports an unrestricted component-oriented view of your software. This is possible because custom components are created in the same environment using the same tools that are used to create applications. This, in turn, encourages developers to take pieces of their software and convert them into new custom components effectively increasing reusability for the developer, other developers on staff, or third parties.

This book will show you how to get the most out of Delphi's component architecture by walking you through the construction of over a dozen different components. So, put on your tool belt and let's get to work!

What Is a Component?

So what exactly is a component? Well, according to my *Random House College Dictionary* (revised edition, by the way) a component is defined as follows:

> **component** (kem po' nent), *adj.* **1.** being or serving as an element (in something larger); composing; constituent; *the component parts.* —*n.* **2.** a component part; constituent; *hi-fi components.* . . .

Real helpful, *not.* I included this definition to illustrate the extreme generality that is associated with the term *component.* Even within the computer industry, the term is still too generic. For example, there are hardware components and software components. Software components are generally described as being self-contained, highly cohesive modules of code that have well-defined interfaces. Of course, this definition could be applied to almost anything.

With the recent rage for visual programming, the term has been refined. Now a component is generally regarded as a binary module of code whose interface is defined by properties, methods, and events. Furthermore, these attributes can be manipulated in a visual development environment at design-time.

But even within visual programming environments, the term *component* is used to represent many different things. For example, Visual Basic Controls (VBXs) and OLE Custom Controls (OCXs) are both labeled software components, even though their implementations differ radically. Likewise, Delphi components are also called software components, and their implementation is likewise dramatically different from both VBXs and OCXs.

Components for Delphi

So for this book what we really want to ask is, "What is a Delphi component?" Defining a Delphi component really depends on your point of view. For example, application developers have a functional perspective in which a component is simply a control that is selected from the palette and dropped onto a form. From there the developer can manipulate the control using Delphi's Form Designer and Object Inspector.

However, since you're reading this book, it's probably safe to assume that your perspective is that of a component developer. In this case, defining a component is a little more involved. The purely technical definition is that a Delphi component is any object that descends from the **TComponent** class within the VCL (Visual Component Library) class hierarchy. A more practical definition is that a component is any piece of a software that you want to treat as a standard-issue "black box" chunk of functionality at design-time.

This is an important concept, because although most components are visual user interface controls, this is by no means a requirement. There are several standard components that are nonvisual, such as the Timer. The important point to remember is that a Delphi component can be any piece of software, just as long as it fits into Delphi's component framework.

What about VBXs and OCXs?

Although Delphi components, VBXs, and OCXs are all called software components, there are a lot of crucial differences between them. The most fundamental difference is that a Delphi component is not a functional specification. Instead, a Delphi component is an object, an instance of a class that exists somewhere within the VCL hierarchy. Therefore, unlike VBXs and OCXs, which can be created using any programming language that supports the construction of dynamic linked libraries (DLLs), Delphi components must be created using Delphi's native Object Pascal language.

This object-oriented approach has two main advantages. First, Delphi components are distributed as compiled source modules that are physically linked into your application's executable file, as opposed to DLLs, which continue to exist as separate files. This reduces the number of DLLs that must be installed when an application is deployed, and reduces the danger of DLL version and namespace conflicts among different applications. (What happens when two applications both install different DLLs named COMMLIB.DLL? Nothing good, believe me . . .) However, the most important advantage of this object-oriented approach is that Delphi components can serve as ancestors to new descendant components. This allows developers to create custom components derived from other custom components. You don't even need the source code for the ancestor component!

For the Future

Visual Basic controls are suffering with the migration toward Windows NT and Windows 95. This is because the VBX specification is designed around the 16-bit nature of Windows 3.X. It is possible to use VBX controls in a 32-bit environment, but a thunking (that is, memory address translation) layer is needed beneath the control, which imposes a significant performance penalty. OLE Custom Controls (OCXs) are designed to be platform independent, and VBX vendors are being encouraged to create OCX versions of their controls. This translation process is not trivial, and often requires that VBXs be redesigned and recoded from scratch.

Fortunately, Delphi components will not suffer this fate, because the Visual Component Library was originally designed with the Win32 API in mind. Therefore, Delphi components can be converted to 32-bit versions with very little effort. In fact, as long as your components do not use 16-bit specific code or make calls to Windows API functions no longer supported under Win32, then your components can be converted to 32-bit versions by simply recompiling the source code with the 32-bit version of Delphi. (Refer to Appendix A for a brief discussion regarding some of the issues involved in moving to Delphi32.)

Reasons to Build Custom Components

There are four primary reasons for building custom Delphi components. They are as follow:

- To provide additional functionality
- To support reusability
- To increase productivity
- To promote consistency

Functionality

The first and most important reason for creating a custom component is to provide functionality that the existing set of components does not provide. For example, you may need a component that is similar to one of the existing components but it does not meet all of your needs. It could be that the existing control is not data-aware, or its appearance is inconsistent with your user interface. It may in fact be that you need a component that is totally different from any existing component.

Reusability

Delphi encourages reusability through its VCL component architecture. By making it relatively easy to create custom components, Delphi encourages developers to view applications as collections of reusable building blocks. One of the best ways to promote reusability is to take isolated pieces of an application, such as a specialized edit field or even a common dialog box, and convert them into components. These components can then be used elsewhere in the same application or even in other applications with the simple click of the mouse.

Productivity

Even though it is relatively easy to change property values using Delphi's Object Inspector, changing four or five properties every time you drop a particular component on the form can be tedious. As an example, consider an OK button. Yes, there is the **Kind** property for the TBitBtn component, but I have my own bitmaps that I prefer to use as glyphs. Furthermore, the default button size is too large for my taste. (By the way, Windows 95–style buttons do not use glyphs.) After dropping a Button component on the form, five different properties must be set in order to create a standard OK button.

To eliminate the tedious task of setting these properties each time an OK button is needed, you could create a custom button component that automatically sets the five properties to the desired values. Therefore, whenever you need an OK button, all you need to do is drop your custom version on the form. There is no need to modify the properties because this is handled by the component itself.

The productivity gains realized in this way are directly proportional to the complexity of the component. For example, if in addition to setting property values, suppose you needed to specify some event handlers. As a component, this code is written only once, but used many times.

Consistency

In addition to enhancing productivity, creating custom components also aids in promoting consistency among forms and even among applications. As an example, consider a development shop where several different applications are being built. Further, suppose that each application's main window will have a status bar. To promote consistency, a status bar component could be created that specifies particular values for the **Height**, **Align**, and **Font** properties. It may even specify standard status panes within the status bar. As long as each application uses the status bar component, that aspect of the interface would be appear to be consistent across all applications produced in that shop.

How Building Components Is Different

Although components and applications are built using the same development environment, building Delphi components is quite different from building Delphi applications. The following list highlights the major differences between building components versus applications:

- Components have different end users
- Component writing is a nonvisual process
- Component writing is highly object-oriented
- Components must follow more conventions
- Components must be flexible
- Components have three different interfaces

Components Have Different End Users

Components are not used by the same people that use applications. The end users of your components will be other application developers, and they will expect

Figure 1.1

The Two Sides of Component Development.

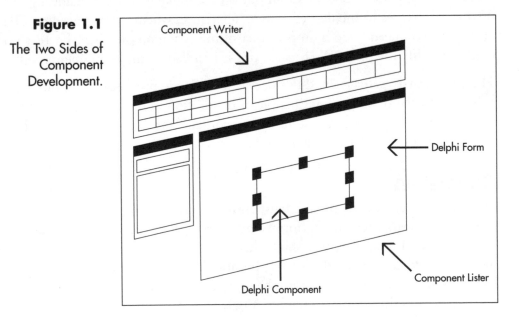

your components to behave in a certain way. Fall short of that expectation, and your components will not be used, or worse, they'll come looking for *you* to help them out! In order to ensure that you do not suffer this fate, be sure to become familiar with the components that come with Delphi.

You will also find that during the development of a component, you will jump to the other side of the computer screen and take on the role of application developer to review your component. Figure 1.1 shows these two sides of component building.

Playing the role of component user serves as a safety check. For example, it's often very useful to step back and ask yourself, "Would I use this component?" Often, the answer will be *yes*. (Let's face it, you developed it, so it must be good, right?) If you answer no, then it's time to reconsider the component's design. However, be careful with this approach. As a rule, never be your own sole expert. It's always best to get some feedback from other developers before making a design decision.

Component Writing Is a Non-Visual Process

Unlike application development in Delphi, building custom components is a nonvisual process. For example, component building is not form-based, so the Form Designer is not used. Likewise, the Object Inspector only displays information pertaining to components already registered with the Delphi development environment, so this is another visual tool that is not applicable. Instead, components are created entirely by writing Object Pascal code.

Fortunately, all is not lost. Although the visual design features of Delphi are not used when building a custom component, the same development environment is. Aside from the obvious use of the Code Editor, component development makes extensive use of the integrated debugger and the ObjectBrowser. Of course, let's not forget online help!

Component Writing Is Highly Object-Oriented

Since components are actually instances of Object Pascal classes, creating them requires a greater knowledge of object-oriented programming than is required for creating Delphi applications. Unlike application developers, component writers must have a solid understanding of key object-oriented programming techniques such as *encapsulation*, *inheritance*, and *polymorphism*.

Building a new component always involves deriving a new class from an existing component type. In essence, the Visual Component Library is extended through inheritance. Furthermore, by descending from an existing class in the hierarchy, a significant amount of functionality is immediately available to the new component type.

However, the most noticeable change between building components and applications is that while applications change values of properties and call methods of components, the component writer must write the methods and properties that define the full behavior of the component in question.

Components Must Follow More Conventions

As a nonvisual process, building components is a more traditional programming task, similar in many respects to traditional programming in Borland and Turbo Pascal. There are also more conventions that should be followed. Of course, being conventions as opposed to rules, you are not forced to follow them—although it is highly recommended that you do so.

In particular, the conventions involved in component writing help to ensure consistency. Remember that the end user of your component is an application developer— more precisely, an application developer using Delphi. Therefore, your end users will have a preconceived idea of how your (or anybody's) components will function within the Delphi environment. For example, suppose that you are creating a new component and it registers a new event in the Object Inspector. By convention, all event names should begin with the word *On*. While it is perfectly legal to use any name you chose, your users will expect to see the event names such as **OnClick.**

 Be sure to check out the *By Convention* sections located throughout the book. Each highlights a particular programming convention common to good Delphi practice.

Components Must Be Flexible

Conventions are not only associated with names, but with behaviors as well. In particular, component users are accustomed to being able to do anything they want to a component at any time. This means that you, as a component writer, need to make your components flexible enough to support this. While this task is not particularly difficult, it requires that the component be designed to support the necessary level of flexibility. Adhering to the conventions outlined in this book will help in this process.

Components Have Three Different Interfaces

When developing an application, there is only one interface of concern—the *runtime interface.* That is, the application only exists when it is being executed. Components, on the other hand, have three different interfaces that must be handled. Like applications, there is the runtime interface. The runtime interface defines how the component can be used at runtime, namely the properties, methods, and events that are available.

Unlike applications, components also have a *design-time interface.* To the component user, this is the most important interface, because this interface defines how the component behaves within the Delphi design environment. It determines which aspects of the component are visible during design.

For the component writer, the most important interface is the *developer interface,* which specifies all of the functionality present in the component. The developer interface is a superset of both the runtime and design-time interfaces. It provides access to implementation-specific elements of the component.

Road Map

This book is organized into four parts, covering virtually every aspect of component building. Although I wrote them to be read in order, each chapter is sufficiently independent to stand on its own. However, because of the dependencies among the various parts of the book, I recommend that all chapters in a particular part be read in their entirety before moving on to the next part. For example, all of the chapters in Part 3 are dependent on the information presented in Parts 1 and 2, but there is very little dependency between these chapters.

Part 1: Laying the Foundation

Part 1 focuses on the fundamental concepts that are involved in component development. The information presented here is from the perspective of the application programmer. The switch to component writer is delayed until the second part. Therefore, the information contained in the first part of this book can be applied to both component development and application development.

As we'll see in Part 2, the object model, properties, and exceptions are all used to implement Delphi's component architecture. Because of this, it is imperative that you have a solid understanding of the information presented in Part 1, specifically the object-oriented features of Delphi.

Since you are more than half through Chapter 1, I'll skip the description of this chapter.

Chapter 2 gets things rolling with a look at Delphi's object model. While it's true that component building requires object-oriented programming, this chapter does *not* attempt to teach object-oriented programming in a generic sense. Instead, Chapter 2 focuses on the syntax and mechanics of Delphi's object-oriented capabilities. This chapter is designed to get an existing BP7 or C++ programmer up to speed with the Delphi object model as quickly as possible.

Chapter 3 continues with an in-depth look at *properties*. In Delphi, properties are formally incorporated into its Object Pascal language and can be used in any class. This chapter presents the technical details behind properties, such as property declaration syntax, access methods, and internal data representation.

Part 1 concludes with Chapter 4, describing how *exceptions*, which are mechanisms for the interception and handling of error conditions, have been incorporated into the Object Pascal language. More importantly, this chapter covers the information necessary for component writers to utilize exceptions. Component writers must understand not only how to respond to exceptions, but how to create them as well.

Part 2: Building Codes

The second part of this book builds on the information presented in the first part by demonstrating how it is applied to Delphi's component architecture. That is, this part of the book describes the rules associated with building components.

Part 2 begins with a detailed look at the anatomy of a component. All components have three main characteristics: *properties*, *methods*, and *events*. Chapter 5 describes each of these in detail and explains how elements from the object model are used to implement them. Several of the conventions used in developing components are also presented in this chapter.

As mentioned earlier, the Visual Component Library is an object-oriented class hierarchy, and building custom components can be viewed as extending that hierarchy. Therefore, it is wise to obtain an understanding of how the VCL is structured and what capabilities it provides. Chapter 6 presents some of the more important VCL classes (for example, **TCanvas**, **TStringList**, etc.), as well as many of the common properties and behaviors that are shared by most typical components.

Otherwise known as the "Your First Component" chapter, Chapter 7 walks you step-by-step through the construction of a few simple components. The components are simple, but the focus is not, in this case, on the components themselves, but rather on the *process* required to create them. The process described in this chapter is used when developing *any* Delphi component, regardless of the complexity of the component. Therefore, Chapter 7 can more accurately be described as an overview of the component building process from construction through testing, all the way to registering the component with Delphi and installing it on the component palette.

Part 3: Under Construction

This is the part in the book where all of the work is being done. In the five chapters in Part 3, more than ten different custom components will be constructed.

Chapter 8 describes the process of adding functionality to an existing component by creating a new descendant class of that component. Although the components presented in Chapter 7 are also descendants (as are all components at some level), the components demonstrated here go beyond simply specifying new default values. Instead, additional properties and methods will be defined in the descendant class.

Chapter 9 focuses on graphical components. These components differ from normal Windows controls in that they never receive the input focus. This chapter describes how the **TGraphicControl** class is used to build graphic controls. Furthermore, the components presented here demonstrate the finer details of the inherited **Canvas** property.

Chapter 10 presents the issues involved in managing the input focus for a custom component. Furthermore, since components are not restricted to single controls,

Chapter 10 also demonstrates the process of building a multi-control component. To wrap up this chapter I've provided a discussion on writing a Delphi component wrapper around an existing Windows control.

Chapter 11 follows, with descriptions of dialog and nonvisual components. Both are similar in that neither type has a visual design-time interface. Creating a nonvisual component simply involves using the **TComponent** class as a base. Creating a dialog component, however, requires a little extra work to manage the display of the dialog box. However, the added work has its benefits, in that once a dialog component is written, it can be placed into a DLL. Therefore, the dialog box can be accessed by any language that can use DLLs.

One of the biggest, if not *the* biggest, areas in component development is in constructing *data-aware* components. Chapter 12 shows how to take an existing component and make it data-aware. The steps involve adding the appropriate fields, creating the data link, and responding to data changes.

Part 4: Hard Hats Required

In the final part of the book, advanced component building techniques are presented.

To start, Chapter 13 takes a much closer look at Delphi's database architecture by discussing the capabilities of *field objects*, which control the attributes of each column in a database table or result set. They are also responsible for supplying data to data-aware controls. In this chapter, the role of field objects will be extended by using them to create *data-aware business components*.

Typically, a component is viewed from the perspective of how it will behave when a program that incorporates it is executed. However, how the component behaves when the Form Designer is active is just as important. Chapter 14 describes how a component can interact with the Form Designer. In particular, this chapter will show you how to build custom property editors and component editors that can then be invoked from Delphi's design environment.

Chapter 15 focuses on debugging components. At design-time, this task can be especially tricky. This chapter presents various tips and techniques for debugging components, including tips on using Delphi's integrated debugger as well as Turbo Debugger for Windows. And if you do not have Turbo Debugger for Windows, a debugging unit is provided that allows minimal debugging at design-time.

Part 4 concludes with a discussion on the steps necessary to create professional quality components. Specifically, Chapter 16 deals with issues such as incorporating online help into your Delphi components. Distribution and installation issues are also addressed in this chapter.

Looking Ahead...

Delphi's extensible component architecture gives developers the freedom to dream up new ideas for components, and the flexibility to implement those ideas quickly and easily. To demonstrate this, during the course of this book, more than a dozen significant components will be constructed. Figure 1.2 gives a sneak preview of the components that will be created as we explore. Of course, before we can start building components, we must continue laying the foundation for further work, with an in-depth look at Delphi's object model.

Figure 1.2

A Palette Full of Components.

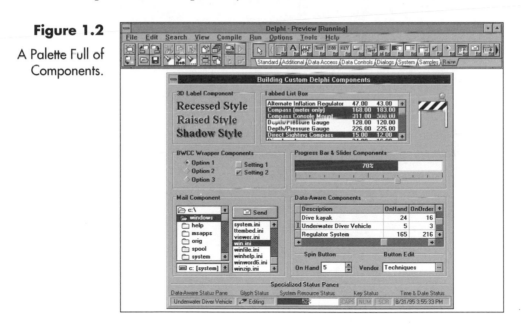

Chapter 2

Delphi's New Object Model

Delphi's New Object Model

Object Pascal has grown a great deal since Borland Pascal 7. It's now component-ready, and you'll need to become familiar with its new features.

As mentioned in the previous chapter, Delphi components are fundamentally different from other component architectures in that Delphi components are completely object-oriented. Because of this, it is imperative that a component developer have a solid understanding of the object-oriented features of Delphi.

Unfortunately, it's beyond the scope of this book to provide a detailed introductory chapter on object-oriented programming. As a result, this and the following chapter are geared towards familiarizing an experienced Delphi, Borland Pascal, or C++ programmer with Delphi's object model. If you do not have any object-oriented programming experience, or are just a little rusty, I would suggest reading *Delphi Programming Explorer* (Jeff Duntemann, Jim Mischel, and Don Taylor, Coriolis Group Books, 1995). See the Coriolis Group Books listings at the end of this book for more details on this and other relevant books from Coriolis.

Taken together, the object-oriented features of a language are commonly referred to as the language's *object model.* Delphi inherits its object model from its underlying language, Object Pascal. Object Pascal's object model is an extension of the one implemented in Borland Pascal version seven (BP7), and shares many similarities with models used in various C++ compilers.

As a result, Object Pascal as implemented in Delphi is far more powerful than BP7 without being overly complex. However, simplicity does not translate to weakness in Object Pascal. With respect to object-oriented features, Object Pascal is on par with C++. In fact, Object Pascal even provides features that are not available in any C++ product. For example, Delphi classes can be defined to include *properties,* which are formal declarations of attributes for a class. Properties are the most powerful addition to the object model, and represent a significant portion of the component architecture. As a result, all of Chapter 3 is dedicated to this topic.

Properties are not the only feature supporting the component architecture. Instead. The entire object model was specifically designed with components in mind. That is, virtually all of the enhancements made to Delphi's implementation of Pascal involved extending the BP7 object model in order to support components. As a result, every aspect of the object model is somehow affected by components, and vice-versa.

In this chapter and the next, we'll take a closer look at the mechanics behind Delphi's object model. These two chapters present a fast-paced overview of the object-oriented building blocks that are needed to create components. The goal of these two chapters is not to teach object-oriented programming, but to familiarize you with Delphi's object-oriented features and syntax. Therefore, it is necessary to have at least a basic understanding of object-oriented programming.

Before we get started, I should point out that although Delphi is a 1.0 release, the Object Pascal language is built upon Borland's award-winning Turbo Pascal compiler technology, and therefore, has many similarities with BP7. Although it is not a prerequisite to know BP7, I will make frequent references to the features of that language in order to aid those moving from BP7 to Delphi.

Delphi Has Class

Borland first introduced *object types* in version 5.5 of Turbo Pascal, and BP7 continues to use the **object** reserved word to define types from which objects are instantiated. Although accurately describing its function, object types are commonly referred to as *classes* in the larger object-oriented community that includes C++ and Smalltalk. Therefore, it is not surprising that Delphi uses the new reserved word **class** to declare object types under its new object model. These new classes have much more power and flexibility than their object type counterparts. The following code fragment shows how to declare a simple Delphi class:

```
type
  TSample = class
    Field1 : Integer;
    Field2 : string;
    procedure Method1;
    function Method2 : Integer;
  end;
```

> ## BY CONVENTION
> Class names always start with the letter 'T' and fields are declared before methods.

To declare a class that descends from **TSample**, the ancestor class is specified within parentheses following the **class** keyword. For example, the following class declaration for **TDescendant** shows that it inherits the fields and methods of the **TSample** class.

```
type
  TDescendant = class( TSample )              { TSample is the ancestor class }
    Field : Real;
    procedure Method;
  end;
```

BP7 object types can be used in the 16-bit version of Delphi by using the **object** keyword. In addition to maintaining compatibility, this allows classes and object types to coexist. Although it is not recommended that both nomenclatures be used in the same module, an application may consist of modules that utilize classes, and ones that utilize object types. However, note that object types are *not* available in the 32-bit version of Delphi and, more importantly, object types cannot be used to create components.

New Visibility Directives

A key concept in object-oriented programming is *information hiding*. The objective is to create classes in which the implementation details are hidden from the outside world. Direct access to a class' underlying data should be restricted to only those methods within the same class. These methods provide the external interface to the data. Therefore, if the implementation of the underlying data changes, users of the class are unaffected because the method interface that is used to access the data remains constant.

As a marketing student learns the "four Ps" of marketing (Product, Price, Place, Promotion), so too must a student of Delphi learn the "four Ps" of information hiding: **public**, **private**, **protected**, and **published**. These are Delphi's four visibility directives. (**Public** and **private** are carryovers from BP7, whereas **protected** and **published** are new with Delphi.) Listed below are the interface sections for two sample units that will be used to describe the rules associated with each directive. And since no object-oriented programming book would be complete without a gratuitous graphics shape example, these units represent a hierarchy of *frame* objects. Let me quickly add that the following source code is for demonstration purposes only, and will *not* be implemented. We have much more exciting things to build than this!

Listing 2.1 Interface Section for the Frames Unit

```
unit Frames;
interface

type
  TSimpleFrame = class
  private
    FSides   : TRect;
    FVisible : Boolean;
  protected
    function GetSides : TRect;
  public
    constructor Create( Bounds : TRect );
    function IsVisible : Boolean;
    procedure Hide;
    procedure Show;
    procedure Draw; virtual;
  end; {== TSimpleFrame Class Declaration ==}


  TColorFrame = class( TSimpleFrame )
  private
    FColor : TColor;
  protected
    function GetColor : TColor;
  public
```

```
    constructor Create( Bounds : TRect; AColor : TColor );
    procedure Draw; override;
  end; {== TColorFrame Class Declaration ==}

implementation
end. {=== Frames Unit ===}
```

Listing 2.2 Interface Section for the TxtFrame Unit

```
unit TxtFrame;
interface

uses
  Frames;

type
  TTextFrame = class( TColorFrame )
  private
    Text : string;
  public
    constructor Create( Bounds : TRect; AColor : TColor; AMsg : string );
    procedure Draw; override;
  end;

implementation
end. {=== TxtFrame Unit ===}
```

The least restrictive directive is **public**. Public items are visible to any program or unit that has access to the unit in which the corresponding class is defined. For example, the **IsVisible** function of **TSimpleFrame** is visible to the **TxtFrame** unit because it uses the **Frames** unit.

The most restrictive directive is **private**, which restricts visibility to the unit in which the class resides. For example, a **TSimpleFrame** object declared outside of the **Frames** unit does not have access to the **FSides** field. Likewise, the **TTextFrame.Draw** method (in the **TxtFrames** unit) *does not* have access to the **FSides** field. However, since the **TColorFrame** class resides *inside* the Frames unit, its **Draw** method does have access to **FSides**. Therefore, within a unit, **private** has the same visibility rules as **public**.

 Object Pascal has no formal implementation of C++ **friend** classes. However, because of the way the **private** directive works, all classes defined in the same unit are friends of one another.

The rules for the **protected** directive fall in between the extremes of **public** and **private**. That is, within a module, protected fields and methods follow the same rules as **private** and **public**. However, outside of the module, only the methods of descendant classes have access to protected items. Therefore, the protected data fields defined in a class in one unit can be accessed by the methods of a derived class in another unit. You don't even need the source code for the ancestor class! As an example, the **TTextFrame.Draw** method has access to its ancestor's **GetColor** method, but a **TTextFrame** object does not.

When creating classes, **private** should only be used for fields and methods that are truly class dependent. That is, class elements that must be hidden from all derived classes. Any fields or methods that a programmer might want to access via a descendant class should be declared as **protected**. If you are unsure, it is better to declare them as **protected**, thus providing access to descendant classes.

The last directive is **published**. It was not used in the sample units shown above because its visibility rules are identical to **public**. The difference between the two is that the **published** directive instructs the compiler to add extra *run-time type information* for the items that appear in that section. Because of this, fields defined in the published section must be of a class type. For example, the following class declaration is invalid:

```
type
  TSample = class
    . . .
  published
    Field1 : Integer;                    { Generates Compiler Error #200 }
  end;
```

The **published** directive is specifically designed for use in component declarations. For now it is only necessary to understand the corresponding visibility rules. The finer details of the published section will be addressed in Chapter 5.

As a final note on visibility directives, fields and methods declared immediately following the class type heading have a default visibility of published if the class is compiled in the {$M+} state or the class descends from a class that was compiled in the {$M+} state. In all other cases, the default visibility is public. For example:

```
type
  TSample = class
    Field1 : Integer;            { Field1 is public }
```

```
public
  . . .
end;

{$M+}
TSample2 = class
  Field2 : TStringList;          { Field2 is published }
public
  . . .
end;
{$M-}

TSample3 = class( TSample2 )
  Field3 : TIniFile;             { Field3 is published }
end;
```

 Always specify a visibility directive to avoid ambiguity.

BY CONVENTION

The sections of a class declaration are specified in the following order: private, protected, public, and published. (As luck would have it, remembering this is easy since the list is in alphabetical order!)

The Object Reference Model

One of the most significant changes between the object model used in BP7 and the one used in Delphi is in the way an object's memory is allocated. Under BP7 and C++, objects can be either statically or dynamically allocated. However, in Delphi, all object instances are dynamically allocated from the heap and referenced via pointers. By itself, this change would not have much impact on coding. For example, OWL programming under BP7, and OWL and MFC programming under C++ requires extensive use of dynamically allocated objects.

The impact comes from Delphi's new reference model, which simplifies the syntax for referencing the fields and methods of objects. Specifically, when you reference an object instance, Delphi automatically assumes that you want to de-reference the pointer. Therefore, the caret symbol ("^") used to de-reference pointers in Pascal is not necessary when de-referencing a Delphi object. Furthermore, it is no longer necessary to declare a separate object pointer type, which is a common practice in BP7 and C++. The following fragments in Listings 2.3 and 2.4 from the **RefMdl_B** and **RefMdl_D** programs demonstrate how object types and classes are declared and used within BP7 and Delphi, respectively.

Listing 2.3 BP7 Reference Model Program

```
program RefMdl_B;                        {= BP7's Reference Model Demonstration =}

uses
  Objects, WinCrt;

type
  PGreeting = ^TGreeting;                    { Object Pointer Type Declaration }
  TGreeting = object( TObject )                     { Descendant of TObject }
    Text : string;
    constructor Init;                  { Constructors called Init by convention }
  end;


constructor TGreeting.Init;
begin
  inherited Init;
  Text := 'Hello';                                  { Initialize Text Field }
end;

var
  Salutation : PGreeting;                       { Declare a Pointer Variable }

begin
  Salutation := New( PGreeting, Init );      { Dynamically Allocate an Object }
  Writeln( 'Greeting: ', Salutation^.Text );
  Salutation^.Text := 'Good Morning';    { Use ^ Notation to Access Text Field }
  Writeln( 'Greeting: ', Salutation^.Text );
  Dispose( Salutation );                          { Don't Forget to Clean Up }
end.
```

Listing 2.4 Delphi Reference Model Program

```
program RefMdl_D;                        {= Delphi's Reference Model Demonstration =}

uses
  WinCrt;

type                                       { Not Necessary to Create Pointer Type }
  TGreeting = class                           { Descends from TObject Implicitly }
    Text : string;
    constructor Create;                { Constructors called Create by convention }
  end;
```

```
constructor TGreeting.Create;
begin
  inherited Create;
  Text := 'Hello';                              { Initialize Text Field }
end;

var
  Salutation : TGreeting;                       { Declare an Object Variable }

begin
  Salutation := TGreeting.Create;   { Object is Created by Calling Constructor }
  Writeln( 'Greeting: ', Salutation.Text );
  Salutation.Text := 'Good Morning';            { De-referencing is Implied }
  Writeln( 'Greeting: ', Salutation.Text );
  Salutation.Free;                              { Call Free to Clean Up }
end.
```

Delphi's implicit de-referencing should look very familiar to Visual Basic programmers, who don't have to deal directly with the intricacies of pointer manipulation. However, this feature of Delphi is only valid with objects of **class** types. Standard pointer variables must still be explicitly de-referenced using the caret symbol.

A Common Ancestor

Take another look at the previous class declarations for the **TGreeting** class. Notice that under Delphi, this class does not specify an ancestor class, whereas the BP7 version descends from **TObject**. This is another new feature that distinguishes Delphi from both BP7 and C++, for *all* classes now have a common ancestor. More precisely,

```
type
  TGreeting = class
    . . .
  end;
```

is equivalent to:

```
type
  TGreeting = class( TObject )
    . . .
  end;
```

Although there are several advantages to requiring that all class have a common ancestor, the most significant is the fact that now all objects can be treated polymorphically. For example, the **AddObject** method of the standard **TStringList** class, which will be covered in detail in Chapter 6, takes two parameters. The first is a string, and the second is a **TObject**. Therefore, a **TStringList** can be used to manage a list of objects. This means that an instance of any class type can be added to a string list.

Constructors and Destructors

Once again, take a look at Listings 2.3 and 2.4. In particular, look at how the **Salutation** object is created and destroyed in both examples. The first example demonstrates the traditional usage of **New** and **Dispose** to create and destroy dynamic variables. In a C++ program, these statements would be replaced with similar calls to **new** and **delete**.

However, the second example shows how the construction and destruction of objects in Delphi has been streamlined. This streamlining is another advantage of having all classes descend from a common ancestor. In particular, **TObject** defines a standard constructor and destructor. The **Create** constructor operates like a function in that it returns a pointer to a newly allocated object. The constructor automatically allocates memory for the object instance and initializes all data fields to zero, whereas the **Destroy** destructor releases the memory and destroys the object instance.

It may seem that **Destroy** is never called in the above program. Actually, it is. It just happens to be an indirect call. Instead of directly calling **Destroy** to dispose of an object, it is safer to use the **TObject.Free** method. **Free** first checks to make sure the object was actually instantiated before attempting to call **Destroy**.

Please note that **New** and **Dispose** have not been eliminated from the Object Pascal language. These two procedures are still used to manage dynamic non-object data structures such as linked lists and integer pointers.

 Object Pascal does not support automatic construction and destruction of objects as in C++, although it sometimes looks like it does. The general rule is that whoever creates an object is responsible for destroying it when it is no longer needed.

Forward Class Declarations

There are often circumstances when it is necessary for two objects to encapsulate a reference to the other object. In BP7 and C++, both of which support static object instances, this is accomplished by encapsulating a pointer to the desired object. In the following BP7 code fragment, two pointer types are created that reference the **TSampleOne** and **TSampleTwo** object types, respectively. Each object declaration then manages a pointer to an instance of the other object type:

```
type                                           {= This is BP7 Code =}
  PSampleOne = ^TSampleOne;
  PSampleTwo = ^TSampleTwo;

  TSampleOne = object
    ObjTwo : PSampleTwo;                { Reference to a TSampleTwo Object }
    . . .
  end;

  TSampleTwo = object
    ObjOne : PSampleOne;                { Reference to a TSampleOne Object }

    . . .
  end;
```

This situation is handled quite differently in Delphi. Since it is no longer necessary to create pointer object types, the concept of creating a *forward* class declaration has been introduced. This is very similar to declaring forward procedure references in standard Pascal. However, the reserved word **class** is used instead of **forward**. For example, the following statement is a forward declaration for the **TSample** class.

```
type
  TSample = class;
```

Now **TSample** can be referenced within another class without having to be completely declared. Please note that the complete declaration of **TSample** must be specified somewhere in the same type declaration block in which the forward reference appears.

The **Controls** unit in Delphi has a fine example of how to use forward class declarations. In the code fragment that follows (taken from that unit), the **TWinControl** class must be declared as forward because the **TControl** class references the **TWinControl** class through its **FParent** field. Note that the order of the class declarations cannot be changed to eliminate the need for the forward declaration. Since **TWinControl** descends from **TControl**, it must come after the declaration of **TControl**, or **TControl** must be declared as a forward reference before **TWinControl**.

```
type                              { Beginning of a Type Declaration Block }
  TWinControl = class;                       { Forward Class Declaration }

  TControl = class( TComponent )
    FParent : TWinControl;          { Reference to Forward Class Declaration }
    . . .
  end;

  TWinControl = class( TControl )    { Declared in same Type Declaration Block }
    . . .
  end;
```

Don't be confused by the notation here. This does not result in an infinite recursion of class declarations as it would under BP7 or C++. Recall the new reference model that is utilized in Delphi—**FParent** is not a static object, but rather a pointer to an object.

Virtual Methods

Many of Delphi's object model enhancements are centered around methods. For example, several enhancements have been made to the way virtual methods are handled in Delphi. Like BP7, Delphi supports two types of virtual methods: *virtual* and *dynamic*. However, unlike BP7, Delphi uses two distinct directives to specify each type. Dynamic methods in Delphi are not specified using a variant of the **virtual** directive followed by an integer expression as in BP7. Instead, the new **dynamic** directive is used. Dynamic methods are still associated with an index, but the index is assigned automatically by the compiler.

The difference between **virtual** and **dynamic** is attributed to the structure of their corresponding method tables (VMTs versus DMTs). It's the classic speed versus size tradeoff. Dispatching dynamic methods is slightly slower than dispatching virtual methods. In turn, dynamic methods are more space efficient. However, the space efficiency gained by dynamic methods is less critical in Delphi. In Delphi, method tables are stored in the code segments, whereas BP7 stores them in the data segment.

Since Delphi uses two different directives to specify how a method is dispatched, how does this affect methods declared in descendant classes? Specifically, how does one override a virtual or dynamic method? In BP7, virtual and dynamic methods were based on the single directive, **virtual**, and obeyed the rule: *once virtual, always virtual.* (A "virtual reality," so to speak!) In Delphi, to override the functionality of an ancestor method, the new **override** directive is used. **Override** is used regardless of how the ancestor's method was declared. Consider the following program:

Listing 2.5 Demonstration of Virtual Method Overriding

```
program VMethods;

uses
  WinCrt;

type
  TBase = class
    procedure VirtualProc; virtual;
    procedure DynamicProc; dynamic;
    procedure BrokenChain; virtual;
  end;

  TDescendant = class( TBase )
    procedure VirtualProc; override;
    procedure DynamicProc; override;
    procedure BrokenChain; virtual;    { Chain Broken b/c redeclared as Virtual }
  end;

{===================}
{== TBase Methods ==}
{===================}

procedure TBase.VirtualProc;
begin
  Writeln( 'TBase.VirtualProc' );
end;

procedure TBase.DynamicProc;
begin
  Writeln( 'TBase.DynamicProc' );
end;

procedure TBase.BrokenChain;
begin
  Writeln( 'TBase.BrokenChain' );
end;

{========================}
{== TDescendant Methods ==}
{========================}
```

```
procedure TDescendant.VirtualProc;
begin
  inherited VirtualProc;
  Writeln( 'TDescendant.VirtualProc' );
end;

procedure TDescendant.DynamicProc;
begin
  inherited DynamicProc;
  Writeln( 'TDescendant.DynamicProc' );
end;

procedure TDescendant.BrokenChain;
begin
  inherited BrokenChain;
  Writeln( 'This method will not be called by TestBroken' );
end;


{= Testing Procedures =}

procedure TestVirtual( P : TBase );
begin
  P.VirtualProc;                          { Test Virtual Method Chain }
end;

procedure TestDynamic( P : TBase );
begin
  P.DynamicProc;                          { Test Dynamic Method Chain }
end;

procedure TestBroken( P : TBase );
begin
  P.BrokenChain;               { Test What Happens When Chain is Broken }
end;


var
  DescObj : TDescendant;

begin
  DescObj := TDescendant.Create;
  { TestVirtual: Displays 'TBase.VirtualProc', then 'TDescendant.VirtualProc' }
  Writeln( '{==== Testing Virtual Chain ====}' );
  TestVirtual( DescObj );

  { TestDynamic: Displays 'TBase.DynamicProc', then 'TDescendant.DynamicProc' }
  Writeln;
  Writeln( '{==== Testing Dynamic Chain ====}' );
  TestDynamic( DescObj );
                               { TestBroken: Displays 'TBase.BrokenChain' ONLY }
  Writeln;
```

```
  Writeln( '{==== Testing Broken Chain ====}' );
  TestBroken( DescObj );

  DescObj.Free;
end.
```

The **override** directive is not used simply for convenience. It is necessary to maintain the polymorphic hierarchy that is established between the two classes. For example, since the **BrokenChain** method is re-declared as **virtual** in the **TDescendant** class, the chain is broken and the call to **TestBroken** only displays "TBase.BrokenChain" as shown in Figure 2.1.

Abstract Methods

Another enhancement related to virtual methods involves the first method in a virtual method hierarchy. Specifically, Delphi has adopted a more formal way of creating *abstract methods*. (Abstract methods are commonly referred to as *pure virtual functions* in C++.) In BP7, abstract methods are created by making a call to the standard **Abstract** procedure in the base class' implementation of the method. If the method is ever executed, the **Abstract** procedure call generates a run-time error 210. Delphi takes a more formal approach to abstract methods by introducing the **abstract** directive which is placed after the method's declaration. This formal designation makes it unnecessary, and illegal, to actually define the method's implementation in the current class. For example,

```
type
  TSample = class
    . . .
    procedure SomeMethod; virtual; abstract;
  end;
```

declares a class with an abstract method. Even though **SomeMethod** is abstract, objects of **TSample** can still be created. However, if **SomeMethod** is called, a run-

Figure 2.1

Output of
VMethods
Program.

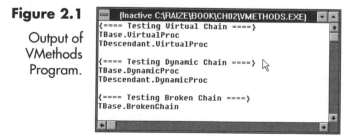

time error 210 is generated. Also note that the **abstract** directive is valid only in the class where the method is first declared, and the method must be either virtual or dynamic.

Message-Handling Methods

Delphi supports a specialized form of dynamic methods called *message-handling methods*. These methods are designed to handle Windows messages more effectively. Message-handling messages have four main characteristics:

- They are always procedures (rather than functions)
- They are declared using the new **message** directive
- They take an integer constant as a dynamic index
- They require a single variable (VAR) parameter

At first glance, message-handling methods appear similar to the *message response methods* used in BP7 OWL programs (and BC++ 3.1 OWL programs as well). However, message-handling methods are much more flexible. Consider the **MsgMain** unit in Listing 2.6. It's a partial listing of the main form unit for the **MsgMthod** sample program.

Listing 2.6 Demonstration of Message Handling Methods

```
unit MsgMain;

interface

uses
  Messages, SysUtils, WinTypes, WinProcs, Classes, Graphics, Controls,
  Forms, Dialogs, ExtCtrls, StdCtrls;

type
  TNewBevel = class( TBevel )
    procedure WMLButtonDown( var Msg : TMessage ); message wm_LButtonDown;
  end;

  TAnotherBevel = class( TNewBevel )
    procedure MouseClick( var MousePt: TWMLButtonDown ); message wm_LButtonDown;
  end;

  TForm1 = class(TForm)
    Label1 : TLabel;
    procedure FormCreate( Sender : TObject );
  public
    Bvl : TNewBevel;
  end;
```

```
var
  Form1 : TForm1;

implementation

{$R *.DFM}

procedure TNewBevel.WMLButtonDown( var Msg : TMessage );
begin
  inherited;
  Canvas.Pen.Color := clBlack;              { Draw Caption in Rectangular Frame }
  Canvas.Rectangle( Msg.LParamLo - 30, Msg.LParamHi - 10,
                    Msg.LParamLo + 30, Msg.LParamHi + 10 );
  Canvas.TextOut( Msg.LParamLo - 20, Msg.LParamHi - 8, Caption );
end;

procedure TAnotherBevel.MouseClick( var MousePt : TWMLButtonDown );
begin
  if ( MousePt.XPos < 150 ) and ( MousePt.YPos < 100 ) then
    inherited                 { Invoke Default Handling if click upper left corner }
  else
  begin                                     { else Draw Caption in Elliptical Frame }
    Canvas.Pen.Color := clBlack;
    Canvas.Ellipse( MousePt.XPos - 30, MousePt.YPos - 15,
                    MousePt.XPos + 30, MousePt.YPos + 15 );
    Canvas.TextOut( MousePt.XPos - 20, MousePt.YPos - 8, Caption );
  end;
end;

procedure TForm1.FormCreate( Sender : TObject );
begin
  Bvl := TAnotherBevel.Create( Self );        { Create a TAnotherBevel Object }
  Bvl.Parent := Self;                         { Set Parent to Show on Form }
  Bvl.SetBounds( 10, 30, 300, 200 );
  Bvl.Caption := 'Delphi';
end;

end.
```

In this example, two descendants of the **TBevel** control are created. Each class declares a message-handling method to handle the **wm_LButtonDown** message. As demonstrated in the source code, two methods handling the same message are not required to have identical method names. In fact, even the parameter names and types can be different.

There are three important points to note about message-handling methods. First, to execute the previously defined method, a variation of the **inherited** keyword is used. For example, in the **TAnotherBevel.MouseClick** method, if the user clicks in the upper left corner of the bevel, the **TNewBevel.WMLButtonDown** method is invoked by calling **inherited** without specifying a method name. Figure 2.2 shows the effect this has on the program.

Second, message-handling methods can always be specified for a class—even if the ancestor class defines a private method handling the same message. And finally, Delphi defines several custom message types that automatically extract the appropriate information from the standard Windows message structure. For example, the **TWMLButtonDown** message type is defined such that the X and Y coordinates of the mouse click, normally embedded into the low and high words of the **LParam** field of the message record, can be accessed by referencing the **XPos** and **YPos** fields, respectively.

Method Pointers

Another new feature of Delphi's Object Model is the introduction of *method pointers*. Method pointers are similar to procedure pointers. However, instead of pointing to stand-alone procedures, they must point to class methods. Method pointers are extremely useful when used between two classes. That is, one class contains a method pointer which is linked to a method of another class. This ability provides the basis for extending an object by *delegation* rather than by deriving a new object and *overriding* its methods.

This process of delegation is how Delphi supports component events (e.g. **OnClick**). Consider the following code fragments, which are taken from a simple application in which a scroll bar is used to change the number of columns that appear in a list box.

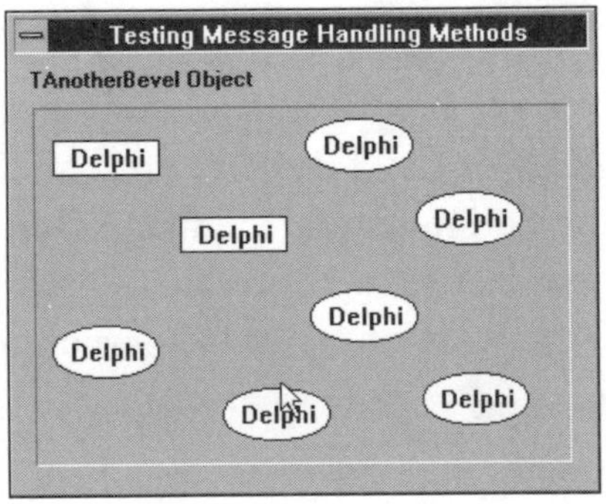

Figure 2.2

Handling the
wm_LButtonDown
Message.

```
type                                {=== Extracted from CLASSES.PAS ===}
  TNotifyEvent = procedure ( Sender : TObject ) of object;


type                                {=== Extracted from STDCTRLS.PAS ===}
  TScrollBar = class( TWinControl )
  private
    FOnChange: TNotifyEvent;
  protected
    procedure Change; dynamic;
  end;

procedure TScrollBar.Change;
begin
  if Assigned( FOnChange ) then     { Does FOnChange Point to a Method? }
    FOnChange( Self );               { If so, then execute that method }
end;


type                                {=== UNIT1.PAS Sample ===}
  TForm1 = class( TForm )
    ScrollBar1 : TScrollBar;
    ListBox1   : TListBox;
    procedure ScrollBar1Change( Sender : TObject );
  private
    { Private declarations }
  public
    { Public declarations }
  end;

procedure TForm1.ScrollBar1Change( Sender : TObject );
begin
  ListBox1.Columns := ScrollBar1.Position;
end;
```

The **TNotifyEvent** type is a method type declaration. It looks very similar to a normal procedural type declaration except that an **of object** clause is placed at the end. Therefore, any variable defined of type **TNotifyEvent** must be assigned to a method that takes a single **TObject** parameter.

The **TScrollBar** class defines a **TNotifyEvent** method pointer called **FOnChange**. Therefore, it is possible to link **FOnChange** to the **TForm1.ScrollBar1Change** method. This can be performed at run-time or at design-time using the Object Inspector. Once the link is made, whenever the user clicks on the scroll bar, the scroll bar component interprets the mouse events and eventually calls its **Change** method. The **Change** method checks to see if the **FOnChange** method pointer actually points to something. If it does, the referenced method (i.e. **ScrollBar1Change**) is executed. By using method pointers, new functionality can be added to an existing class without having to create a descendant class.

Class References and Virtual Constructors

Let's continue our discussion of methods by focusing specifically on constructors. Simply stated, in Delphi, constructors can be virtual. However, virtual constructors by themselves are not very useful. Virtual constructors do not exist in BP7 because there is no way to utilize them. So, along with virtual constructors, Delphi introduces the notion of *class reference types* (sometimes called *metaclasses*).

Consider the following, simplified version of the DynaInst demo program that ships with Delphi. Figure 2.3 shows the main and only window for the **ClassRef** sample program. The user is given the option of selecting one of three controls to create. The program itself isn't very interesting, but the code used to create the selected control is quite powerful.

Class reference types are typically used to treat a number of different classes as a single class. For example, in the method shown below, the actual control to be created is not known until the user presses the Create button. However, since all controls are descendants of the **TControl** class, it is possible to use a class reference type to create the desired control. Specifically, the **TControlClass** is declared as being a class reference type for the **TControl** class. Therefore, any instance of **TControlClass** can be assigned to any *class* that descends from **TControl**. For example, in the following code, the **Reference** variable is assigned to **TEdit** if the **OptEdit** radio button is checked by the user.

However, the key portion of this method is the point where the control is actually created. Since the type stored in the **Reference** variable is used to create the desired control, the same source code is used to create all three types of controls:

Figure 2.3

Dynamically
Creating
Control.

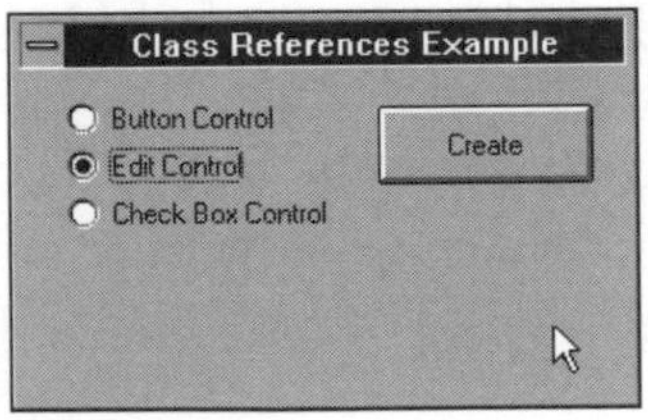

Class References Example

○ Button Control
● Edit Control   Create
○ Check Box Control

```
TControlClass = class of TControl;               { From CONTROLS.PAS File }
                                           { Class Reference Type Declaration }


procedure TForm1.BtnCreateClick( Sender : TObject );
var
  Reference : TControlClass;
  Instance  : TControl;
begin
                        { Set the Reference variable to the selected Control Type }
  if OptButton.Checked then
    Reference := TControlClass( TButton )
  else if OptEdit.Checked then
    Reference := TControlClass( TEdit )
  else
    Reference := TControlClass( TListBox );

  Instance := Reference.Create( Self );                    { Create the Control }
  Instance.Parent := Self;                 { Specify Parent, So Control Shows Up }
  Instance.Left := 50;
  Instance.Top := 100;
end;
```

Virtual constructors are very powerful indeed—especially when used with class references. Actually, it is through the same mechanism demonstrated above that Delphi's form designer is able to create components as they are dropped onto forms.

Class Methods

Next on our list of object model features is *class methods*. Class methods are like regular methods except that class methods can be executed via a class reference. Although class methods can also be called from an object instance, the implementation of class methods cannot reference any fields or normal methods of the class type. However, constructors and other class methods may be referenced. As a result, class methods usually modify global data, or return information about the class.

Class methods combine the benefits of belonging to a class with the accessibility of a normal procedure or function. Even though these methods can be called without creating an object instance, class methods are still bound by the access rights specified in the class declaration. Specifically, if a class method is declared in the **private** section, that method can only be called from within the unit that defines the class.

The following program declares a simple class that contains a class method. First, the class method is invoked without creating a **TSample** object and the returned string is displayed in the WinCrt window. The string displayed is the same one that will be displayed when **GetClassName** is called through the **AnObj** object:

```
program ClsMthod;
uses
  WinCrt;

type
  TSample = class
    ID : Integer;
    class function GetClassName : string;        { Class Method Declaration }
  end;
                                    { 'class' is also used in method definition }
  class function TSample.GetClassName : string;
  begin
    Result := 'The Sample Class';        { Not Dependent on Any Class Data }
  end;

var
  AnObj : TSample;
  S     : string;

begin
  S := TSample.GetClassName;                  { Invoke the Class Method }
  Writeln( S );                          { Displays 'The Sample Class' }

  AnObj := TSample.Create;                  { Create Obj Object Instance }
  S := AnObj.GetClassName;              { Call the Method the Normal Way }
  Writeln( S );                          { Displays 'The Sample Class' }
  AnObj.Free;
end.
```

The class method syntax does impose a restriction in Delphi that does not exist in BP7. In BP7 it is possible to execute a method that is defined in any earlier ancestor class, even if the method has been overridden in the immediate ancestor class. However, since the syntax for doing this and calling a class method are identical, this feature has been removed from Delphi. Therefore, only methods from the immediate ancestor can be executed by using the **inherited** keyword.

Runtime Type Information

When dealing with polymorphism and hierarchies of classes, there are many times when it is necessary to determine the type of object to which an object pointer points. In BP7, this is accomplished, to some extent, using the **TypeOf** function.

The **TypeOf** function returns a pointer to an object's VMT. This value is then compared to the value returned from **TypeOf** for particular type. If the VMT pointers match, the pointer points to an object of that type. The following BP7 example demonstrates this:

```
if TypeOf( P^ ) = TypeOf( TSomeObj ) then          {= This is BP7 Code =}
  { P points to TSomeObj object }
else
  { P points to some other object }
```

Unfortunately, this process only works if you are looking for an exact match. Assignment compatibility between objects extends to descendent classes as well. If you simply want to determine whether an object is assignment compatible with a given object type using **TypeOf**, you would have to test all descendant object types for a match as well.

Fortunately, Delphi provides an easier way to do this, through r*untime type information* (RTTI). More precisely, the new **is** operator provides access to RTTI to determine if an object's type is that of a particular class or one of its descendants. The **is** operator is a Boolean operator that takes as arguments an object instance and a class type. For example, the following method can be used to implement a Copy toolbar button.

```
procedure TForm1.SpeedButton1Click( Sender : TObject );
begin
  if ActiveControl is TCustomEdit then
    TCustomEdit( ActiveControl ).CopyToClipboard;
end;
```

The **is** operator is used to check if the currently active control is a descendant of **TCustomEdit**. If **ActiveControl** is compatible with **TCustomEdit** (for example, **TEdit**, **TMemo**, **TMaskEdit**), then the **CopyToClipboard** method is called.

Delphi also provides the new **as** operator which uses RTTI to ensure safe type-casting. The statement **ActiveControl as TCustomEdit** is roughly equivalent to **TCustomEdit(ActiveControl)**. However, the **as** operator goes an extra step to ensure that the typecast is valid. If the typecast cannot be made, an **EInvalidCast** exception is raised. (Exceptions will be covered in Chapter 4.)

The **as** operator is used quite extensively in the VCL code, especially in **with..do** blocks. For example,

```
with ActiveControl as TCustomEdit do . . .
```

is often used in place of

```
if ActiveControl is TCustomEdit then
  with TCustomEdit( ActiveControl ) do . . .
```

Looking Ahead...

As you can see, Delphi's object model is quite extensive—and we haven't even finished covering it yet. The discussion continues in the next chapter, with the most significant feature of Delphi's object model, *properties*.

Chapter 3

Properties

Properties

CHAPTER 3

Delphi's properties add tremendous power to the Object Pascal object model by implementing "smart data" that can execute code when it is read from or written to.

In the previous chapter, the basics of Delphi's object model were presented in such a way that those of you familiar with Borland Pascal or some variation of C++ would be able to get on board quickly. This chapter wraps up Delphi's object model by focusing on a feature not found in any other language: *properties*. Properties play such an important role in component development that I need an entire chapter to provide adequate coverage.

Logical Properties

The notion of a property is not a new concept. On the contrary, properties are very familiar to object-oriented programmers. This is partly due to the fact that things in the real world, which classes are designed to mimic, possess properties. Properties are characteristics or traits that distinguish one object from others. For example, two bookcases can be uniquely identified by finding the differences in their properties such as *color*, *height*, and *shelf count*. Even if two bookcases are the same style and color, and have the same number of shelves, they can still be differentiated by their *location*. Therefore, location is another property.

In other languages, properties of a class are usually represented by data fields. Since information hiding is always desired, these data fields are typically declared in the **private** section. In this case, the property data can be accessed only through publicly declared methods. These methods are called *access methods*.

Listing 3.1 shows a BP7 program that implements a bookcase object, complete with properties. This program, albeit simple, demonstrates how traditional languages implement properties and, more importantly, how those properties are used in a program. The goal of this sample program is to create a three shelf bookcase with a width of thirty inches and a depth of ten inches. After the number of shelves is modified, the total shelf space (in square inches) in calculated.

Listing 3.1 BP7 Implementation of Properties

```
program BP7Book;

uses
  WinCrt;

type
  TBookcase = object              { BP7 Program! Notice use of object not class }
  private
    Width       : Integer;                        { Property Value Holders }
    ShelfCount : Integer;
  public
    Depth : Integer;                                   { Public property }

    procedure Init( W, D, C : Integer );
    function GetWidth : Integer;                       { Access Methods }
    procedure SetWidth( Value : Integer );
    function GetShelfCount : Integer;
    procedure SetShelfCount( Value : Integer );
  end;



{======================}
{== TBookcase Methods ==}
{======================}

procedure TBookcase.Init( W, D, C : Integer );
begin
  Width := W;
  Depth := D;
  ShelfCount := C;
end;

function TBookcase.GetWidth : Integer;
begin
  GetWidth := Width;
end;

procedure TBookcase.SetWidth( Value : Integer );
begin
  Width := Value;
end;


function TBookcase.GetShelfCount : Integer;
begin
```

```
    GetShelfCount := ShelfCount;
end;

procedure TBookcase.SetShelfCount( Value : Integer );
begin
  ShelfCount := Value;
end;


var
  Bookcase   : TBookcase;
  ShelfSpace : Integer;

begin
  Bookcase.Init( 30, 10, 3 );                    { 30" Wide, 10" Deep, and 3 Shelves }
  Bookcase.SetShelfCount( 5 );                         { Change Shelf count to 5 }
  with Bookcase do
    ShelfSpace := GetWidth * Depth * GetShelfCount;
  Writeln( 'Shelf Space = ', ShelfSpace );
end.
```

Since the data fields for **Width** and **ShelfCount** are declared as private, the only way to modify their values is through the use of their respective **get** and **set** methods. On the other hand, since **Depth** is a public field, it can be modified directly.

Now some of you might suggest handling all of the properties in the same manner as **Depth**—eliminate their access methods and make them public. For an example like this, I would have to agree. However, I would also argue that there are several advantages to using the access methods. First and foremost is that by keeping the data fields private, their implementations can change without affecting anything outside of the class. This is the same argument that has been used to promote object-oriented programming in general. You might, for example, store the bookshelf's dimensions in metric measurements internally, but provide separate methods to return those dimensions as either English or metric values, as desired. Later on, if you decide to store the dimensions as English values, the view from *outside* the object does not change at all.

Access methods also provide the means to perform additional work during the assignment or retrieval of a property value. This additional work is commonly referred to as *side effects*. Incorporating side effects adds a tremendous amount of flexibility to your property, especially when the class is used in a visual environment. For example, if our bookcase has a visual representation and we were utilizing a side effect, then by changing the **Width**, the visual representation would be updated by the **SetWidth** method.

Formal Properties

In Delphi, properties have a more formal role than they do in other languages. The reason for this is that Delphi incorporates the notion of properties directly into its object model. So, along with data fields and methods, a class may contain property declarations. Properties provide a layer on top of the access methods described above. Yes, Delphi properties also depend on access methods. However, unlike the traditional OOP approach, these access methods are never called directly from an object instance. Instead, the corresponding property is used to invoke the desired access method.

An example will help explain this. The program in Listing 3.2 is functionally equivalent to the BP7 version in Listing 3.1 except that this new version utilizes Delphi properties. First of all, take a close look at the new class declaration for **TBookcase**. The class still contains data fields to hold the values of the corresponding properties, and access methods to alter that data. However, the most noticeable difference is that the **public** section is now filled with property declarations.

Listing 3.2 Delphi Implementation of Properties

```
program Book1;

uses
  WinCrt;

type
  TBookcase = class
  private
    FWidth      : Integer;                        { Internal Data Fields }
    FDepth      : Integer;
    FShelfCount : Integer;
     function GetWidth : Integer;                    { Access Methods }
    procedure SetWidth( Value : Integer );
    procedure SetDepth( Value : Integer );
    function GetShelfSpace : Integer;
  public
    property Width : Integer read GetWidth write SetWidth;
    property Depth : Integer read FDepth write SetDepth;
    property ShelfCount : Integer read FShelfCount write FShelfCount;

    property ShelfSpace : Integer read GetShelfSpace;     { Read Only Property }
  end;
```

```
{=====================}
{-- TBookcase Methods --}
{=====================}


function TBookcase.GetWidth : Integer;
begin
  Result := FWidth;                               { Reference Private Field }
end;

procedure TBookcase.SetWidth( Value : Integer );
begin
  if Value <> FWidth then
    FWidth := Value;                              { Reference Private Field }
end;


procedure TBookcase.SetDepth( Value : Integer );
begin
  if Value <> FDepth then            { Don't change unless new value is }
    FDepth := Value;                        { different from current value }
end;


function TBookcase.GetShelfSpace : Integer;
begin
  Result := FWidth * FDepth * FShelfCount;       { Calculate Total Shelf Area }
end;


var
  Bookcase : TBookcase;

begin
  Bookcase := TBookcase.Create;                     { Use default constructor }
  with Bookcase do
  begin
    Width := 30;                                { Assignment using property }
    Depth := 10;
    ShelfCount := 5;
    Writeln( 'Shelf Space = ', ShelfSpace );   { Reference ShelfSpace Property }
  end;
end.
```

As in the BP7 version, the **TBookcase** class declares three properties: **Width**, **Depth**, and **ShelfCount**. However, in this example, we use the reserved word **property** to specify the public interface of the class. A property declaration has the following syntax:

```
property PropName : PropType read GetMethod write SetMethod;
```

There are four key pieces of information to the property declaration. First is the property name. This identifier is used throughout your source code to reference the property value. This gives properties the appearance of data fields, but the similarity is in appearance only. Each property declaration must also specify the property's type. This is specified in typical Pascal fashion—following the property name and a colon.

Following the name and type specification is the read clause. The **read** directive is used to indicate the method that will be used to retrieve the property's value. The method must be a function whose return type is the same as the property's type. Following the read clause is the write clause in which the **write** directive is used to specify which method will be used to assign a value to the property. The method must be a procedure which has a single parameter. Of course, the parameter's type and that of the property must match. Furthermore, both read and write access methods must reside in the same class as the property. It is not possible to specify a stand-alone function or procedure in either clause.

The main program block of Listing 3.2 demonstrates that Delphi properties are used in the same manner as an object's data fields. However, looks can be deceiving. Whenever the property is referenced, the compiler translates the statement into an appropriate method call. For example, to assign a value to the **Width** property, simply use an assignment statement.

```
Bookcase.Width := 36;
```

However, note well: The compiler translates this statement into the following statement:

```
Bookcase.SetWidth( 36 );
```

To retrieve the property's value, simply reference the property name. For example:

```
W := Bookcase.Width;
```

Likewise, the compiler translates this statement into the following:

```
W := Bookcase.GetWidth;
```

Internal Data Storage

The private data fields in **TBookcase** provide the internal data storage for all of the properties used by this class. These fields actually hold the values of the properties. Recall that a property is simply a processing layer on top of the access methods and does not have any data storage of its own.

> **By Convention**
>
> A property's internal data storage field starts with the letter *F* followed by the property name. For example, the internal data field for the **Height** property is **FHeight**.

In this particular class, the data types of the private data fields and their corresponding properties are equivalent. Although this is a common arrangement, it is not a requirement. In fact, it is not even necessary for a property to have an individual storage field. A property may represent a conceptual value that is derived from other values, as the following example demonstrates.

Consider a thermometer class that has a single data field that stores temperature. Further suppose that the temperature is stored using the Kelvin temperature scale. The Kelvin scale is similar to the Celsius scale in that a temperature change of one degree is the same in both scales. However, in the Kelvin scale there are no negative temperatures. Zero degrees Kelvin represents absolute zero, which is equivalent to -459.69°F.

Although the Kelvin scale is used quite extensively in the scientific community, most people would not find it very useful. One does not often come across absolute zero. Heck, even the winters in my home town of Chicago rarely get that cold! Therefore, the thermometer class declares two properties, **Celsius** and **Fahrenheit**, to accommodate general users. However, these properties do not need their own data storage. Instead, the access methods for each property convert the internal Kelvin temperature value using an appropriate conversion formula.

Take another look at the class declaration for **TBookcase**. Specifically, notice the usage of the visibility directives. Since the internal data fields are part of the implementation of the property, they appear in the **private** section. How does this affect descendant classes? Since these data fields are implementation dependent, there is no reason to have these fields visible to descendants. Instead, a descendant should access the property itself and not the internal representation.

This allows the original class to change the internal representation without affecting descendant classes.

Direct Access

The three main property declarations from the **TBookcase** class have been rewritten below so that we may focus on a feature that is available when a property *does* have an internal data field.

```
property Width : Integer read GetWidth write SetWidth;
property Depth : Integer read FDepth write SetDepth;
property ShelfCount : Integer read FShelfCount write FShelfCount;
```

The **Width** property follows the standard format described above by specifying both a read and write access method. However, the **Depth** property only specifies a write access method. In its read clause, the internal data field is specified instead. This causes the property value to be retrieved directly from the private data field. Since side effects are rare in the implementation of a read access method, it is very common to declare properties in this manner. The only requirement for doing so is that the internal data field and the property must be of the same type.

The write access method can also be replaced with a reference to an internal data field. The **ShelfCount** property avoids using access methods altogether by specifying the **FShelfCount** field in both the read and write clauses. Although it appears that there is nothing gained from doing this, there are times when providing a simple property layer is quite advantageous, but we will save that discussion for Chapter 5.

Access Methods

In real estate, the three most important features of a property are location, location, location. In Delphi, the three most important features of a property are access, access, access. As alluded to earlier, properties represent a programming interface on top of a set of access methods. Ultimately, the property is used by the developer as a conduit to the property's data. How that conduit gets to the data is governed by the access methods.

Read Methods

So far, we have seen that access methods are responsible for managing the underlying data that supports a property. A read access method, if specified, must be a function that takes no parameters and returns a value which has the same type as the property. Since the read access method can be a function, properties can be any type that can be returned by a function.

In Delphi, functions can return all types except old style objects types (using the **object** keyword) and file types. Note that classes are not exempt from being returned from a function. This means that a property could be an object instance of a class. In fact, object properties are used quite extensively in the VCL. For example, the common **Font** property is an instance of the **TFont** class which in turn, has its own properties.

The **GetWidth** read method shown in Listing 3.2 simply returns the value stored in **FWidth**. Because this type of read access is very common, read methods are usually replaced with direct access references to the data field as described in the previous section. Read methods are necessary when a property does not have an internal data field, or when the data must be manipulated before it can be delivered to the caller.

Consider the **GetShelfSpace** access method. This method is used by the **ShelfSpace** property and demonstrates two important features. First, there is no data field corresponding to **ShelfSpace**. Instead, the **GetShelfSpace** method calculates the property value by multiplying the area of each shelf by the number of shelves. Second, only a read clause is specified for this property. This makes **ShelfSpace** a *read-only* property. (Since there is no single data value representing the shelf space, this makes sense. You can only change the shelf space value by changing the dimensions of the shelves themselves.) Therefore, the **ShelfSpace** property cannot appear on the left hand side of an assignment statement.

> ### By Convention
> Read access methods start with *Get* followed by the property name while write access methods start with *Set* followed by the property name. For example, the access methods for the **Height** property would be **GetHeight** and **SetHeight**.

Write Methods

Turning our focus to the write clause, a write access method, if specified, must be a procedure that takes a single parameter. This parameter may be either a variable or value parameter, but must be of the same type as the property. Write methods are more common than read methods because of the frequent need to invoke side-effects.

Although the main goal of a write method is to assign a new value to the property's internal storage field, it is often desirable to perform other tasks that are affected by a change in the property. For example, the following write method for the **Height** property ensures that a change in height will be reflected in the display by making a call to **Invalidate**, which will force the object to redraw itself.

```
procedure SetHeight( Value : Integer );
begin
  if Value <> FHeight then              { Only Change if Value is Different }
  begin
    FHeight := Value;
    Invalidate;           { Side-effect:  Make sure display reflects new height }
  end;
end;
```

In the above method, notice that the property data is only modified if the new value is different than the current value. This type of processing is very common in write methods and helps to avoid unnecessary assignments and redundant side-effects that would otherwise waste considerable processing time.

If a property only specifies a write clause, the property becomes a *write-only* property. A write-only property's value can be modified, but it cannot be retrieved. Not surprisingly then, write-only properties are very rare and generally not very useful.

 Since a property can be used within the methods of a class, it is very easy to get into an infinitely recursive situation. For example, the following **SetHeight** method is infinitely recursive because the new value is assigned to the property value, which results in another call to **SetHeight**, and so on.

```
procedure SetHeight( Value : Integer );
begin
  if Value <> FHeight then
  begin
    Height := Value; { WARNING! Assigning Value to Property! }
    Invalidate;
  end;
end;
```

To avoid this problem, assign the new value to the internal data field, **FHeight**.

Array Properties

Not all properties can be represented by a single value. For example, suppose we want to add a new property to the **TBookcase** class that allows us to label each shelf. If the number of shelves in the bookcase were fixed, then we could create a set of properties to manage the shelf labels—one label per shelf. However, if the bookcase can have any number of shelves, it is not possible to create a separate property for each shelf.

Fortunately, this problem can be solved using *array properties*. Array properties allow multiple property values to be referenced using the same property name. Each value is referenced by specifying a different index into the array. Listing 3.3 shows the source code for the **Book2** program. This program demonstrates a new version of the **TBookcase** class which implements the proposed **ShelfLabels** array property. Figure 3.1 shows the output from this program.

Listing 3.3 TBookcase with an Array Property

```
program Book2;

uses
  WinCrt;

type
  TShelfLabels = array[ 0..10 ] of string;

  TBookcase = class
  private
    FWidth       : Integer;                        { Internal Data Fields }
    FDepth       : Integer;
    FShelfCount  : Integer;
    FShelfLabels : TShelfLabels          { Internal Array to Hold Shelf Labels }
     function GetWidth : Integer;                          { Access Methods }
    procedure SetWidth( Value : Integer );
    procedure SetDepth( Value : Integer );
    function GetShelfSpace : Integer;
    function GetShelfLabels( Index : Integer ) : string;
    procedure SetShelfLabels( Index : Integer; const Value : string );
  public
    constructor Create;
    property Width : Integer read GetWidth write SetWidth;
    property Depth : Integer read FDepth write SetDepth;
    property ShelfCount : Integer read FShelfCount write FShelfCount;
    property ShelfSpace : Integer read GetShelfSpace;
```

```
    { Array Property }
    property ShelfLabels[ Index : Integer ] : string read GetShelfLabels
                                            write SetShelfLabels;
  end;


{=======================}
{-- TBookcase Methods --}
{=======================}


constructor TBookcase.Create;
begin
  inherited Create;
  FShelfCount := 5;
end;

function TBookcase.GetWidth : Integer;
begin
  Result := FWidth;
end;

procedure TBookcase.SetWidth( Value : Integer );
begin
  if Value <> FWidth then
    FWidth := Value;
end;


procedure TBookcase.SetDepth( Value : Integer );
begin
  if Value <> FDepth then
    FDepth := Value;
end;


function TBookcase.GetShelfSpace : Integer;
begin
  Result := FWidth * FDepth * FShelfCount;
end;


function TBookcase.GetShelfLabels( Index : Integer ) : string;
begin
  Result := FShelfLabels[ Index ];          { Read Value from Internal Array }
end;

procedure TBookcase.SetShelfLabels( Index : Integer; const Value : string );
begin
  if Value <> FShelfLabels[ Index ] then
    FShelfLabels[ Index ] := Value;         { Write Value to Internal Array }
end;
```

```
var
  Bookcase : TBookcase;
  Lbl      : string;
  I        : Integer;

begin
  Bookcase := TBookcase.Create;                         { Use inherited constructor }
  with Bookcase do
  begin
    Width := 30;                                         { Assignment using property }
    Depth := 10;
    ShelfCount := 5;
    ShelfLabels[ 0 ] := 'Fiction A-M';
    ShelfLabels[ 1 ] := 'Fiction N-Z';
    ShelfLabels[ 2 ] := 'Nonfiction A-Z';
                                                         { Display Bookcase Information }
    Writeln( 'Shelf Space = ', ShelfSpace );
    Writeln;
    Writeln( 'Shelf Labels' );
    for I := 0 to Pred( ShelfCount ) do
      Writeln( '  Shelf ', I + 1, ' ', ShelfLabels[ I ] );
  end;
end.
```

Array properties are declared in much the same way as normal properties, with only a couple of restrictions. First, the array property must specify an *index parameter list* after the property name. This parameter list is enclosed in brackets just like an array, but it is formatted like the parameter list of a procedure or function. The purpose of the parameter list is to indicate the number and type of indexes that will be used by the property. The second restriction is that the read and write clauses, if specified, must reference an access method. In the following fragment from Listing 3.3, the **ShelfLabels** property is declared as being a one-dimensional array of strings indexed by an integer value.

```
property ShelfLabels[ Index : Integer ] : string read GetShelfLabels
                                            write SetShelfLabels;
```

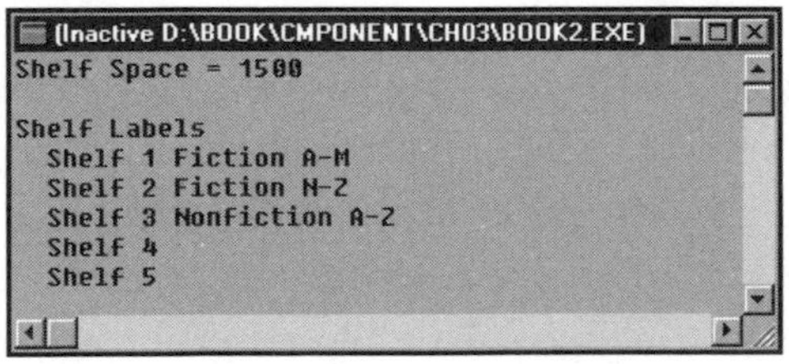

Figure 3.1

Output of
Book2
Program.

Aside from the obvious differences between properties and standard variables, array properties differ in two significant ways from regular arrays. First, unlike standard arrays, property arrays may be indexed on non-ordinal data types. For example, it is possible to specify a string as the index type. Second, array properties cannot be referenced as a whole like regular arrays. That is, you must reference an individual item in the array rather than the array as a unit.

Access Methods for Array Properties

As mentioned above, it is not possible to specify a data field in either the read or write clause for an array property declaration. The reason for this restriction is that the access methods are passed an index value which is used to determine the item in the array to manipulate.

The read method for an array property must be a function that takes one parameter and returns a value matching in type to that of the property. In addition, the index declared in the read method must match the type of index declared in the property declaration. Here is the declaration for the read method used for the **ShelfLabels** property:

```
function TBookcase.GetShelfLabels( Index : Integer ) : string;
```

Likewise, the write access method of an array property must accept an index parameter list that identifies the array element to modify. The last parameter to such a method must be the new value for the array element.

```
procedure TBookcase.SetShelfLabels( Index : Integer; const Value : string );
```

 When dealing with string properties, such as **ShelfLabels**, specify the new value parameter in the property's write method as a *constant parameter*. When a string is passed to a method as a value parameter, a local copy of the string is made for use within the method. When a string is passed using the **const** keyword, only a reference to the string (that is, a pointer) is passed to the method. However, the contents of the string cannot be modified. This results in more efficient code without sacrificing protection.

Multi-Dimensional Array Properties

Just like their standard array variable counterparts, array properties may be declared with more than one index. Declaring a multi-dimensional array property simply requires extending the index parameter list with additional index declarations. In the following example, the **Entry** property of a **TMatrix** class is declared.

```
type
  TMatrix = class
  private
    . . .
    function GetEntry( ACol, ARow : Integer ) : Real;
    procedure SetEntry( ACol, ARow : Integer; Value : Real );
  public
    property Entry[ ACol, ARow : Integer ] : Real read GetEntry write SetEntry;
  end;
```

The **Entry** property is an array property with two indexes indicating the row and column of the desired matrix entry. In addition to modifying the property declaration to accommodate the additional indexes, the parameter lists for both access methods must be adjusted.

Default Array Properties

If a class defines one or more array properties, one of these properties may be deemed the *default* property. In the following class declaration, the **ShelfLabels** property is specified as being the default property by appending the **default** directive after the write clause.

```
type
  TBookcase = class
  private
    . . .
  protected
    . . .
  public
    property ShelfLabels[ Index : Integer ] : string read GetShelfLabels
                                    write SetShelfLabels default;
  end;
```

If a class has a default array property, the property array can be referenced without specifying the property name. In effect, this makes the object appear to be indexed. For example, the following statements:

```
S := Bookcase[ 3 ];
Bookcase[ 1 ] := 'Comics/Humor';
```

are equivalent to:

```
S := Bookcase.ShelfLabels[ 3 ];
Bookcase.ShelfLabels[ 1 ] := 'Comics/Humor';
```

Indexed Properties

Indexes can also pay another role with respect to properties. Multi-dimensional properties use an index to differentiate multiple property values referenced by the same name. An index can also be used to differentiate multiple property names supported by a single access method.

Listing 3.4 shows another version of the **TBookcase** class in which the private data fields for **FWidth**, **FDepth**, and **FHeight** have been replaced by a single **FDimensions** array. The corresponding property declarations for these three fields have also been modified and are shown below:

```
property Width : Integer index 1 read GetDimension write SetDimension;
property Height : Integer index 2 read GetDimension write SetDimension;
property Depth : Integer index 3 read GetDimension write SetDimension;
```

Notice that each property specifies the same read and write methods. The properties are distinguished by the index specifier positioned in front of the read clause. The corresponding index specifier is passed to the access methods whenever one of these properties are referenced. For example, the following statements:

```
Bookcase.Height := 50;
W := Bookcase.Width;
```

are equivalent to

```
Bookcase.SetDimension( 2, 50 );
W := Bookcase.GetDimension( 1 );
```

Listing 3.4   TBookcase Utilizing Indexed Properties

```
program Book3;

uses
  WinCrt;
```

```
type
  TBookcase = class
  private
    FDimensions : array[ 1..3 ] of Integer;
    FShelfCount : Integer;
    function GetDimension( Index : Integer ) : Integer;
    procedure SetDimension( Index : Integer; Value : Integer );
    function GetShelfSpace : Integer;
  public
    constructor Create;

    { Indexed Properties }
    property Width : Integer index 1 read GetDimension write SetDimension;
    property Height : Integer index 2 read GetDimension write SetDimension;
    property Depth : Integer index 3 read GetDimension write SetDimension;

    property ShelfCount : Integer read FShelfCount write FShelfCount;
    property ShelfSpace : Integer read GetShelfSpace;
  end;


{=====================}
{== TBookcase Methods ==}
{=====================}


constructor TBookcase.Create;
begin
  inherited Create;
  FShelfCount := 5;
end;

function TBookcase.GetDimension( Index : Integer ) : Integer;
begin
  Result := FDimensions[ Index ];
end;

procedure TBookcase.SetDimension( Index : Integer; Value : Integer );
begin
  if Value <> FDimensions[ Index ] then
    FDimensions[ Index ] := Value;
end;


function TBookcase.GetShelfSpace : Integer;
begin
  Result := Width * Depth * FShelfCount;  { Reference Width & Depth Properties }
end;


var
  Bookcase : TBookcase;
```

```
begin
  Bookcase := TBookcase.Create;                    { Use inherited constructor }
  with Bookcase do
  begin
    Width := 30;                                    { Assignment using property }
    Height := 20;
    Depth := 10;
    ShelfCount := 5;
                                                    { Display Bookcase Information }
    Writeln( 'Shelf Space = ', ShelfSpace );
  end;
end.
```

Properties and Class Hierarchies

It is not a requirement to have properties declared in the **public** section. On the contrary, it is often very useful for properties to be declared in the **protected** section of a class. The base classes in a class hierarchy often make use of this feature. (The VCL certainly does, but I digress—more on that in Chapter 8.) Although a class may hide a property in this fashion to take advantage of certain side effects that have been coded into its access methods, a property is usually declared **private** or **protected** so that descendant classes can decide whether or not to expose it to users.

The following is a simple class declaration which contains two property declarations in the **protected** section. Therefore, instances of the **TBase** class do not expose the **Color** or **Font** properties to users of the class:

```
type
  TBase = class
  private
    FColor : TColor;
    FFont  : TFont;
  protected
    procedure SetColor( Value : TColor );
    procedure SetFont( Value : TFont );
                                                    { Protected Properties }
    property Color : TColor read FColor write SetColor;
    property Font : TFont read FFont write SetFont;
  public
    . . .
  end;
```

A descendant class, such as the one shown below, inherits both of these properties, and has the opportunity to redeclare their visibility. In this example, the

TDescendant class redeclares the **Color** property in the **public** section so that instances of this class obtain access to this property. Since the **Font** property is not redeclared, it remains protected and thus invisible to object instances.

```
type
  TDescendant = class( TBase )
  private
    . . .
  protected
    . . .
  public
    property Color;                              { Move Color to public section }
  end;
```

Notice that it is not necessary to specify the type or access methods when redeclaring a property. Since Delphi already knows this information from the ancestor class, it is not necessary. This particular feature will surface again in Chapter 8 during the discussion of Delphi's *custom* component classes.

Limitation of Using Properties

As powerful as properties are, they do have their limitations. For example, it is not possible to make a property *less* visible in a descendant class. This means that you cannot redeclare a **public** property to be **protected** (or **private**) in a descendant class. Consider the following version of the **TBase** class from the previous example:

```
type
  TBase = class
  private
    FColor : TColor;
    procedure SetColor( Value : TColor );
  public
    property Color : TColor read FColor write SetColor;
  end;
```

As before, we will create a descendant class, but this time we will try to hide the **Color** property instead of making it visible. Although the **Color** property is redeclared in the **protected** section of the class, doing so will not produce the desired effect. Specifically, the class declaration will compile, but the property will still be visible to instances of **TDescendant**.

```
type
  TDescendant = class( TBase )
  private
    . . .
  protected
    property Color;                  { Moving to protected section has no effect }
  public
    . . .
  end;
```

Properties suffer from another limitation in that you cannot pass a property to a procedure or function that expects to receive a variable parameter. As an example, consider the following property declaration which belongs to an employee class:

```
property FullName : string read FFullName write SetFullName;
```

If you wanted to remove the employee's first name from this property, you might be tempted to use the standard **Delete** procedure, such as:

```
Employee := TEmployee.Create;                { Construction of Employee Object }
. . .
Delete( Employee.FullName, 1, Pos( ' ', Employee.FullName ) );        { Invalid }
```

However, this statement will generate an *invalid variable reference* compiler error because the first parameter to **Delete** must be a variable parameter.

Fortunately, there is a simple way to correct the problem. The solution is to create a local variable of the same type as the property and before calling the procedure in question, assign the property to the local variable, creating a temporary copy of the property's value. Then, pass the local variable to the procedure. Of course, if the procedure does indeed change the local variable's contents, it's your responsibility to copy the new value back into the property. The following shows how this can be accomplished for the above example:

```
S := Employee.FullName;                      { S declared as a string variable }
Delete( S, 1, Pos( ' ', Employee.FullName ) );              { Valid Statement }
Employee.FullName := S;
```

Oh, and there's one other limitation to properties. As I have shown, properties can easily be used to create a bookcase. However, much to my wife's chagrin, I have yet to write a method to *dust* said bookcase!

Looking Ahead...

This chapter covered the ground rules for properties. As you can see, properties are a significant enhancement to Delphi's object model. However, properties are much more important when creating components. This will become apparent in Chapter 5 when the component architecture is introduced. Properties play a significant role in that architecture. But before we jump into the that, there is one more fundamental concept that must be addressed before we can start building components. Next stop—*exceptions*.

Chapter 4

Exception Handling in Delphi

Exception Handling in Delphi

Delphi enhances Object Pascal with an elegant mechanism to recover from any code-related or even hardware-oriented mishap.

It was stated back in Chapter 2 that the virtually all of the enhancements made to Delphi's implementation of Pascal involved extending the BP7 object model. Although accurate, this statement does overlook one of Delphi's most significant enhancements to Object Pascal, the ability to handle *exceptions*.

Exceptions are indicators of error conditions. Implemented as object instances, exceptions provide a way for developers to selectively respond to errors in a consistent manner. Responses involve executing clean-up code, correcting the error, or a combination of both. More importantly, however, exceptions enable developers to separate the error checking from the algorithm. In fact, using exceptions can actually simplify your code.

Exceptions are equally important, if not more so, to component developers than to application developers. Like application developers, component developers must understand how to deal with exceptions that occur in an appropriate manner. However, responding to exceptions is only half the battle for component developers. Since components are used by application developers, any error condition that occurs within a component should be presented to the application developer as an exception. Component developers must therefore understand not only how to respond to exceptions, but how to create them as well.

What Is an Exception?

An exception is an indication that an error has occurred somewhere in your application. In Delphi, an exception is actually an object that contains information identifying the error that occurred and its location. Exceptions are generated, or *raised*, under two circumstances. Errors occurring in the run-time library (RTL), the visual component library (VCL), or the operating system will cause exceptions to be raised. In addition, your application code may explicitly raise an exception if the need arises.

It is important to realize that once an exception is raised, it stays raised until it is handled or until the application terminates. Therefore, when an exception is raised, an application must respond to the exception by either executing some termination code, handling the exception, or both.

Why Use Exceptions?

Exceptions make it easier to write robust applications—and components, for that matter. Specifically, a *robust* application handles errors in a consistent manner, allows for the possibility of recovering from an error, and exits gracefully if the application must in fact terminate.

To further explain the advantages of exceptions, consider the following scenario: You've been given the task of writing an application that processes records in a file and updates a remote database with the information stored in the records. Think of it as an import process. In order to create a robust application, there are many tests that must be performed during the course of the process. For example, the input file must be tested for existence and the database connection must be verified as usable. Furthermore, the information in the file records may need to be modified before it can go into the database. If calculations are performed, those results must be tested for validity. Any of these conditions may cause your application to behave unexpectedly, unless you prepare for them.

Preparing for these conditions usually requires cluttering your code with tests that check for errors. The problem with this is that all of these tests can take away from the normal flow of your algorithm—not to mention wasting time checking perfectly valid data. Exceptions provide the means by which the algorithm is separated from the error checking. That is, instead of *proactively* testing for error conditions, a *reactive* approach is taken by recovering from errors after they occur. Therefore, the code implementing the algorithm does not have to be laden with tests for error conditions. This can simplify your code and make it easier to read.

Guarding Program Statements

Recall that an application responds to an exception either by executing some termination code, handling the exception, or both. In order to respond to an exception, the exception must occur within a *guarded block* of code. A guarded block is simply an Object Pascal block of statements. However, if an exception occurs at a given statement in the block, the statements that follow do not get executed. Instead, control immediately jumps to a related *response* block of statements. The response block specifies the termination code to execute or how to handle the exception.

The guarded block and response block together make up what's called a *protected block*. (Do not get this concept confused with the **protected** directive used in class declarations, or with protected mode as supported by the CPU.) Object Pascal has two types of protected blocks, one for each type of response. The **try..finally** protected block is used to specify termination code responses, and the **try..except** block is used to specify exception handlers. Both blocks are terminated with the standard **end** reserved word. The code fragment below shows the layout of both types of blocks.

```
try                                        try
  { Guarded Block of Statements }            { Guarded Block of Statements }
finally                                    except
  { Termination Code-Response Block }        { Exception Handlers-Response Block }
end;                                       end;
```

Protecting Resources

One of the most common problems developers experience when developing Windows applications is forgetting to free GDI resources. Problems of this nature are very difficult to locate. However, evidence of their existence is usually detected after the program is executed four or five times. This is especially true if you forget to release a device context. Anyone who has experienced this can tell you that Windows does not behave well when all of its device contexts are used up.

Fortunately, the Visual Component Library (VCL) does a very good job of protecting the programmer from having to worry about device contexts and other GDI objects. However, applications use more than just Windows resources. For example, an application must ensure that opened files get closed, allocated memory gets released back to the heap, and object instances get destroyed. Resource allocations can be protected using **try...finally** blocks. This type of block helps to ensure that resources are released even in the event of an error.

No Protection

Figure 4.1 shows the main window for the Stats1 program. This program is used to record the scoring statistics for a basketball player. When the user presses the Save button, the information recorded in the dialog box is saved in the file specified in the File Name field. If successful, all of the fields are cleared and the user can enter another player's scoring information. The majority of code that supports this application can be found in the **BtnSaveClick** method, which is shown in Listing 4.1.

Listing 4.1   MAINFRM1.PAS - Saving Player Stats (Version 1)

```
procedure TFrmMain.BtnSaveClick( Sender : TObject );
var
  F : TextFile;
begin
  AssignFile( F, EdtFileName.Text );
  Append( F );                       { Open the File—File Pointer Placed at EOF }

  Writeln( F, 'Opponent: ', CbxOpponent.Text );
  Writeln( F, 'Date:     ', EdtGameDate.Text );
  Writeln( F, 'Player:   ', CbxPlayer.Text );

  Writeln( F, 'FGM: ', SpnFGM.Value );
  Writeln( F, 'FGA: ', SpnFGA.Value );
  Writeln( F, 'FG%: ', Percentage( SpnFGM.Value, SpnFGA.Value ) );          {##}

  Writeln( F, 'FTM: ', SpnFTM.Value );
  Writeln( F, 'FTA: ', SpnFTA.Value );
  Writeln( F, 'FT%: ', Percentage( SpnFTM.Value, SpnFTA.Value ) );          {##}
  Writeln( F );                                    { Put a blank line between games }

  CloseFile( F );                       { Must Close File or Data Will NOT be Saved }
  ClearFields;                              { Reset All Fields to Initial Values }
end;
```

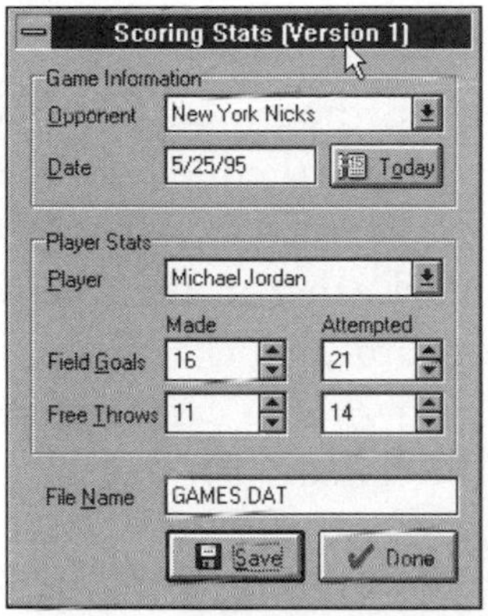

Figure 4.1

Another Great Game for Michael.

First, the specified file is opened. The **Append** procedure is used to open the file. Using **Append** forces the file pointer to be placed at the end of the file. Next, all of the data entered by the user is written to the file. Notice that some additional data is written to the file that wasn't specified by the user. Specifically, the field goal and free throw percentages. These percentages are calculated using the following method, which is also found in the MAINFRM1.PAS file:

```
function TFrmMain.Percentage( Made, Attempts : Integer ) : Real;
begin
  Result := Made / Attempts * 100;
end;
```

Finally, the file is closed and all the fields are reset back to their initial values. This allows the user to enter multiple players without having to close the dialog box. When finished, the user simply presses the Done button.

Unfortunately, there is a potential problem in the **BtnSaveClick** method. What would happen if the user forgets to enter in a value for the field goals attempted field? Since the four spin buttons have an initial value of zero, if one of the attempted fields is not specified, then the call to **Percentage** will generate a divide by zero error. This error manifests itself as an **EZeroDivide** exception. The exception causes the application to immediately jump out of this block (that is, the **Percentage** method) and display a message indicating the error. Unfortunately, since none of the statements in this method are guarded, the call to **CloseFile** never gets executed, and the information previously written to the file will be lost.

Preventing Resource Leaks

Listing 4.2 shows the **BtnSaveClick** method used in the **Stats2** program. This version uses a **try...finally** block to protect the file resource. More precisely, the code that uses the file is located in the guarded section, whereas the code to close the file is placed in the response block (that is, the **finally** portion). As stated earlier, if an exception occurs in the guarded block, execution immediately jumps to the code listed in the response block—in this case the **finally** block. Therefore, if an exception occurs, the file will be closed.

Listing 4.2   MAINFRM2.PAS - Saving Player Stats (Version 2)

```
procedure TFrmMain.BtnSaveClick( Sender : TObject );
var
  F : TextFile;
begin
  AssignFile( F, EdtFileName.Text );
  Append( F );                     { Open the File—File Pointer Placed at EOF }
  try
    Writeln( F, 'Opponent: ', CbxOpponent.Text );
    Writeln( F, 'Date:     ', EdtGameDate.Text );
    Writeln( F, 'Player:   ', CbxPlayer.Text );

    Writeln( F, 'FGM: ', SpnFGM.Value );
    Writeln( F, 'FGA: ', SpnFGA.Value );
    Writeln( F, 'FG%: ', Percentage( SpnFGM.Value, SpnFGA.Value ) );

    Writeln( F, 'FTM: ', SpnFTM.Value );
    Writeln( F, 'FTA: ', SpnFTA.Value );
    Writeln( F, 'FT%: ', Percentage( SpnFTM.Value, SpnFTA.Value ) );
    Writeln( F );                               { Put a blank line between games }
  finally
    CloseFile( F );                          { File will Always get Closed }
    ClearFields;                    { Reset All Fields to Initial Values }
  end;
end;
```

Statements that have the potential of generating an exception should be guarded and placed in the **try** portion of a protected block. Likewise, code that *must* be executed should be placed in the **finally** portion of the block. The key to this construct is that the code in the **finally** block *always* gets executed, whether or not an exception was raised. This makes it perfectly suited for protecting resource allocations. However, to actually *recover* from the exception in a graceful way, we need to create exception *handlers*.

Exception Handlers

Exceptions are not fatal to execution. This is one of the major advantages of using exceptions. By handling an exception, you are given the opportunity to recover from an error condition and continue running, or terminate gracefully. Delphi applications can even recover from a general protection fault! This ability to recover from error conditions is vital in producing quality applications.

So how are exceptions handled? As mentioned earlier, the new **try...except** construct provides the means of creating exception handlers. Program statements that have the potential of generating exceptions are placed in the **try** part of the block, just as with **try...finally** blocks. Within the **except** part of the block, exception handlers are created for exception classes. Recall that exceptions are objects. Therefore, each exception must belong to a certain class. You create exception handlers by writing code to handle a particular class of exceptions. An exception handler has the following format:

```
on <ExceptionClass> do
begin
  { Code to Handle the Exception };
end;
```

To demonstrate how to create an exception handler, let's take a closer look at the **Percentage** function that is implemented in the Stats2 program. As stated earlier, if the **Attempts** parameter is zero, then the division operation generates an **EZeroDivide** exception. Instead of having the application handle the exception, let's write an exception handler to handle it ourselves. The following is what the **Percentage** function looks like with an exception handler.

```
function TFrmMain.Percentage( Made, Attempts : Integer ) : Real;
begin
  try
    Result := Made / Attempts * 100;
  except
    on EZeroDivide do
      Result := 0;
  end;
end;
```

In this new version, if the **Attempts** parameter is zero, an **EZeroDivide** exception is *still* generated. However, since the division occurs in a guarded block, execution immediately jumps to the response section (that is, the except block). Once inside the except block, the search for an exception handler begins. If a matching exception handler is found then the code specified in the handler is executed. If a matching handler is not found, then the search is continued to the next outer block. Information stored on the stack is used to identify the next guarded block of code.

To further clarify this, let's take another look at the **Percentage** function. **EZeroDivide** is not the only exception that can be raised from improper division. The **EInvalidOp** exception will be raised if both the numerator and denominator are zero. If this were to happen, execution jumps to the except block, and the search for an appropriate handler begins. However, an appropriate handler is not specified in this protected block. Therefore, the stack is searched for the next protected block. That would be in the **BtnSaveClick** method.

But the protected block in **BtnSaveClick** is a **try..finally** block. Therefore, the search for an exception handler is put on pause, and the code in the finally portion is executed. Once the termination code is completed, execution jumps out of the **BtnSaveClick** method. That is, the search for an exception handler resumes. This process continues until an appropriate handler is found. So when does the search stop? Every Delphi application has a default exception handler which will handle all exceptions not handled earlier.

Exception Classes

Since the division operation can generate two types of exceptions, it would make sense to add an additional handler to the **except** block. The following version of **Percentage** (taken from the Stats3 program) demonstrates that any number of handlers can be placed in an except block.

```
function TFrmMain.Percentage( Made, Attempts : Integer ) : Real;
begin
  try
    Result := Made / Attempts * 100;
  except
    on EZeroDivide do                          { Denominator is Zero }
      Result := 0;

    on EInvalidOp do                 { Numerator and Denominator are Zero }
      Result := 0;
  end;
end;
```

Actually, there is an easier way to write this method. It relies on the object-oriented nature of exceptions. All exception types defined in Delphi are descendants from a base class called **Exception**. An entire hierarchy exists with the **Exception** class as the root. For example, **EZeroDivide** is a descendent of **Exception**. However, it is not a *direct* descendent. Instead, **EZeroDivide** descends from **EMathError**. **EMathError** in turn descends from **Exception**. Likewise, **EInvalidOp** descends from **EMathError**. Therefore, because of the type compatibility rules of Object Pascal, we can create an exception handler which handles a class of exceptions.

```
function TFrmMain.Percentage( Made, Attempts : Integer ) : Real;
begin
  try
    Result := Made / Attempts;
  except
    on EMathError do                              { Handles All Math Errors }
      Result := 0;                       { Including EZeroDivide & EInvalidOp }
  end;
end;
```

The exception handler for **EMathError** will handle any exception of that same type or of a descendent type. Therefore, this single exception handler will handle both **EZeroDivide** and **EInvalidOp** exceptions.

Exception in the RTL

As the previous examples have demonstrated, Delphi's run-time library is exception-aware. Figure 4.2 shows the seven basic classes of exceptions raised by the RTL. We have already seen the floating-point exceptions in action. The integer math exceptions work much the same way. The heap exceptions indicate memory errors, such as attempting to dispose of a pointer that has already been disposed. The typecast exception is raised when the **as** operator is used to cast an object into an incompatible type.

There are several functions in Delphi that convert data to alternate forms. When a problem occurs during the conversion, an **EConvertError** exception is raised. File I/O errors generate **EInOutError** exceptions, and hardware exceptions result from a system fault the processor cannot handle, or from the application generating an interrupt to break execution. Other than the infamous general protection fault, your applications should rarely experience hardware exceptions.

It should be noted that the RTL never raises an **EMathError**, **EIntError**, or **EProcessorException** exception. These classes define common characteristics for the exceptions that descend from them. In addition, the exception classes shown in Figure 4.2 do not represent all of the predefined exceptions in Delphi. The hierarchy shows only those exceptions that can be raised by the RTL. There are several more exceptions defined within the Visual Component Library which may be raised during the course of an application. For example, trying to access a list box element that does not exist results in an **EListError** exception. (Appendix B lists the entire exception hierarchy defined in Delphi.)

Re-raising an Exception

It is important to realize that you do not have to provide handlers for every kind of exception within every **try...except** block. In this respect, exceptions are analogous to Windows messages. Just as a window does not have to respond to every message that it receives, an exception block does not have to handle every exception. If a window does not process a message, the message is sent to the window's owner. Likewise, if an exception block does not handle an exception, the exception is propagated up the call stack to the next block of code that can handle the exception. Because exceptions are implemented through the call stack, they have a scope associated with them which allows for localized handling. The **Percentage** function from the Stats2 or Stats3 programs provide an example of this.

Figure 4.2

The Delphi RTL Exception Class Hierarchy.

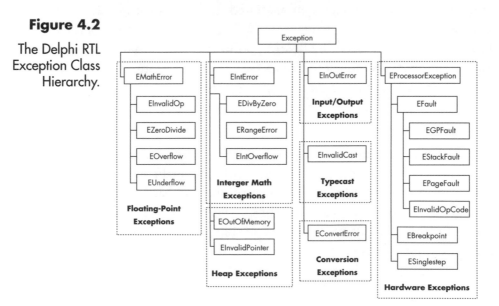

Using another comparison, exception handlers are like virtual methods in that they can be used to *override* or *augment* the handling performed by ancestor blocks. Under normal circumstances, exception handlers simply override any previously defined handlers. All of the previous handlers in this chapter are of this type.

Augmenting an exception handler, on the other hand, means that you want to provide some localized handling of the exception, but still want previously defined handlers to handle the exception. This process of augmenting an exception handler is accomplished by *re-raising* the exception. To re-raise an exception, handle the exception as normal, and then at the end of the handler code, use the new reserved word **raise** as a procedure call. The general syntax is shown in the following code fragment:

```
try
  { Guarded Statements }
except
  on ESomeException do
  begin
    { Local Handling of Exception }
    raise;  { Re-raise the Exception }
  end;
end;
```

Since the local exception handler has already handled the exception, calling **raise** forces the exception to move up the ancestor block chain looking for the next handler. The third version of the Stats program, presented in the next section, demonstrates this technique.

Using the Exception Object

As stated previously, an exception is an object that contains information identifying an error and its location. Up to this point, we have not used the exception object. Delphi's syntax for exceptions allows for the creation of a temporary exception object that can be used within an exception handler. The object has the same type as the handler in which it is declared. The following syntax is used to declare a temporary exception object.

```
try
  { Guarded Statements }
except
  on E : ESomeException do           { E is Temporary Exception Object }
```

```
begin
  { E Can Only be Used in Handler }
  end;
end;
```

Let's take one last look at the **BtnSaveClick** method. In particular, the **Append** procedure has one interesting little side effect. That is, if the file specified does not exist, an **EInOutError** exception is raised. This type of exception does not pose a threat to the remaining code because the Append call is unguarded. Therefore, when the exception occurs, execution jumps out of the method and a generic message box is displayed. By writing an exception handler for the **Append** call, we can use the exception object to display a more appropriate and user friendly message box.

Listing 4.3   MAINFRM3.PAS - Saving Player Stats (Version 3)

```
procedure TFrmMain.BtnSaveClick( Sender : TObject );
var
  F : TextFile;
  Ans : Word;
begin
  AssignFile( F, EdtFileName.Text );
  try
    Append( F );                       { Call will fail if file does not exist }
    try
      Writeln( F, 'Opponent: ', CbxOpponent.Text );
      Writeln( F, 'Date:     ', EdtGameDate.Text );
      Writeln( F, 'Player:   ', CbxPlayer.Text );

      Writeln( F, 'FGM: ', SpnFGM.Value );
      Writeln( F, 'FGA: ', SpnFGA.Value );
      Writeln( F, 'FG%: ', Percentage( SpnFGM.Value, SpnFGA.Value ) );

      Writeln( F, 'FTM: ', SpnFTM.Value );
      Writeln( F, 'FTA: ', SpnFTA.Value );
      Writeln( F, 'FT%: ', Percentage( SpnFTM.Value, SpnFTA.Value ) );
      Writeln( F );
    finally
      CloseFile( F );                          { File will Always get Closed }
      ClearFields;                     { Reset All Fields to Initial Values }
    end;
  except
    on E : EInOutError do               { Declare Temporary Exception Object E }
    begin
      if E.ErrorCode = 2 then    { If 'File Not Found', then Display Custom Msg }
      begin
        Ans := MessageDlg( 'Could not find file: ' + EdtFileName.Text + '.'#13 +
```

```
                          'Would like to create it?',
                          mtError, [ mbYes, mbNo ], 0 );
        if Ans = mrYes then
           FileCreate( EdtFileName.Text );
      end
      else
         raise;                              { Otherwise, Reraise the Exception }
    end;
  end;
end; {= TFrmMain.BtnSaveClick =}
```

If an exception is raised during the call to **Append,** control jumps immediately to the exception handler. Note that the nested **try...finally** block is skipped. Once in the handler, the temporary exception object E is used to determine what type of I/O error occurred. The **ErrorCode** field of the **EInOutError** class specifies the error that caused the exception. An error code of two indicates that the file was not found. Therefore, the handler tests for this error code, and if successful, a more appropriate message box is displayed indicating the file name that could not be found. If a different I/O error is raised, the exception handler simply re-raises the exception and passes it on up the chain for someone else to handle.

Exceptions in Delphi Components

The examples presented thus far have been based on exceptions being raised as a result of errors occurring in the run-time library. But this is not the only source of exceptions. Delphi components also generate exceptions when used improperly.

Consider the many components that manage a list of items. For example, a ListBox manages a list of strings, a TabSet manages a list of tabs, and a Notebook manages a list of pages. Each component provides an indexed property that can be used to access items on their respective list. If an index outside the current range of items is used to access the list, then an **EListError** or **EStringListError** exception is raised.

From an application developer's point of view, exceptions generated by components are treated the same way as exceptions generated by the runtime library. However, from the component developer's viewpoint, the component is responsible for raising an exception in the event of an error. Therefore, component developers must understand not only how to respond to exceptions, but how to create them as well.

Creating a Custom Exception

There are two steps that must be performed in order to utilize a new exception. First, the new exception must be defined. Second, you must define the class from which the new exception object will be created. Under most circumstances, you will define a new exception class as a descendent of the **Exception** class (see Figure 4.2). The **Exception** class allows you to specify a string to be associated with the exception. Since **Exception** defines all of the necessary methods, the type definition for most exceptions is quite simple. For example,

```
type
  ENewException = class( Exception );
```

defines a new exception class called **ENewException**. Although the majority of exception classes do not provide any additional fields or methods, it is quite possible to do so. For instance, in the previous example the **ErrorCode** value was checked to determine if an **EInOutError** exception is raised. The **ErrorCode** field is not defined in the base **Exception** class. Instead, it is part of the **EInOutError** class declaration:

```
type
  EInOutError = class( Exception )
  public
    ErrorCode : Integer;
  end;
```

After a new exception class is defined, you can start utilizing it in your code. To utilize a new exception, simply write the code that will raise the exception. To raise an exception, construct an object instance of the new exception class and then use the **raise** reserved word to invoke it as an exception. For example, Listing 4.4 shows the GetFullName function from the Custom sample program that demonstrates how to raise a custom exception.

Listing 4.4   CUSTOM.PAS - Using a Custom Exception

```
function TFrmSearch.GetFullName( EmpNo : Integer ) : string;
begin
  if not TblEmployee.FindKey( [ EmpNo ] ) then
  begin
          { Raise a Custom Exception Indicating that Employee Was Not Found }
    raise EEmployeeNotFound.CreateFmt( 'Employee #%d is not in the database',
```

```
                                    [ EmpNo ] );
    end;

    Result := TblEmployee.FieldByName( 'FirstName' ).AsString + ' ' +
              TblEmployee.FieldByName( 'LastName' ).AsString;
end;
```

The **GetFullName** function searches the Employee table in the DBDEMOS database for the employee record matching the employee number passed in via the parameter. If the record is found, the function returns the employee's full name by concatenating the first and last name fields into a single string. If a matching record is not found, the custom **EEmployeeNotFound** exception is raised. It is defined as:

```
EEmployeeNotFound = class( Exception );
```

However, note that the exception object is created using one of the alternate constructors. In this example, the **CreateFmt** constructor is used to format the message string so that it contains the employee number being searched for. Figure 4.3 shows how this message appears to the user if the employee number entered does not exist.

The **Exception** class defines many other constructors, which provide various ways of formatting the message string. For example, the **CreateRes** and **CreateResFmt** constructors are provided for retrieving the message from a string table resource.

Do not place a period at the end of an exception message. Delphi does this automatically when the message is displayed.

Figure 4.3

Custom Exception with Custom Message.

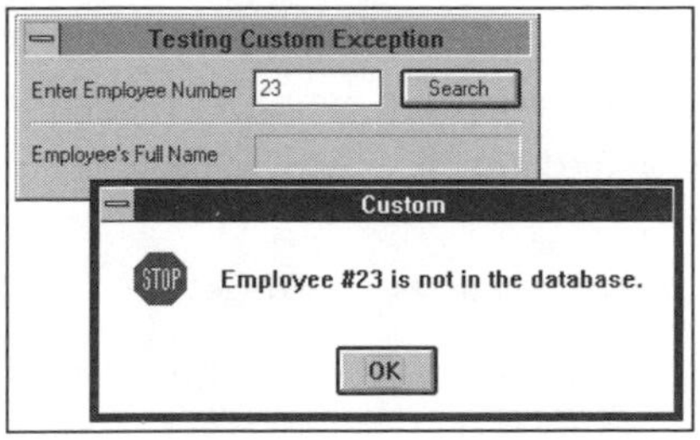

As a final note, although you must create the exception object by calling one the constructors, you do not have to worry about destroying the object. That is, once an exception handler actually handles the exception, the object is destroyed automatically.

Silent Exceptions

As noted earlier, all Delphi applications have a default exception handler which will handle any exceptions that are not specifically handled in your code. The default action of this handler is to display the exception message string in a message box as demonstrated in Figure 4.3.

For those times when it is not desirable to display a message box, a silent exception can be used. Silent exceptions have the same effect as other exceptions insofar as when one is raised the current process is aborted and the stack is unwound until an appropriate handler is found. However, if a silent exception reaches the default exception handler, the application does not display a message box.

Delphi has one predefined silent exception: **EAbort**. Custom silent exceptions can be created by defining an exception class that descends from this class. Silent exceptions must be descendants of **EAbort** because the default exception handler uses the **is** operator to test the exception object against the **EAbort** class. Only if the exception is a descendant of **EAbort** will the handler avoid displaying a message box.

An **EAbort** exception can be raised like any other exception by constructing an object instance and using the reserved word **raise**. However, Delphi provides a much easier way to generate this type of exception. The **Abort** procedure takes no parameters and automatically raises a silent exception. The following code fragment uses the **Abort** procedure to abort the post process on the Employee database table if the record to be posted specifies a first name but not a last name.

```
procedure TForm1.TblEmployeeBeforePost( DataSet : TDataset );
begin
  if ( TblEmployee.FieldByName( 'FirstName' ).AsString <> '' ) and
    ( TblEmployee.FieldByName( 'LastName' ).AsString = '' ) then
    Abort;                          { Aborts Current Process which is the Post }
end;
```

Different Exception Models

Exceptions in Object Pascal have many similarities to exceptions in C++ and Win32. For example, Object Pascal exceptions are similar to C++ in that both are *type*-based. That is, exception objects are created from exception classes. Furthermore, Object Pascal exceptions are similar to Win32 exceptions in syntax and structure. Table 4.1 shows how the three models compare with one another. The

Table 4.1	Object Pascal, C++, and Win32 Exception Models			
Exception Model	**Exception Types**	**Resumable**	**Exception Handling**	**Termination Handling**
Object Pascal	Any	No	try <guarded block>; except on <class1> do HandlerBlock1; on <class2> do HandlerBlock2; end;	try <guarded block>; finally <term. block>; end;

C++	Any	No	try
			<guarded block>;
			}
			catch(<type1>)
			{
			 handlerBlock1;
			}
			catch(<type2>)
			{
			 handlerblock2;
			}
				Not Available in C++

Win32	unsigned int	Yes	_try
			{
			<guarded block>;
			}
			_except(<filter>)
			{
			 handlerBlock;
			}
				_try
				{
				<guarded block>;
				}
				_finally
				{
				<term. bllock>;
				}

Resumable column indicates whether or not the exception model supports resuming execution at the point where the exception was raised. Of course, the exception must first be handled successfully. Only Win32's model supports resumable exceptions. When an exception is raised in Win32, the current state of the thread in which the exception was raised is saved in a context structure allowing the original state to be re-established.

Looking Ahead...

Let's face it—run-time errors will continue to occur in software. There's no getting away from them. However, with the introduction of exceptions in Object Pascal, developers have a powerful new tool to battle them. Traditional programming requires that the developer proactively test for error conditions. With exceptions, a reactive approach is taken by recovering from errors after they occur.

Exceptions are used quite extensively in Delphi. The run-time library is exception-aware, as is the Visual Component Library. For the component developer, exceptions provide a clean and consistent way of reporting error conditions to application developers. Furthermore, Delphi developers expect errors to be reported via exceptions. As we'll see in the remaining chapters, to build professional quality components, you cannot take exception to exceptions!

Part 2

The Delphi
Component Architecture

Chapter 5

Component Anatomy 101

Component Anatomy 101

Delphi's components, like Gaul, can be divided into three parts: properties, methods, and events. How these are constructed, and how they interact, are fundamental to understanding the way components are created.

This chapter describes the general anatomy of Delphi components. Implemented as Object Pascal classes, components can be dissected into three distinct categories of parts: *properties, methods,* and *events*. Each category is supported by one or more features of Delphi's object model. After taking a brief look at the evolution of the component, I'll discuss each category in detail.

The Component Kingdom

When you drop a component onto a form, the Delphi Form Designer creates an instance of the selected component. Actually, we know from Chapter 2's discussion of virtual constructors that the Form Designer simply creates a new object from the corresponding component class. Actual components, however, are not defined by just any class declaration. All components ultimately trace their ancestry back to the **TComponent** class.

The **TComponent** class provides the basic functionality required for a component to behave like a component. For example, **TComponent** implements the

Name and **Tag** properties that are inherited by all components. Furthermore, **TComponent** provides the methods and properties that allow components to be manipulated by the Form Designer. In other words, for a component to be manipulated at design-time, it must descend from **TComponent**.

Although all component classes ultimately descend from **TComponent**, you will rarely create a custom component that is a *direct* descendant of **TComponent**. This is because this base component class does not provide any visual representation. It is much more common to create new components that descend from an existing class somewhere further down the class hierarchy. However, the actual class from which you chose to inherit will depend on the type of component you wish to create.

The easiest way to create a custom component is to inherit from an existing component that comes close to being what you want, and alter its behavior. For example, to create a specialized edit field, don't create the entire component from scratch. Instead, define your new component to be a descendant of the **TEdit** class and make the necessary modifications. Chapters 7 and 8 provide several examples of this process.

Slightly more difficult to implement are graphic controls. Graphic components descend from **TGraphicControl** and have a visual representation, but do not receive the input focus. An example of a graphic component is **TLabel**. Since graphic controls cannot be focused, they do not need a window handle. Therefore, graphic components are system resource friendly. In fact, Windows does not even know about these types of components, because graphic controls do not supply a window class to Windows. Chapter 9 focuses on building graphic components.

What if you want to build a component that needs the input focus? In this case, there are two predefined classes from which you can inherit: **TWinControl** and **TCustomControl**. **TWinControl** is used when creating a Delphi component based on an existing Windows control. For example, the standard edit field component, **TEdit**, is a descendant of **TWinControl**. To create a truly custom control, the **TCustomControl** class is used. Since **TCustomControl** is a direct descendant of **TWinControl**, it automatically inherits all of the necessary functionality. It differs from **TWinControl** by providing a **Canvas** property, which is used to draw the custom component. **TWinControl** does not provide a **Canvas** property because an existing Windows control should already know how to paint itself. Chapter 10 demonstrates the subtle differences between these two classes.

All of the component classes described above refer to visual components. However, not all components need to be visual. The **Timer** component is a common example of a nonvisual component. Creating a nonvisual component is one of those rare cases where the new component type descends directly from **TComponent**. Nonvisual components are covered in detail in Chapter 11.

Table 5.1 summarizes the available parent classes and when to use each one as an ancestor for a new component class.

Components versus Objects

Although components are implemented using Object Pascal classes, a class declaration is *not* a component declaration unless it descends from **TComponent**. Instances of classes that are derived from **TComponent** are called *components*, and instances of all other classes are called *objects*. The major difference between these two entities is that components can be manipulated on a form, whereas objects cannot.

This does not mean that objects do not have their place in Delphi. On the contrary, there are dozens of object types defined in the VCL to provide basic services. For example, **TFont** and **TIniFile** are classes that do not descend from **TComponent** but are used quite extensively in the VCL. You cannot drop a **TFont** component onto a form and manipulate it at design-time, but you can manipulate the **Font** property (which is of type **TFont**) of the **Label** component at design-time. The distinction is subtle, but nonetheless important.

A Component Skeleton

Since all components are descendants of **TComponent**, they all share a similar structure. The most obvious aspect of that structure is that all components are

Table 5.1   Delphi Base Classes for Component Building

Inherit from	To create	Examples in
An existing component	a modified version of a working component.	Chapters 7 & 8
TGraphicControl	a graphical component that does not require input focus.	Chapter 9
TWinControl	a component that requires a window handle or to create a wrapper for an existing windows custom control.	Chapter 10
TCustomControl	an original component.	Chapter 10
TComponent	a nonvisual component.	Chapter 11

defined using a class declaration. The following skeleton class represents the basic elements of a Delphi component:

```
type
  TSkeletonComponent = class( TComponent )
  private
    FNewProp     : TPropType;              { Internal Data Holds Property Value }
    FRunTimeProp : TPropType;     { Internal Data Holds Run-Time Property Value }
    FOnNewEvent  : TEventType;        { Internal Method Pointer Supports Event }

    function GetNewProp : TPropType;                        { Access Methods }
    procedure SetNewProp( Value : TPropType );
    procedure SetRunTimeProp( Value : TPropType );
  public
    constructor Create( AOwner : TComponent ); override;
    destructor Destroy; override;
    procedure NewMethod;               { New Method Implements Behavior  }
    procedure NewEvent;             { Method to Invoke OnNewEvent Event }
    property RunTimeProp : TPropType read FRunTimeProp write SetRunTimeProp;
  protected
    property NewProp : TPropType read GetNewProp write SetNewProp;
    property Height;                          { Redeclare Property }
    property Width;
                                                         { Events }
    property OnNewEvent : TEventType read FOnNewEvent write FOnNewEvent;
    property OnClick;                          { Redeclare Event }
  end;
```

The structure of this skeleton component should look familiar. That's because component class declarations, like this one, utilize the object model features that were covered in Chapters 2 and 3. However, no matter how many features are utilized, a component is always described by its properties, methods, and events.

Properties

Although properties were covered in detail in Chapter 3, this section focuses on how properties are used in a component. Properties are the single most important aspect of any component, and their importance cannot be overstated. Properties define the primary interface through which users manipulate the component. Well-designed properties make components more usable.

Properties represent the most significant aspect of component design because of their ability to be modified at design-time using the Object Inspector. This is significant because it lets users customize components before executing the application. Since properties provide the primary interface to a component, generally components will have many more properties than methods. From the component user's point of view, it is better to err on the side of too many properties than too few.

As described in Chapter 3, properties can be used to hide implementation details from the user as well as to create side effects. Side effects are quite common in component building. Any property that contributes to the visual representation of a component will most surely rely on a side effect whenever the value of the property is changed. For instance, changing the **Height** property of a **TPanel** not only updates the internal storage holding the **Height** value, but also causes the component to repaint itself. Repainting a component is a typical side effect.

Property Types

The same rules that apply to class properties also apply to component properties. For example, since properties can be implemented using a read access method, they can be any type that is valid as a function result. This includes all of the standard types except file types and BP7-style object types. Fortunately, class types *can* be returned from a function, and therefore make good candidates for properties.

At design-time, the published properties of a component appear in the Object Inspector. A property's type determines *how* it appears in the Object Inspector. When a property is selected in the Object Inspector, a property editor is used to modify its value. There are several standard property editors that come built into Delphi. There are editors for all of the standard types. Table 5.2 describes the more common editors, and Figures 5.1 through 5.4 show the visual representation of the four basic types of editors.

Although this list of four property editors handles a significant portion of all property fields, you are not limited to this set of editors. In Chapter 14, we'll learn how to build custom property editors.

Table 5.2	Property Editors Available in the Object Inspector
Property Type	**Property Editor Description**
Simple	Simple property values such as numbers, strings, and so on are edited directly on the property line.
Enumerated	All of the enumerated values defined for the type are displayed in a combo box. The values in the enumeration may be cycled by double clicking in the property line.
Set	On the property line, set types appear as Pascal sets. If the line (or set) is expanded, each potential member of the set is treated as a Boolean value.
Object	The object type appears on the property line. If the object has published properties, the object property may be expanded and each sub-property may be edited.

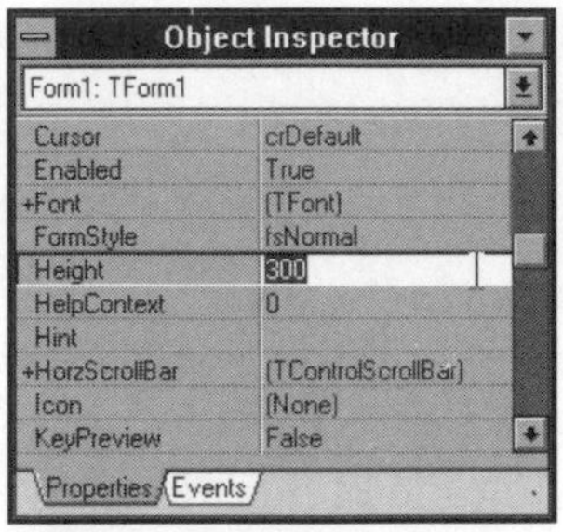

Figure 5.1

Simple Type
Property Editor.

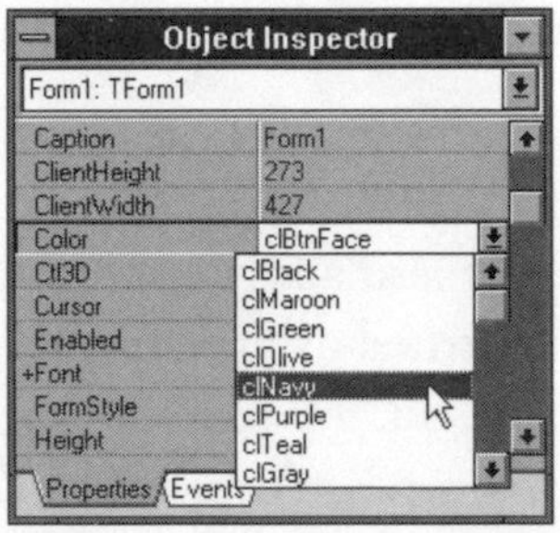

Figure 5.2

Enumerated
Type Property
Editor.

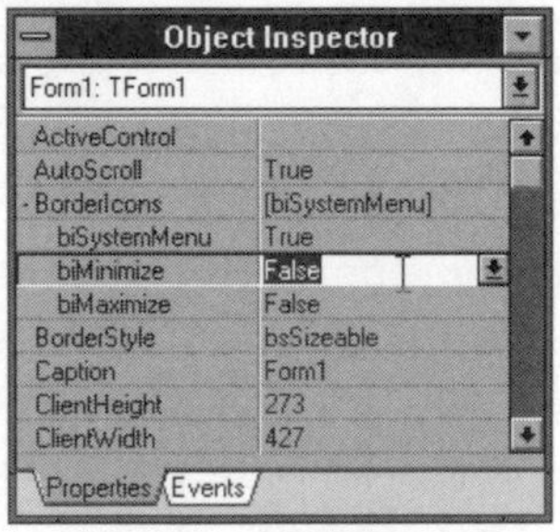

Figure 5.3

Set Type
Property Editor.

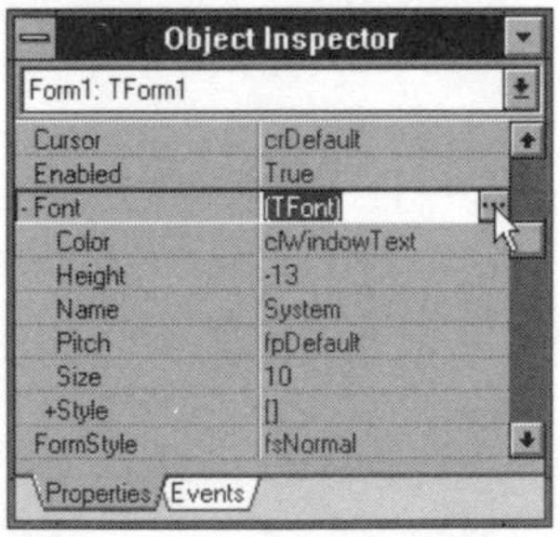

Figure 5.4

Object Type
Property Editor.

Storage Specifiers

When a developer uses the Object Inspector to change the properties of a form, or the properties of a component on the form, the resulting changes get recorded in the form (*.DFM) file. Delphi form files are actually Windows resource files, and when an application is compiled, the form file is attached to the application just like a normal resource. When the application starts, the form's description is loaded from the resource.

But what exactly is stored in the form file? A form file specifies a list of the form's properties and their values. In addition, the file will include similar lists for each component on the form. The contents of each list are determined by each individual component, including the form, when the form is saved. By default, when a component is stored, its list will include the values of its **published** properties that differ from their default values. When the form is loaded, each component is first constructed, thereby initializing all properties with their default values. Then the non-default property values stored in the form file are read in and the new component's properties are updated.

Under most circumstance, you as a component writer will not have to modify this default process. However, there are times when more control is needed over what properties actually get stored in the form file. When declaring simple properties for a component class, *storage specifiers* may be added to the property declaration. The **default**, **nodefault**, and **stored** specifiers are implemented as directives. These directives affect the runtime type information that is generated for **published** properties. Although storage specifiers have no effect on how a property is used, the Form Designer uses the RTTI (RunTime Type Information) generated by the specifiers to determine how to store a component's properties. The **stored** directive controls whether or not a property is actually stored in the form file, and the **default** and **nodefault** directives control a property's default value.

Let's discuss the **default** directive in more detail. Recall that **default** was shown in Chapter 3 to indicate the default array property for a class. The **default** directive does double duty when used in a component declaration. When the **default** directive is used on a non-array property, the directive is followed by a value that will serve as the default value for the component. The syntax for specifying a default value is shown in the following declaration:

```
property Height : Integer read FHeight write SetHeight default 25;
```

A common misconception regarding this directive is that by specifying a default value when the component is constructed, the specified property automatically gets set to the default value when the component is constructed. Unfortunately, this is not the case! *You* are still responsible for initializing property values in the constructor of the component. The **default** directive is used by the Form Designer to determine whether or not a particular property value gets stored in the form file. If the current value of the property is the same as the specified default value, then the property value is *not* stored in the form file.

Not all properties can specify default values. The **default** directive is only valid for ordinal and small set properties. If the **default** storage specifier is used in a non-array property declaration, it must be followed by a constant of the same type as the property.

 Use the **default** directive wherever possible, especially on published non-array properties. Providing default values for your component's properties can dramatically reduce the number of values that must be saved to the form file. This in turn helps to reduce form load times.

The second storage specifier is the **nodefault** directive. This directive is used to specify that the corresponding property has no default value. The **nodefault** directive is particularly useful when redeclaring a property that was defined with a default value in an earlier class. By terminating the new property declaration with **nodefault**, the corresponding property will be treated as though it does not have a default value. However, since properties automatically behave as though **nodefault** is specified, actually specifying the **nodefault** directive in a property declaration is quite rare. In fact, there is not a single occurrence of **nodefault** in the entire VCL.

The final storage directive is **stored**. This directive is used to specify whether or not a non-array property is stored in a form file. In a property declaration, the **stored** directive must be followed by one of the following values:

- One of the two predefined Boolean constants (that is, True or False)
- The name of a Boolean field of the class
- The name of a parameterless function method returning a Boolean value

As an example, consider the **Color** property that is inherited by all of the visual components. The **Color** property is declared using the **stored** directive with a function call in the following manner:

```
property Color : TColor read FColor write SetColor
                stored IsColorStored default clWindow;
```

The **IsColorStored** function is defined as follows:

```
function TControl.IsColorStored : Boolean;
begin
  Result := not ParentColor;
end;
```

Therefore, if a component has **ParentColor** set to **True**, there is no need to store the **Color** value for the component, because it will just use the **Color** value of its parent.

All three storage specifiers work together to minimize the amount of data that needs to be stored in form files. When saving a component's state to a form file, the Form Designer iterates over all of the component's **published** properties. For each property, the expression following the stored specifier (if present) is evaluated. If the result is **False**, the property is not saved. If the result is **True**, the current value of the property is compared with the value specified by the **default** directive (if present). If the values match, the property is not stored. If the values do *not* match or if **nodefault** was specified, the property value is stored in the form file.

Methods

Although properties provide the primary interface between the component and the user, they only capture the attributes of the component. Properties do not represent behaviors. For example, several components have the ability to cut, copy, and paste text to and from the clipboard. These actions are behaviors and are not invoked through properties. Instead, methods are created for each type of behavior.

Minimize Method Interdependencies

Note well: *Component users will use your components in ways you never dreamed.* Given this axiom of component building, you must design your components in such a way that you minimize the preconditions imposed on the component user. Here are a few things to avoid when creating new methods.

First, a component should always be created in a valid state. Do not force the user to execute a method before the component can be used! (If you do this, you won't have to worry about your component being used in an invalid state—it just won't be used!) Second, never impose an order in which methods must be called. And finally, avoid creating methods that cause other methods or properties to become invalid.

This last guideline can be a little tricky to handle. There will certainly be times when a method will change the state of the component, which in turn may invalidate some other method or property. In circumstances such as these, the best approach is to correct the errors in the method before executing the method's main block of code. Of course, this assumes the error is correctable. If not, it might be a prime spot to raise an exception.

 Since methods are accessible at runtime by component users, it is important to name your methods appropriately. Method names should be descriptive and use active verbs. Likewise, function names should indicate what they return. Here are a few examples of appropriate and inappropriate method names:

Appropriate	**Inappropriate**
`procedure CutToClipboard`	`procedure Cut`
`procedure SetHeight`	`procedure SetH`
`function GetTextLen`	`function Len`

Exposing Behaviors

Methods can reside in either the *public, protected,* or *private* sections of a component declaration. Deciding on where a particular method should be located depends on how it will be used. Methods that are to be accessible to the user at runtime must be placed in the public section. Implementation-specific methods, however, should at least reside in the protected section. This prevents users of your component from accidentally executing one of the implementation-specific methods. Methods that should be accessible from descendant classes should also be located in the protected section.

The private section usually contains the access methods for the properties defined in that component. Since the access methods are accessible through the properties, there is no need to make them visible to anyone outside of the current class. This makes sense when you consider that the internal data storage for a property is always private. Like component users, descendant components reference property values through the property name, and not by directly calling the access methods. Moving the access methods from the protected section to the private section prevents descendant classes from inadvertently modifying the internal property value. It also hides implementation-specific details from descendant classes.

Constructors

Before leaving the subject of methods, let's take a closer look component constructors. All Delphi components must provide a constructor that has the following form:

```
constructor Create( AOwner : TComponent ); override;
```

Of course, not every component class needs to define a new constructor. You could inherit a constructor from an ancestor. In either case, the constructor takes a single parameter of type **TComponent**.

Like any other class, a component's constructor is called when an instance of the class needs to be created. For components, the **Create** constructor is where default values for properties are set. For example,

```
constructor TSampleControl.Create = class( TWinControl )
begin
  inherited Create( AOwner );
  FHeight := 25;                                    { Set default values }
  FWidth := 50;
  FColor := clWindows;
end;
```

Constructor Tip, Part 1: Don't forget to specify the **override** directive after the constructor declaration. It is syntactically legal to omit the directive, but doing so will prevent the component from being dropped onto a form. Recall that the Form Designer creates new components by invoking the selected components' virtual constructor. By omitting the **override** directive, the chain is broken, and the correct component will not be created.

Constructor Tip, Part 2: Don't forget to call the inherited **Create** constructor!

Events

Both properties and methods have a direct correlation with elements in the object model. The last major group of Delphi components, *events*, are implemented using a combination of object model features. From the component user's perspective, events are indications that a system event has occurred. For example, a key was pressed or the mouse pointer was moved. The user responds to these events by writing *event handlers*. Event handlers are typically methods located in the form containing the component that generated the event.

For example, the Button component has a event called **OnClick**. Whenever the user clicks the mouse on the button component, an **OnClick** event is generated. The user can respond to the click event by creating an event handler using the Object Inspector. The event handler is created as a method in the form containing the button. Inside this method, the user writes code to perform the necessary actions whenever the button is pressed. In essence, the user has modified the behavior of the button component. This is an important point. Events allow users to customize the behavior of components without having to create new ones.

The component developer (rather than the component user) has quite a different view of events. From this perspective, events are hooks into the component's normal processing. As described above, these hooks are used by component users to link custom code to a particular component.

Events are implemented using method pointers. Recall from Chapter 2 that method pointers provide a way for one object to execute a method defined in another object. Method pointers provide the linking capability necessary to support event handling. However, method pointers are not manipulated directly. Instead, properties are defined for each event. By creating event properties, the Object Inspector can be used to connect custom code to individual components at design time.

Event Structure

Consider the following code fragment, which shows some of the standard events declared in the **TControl** class:

Listing 5.1   TControl's Events

```
type
  TControl = class( TComponent )
  private
    FOnClick : TNotifyEvent;
    FOnDblClick : TNotifyEvent;
    FOnMouseDown : TMouseEvent;
    FOnMouseMove : TMouseMoveEvent;
    . . .
  protected
    property OnClick : TNotifyEvent read FOnClick write FOnClick;
    property OnDblClick : TNotifyEvent read FOnDblClick write FOnDblClick;
    property OnMouseDown : TMouseEvent read FOnMouseDown write FOnMouseDown;
    property OnMouseMove : TMouseMoveEvent read FOnMouseMove write FOnMouseMove;
    . . .
  public
  end;
```

Notice that events are composed of two pieces. First an event requires an internal data field, which is used to hold the method pointer. Second, a corresponding property is created to allow event handlers to be connected at design-time.

So how does Delphi know which properties to display on the Properties page of the Object Inspector and which ones to display on the Events page? The Object Inspector uses the runtime type information stored for each property to determine the correct page. Only properties that are of method types appear on the Events page. Therefore, **TNotifyEvent**, **TMouseEvent**, and **TMouseMoveEvent** are method types that are defined as follows:

```
type
  TNotifyEvent = procedure( Sender : TObject ) of object;
  TMouseEvent = procedure( Sender : TObject; Button : TMouseButton;
                           Shift : TShiftState; X, Y : Integer ) of object;
  TMouseMoveEvent = procedure( Sender : TObject; Shift : TShiftState;
                              X, Y : Integer ) of object;
```

The method type associated with an event determines the parameters that are passed to the event handler. Furthermore, an event handler must have the same number and type of parameters as defined in the method type. Since these method types are used to implement event handlers, they are often called *event handler types*.

By Convention

Event handler types are declared as procedures. Although the compiler supports declaring method types that are functions, functions should not be used for event handlers. Since an empty function returns an undefined result, an empty event handler defined as a function may not always be valid.

Standard Events

All Delphi components inherit a set of standard events. Table 5.3 lists these events and when they occur. In addition to the standard events, components that descend from **TWinControl** inherit a set of window control events. These events are summarized in Table 5.4.

By default, all of these events are declared as **protected** (see Listing 5.1). Therefore, the standard events are not visible to component users. Descendant components are responsible for giving access to individual events by redeclaring the event prop-

Table 5.3   Events Common to ALL Components

Event Property	Occurs when a user
OnClick	clicks the component with the left mouse button
OnDblClick	double-clicks the component with the left mouse button
OnMouseDown	presses any mouse button with the cursor positioned over the component (paired with OnMouseUp)
OnMouseMove	moves the mouse over a component
OnMouseUp	releases a mouse button that was pressed while the mouse pointer was over a component (paired with OnMouseDown)
OnDragOver	drags an object over a component
OnDragDrop	drops an object that was being dragged
OnEndDrag	drops an object or terminates a dragging operation

Table 5.4   Window Control Events

Event Property	Occurs when a user
OnEnter	moves the input focus to a component
OnExit	removes the input focus from a component
OnKeyDown	presses a key while the component has the input focus
OnKeyUp	releases a key while the component has the input focus
OnKeyPress	presses a single character key

erties. For example, the **TEdit** component publishes the **OnClick** event by redeclaring the property in its **published** section. The class declaration looks like this:

```
type
  TEdit = class( TCustomEdit )
  private
    . . .
  published
    property OnClick;                        { Redeclared Onclick to be Published }
  end;
```

Standard Event Dispatching

Each of the events listed in Tables 5.3 and 5.4 have a corresponding protected method called an *event dispatch method*. These dispatch methods are responsible for executing the method referenced by the event's method pointer. The methods are named after the event sans the "On" prefix. For example, the event dispatch method for the **OnClick** event is called **Click**. Of course, there has to be an exception or two. The dispatch methods for the **OnEnter** and **OnExit** events replace "On" with "Do."

Suppose you wanted to change the way a custom component responds to a particular event. At first glance, you may be tempted to write the code to handle the event and then hook it to the event property. As a component user, this is the correct approach. However, as a component developer, this approach has a severe limitation. In particular, if the user decides to specify an event handler for the same event, your handler code will never be executed because the user has changed where the event handler's method pointer points to. It is no longer pointing to one of your methods but to one of the user's methods.

The correct approach is to override the event's dispatch method. As an example, consider a descendant of **TButton** called **TBeepButton**, which sounds a beep whenever pressed. This functionality is provided by simply overriding the **TButton.Click** method and adding the call to **MessageBeep**. The call to inherited **Click** is important because the inherited dispatch method is responsible for executing the user's event handler associated with this event.

```
type
  TBeepButton = class( TButton )
  protected
    procedure Click; override;               { Override Dispatch Method }
  end;
```

```
procedure TBeepButton.Click;
begin
  inherited Click;            { Default Dispatching - User Defined Handler }
  MessageBeep( 0 );                        { Custom Processing Goes Here }
end;
```

Creating Custom Events

Creating a new event is not a high-volume task in component development. The set of events provided by the VCL are usually adequate for handling your event needs. However, there will be times when you need to create a new event. The steps involved to do so include determining what action(s) triggers the event, declaring the event property, defining the method type, and finally dispatching the event once it occurs.

Before we get into the four tasks of creating events, a word of caution. The single most important issue regarding custom events is that events are optional. The code you write to trigger the event must not in any way be dependent on the existence of an associated event handler. Furthermore, your code should not depend on the component user responding to an event in any specific way.

The first task in creating a new event is to determine what actions trigger the event to occur. The trigger action may be some system event like a mouse click, or possibly a state change occurring in the component. It is even possible that multiple actions trigger the same event. Therefore, the common practice is to create a single event dispatch method for each type of event your component will manage. When your component detects an action that triggers the event (for example, **wm_LButtonDown**), all that needs to be done is call the dispatch method.

To aid in the discussion, consider the following scenario. We have a **TNumLockStatus** panel that knows how to detect changes in the NumLock key status, and we want to create an event that occurs whenever the NumLock key status changes.

The second task is to create an internal data field that will be used to hold the method pointer. This involves selecting (or creating) a method type that will adequately capture the information associated with the event. For example, mouse events use the **TMouseEvent** event handler type, which provides parameters indicating the X and Y positions of the mouse pointer.

Continuing with the **NumLock** example, the following code fragment shows the declarations for the **TNumLockEvent** event handler type and the **FOnNumLock** internal method pointer. The method type specifies an extra parameter that will be set to the new state of the NumLock key after a change.

```
type
  TNumLockEvent = procedure ( Sender : TObject; LockOn : Boolean ) of object;

  TNumLockStatus = class( TPanel )
  private
    FOnNumLock : TNumLockEvent;                              { Method Pointer }
    . . .
  end;
```

The third task involves declaring a new property that will read and write to the internal method pointer. There is one important point regarding this property declaration. The access clauses of an event property cannot specify methods. A method pointer must be specified for each value.

> ### By Convention
> Event properties start with the word "On" followed by the event name. For example, the property name for the Paint event is called **OnPaint**.

Now the **TNumLockStatus** class can be extended to incorporate the **OnNumLock** event property:

```
type
  TNumLockEvent = procedure ( Sender : TObject; LockOn : Boolean ) of object;

  TNumLockStatus = class( TPanel )
  private
    FOnNumLock : TNumLockEvent;                              { Method Pointer }
    . . .
  published
    property OnNumLock : TNumLockEvent read FOnNumLock write FOnNumLock;    { ** }
  end;
```

The final task in creating a custom event is to write the dispatch method for the event. Recall that the dispatch method is responsible for executing an attached event handler. This last block of code wraps up the **NumLockStatus** example by implementing the **NumLock** dispatch method. Whenever the status of the NumLock key changes, the detection code (not shown) calls the **NumLock** method. The dispatch method then executes the attached event handler only if one is present.

```
type
  TNumLockEvent = procedure ( Sender : TObject; LockOn : Boolean ) of object;

  TNumLockStatus = class( TPanel )
  private
    FNumLock : TNumLockEvent;                          { Method Pointer }
  protected
    procedure NumLock;                                 { Dispatch Method }
  published
    property OnNumLock : TNumLockEvent read FNumLock write FNumLock;
  end;

procedure TNumLockStatus.NumLock;
begin
  if Assigned( FNumLock ) then                    { Is there an event handler? }
    FNumLock( Self, IsNumLockOn );                        { If so, execute it }
end;
```

 The **Assigned** function is used in the dispatch method to check that the method pointer actually points to something. You might be tempted to write something like this:

```
if FNumLock then
  FNumLock( Self, IsNumLockOn );
```

However, the reference to **FNumLock** in the **IF** test actually instructs the compiler to execute the method referenced by **FNumLock**. The other alternative is to use the @ operator. The **Assigned** function is not limited to method pointers. It can be used with any pointer type.

Looking Ahead...

I stated several times in Part One that Object Pascal's object model is the foundation of Delphi's Component Architecture. This chapter further emphasized that relationship by showing a low-level view of how particular features of the object model are used to create the three basic features of components: properties, methods, and events. In the next chapter, the Visual Component Library is presented, with specific focus on a few of the classes that are used frequently during component development.

Chapter 6

The Visual Component Library

The Visual CHAPTER 6
Component
Library

All Delphi components belong to the Visual Component Library (VCL), either directly or through inheriting from a VCL ancestor. To create components, you'd be well advised to become a very close friend of the VCL.

For the application developer, the Visual Component Library (VCL) is a framework consisting of a set of components that are used to construct applications. For the component writer, the VCL represents an extensible class hierarchy containing a vast amount of functionality that can be incorporated, through the mechanism of inheritance, in custom components. The VCL is extensible in that new components become part of this hierarchy and thus can serve as ancestors for still other components in the future.

Out of the box, the VCL is quite extensive, with over 130 different public classes—not to mention more than 50 additional implementation-specific classes. To give you an idea of just how much information is captured in the VCL, consider the fact that the *VCL Reference Guide* has over 1,000 pages. And the reference guide is written from the perspective of a component user, not a component *writer*! Therefore, I will not even attempt to cover *all* of the classes in the VCL. Instead, this chapter maps out the important classes that will be used in building custom components.

If you're serious about building custom components, get the VCL source code! It comes with the Delphi Client/Server package and is sold as an add-on for Delphi for Windows. The source code is a fantastic reference, and there's no better way to learn how to build components than to see how the people at Borland actually did it!

The VCL Hierarchy

The term *Visual Component Library* is a bit misleading. This is mostly due to the fact that not all components are visual. The VCL includes nonvisual components as well. The confusion is further compounded in that many classes that are not even components are considered to be part of the VCL.

Figure 6.1 displays the base classes that form the structure of the VCL. At the top is **TObject**, which is the ultimate ancestor for all classes in Object Pascal. Descending from it is **TPersistent**, which provides the necessary methods to create *streamable objects.* A streamable object is one that can, oddly enough, be stored on a *stream.* A stream is an object that encapsulates a storage medium that can store binary data (for example, memory or disk files). Since Delphi implements form files using streams, **TComponent** descends from **TPersistent**, giving all components the ability to be saved in a form file.

Figure 6.1

The Base Classes of the VCL.

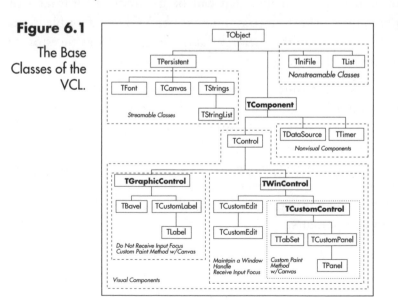

The **TComponent** class is essentially the top of the component hierarchy, and is the first of the four base classes used to create new components. Direct **TComponent** descendants are nonvisual components. The **TControl** class implements the necessary code for visual components. From the diagram in Figure 6.1, notice that there are two basic types of visual controls: graphic controls and windowed controls. Each is represented by its own hierarchy descending from **TGraphicControl** or **TWinControl**, respectively. The main difference between these types of components is that graphic controls do not maintain a window handle, and thus cannot receive the input focus.

Windowed components are further broken up into two categories. Direct descendants of **TWinControl** are wrappers around existing controls that are implemented within Windows and, therefore, already know how to paint themselves. The standard Windows controls like the edit field are direct descendants of **TWinControl**. For components that require a window handle but do not encapsulate an underlying Windows control that provides *visualization* (that is, the ability to repaint itself), the **TCustomControl** class is provided.

There are a number of supporting classes within the VCL that are not components, because they do not descend from **TComponent**, but which are nonetheless extremely useful to component writers. Some of these classes are streamable (like **TStringList**) and others, like **TIniFile**, are not. These supporting classes are used in implementing a component as well as serving as property types. However, only the streamable classes (that is, those derived from **TPersistent**) can be used for properties that are to be stored in the form file along with the other properties of the component.

 To get an overall view of the classes that make up the VCL, use the ObjectBrowser. The ObjectBrowser is a powerful tool for navigating through the entire hierarchy as well as viewing the details of each class. The ObjectBrowser is activated through the View|Browser menu item.

The Component Classes

The four shaded classes in Figure 6.1 represent the base classes from which you will derive new custom components. These classes were introduced in Chapter 5, and now we'll take a closer look at just what these classes provide.

TComponent

The **TComponent** class provides the properties and methods that enable components to be managed by the Form Designer. Besides the **Name** and **Tag** properties, **TComponent** introduces a couple of properties useful to component writers. One of the most useful is **ComponentState**. This property holds a set of values that indicate the current state of the component. The possible values are described in Table 6.1.

A common usage of the **ComponentState** property is to determine whether the component is being manipulated at run-time or design-time. For example, the Image component uses this property to determine if a dashed border should be drawn around the control. The following fragment from the **TImage.Paint** method shows that by checking if **csDesigning** is in the **ComponentState** set, the dashed border is only drawn at design-time.

```
procedure TImage.Paint;
begin
  if csDesigning in ComponentState then
  begin                               { Draw Dashed Border only at Design-Time }
    with inherited Canvas do
    begin
      Pen.Style := psDash;
      Brush.Style := bsClear;
      Rectangle( 0, 0, Width, Height );
    end;
  end;
  . . .                    { Continue Drawing the Image within Bounds of Component }
end;
```

The **TComponent** class also introduces the concept of *ownership* that is propagated throughout the VCL. There are two properties that support ownership:

Table 6.1	ComponentState Flags
Flag	**Component State Description**
csDesigning	The component is in Design mode (that is, it is on a form being manipulated by the Form Designer).
csDestroying	The component is about to be destroyed.
csLoading	The component is being loaded from a form file.
csReading	The component is reading its property values from a stream.
csWriting	The component is writing its property values to a stream.

Owner and **Components**. Every component has an **Owner** property that references another component as its owner. Likewise, a component may own other components. In this case, all owned components are referenced in the **Components** array property. A component's constructor takes a single parameter that is used to specify the new component's owner. If the passed-in owner exists, then the new component is added to the owner's **Components** list.

Aside from using the **Components** list to reference owned components, the most important service this property provides is *automatic destruction* of owned components. This is an important point even for application developers. As long as the component has an owner, it will be destroyed when the owner is destroyed. For example, since **TForm** is a descendant of **TComponent**, when a form is destroyed, all components owned by the form are destroyed and their memory freed.

Turning to the methods of **TComponent**, one of the most useful is the **Notification** method. This method is called whenever a component is inserted into or removed from the owner's **Components** list. The owner sends a notification to each member of the **Components** list. The **Notification** method is overridden in descendant classes to ensure that a component's references to other components remain valid.

Providing a **Notification** method is especially important for design time operation. Consider the form shown in Figure 6.2, which contains two components: **Label1** and **Edit1**. **Label1** references **Edit1** through its **FocusControl** property. When **Label1** is selected, the Object Inspector displays the focused control's name by accessing the **FocusControl.Name** property (that is, **Edit1**). Now, suppose **Edit1** is deleted from the form. If **Label1** is *not* notified of this change, its **FocusControl** property becomes invalid because it is pointing to the memory location that used to be occupied by **Edit1**. Therefore, if **Label1** is selected again,

Figure 6.2

The FocusControl Property at Work.

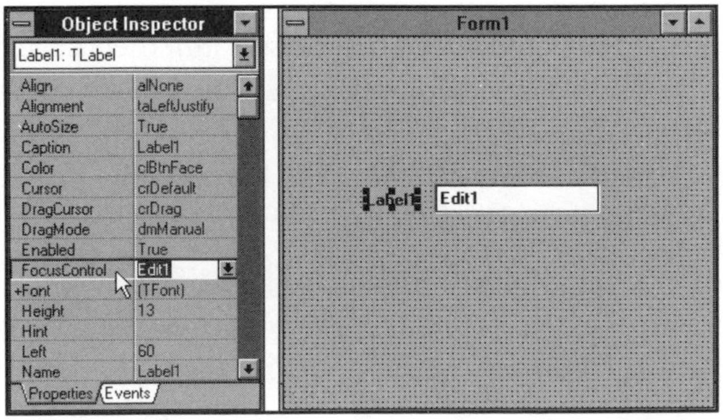

a GPF occurs when the Object Inspector tries to access **FocusControl.Name.** Fortunately, the **TLabel** component *does* provide a **Notification** method to prevent this.

Since the **Notification** method is called whenever a component is inserted or removed from a form, the label's **Notification** method, shown below, tests if the component being removed is the one referenced by the label's **FocusControl** property. (**FFocusControl** is the internal data storage for the property.) If so, then the reference is set to **nil** and the GPF is avoided.

```
procedure TLabel.Notification( AComponent: TComponent; Operation: TOperation );
begin
  inherited Notification( AComponent, Operation );
  if ( Operation = opRemove ) and ( AComponent = FFocusControl ) then
    FFocusControl := nil;
end;
```

There is one more method defined in **TComponent** that is of particular interest to component writers. The **Loaded** method is a virtual method that is called immediately after all the property values of a component are read in from a form file. Since the call to **Loaded** occurs *before* the form and component are displayed, you can perform initialization steps without worrying about causing excessive repaints. The MediaPlayer component has a fine example of overriding the **Loaded** method.

```
procedure TMediaPlayer.Loaded;
begin
  inherited Loaded;
  if ( not ( csDesigning in ComponentState ) ) and FAutoOpen then
    Open;
end;
```

The MediaPlayer's version of **Loaded** first calls its inherited **Loaded** method. This should always be done when overriding the **Loaded** method. This ensures that any inherited properties are correctly initialized. In addition, the **TComponent.Loaded** method is responsible for updating the **ComponentState** property by removing the **csLoading** flag from the set.

Next, the method checks if the component is being loaded at run-time and if the **AutoOpen** property is set to **True.** If both conditions are met, the MediaPlayer tries to open the media file.

TControl

Although not one of the shaded classes, the **TControl** class provides a majority of the properties, methods, and events used by all visual components in Delphi. For example, Table 6.2 shows some of the properties and events that are introduced in **TControl**.

Very few of these properties and events are declared with the **published** directive. This allows descendant classes to determine which properties and events will appear in the Object Inspector. This is a common theme in the VCL because although a property can be made more visible in a descendant class by redeclaring it (see the "Properties and Class Hierarchies" section in Chapter 3), it cannot be made *less* visible.

There are many classes that implement the properties, methods, and events of a component but do not publish their properties and events. They leave this task to descendant classes. The **TControl** class is an example of this. Likewise, there are numerous *Custom* classes in the VCL that behave similarly. For example, the **TCustomEdit** class provides all of the properties and methods to support the edit field control, but very few of the properties and events are made visible. The **TEdit** class redeclares the properties and events to be published.

Going back to **TControl**, there are a couple of properties introduced in this class that are important to component writers. First of all, the **TControl** class introduces the notion of *parent controls* in the VCL. The term "parent" used here is a Windows-specific term. Although similar to "owner," a control's parent is the

Table 6.2 Properties and Events of TControl	
Properties	
Position Properties	Left, Top, Width, Height, Align
Client Area Properties	ClientRect, ClientWidth, ClientHeight
Appearance Properties	Visible, Enabled, Font, Color
String Properties	Caption, Hint, Text
Mouse Properties	Cursor, DragCursor, DragMode
Events	
Left Mouse Button Events	OnClick, OnDblClick
General Mouse Events	OnMouseDown, OnMouseMove, OnMouseUp
Drag and Drop Support	OnDragDrop, OnDragOver, OnEndDrag

Table 6.3 ControlStyle Flags	
Flag	**Control Style Description**
csAcceptsControls	The control becomes the parent of any controls dropped on it at design time. Only applicable to Windowed controls.
csCaptureMouse	The control captures mouse events. (That is, MouseUp events are sent to control even if mouse was released outside the bounds of the control.)
csDesignInteractive	At design-time, right mouse button clicks are translated to left mouse button clicks.
csClickEvents	When the mouse is pressed and released on the control, an OnClick event is generated.
csFramed	The control has a frame. Needed for Ctl3D effects.
csSetCaption	The control's Caption or Text properties are set to match the Name property. Only occurs if Caption/Text has not been explicitly set.
csOpaque	The control hides any items behind it, as opposed to being transparent.
csDoubleClicks	When the mouse is double-clicked on the control, an OnDblClick event is generated.
csFixedWidth	The width of the control is not effected by scaling.
csFixedHeight	The height of the control is not effected by scaling.

window (not the component) that contains the control. Therefore, parents must be **TWinControl** objects or descendents, because a window handle is necessary in order to contain other controls.

The second property of interest to the component writer is the **ControlStyle** property. This property indicates the various styles applicable only to visual components. The **ControlStyle** set can contain any number of the flags specified in Table 6.3. The **ControlStyle** set is usually manipulated in the **Create** constructor of a component, and we'll see several examples of this in upcoming chapters.

The **TControl** class also implements many methods used by visual components. For example, the event dispatch methods (for example, **Click**, **MouseUp**) supporting all of the events listed previously are introduced in **TControl**. It is very common for custom components to override these dispatch methods to provide custom handling of events without disturbing the delegation model.

TGraphicControl

The **TGraphicControl** class is the base class for components that do not need to receive the input focus or serve as a parent to other controls. Both of these tasks require a window handle, which is not available in this class.

Even though graphic controls do not have a window handle, they are still able to respond to mouse events. This is made possible by the control's parent. The parent of a control must be a **TWinControl** (for example, a Form or Panel), and **TWinControl** components respond to mouse messages by determining if the mouse event occurred within the bounds of any of its child controls. If so, then the message is sent to the child control.

By default, **TGraphicControl** objects have no visual appearance of their own. However, a virtual **Paint** method and **Canvas** property are provided for descendants. The **Paint** method is called whenever the control needs to be painted, and the **Canvas** property is used as a "surface" for the actual drawing of the control. The **TCanvas** class is described in detail a little later on in this chapter.

 WARNING: Although it is possible to set a graphic control's **ControlStyle** to include **csAcceptsControls**, it is not valid to do so. Since a graphic control does not have a window handle, when you attempt to drop a component on top of it, Delphi will attempt to insert the dropped component into the *window* of your graphic control. Since this is not possible without a window handle, you will experience a severe GPF.

TWinControl

The **TWinControl** class is used as the base class for creating components that encapsulate existing window controls that perform their own painting. This includes the standard Windows controls like edit fields and check boxes, as well as custom controls implemented as dynamic link libraries. Since VBX controls are implemented as DLLs, the VBX component wrapper class that Delphi generates when installing a VBX control descends from **TWinControl**.

As mentioned earlier, the **TWinControl** class provides the **Handle** property, which is a reference to the underlying control's window handle. In addition to this property, the **TWinControl** class implements the properties, methods, and events that support keyboard events and focus changes. These additions are summarized in Table 6.4.

Table 6.4 Properties, Methods, and Events for TWinControl	
Properties	
Focus Properties	TabStop, TabOrder
Appearance Properties	Ctl3D, Showing
Methods	
Event Dispatch Methods	DoEnter, DoExit, KeyDown, KeyPress, KeyUp
Focus Methods	CanFocus, Focused
Alignment Methods	AlignControls, EnableAlign, DisableAlign, Realign
Window Methods	CreateWnd, CreateParams, CreateWindowHandle, RecreateWnd, DestroyWnd
Events	
Focus Events	OnEnter, OnExit
Keyboard Events	OnKeyDown, OnKeyPress, OnKeyUp

The are two methods in **TWinControl** that deserve a closer look. The **CreateParams** and **CreateWnd** virtual methods are often overridden by component writers. Both methods are called during the creation of the underlying Windows control. Whenever the window needs to be created, **CreateWnd** is called. **CreateWnd** first calls **CreateParams** to initialize a window-creation parameter record, and then calls **CreateWindowHandle** to create the actual window handle using the parameter record. **CreateWnd** then adjusts the size of the window and finally sets the control's font.

A component writer will typically override the **CreateParams** method when the window handle to be created needs to be created using additional Windows style settings. The method takes a **TCreateParams** record as its single parameter. As an example, the **TBitBtn** component overrides this method to specify that BitBtn windows be created with the **bs_OwnerDraw** style.

```
procedure TBitBtn.CreateParams( var Params : TCreateParams );
begin
  inherited CreateParams( Params );
  Params.Style := Params.Style or bs_OwnerDraw;
end;
```

CreateWnd, on the other hand, will typically be overridden when some initialization code that depends on the existence of the window handle must be executed. For example, the **TCustomEdit** component class overrides **CreateWnd** so that it may send the **em_LimitText** Windows message to the underlying edit window. This message sets the maximum length of text allowed by the edit field. Notice that writing the call as **inherited CreateWnd** ensures that the **Handle** property will be set correctly for use in the call to **SendMessage**:

```
procedure TCustomEdit.CreateWnd;
begin
  . . .
  inherited CreateWnd;
  . . .
  SendMessage( Handle, EM_LIMITTEXT, FMaxLength, 0 );
  . . .
end;
```

We will see more examples of overriding both of these methods, **CreateParams** and **CreateWnd**, in future chapters.

TCustomControl

The **TCustomControl** class is a combination of the **TWinControl** class and the **TGraphicControl**. By descending from **TWinControl**, **TCustomControl** inherits the ability to manage a window handle and all the features that go with it. However, it is similar to **TGraphicControl** in that it provides a virtual **Paint** method with an associated **Canvas** property. The **TCustomControl** class is used as a base for components that must provide their own painting routines.

The Supporting Cast

As mentioned earlier, the VCL contains more than just components that can be dropped onto a form. Non-component objects are very much in evidence, and play a key part in the VCL's overall mission. The *VCL Objects*, as they are called in the Delphi documentation, are very useful to component writers as implementation tools and as property types. The **TCanvas** and **TStrings** classes are two of the most useful.

A Canvas to Paint On

The **TForm** class is actually a descendant of **TWinControl** and provides a **Canvas** property that can be used in order to draw in the form's client area. In the same manner the **TGraphicControl** and **TCustomControl** classes provide a **Canvas** property that is used by the component writer to give a component its visual appearance. Although the **Canvas** property is seldom used by application developers, this is not true for component writers. As I have pointed out earlier, graphic controls and custom controls will need custom painting.

The **Canvas** properties are of type **TCanvas**, which is roughly equivalent to a Windows device context. The **Canvas** property gives the developer a fast and straightforward way of drawing on a window as opposed to using the Windows GDI. Using the Windows GDI requires quite a bit of overhead. Consider the steps that it takes to draw a colored rectangle with a dashed border on a window: First, the dashed pen must be created because the default pen is solid. Next, a colored brush must be created. This brush will be used to color in the rectangle. Step three involves selecting the new pen and brush into the device context. Next, the rectangle is drawn. Unfortunately, this is not the end of the process. The original drawing objects must be selected back into the device context. Therefore, you must keep the old objects around. After selecting the old objects back into the device context, you need to delete the new objects that you created. And that's what it takes to draw a colored rectangle on a window. Sometimes it makes doing your taxes seem like a snap.

The **Canvas** property simplifies many of the tasks that must be performed when drawing on windows. First of all, the entire (somewhat peculiar) concept of selecting "into" and "out of" a device context is removed from the process. Instead, the **Canvas** property, or more precisely the **Canvas** object, has properties that represent all of the drawing objects, such as **Pen**, **Brush**, and **Font**. With the **Canvas** property, there is no longer a need to create the new brush that is used to fill the rectangle. Instead, the **Brush** property of the **Canvas** is simply changed to reflect the desired color. Furthermore, the **Canvas** property handles restoring the original drawing objects, and thus removes this burden from the programmer.

To demonstrate the significance of the overhead required by normal Windows GDI programming, consider Listing 6.1. This listing contains two procedures that perform the same task. However, the first one is written in OWL using normal GDI calls, whereas the second is written in Delphi and uses the **Canvas** property. Aside from being far simpler, using the **Canvas** can provide a performance boost because it caches the drawing objects that are used in your application.

Listing 6.1   GDI Calls versus the Canvas Property

```
{ OWL Paint method making direct GDI calls }

procedure TMainWindow.Paint( PaintDC : HDC;
                             var PaintInfo : TPaintStruct );
var
  OldBrush, RedBrush : HBrush;
  OldPen, DashPen    : HPen;
begin
  DashPen := CreatePen( ps_Dash, 1, RGB( 0, 0, 0 ) );
  RedBrush := CreateSolidBrush( RGB( 255, 0, 0 ) );

  OldPen := SelectObject( PaintDC, DashPen );
  OldBrush := SelectObject( PaintDC, RedBrush );

  Rectangle( PaintDC, 10, 10, 200, 200 );

  SelectObject( PaintDC, OldPen );
  SelectObject( PaintDC, OldBrush );

  DeleteObject( DashPen );
  DeleteObject( RedBrush );
end;



{ Delphi FormPaint method using Canvas property }

procedure TForm1.FormPaint( Sender : TObject );
begin
  Canvas.Brush.Color := clRed;
  Canvas.Pen.Style := psDash;
  Canvas.Rectangle( 10, 10, 200, 200 );
end;
```

Component writers will use the **Canvas** property quite a bit—especially if they are building a graphic or custom component. The **TCanvas** class provides many methods that map to corresponding GDI function calls. Some of the more useful ones for component writers are summarized in Table 6.5. As you can see there are quite a bit of rectangle-oriented methods listed. This is because most user interface controls are rectangular in nature.

It should be noted that the **TCanvas** class does not provide methods for all of the GDI functions but only for the common ones. But what if you need to use one of the GDI functions? Do you need to go back to using device contexts? Well, not exactly. The **TCanvas** class provides a **Handle** property for just this reason. The

Table 6.5 Useful TCanvas Methods	
Method	**Description**
MoveTo	Moves the current pen position to a new point.
LineTo	Draws a line from the current pen position to the specified point.
Rectangle	Draws a rectangle at the specified coordinates.
FrameRect	Draws a rectangle using the current brush to draw the border. The interior of the rectangle is not filled.
DrawFocusRect	Draws the Windows *focus* rectangle at the specified coordinates.
FillRect	Fills the specified rectangle using the current brush.
CopyRect	Copies part of an image from another canvas into the current canvas.
TextHeight	Returns the height in pixels of a text string if it were rendered using the current font.
TextWidth	Returns the width in pixels of a text string if it were rendered using the current font.
TextOut	Displays text at the specified coordinates.
TextRect	Displays text using a clipping rectangle. Text that would appear outside the rectangle is not drawn.

Handle property represents the actual device context that is being used. There-fore, any GDI function can be called by using the **Handle** property wherever a device context handle is needed. For example, the following code fragment from the **Paint** method of the progress bar component that I'll present in Chapter 9 uses the **SetTextAlign** GDI function:

```
begin
  . . .
  SetTextAlign( Canvas.Handle, ta_Center or ta_Top );
  . . .
end;
```

For more information on using the **TCanvas** object, refer to Chapters 11 and 12 in the *Delphi User's Guide*.

String Lists

If you've been developing applications in Delphi for any length of time, you've been bombarded with string lists. They're everywhere. List boxes and combo boxes, memo controls and tab sets, notebook pages and outlines. They all have a **TStrings** property that is accessible through the Object Inspector. This gives the compo-nent user a clean and consistent way of managing a list of strings.

As a component writer, you'll eventually have to incorporate a string list property into one of your components. The actual details of doing so are deferred until Chapter 11, but I mention it here to point out a trap that many component writers fall victim to—that is, deciding which class to use for the property type, **TStrings** or **TStringList**. The problem occurs because the correct answer is a combination of both. The **TStrings** class is an abstract class that defines all of the behaviors associated with a string list. However, the **TStrings** class does not provide any features to actually *hold* the list of strings. Descendants of **TStrings**, like **TStringList**, are responsible for that.

With this in mind, component writers are often quick to select **TStringList**, but this is short-sighted. One of the more powerful features of the **TStrings** class is that you can copy the strings in one list to another using the **Assign** method. If you declare your property to be a **TStringList** property, then you will only be able to assign other **TStringList** type properties to it. A better approach is to declare the property as **TStrings**.

But what about the fact that **TStrings** cannot hold the list of strings? This is solved by having the property reference an object of type **TStringList** or some other descendant of **TStrings**. The property (of type **TStrings**) provides the interface while the underlying object it references (of type **TStringList**) provides the storage.

A classic example of this approach is found in the **TCustomListBox** class. The **Items** property and its internal data storage field, **FItems**, are both declared as **TStrings**. However, in the constructor of **TCustomListBox**, the **FItems** field is assigned to an instance of **TListBoxStrings**. Since the underlying Windows list box control actually manages the list of strings, the **TListBoxStrings** class serves as a translator between the methods defined in the **TStrings** class and the Windows messages that must be sent to the control to actually manipulate the strings.

Persistent Data

In this section we'll be going over how Delphi stores components in a form file. Usually a component writer can rely on the default processing of Delphi's streaming mechanism to ensure that component data is correctly stored in the form file. However, there are situations when it becomes necessary to store additional information about the component that the default processing doesn't know how to handle. After reviewing the form saving process, an example demonstrating how to specify additional persistent data will be presented.

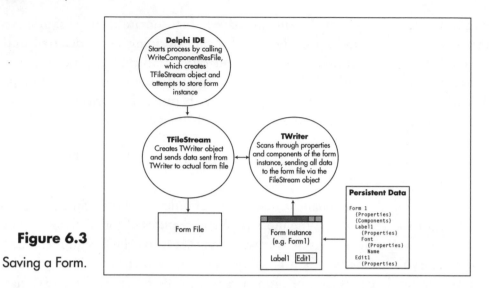

Figure 6.3

Saving a Form.

To start off, Figure 6.3 gives a graphical overview of the steps that occur when a form is saved. The process is begun with Delphi making a call to **Write-ComponentResFile**, a global procedure declared in the **Classes** unit. The form's file name and instance variable are passed to the procedure. For example:

```
WriteComponentResFile( 'UNIT1.DFM', Form1 );
```

A **TFileStream** object is created next, and this object is responsible for moving the data in and out of the physical disk file. Delphi form files are actually stored as Windows resource files, and the stream object is responsible for creating the correct resource header information before the form's data is actually stored.

After the stream is set up, the file stream object creates a **TWriter** object, which is used to determine what data is to be stored in the stream. The **TWriter** object first starts with the form instance, in this example **Form1**, and parses out all of the form's storable properties and sends the property values to the stream. After the form's properties are processed, the **TWriter** object goes through all of the components that are in **Form1**'s **Components** list. For each component in the list, the property values of that component are determined and sent to the stream. Since properties can be objects, some component properties may in turn have their own properties that need to be sent to the stream. An example of this is the **Font** property of the Label component. Fortunately, the recursive nature of this process handles sending the font's **Name** property to the stream as well. The process continues until all components on the form are sent to the stream.

This is only a summary of the process that occurs when a form is saved. The process itself is much more complex in coding terms yet is quite elegant. Interestingly enough, you can actually test out this process because the **WriteComponentResFile** is a global procedure. Just don't specify a file name of one of your existing forms! Reading the form back into Delphi is handled by a similar process involving a **TReader** object instead of a **TWriter**.

Saving Unpublished or Non-Standard Properties

The above process will handle saving most of the properties that your components will use. This is possible because the **TWriter** object uses Run-Time Type Information (RTTI) to determine which properties can be stored in the form file. This means that only published properties will be written to the form file by default. Fortunately, unpublished properties and non-standard property types can also be stored in the form file by instructing Delphi how to interpret the data.

The **TPersistent** class introduces a virtual method called **DefineProperties,** which provides the means of instructing Delphi how to store special property data. This method will be overridden by component writers under two circumstances. First, the component itself will override **DefineProperties**. This is usually done when it is necessary to store unpublished property values of the component in the form file. The second circumstance under which the overriding of **DefineProperties** occurs is when the property type that needs to be saved is a class type. In this case, the property class will override the method.

In either case, the process is the same. **DefineProperties** is passed a **TFiler** object as its only parameter. The **TFiler** class is an abstract class that serves as the immediate ancestor to both **TReader** and **TWriter**. A **TFiler** reference is used because this method is called during both the read and write operations. For example, when the object is being read in from a stream, the **TFiler** parameter will actually reference a **TReader** object. Within the method, the various properties that need to be stored, or loaded, are specified using the **TFiler.DefineProperty** method. Let's take a look at a real example.

The TIntegerList Class

The **TIntergerList** class is similar to **TStringList**, but instead of dealing with strings, it deals with integers. The methods for adding, deleting, and finding integers on the list are the same as those used in **TStringList** and will not be covered here. However, in order for this class to effectively serve as a property type, it must provide the ability to load and store the list of numbers to and from the form file. This is an example of the second circumstance described above for overriding the **DefineProperties** method.

Listing 6.2 shows **TIntegerList**'s streaming methods. (Listing 6.3 shows the complete source code for the **IntList** unit, which contains the **TIntegerList** class, but because of the length of the **TIntegerList** class, the particular methods of interest are shown again in Listing 6.2.) The first method of interest is **DefineProperties**, which is overridden in this class to specify three properties that will become the persistent data for the class. The three properties are the minimum and maximum range limits and the list of integers.

As mentioned above, the **TFiler.DefineProperty** method is used to specify how each property is managed. The **DefineProperty** method takes four parameters. The first is a string that will be used as the property's name in the form file. This does not have to be the same as the actual property name. The second and third parameters are methods responsible for reading and writing the desired data, respectively. The final parameter is a Boolean expression that indicates whether or not the property has any data to store. This last parameter is only used during the write process.

Listing 6.2   TIntegerList's Streaming Methods

```
procedure TIntegerList.DefineProperties( Filer : TFiler );
begin
  Filer.DefineProperty( 'Min', ReadMin, WriteMin, FMin <> 0 );
  Filer.DefineProperty( 'Max', ReadMax, WriteMax, FMax <> 0 );
  Filer.DefineProperty( 'Integers', ReadIntegers, WriteIntegers, Count > 0 );
end;


procedure TIntegerList.ReadMin( Reader : TReader );
begin
  FMin := Reader.ReadInteger;
end;

procedure TIntegerList.WriteMin( Writer : TWriter );
begin
  Writer.WriteInteger( FMin );
end;


procedure TIntegerList.ReadIntegers( Reader : TReader );
begin
  Reader.ReadListBegin;                    { Read in the Start of List Marker }
```

```
  Clear;                                          { Clear Current List }
  while not Reader.EndOfList do
    Add( Reader.ReadInteger );                 { Add Stored Integers to List }
  Reader.ReadListEnd;                        { Read in the End of List Marker }
end;

procedure TIntegerList.WriteIntegers( Writer : TWriter );
var
  I : Integer;
begin
  Writer.WriteListBegin;           { Be sure to Write the Start of List Marker }
  for I := 0 to Count - 1 do
    Writer.WriteInteger( GetItem( I ) );      { Write All Integers to Writer }
  Writer.WriteListEnd;                      { Write the End of List Marker }
end;
```

After defining the properties, the next step is to write the methods that do the actual work of reading and writing the data. Listing 6.2 includes the read and write methods for the **Min** and **Integers** properties. As you can see, these methods have a specific format. The read methods take a single **TReader** parameter, whereas the write methods are passed a **TWriter** object.

TReader and **TWriter** provide several methods to facilitate transferring data to and from a stream. For example, the **Min** property is read in from the form file by calling **Reader.ReadInteger**, and it is written to the file using **Writer.WriteInteger**. The methods for managing the list are a little more interesting. Whenever you need to write a list of data to the stream under a single property name, you must first call the **WriteListBegin** method. This method inserts a start-of-list marker into the stream to indicate the start of the list for the read process. Next, the list values are written using one of the appropriate methods of **TWriter** (for example, **WriteString**, **WriteFloat**). In this example, our list is made up of integers, so **WriteInteger** is used. When all of the list items have been written, the **WriteListEnd** method is called to insert the end-of-list marker.

Reading the list back is accomplished with a similar approach. First, the stream is checked for the start-of-list marker. Next, the list is cleared, to get ready to add the new numbers on the stream. Notice that **Clear** is called after **ReadListBegin**. This is done in case the start-of-list marker is not found. If this happens, an exception is raised and the process stops. Calling **Clear** before **ReadListBegin** would cause the list to be cleared even in the event of an error. Moving on, the **ReadIntegers** method then continues to add the integers that are read in from the stream to the internal list until the **EndOfList** function returns **True**. And finally, the end-of-list marker is read to complete the process.

This approach can be used whenever you want to make property values persistent. By the way, we'll be seeing the **TIntegerList** class again in Chapter 8, where it will be used for a **TabStops** property.

Listing 6.3   INTLIST.PAS—TIntegerList Class

```
{=========================================================================}
{= This unit provides a TIntegerList class which mimics the TStringList class =}
{= except that this class manages a list of Longints.                      =}
{=========================================================================}

unit IntList;

interface

uses
  Classes;

type
  EOutOfRange  = class( EListError );

  TIntegerList = class( TPersistent )
  private
    FList        : TList;
    FDuplicates  : TDuplicates;
    FMin         : Longint;
    FMax         : Longint;
    FSizeOfLong  : Integer;
    FSorted      : Boolean;
    procedure ReadMin( Reader : TReader );
    procedure WriteMin( Writer : TWriter );
    procedure ReadMax( Reader : TReader );
    procedure WriteMax( Writer : TWriter );
    procedure ReadIntegers( Reader : TReader );
    procedure WriteIntegers( Writer : TWriter );
    procedure SetSorted( Value : Boolean );
    procedure QuickSort( L, R : Integer );
  protected
    procedure DefineProperties( Filer : TFiler ); override;
    function Find( N : Longint; var Index : Integer ) : Boolean; virtual;
    function GetCount : Integer;
    function GetItem( Index : Integer ) : Longint;
    procedure SetItem( Index : Integer; Value : Longint ); virtual;
    procedure SetMin( Value : Longint );
    procedure SetMax( Value : Longint );
    procedure Sort; virtual;
  public
    constructor Create;
```

```
    destructor Destroy; override;

    function Add( Value : Longint ) : Integer; virtual;
    procedure AddIntegers( List : TIntegerList ); virtual;
    procedure Assign( Source : TPersistent ); override;
    procedure Clear; virtual;
    procedure Delete( Index : Integer ); virtual;
    function Equals( List : TIntegerList ) : Boolean;
    procedure Exchange( Index1, Index2 : Integer); virtual;
    function IndexOf( N : Longint ) : Integer; virtual;
    procedure Insert( Index : Integer; Value : Longint ); virtual;
    procedure Move( CurIndex, NewIndex : Integer ); virtual;

    property Duplicates : TDuplicates read FDuplicates write FDuplicates;
    property Count : Integer read GetCount;
    property Items[Index: Integer]: Longint read GetItem write SetItem; default;
    property Min : Longint read FMin write SetMin;
    property Max : Longint read FMax write SetMax;
    property Sorted: Boolean read FSorted write SetSorted;
  end;


implementation

uses
  WinTypes;

{=========================}
{== TIntegerList Methods ==}
{=========================}

constructor TIntegerList.Create;
begin
  inherited Create;
  FList := TList.Create;
  FSizeOfLong := SizeOf( Longint );
end;


destructor TIntegerList.Destroy;
begin
  Clear;
  FList.Free;
  inherited Destroy;
end;


procedure TIntegerList.Assign( Source : TPersistent );
begin
  if Source is TIntegerList then
  begin
    Clear;
```

```
    AddIntegers( TIntegerList( Source ) );
  end
  else
    inherited Assign( Source );
end;


procedure TIntegerList.DefineProperties( Filer : TFiler );
begin
  Filer.DefineProperty( 'Min', ReadMin, WriteMin, FMin <> 0 );
  Filer.DefineProperty( 'Max', ReadMax, WriteMax, FMax <> 0 );
  Filer.DefineProperty( 'Integers', ReadIntegers, WriteIntegers, Count > 0 );
end;


procedure TIntegerList.ReadMin( Reader : TReader );
begin
  FMin := Reader.ReadInteger;
end;


procedure TIntegerList.WriteMin( Writer : TWriter );
begin
  Writer.WriteInteger( FMin );
end;


procedure TIntegerList.ReadMax( Reader : TReader );
begin
  FMax := Reader.ReadInteger;
end;


procedure TIntegerList.WriteMax( Writer : TWriter );
begin
  Writer.WriteInteger( FMax );
end;


procedure TIntegerList.ReadIntegers( Reader : TReader );
begin
  Clear;                                         { Clear Current List }
  Reader.ReadListBegin;              { Read in the Start of List Marker }
  while not Reader.EndOfList do
    Add( Reader.ReadInteger );              { Add Stored Integers to List }
  Reader.ReadListEnd;                  { Read in the End of List Marker }
end;


procedure TIntegerList.WriteIntegers( Writer : TWriter );
var
  I : Integer;
```

```
begin
  Writer.WriteListBegin;              { Be sure to Write the Start of List Marker }
  for I := 0 to Count - 1 do
    Writer.WriteInteger( GetItem( I ) );            { Write All Integers to Writer }
  Writer.WriteListEnd;                              { Write the End of List Marker }
end;


procedure TIntegerList.SetSorted( Value : Boolean );
begin
  if FSorted <> Value then
  begin
    if Value then
      Sort;
    FSorted := Value;
  end;
end;


function TIntegerList.GetCount : Integer;
begin
  Result := FList.Count;
end;


function TIntegerList.GetItem( Index : Integer ) : Longint;
begin
  Result := PLongint( FList.Items[ Index ] )^;
end;


procedure TIntegerList.SetItem( Index : Integer; Value : Longint );
begin
  if ( FMin <> FMax ) and ( ( Value < FMin ) or ( Value > FMax ) ) then
    raise EOutOfRange.CreateFmt( 'Value must be within %d..%d', [ FMin, FMax ]);

  PLongint( FList.Items[ Index ] )^ := Value;
end;


procedure TIntegerList.SetMin( Value : Longint );
var
  I : Integer;
begin
  if Value <> FMin then
  begin
    for I := 0 to Count - 1 do
    begin
      if GetItem( I ) < Value then
        raise EOutOfRange.CreateFmt( 'Unable to set new minimum value.'#13 +
                                     'List contains values below %d',[ Value ]);
```

```
      end;
    FMin := Value;
    if FMin > FMax then
      FMax := FMin;
  end;
end; {= TIntegerList.SetMin =}


procedure TIntegerList.SetMax( Value : Longint );
var
  I : Integer;
begin
  if Value <> FMax then
  begin
    for I := 0 to Count - 1 do
    begin
      if GetItem( I ) > Value then
        raise EOutOfRange.CreateFmt( 'Unable to set new maximum value.'#13 +
                                     'List contains values above %d',[ Value ]);
    end;
    FMax := Value;
    if FMax < FMin then
      FMin := FMax;
  end;
end; {= TIntegerList.SetMax =}


procedure TIntegerList.AddIntegers( List : TIntegerList );
var
  I : Integer;
begin
  for I := 0 to Pred( List.Count ) do
    Add( List[ I ] );
end;


function TIntegerList.Add( Value : Longint ) : Integer;
begin
  Insert( Count, Value );
end;


procedure TIntegerList.Clear;
var
  I : Integer;
begin
  for I := 0 to Pred( FList.Count ) do
    Dispose( PLongint( FList.Items[ I ] ) );
  FList.Clear;
end;
```

```
procedure TIntegerList.Delete( Index : Integer );
begin
  Dispose( PLongint( FList.Items[ Index ] ) );
  FList.Delete( Index );
end;


function TIntegerList.Equals( List : TIntegerList ) : Boolean;
var
  I, Count : Integer;
begin
  Count := GetCount;
  if Count <> List.GetCount then
    Result := False
  else
  begin
    I := 0;
    while ( I < Count ) and ( GetItem( I ) = List.GetItem( I ) ) do
      Inc( I );
    Result := I = Count;
  end;
end; {= TIntegerList.Equals =}


procedure TIntegerList.Exchange( Index1, Index2 : Integer );
begin
  FList.Exchange( Index1, Index2 );
end;


{= Find - Implements a binary search which is called by IndexOf only if the  =}
{=        list is sorted.                                                    =}

function TIntegerList.Find( N : Longint; var Index : Integer ) : Boolean;
var
  L, H, I : Integer;
begin
  Result := False;
  L := 0;
  H := Count - 1;
  while L <= H do
  begin
    I := ( L + H ) shr 1;
    if PLongint( FList[ I ] )^ < N then
      L := I + 1
    else
    begin
      H := I - 1;
      if PLongint( FList[ I ] )^ = N then
      begin
        Result := True;
        if Duplicates <> dupAccept then
```

```
        L := I;
      end;
    end;
  end;
  Index := L;
end; {= TIntegerList.Find =}


function TIntegerList.IndexOf( N : Longint ) : Integer;
var
  I : Integer;
begin
  Result := -1;

  if not Sorted then
  begin
    for I := 0 to Pred( GetCount ) do
    begin
      if GetItem( I ) = N then
        Result := I;
    end;
  end
  else if Find( N, I ) then
    Result := I;
end; {= TIntegerList.IndexOf =}


procedure TIntegerList.Insert( Index : Integer; Value : Longint );
var
  P : PLongint;
begin
  if ( FMin <> FMax ) and ( ( Value < FMin ) or ( Value > FMax ) ) then
    raise EOutOfRange.CreateFmt( 'Value must be within %d..%d', [ FMin, FMax ]);

  New( P );                                 { Allocate Memory for Integer }
  P^ := Value;
  FList.Insert( Index, P );             { Insert Integer onto Internal List }
end;


procedure TIntegerList.Move( CurIndex, NewIndex : Integer );
begin
  FList.Move( CurIndex, NewIndex );
end;


procedure TIntegerList.QuickSort( L, R : Integer );
var
  I, J : Integer;
  P    : PLongint;
begin                                   {= Generic QuickSort Procedure =}
  I := L;
```

```
    J := R;
    P := PLongint( FList[ ( L + R ) shr 1 ] );
    repeat
      while PLongint( FList[ I ] )^ < P^  do
        Inc( I );
      while PLongint( FList[ J ] )^ > P^ do
        Dec( J );
      if I <= J then
      begin
        FList.Exchange( I, J );
        Inc( I );
        Dec( J );
      end;
    until I > J;
    if L < J then
      QuickSort( L, J );
    if I < R then
      QuickSort( I, R );
end; {= TIntegerList.QuickSort =}


procedure TIntegerList.Sort;
begin
  if not Sorted and ( FList.Count > 1 ) then
    QuickSort( 0, FList.Count - 1 );
end;

end.
```

Looking Ahead...

In the next chapter, we will finally get our hands dirty and construct a few components. You won't see these components in a third-party custom component package, but they can be quite useful. Actually, simplicity is preferred in the next chapter because the focus is on the *process* of creating Delphi components. Chapter 7 will take you step-by-step through the entire process of building a custom component. You will start by constructing a few new components, then these components will be tested, and finally the new components will be registered with Delphi so they appear on the component palette.

Chapter 7

An Overview of the Component Building Process

An Overview of the Component Building Process

Building Delphi components is far different from building Delphi applications, although nearly all of the tools are the same.

U p to this point, we've been packing our toolbox with a number of different tools that will be used when building components. Well, now it's time to open that toolbox and start building. Our first project will be to build a descendant of the Button component. The component is quite simple, but it is an excellent way to demonstrate the *process* of building a component. This chapter covers the steps necessary to construct, test, and register a component in Delphi.

Although the process of building the component is paramount, this chapter does illustrate how to override default values. For instance, when a button is dropped onto a form, it has a width of 89 pixels and a height of 33. This is a big button. I always resize them after dropping them onto a form. While this is not a difficult task, it's tedious and time-consuming. Therefore, we will build a new button component that overrides the default values for the **Width** and **Height** properties.

The Process

Regardless of complexity, the process described in this chapter can be used when developing any Delphi component. Figure 7.1 provides a graphical view of the

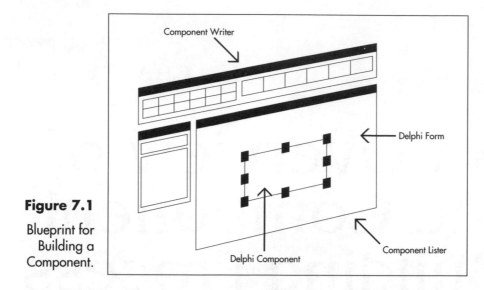

Figure 7.1

Blueprint for Building a Component.

steps involved in building a custom component. Yes, it looks like a flowchart. But since incorporating flowcharts into programming books was outlawed in the eighties, let's just call it a blueprint.

The process begins with some initial setup, namely the creation of a directory to hold the component unit and a test application. Components are built inside Delphi units. They are structured very much like a Delphi form unit with the class declaration for the component appearing in the interface section and the actual method definitions appearing in the implementation section. The fact that a component unit and a form unit are structured similarly is no coincidence. Remember that **TForm** is a descendant of **TComponent**, and when you create a new form in Delphi, you are in essence creating a new form component.

The next step is to create the component unit. As Figure 7.1 shows, this can be performed either manually or by using the Component Expert. The Component Expert actually does more than simply create the unit. It also generates placeholders for all of the basic elements required in a component unit. These placeholders include a partially filled uses clause, an empty class declaration, and a **Register** procedure. The dashed box in Figure 7.1 corresponds to the tasks that must be performed to produce the same output as the Component Expert.

After the basic elements of the unit are specified, either manually or by using the Component Expert, the next step is to fill out the class declaration and write the supporting methods. Once the coding tasks are completed, the component can be tested. Since components have two distinct interfaces, runtime and design-time, testing is performed in two steps. Runtime testing can commence as soon as coding is finished, but design-time testing can only occur once the component has been registered with Delphi and appears on the component palette.

Each of these steps will be covered in detail in the remaining sections of this chapter.

A Building Site

The first step in building a new component is to locate a building site. By this I mean creating a new directory for the component unit and its associated test program. To start, the directory will hold just the component unit file, but during the testing stage, the directory will contain all of the files associated with a separate Delphi project.

At first, you may be tempted to place all of your component units in a single directory. This is certainly possible, but after developing three or four component units with test projects for each, the directory becomes so cluttered with files that it becomes difficult to manage. Using a separate directory structure simply helps to organize all the files associated with multiple components. It also prevents "namespace collisions" between files that are part of different projects but have the same names.

Creating the Component Unit

The source code for a component resides in a Delphi unit. While it is possible to place any number of components into a single unit, generally only similar kinds of controls are placed in the same unit. For example, in the next chapter, we will be creating an enhanced list box component, but it will reside in its own unit rather than the one containing this chapter's button component. Keeping the number of components that a unit contains to a minimum has all the same benefits that stem from modular program design. This can be especially important when several developers are building the components in parallel.

There are two ways to create a component unit:

- Manually
- Using the Component Expert

As its name implies, the Component Expert simplifies the task of creating a component unit. Actually, creating the unit is not what the Component Expert specializes in. The Component Expert does more than create the unit file. It generates a syntactically correct Delphi unit that contains a basic implementation of a component. This unit could then be immediately installed onto the Delphi component palette.

The Expert does *not* generate any functionality. It simply provides a framework or foundation around which to build the component. We'll cover the Component Expert shortly. But first, the next section will demonstrate how to perform all of the steps that the Component Expert does automatically.

Manual Labor

Actually creating the unit file is a simple matter of selecting the File|New Unit menu item in Delphi. The real work of creating a working component unit can be broken down into four basic tasks:

- Specifying the uses clause
- Declaring the component class
- Implementing component methods
- Writing a **Register** procedure

The uses clause must specify at least the Classes unit, but typically, you will also need to include the Controls and Forms units. If your component descends from an existing visual component, the unit where that component is declared will also need to be specified. Other common units to include are Messages, WinTypes, WinProcs, Graphics, and SysUtils.

Our button component will need the Classes, Controls, and Forms units. And since this new component will be a direct descendant of the **TButton** class, the StdCtrls unit, which contains the **TButton** class declaration, must be added as well.

The next task, declaring the component class, is a crucial step in the process because it defines the different interfaces the component will have. Of course, before we can declare the interfaces of the component, we need to give the component, and its class, a name. Like most aspects of component building, there are conventions for naming components.

Naming Conventions

The name you choose for your component class will dictate how the component will be referenced in the Delphi environment. If the class starts with a *T*, which it should by convention, Delphi strips off the first character and uses the remaining string as the name of the component. If the class name does *not* start with a *T*, then the entire class name is used. The resulting name is displayed as a hint when the cursor is positioned over the component in the component palette. Likewise, this same name with a numeric suffix (for example, **Button4**) is used as the default name for each component of this type that you drop on a form.

In addition to *T*, it has become commonplace to use an additional prefix when naming components. The prefix serves as an identifying string indicating the author of the component, for example, the author's initials. But the prefix does not have to represent a single person. It may be the name or abbreviation of a company, or even a product name. Table 7.1 shows some examples of names used in some component packages currently on the market.

Component prefixes also tend to be more practical. In order for Delphi to install a component, its component name must be unique. Therefore, if you purchase two component packages that each contain a **TVirtualListBox** component, Delphi will only allow one of those components to be installed. This problem is further compounded by individuals building their own custom components which can cause additional namespace conflicts.

Following this convention, I will use a prefix for all of the components presented in this book. Each of the components will start with an *Rz* prefix, which is an abbreviation for *Raize*, the collective name of the components I have created for this book. Something like *Raize Custom Components*. (The fact that my company's name is Raize Software Solutions is purely coincidental.)

In addition to selecting the component name, a name for the unit file must also be selected. Do not underestimate the importance of this task. To avoid ambiguity, it is best to have unique file names. For example, it would not be wise to use the unit name of Buttons for the component presented in this chapter, because

Table 7.1 Component Names

Sample Component	Prefix	Company	Product
TOvcEditor	Ovc	TurboPower Software	Orpheus
TEPMenuButton	EP	Eschalon Development	Eschalon Power Controls
TVisualLED	Visual	Shoreline Software	VisualPROS
TwwTable	ww	Woll2Woll Software	Info*Power*

Delphi already has a unit of this name. As a result, like component names, unit names are commonly prefixed with an identifier string. Keeping the unit files unique is especially important when installing multiple components from many different sources.

Back to Work

Now that we have a name for our button component, we can get back to declaring the **TRzButton** class. Before diving into naming conventions, it was mentioned that the class declaration is where the different interfaces of the component are declared. Specifically, from a user's point of view, the public and published sections of the class declaration are the most important, because they define the *runtime* and *design-time* interfaces, respectively.

Properties, methods, and events declared in the public section make up the runtime interface. These items can only be called or referenced when the application using the component is running. Properties and events declared in the published section are also available at runtime, but more importantly are available through the Object Inspector at design-time as well. Notice that methods are always declared as public and are thus limited to runtime usage.

The Component Expert does not fill in the sections of the component class that it generates. It simply generates the four different sections of the class. Therefore, it is sufficient for now to simply declare the **TRzButton** class in the interface section of the unit as an empty class. The properties, methods, and events of the component will be added later. The following code fragment shows the current state of the RzBtn unit:

```
unit RzBtn;

interface

uses
  Classes, Controls, Forms, StdCtrls;

type
  TRzButton = class( TButton )
  end;

implementation
```

The last task performed by the Component Expert lies in generating the **Register** procedure. The **Register** procedure is used by Delphi to install the components that reside in the unit. Since the **Register** procedure is called from outside the unit, its procedure heading must appear in the interface section of the unit. The actual procedure appears in the implementation section.

The **Register** procedure uses the **RegisterComponents** procedure to register all of the components that are defined in the unit. The first parameter specifies in which tab of the component palette the new components will appear. If the tab does not exist, it is created. The second parameter is a set of component types that are to be registered. Listing 7.1 shows the RzBtn unit complete with a **Register** procedure. This unit could now be installed onto the component palette. The call to **RegisterComponents** indicates that the RzButton component will be installed onto the Raize tab of the component palette.

Listing 7.1 Stripped Down RzBtn Unit

```
Unit RzBtn;

interface

uses
  Classes, Controls, Forms, StdCtrls;

type
  TRzButton = class( TButton )
  end;

procedure Register;

implementation

procedure Register;
begin
  RegisterComponents( 'Raize', [ TRzButton ] );
end;

end.
```

Using the Component Expert

The Component Expert performs all of the steps described in the previous section automatically, thereby making it a useful tool when building a new component unit. This section describes how to use the Component Expert.

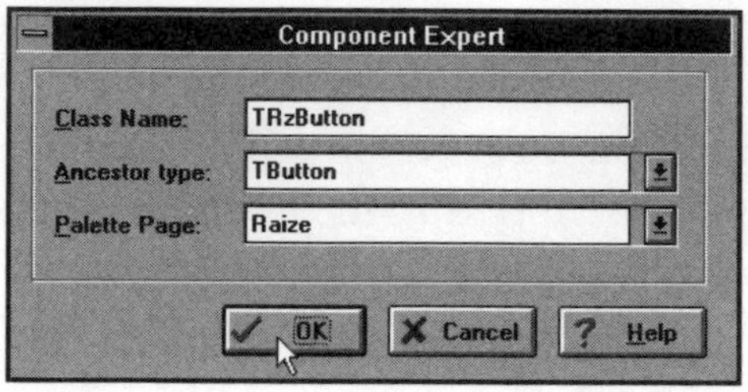

Figure 7.2

The Component Expert Dialog Box.

Figure 7.2 shows the Component Expert dialog box, which is displayed when the File|New Component menu item is selected.

The Component Expert requires the following three pieces of information:

- The name of the new component class
- The ancestor class from which the new component will descend
- A tab name on the component palette

First, enter the name to be used for the component class. Recall that component class names must be unique and that the Component Expert will not let you enter the name of a class that is already registered in Delphi. After entering the name to be used for the component class, the ancestor class must be chosen. Either type in the name of the class from which your new component will descend, or use the drop-down list. The list contains all of the components currently registered in Delphi and is generally safer than entering the name by hand because you won't commit any typing errors.

The last step is to select the component palette page where your new component will appear once it is registered with Delphi. The drop-down list contains all of the current pages in the palette. If you would like to create a new page, just enter the new name in this field. Once all of the data is entered, press the OK button to instruct Delphi to create the new unit. For the values shown in Figure 7.2, the Component Expert generates the source code shown in Listing 7.2.

Listing 7.2 Component Template from Component Expert

```
unit Unit2;

interface

uses
  SysUtils, WinTypes, WinProcs, Messages, Classes, Graphics, Controls,
  Forms, Dialogs, StdCtrls;
```

```
type
  TRzButton = class(TButton)
  private
    { Private declarations }
  protected
    { Protected declarations }
  public
    { Public declarations }
  published
    { Published declarations }
  end;

procedure Register;

implementation

procedure Register;
begin
  RegisterComponents('Raize', [TRzButton]);
end;

end.
```

Notice from Listing 7.2 that the name of the unit is Unit2. (Depending on the current state of Delphi when you run the Component Expert, the name might be Unit3, Unit4, etc.) Since the Component Expert does not let you specify the name of the unit, it is wise to immediately save the newly generated unit under a more appropriate name.

Also notice that the **uses** clause is populated with more units than the minimum required to compile the unit under construction. By adding many of the common units to the **uses** clause, most of the functionality that will be added to a component will be available from this list of units. Fortunately, adding extra units to the **uses** clause does not waste resources. Because of Delphi's *smart linking*, only those program elements that are referenced somewhere in the source code are actually linked into the final executable.

Although the Component Expert is a great tool for getting started with a component, it can only be used to create a *new* component unit. It cannot add components to existing unit files. This has to be done manually.

Customizing the Component

Once the framework for the component is created, the next step in the overall process is to write the actual code that will customize the bare framework and thereby make it a whole new component. This includes defining the properties, methods, and events of the component as well as implementing the necessary support methods in the implementation section of the unit.

This part of the process will vary widely, depending on the type of component that you are creating. For simply overriding default values, all that is required is that the constructor for the component be overridden. The components presented in the later chapters are much more involved. Listing 7.3 shows the RzButton component complete with a class declaration and an overridden constructor.

Listing 7.3 The RzButton Component

```
unit RzBtn;

interface

uses
  Classes, Controls, Forms, StdCtrls;

type
  TRzButton = class( TButton )
  public
    constructor Create( AOwner : TComponent ); override;
  published
    property Height default 26;
    property Width default 80;
  end;


procedure Register;

implementation

constructor TRzButton.Create( AOwner : TComponent );
begin
  inherited Create( AOwner );    { Don't Forget to Call Ancestor's Constructor }

  Width := 80;                                    { Set New Default Values }
  Height := 26;
end;


{========================}
{== Register Procedure ==}
{========================}

procedure Register;
begin
  RegisterComponents( 'Raize', [ TRzButton ] );
end;

end.
```

Declaring the Constructor

Let's start with the class declaration. All components inherit a virtual constructor called **Create** from the **TComponent** class. Even if the constructor is overridden in a descendant class because it's declared as virtual, its parameter list cannot be changed. The constructor takes a single argument, which is a reference to the component that will *own* the new component. Recall from Chapter 5 that the owner is responsible for destroying all of the components on its **Components** list.

When overriding default values, the only method that must be implemented is the constructor. Listing 7.3 shows that the **Create** constructor is declared in the public section of the class. This is done so that the Form Designer has access to the constructor. In fact, the **Create** constructor for a component is always placed in the public section.

In addition to declaring the constructor in the correct section, you must remember to add the **override** directive to its declaration. If the **override** directive is missing, the component will still compile, but when the component is created at design-time by the Form Designer, the wrong constructor will be called. Omitting the **override** directive breaks the virtual hierarchy chain between the constructors, and when the Form Designer creates a new component, it utilizes polymorphism to determine the correct constructor to call. But since the virtual chain is broken, the **TButton.Create** constructor will be called instead of **TRzButton.Create**.

Redeclaring New Property Defaults

When overriding default values for a component, it is beneficial to redeclare the properties that are being overridden and specify the new default value. Recall from Chapter 5 that the **default** directive is used for ordinal properties to determine if the current property value gets stored in the form file. When providing a new default value for an inherited property, use the **default** directive in the following way:

```
property Height default 26;
```

While it is not required to redeclare the property with a new default value, it is more efficient to do so. When a form is saved, the properties whose current values differ from their default values are stored in the form file. When the component is loaded from the form file, it is first created, which sets the properties to their default values. Then the property values stored in the form file are loaded, and the component's current property values are updated accordingly.

This process is inefficient if the constructor sets a property to the same value that is stored in the form file. The property is thus set twice! When you override a property value, unless you use the **default** directive, that property will *always* be in the form file because the Form Designer will use the *old* default value to determine if the property gets stored in the form file.

Implementing the Constructor

At this point, the only thing left to do is to implement the constructor. Again, because the constructor is virtual, it should call the inherited constructor first. This ensures that the component is properly created. When overriding default values, it is especially important to do this because the inherited constructors are responsible for setting the original default values that we are trying to override. If the inherited constructor is called *after* setting the new default values, the original values will be reused.

Testing the Runtime Interface

Just as in application programming, once the implementation code for the component has been written, it's time to test it. Testing a component is a little different from testing a complete Delphi application. The difference stems from the fact that components have two separate, although similar, interfaces that need to be tested. When a component is used in an application, the runtime interface of the component determines the behavior of the component. However, when a component is dropped onto a form within the Delphi environment, your component's behavior is dictated by its design-time interface. Both of these interfaces need to be tested in order to create a quality component. It is quite possible to create a component that behaves properly at runtime but improperly at design-time, and viceversa.

We'll first test the runtime interface of the component. We start with this one for several reasons. First, it's much easier to test the runtime behavior of a component than its design-time behavior. Second, for most components, the design-time interface of a component is very similar to the runtime interface. Testing the runtime environment first helps to ensure that the component works properly at design-time. And third, the integrated debugger can be used for runtime debugging. This option is not available at design-time because although Delphi was written in Delphi, you cannot use Delphi to debug Delphi.

Creating the Test Application

To test our new RzButton component, we need to create a test application. This is a primary reason for creating a separate directory for each component unit. The directory contains the source file for the component and all the files associated with the test project. Keeping the test application around also makes it easier to maintain your components, because when it comes time to modify a component, you will already have the test application already built into the same directory with the component proper.

So how will we test our new component when it doesn't appear on the component palette? Instead of using the Form Designer to drop a component onto the form and then use the Object Inspector to change some of its properties, we will dynamically create an instance of the component when the form of our application is created. Dynamically creating a component allows us to create the component *without having to register it with Delphi*. Registration is the process by which Delphi becomes aware of the components that reside on the component palette. Registration must be performed in order to test the design-time behavior of a component, but for testing the runtime behavior it isn't necessary.

In the same directory where your component unit exists, create a new project. If you are using the Gallery option in Delphi, select the B*lank Project* option. All you will need to test a component is a single form.

Dynamically creating the component is summarized by the following steps:

1. Add the component unit to the form's **uses** clause.

2. Add a field in the form class that will be a reference to the component.

3. Create the component in the form's **OnCreate** event.

4. Set the **Parent** property of the component.

5. Set additional properties of the component as required.

Listing 7.4 contains the source code for the MainForm unit of the TestBtns project, which will be used to test the RzButton component.

Listing 7.4 Test Project for RzButton

```
unit Mainform;

interface

uses
  SysUtils, WinTypes, WinProcs, Messages, Classes, Graphics, Controls,
  Forms, Dialogs, RzBtn, StdCtrls;
```

```
type
  TForm1 = class(TForm)
    procedure FormCreate(Sender: TObject);
  private
    { Private declarations }
  public
    { Public declarations }
    BtnTest : TButton;
end;

var
  Form1: TForm1;

implementation

{$R *.DFM}

procedure TForm1.FormCreate(Sender: TObject);
begin
  BtnTest := TRzButton.Create( Self );
  BtnTest.Parent := Self;
  BtnTest.Left := 100;
  BtnTest.Top := 100;
  BtnTest.Caption := 'Smaller';
end;

end.
```

The first step is straightforward enough. Since we will be referencing the type of the new component, we need to include the new component unit in the form's **uses** clause. The second step involves adding an object field to the public portion of the form class. This object field will be used to reference the component that will be created, and thus its type is that of the newly created component class. For the current test program, the **BtnTest** field is declared of type **TRzButton**.

 Never add, delete, or modify any of the fields that appear above the **private** directive in a Delphi form class. This area is managed by the Form Designer, and the fields that appear in this section correspond to the components that are stored in the form file. Modifying the fields in this area can make your form file invalid.

```
type
  TForm1 = class(TForm)
    Label1: TLabel;     { This area is managed internally by Delphi }
```

```
    Edit1: TEdit;  { Do Not modify the components in this section }
  private
    { Private declarations }    { Only add fields and methods to the
private }
  public
    { Public declarations }   { or public sections }
  end;
```

The remaining steps all involve the **OnCreate** event handler for the form. The shortcut for creating the **OnCreate** event handler is to double click on an empty area of the form. This creates the **FormCreate** method in which the BtnTest component will be created.

The first task that must be performed within the **FormCreate** method is to create an instance of the new component by calling the constructor of the component. The only decision that needs to be made is what to specify as the owner of the component. Under most circumstances, the owner will be the form. In the **FormCreate** method of Listing 7.4, the **TRzButton** constructor is passed the parameter **Self** indicating that the main form will serve as the owner of the new component.

After the component is created, one of the most important tasks must still be performed: setting the **Parent** property. Setting the **Parent** property puts the current component on the parent's **Controls** list. A TWinControl component, which is the only type of component that can accept controls dropped onto it, uses the **Controls** list to establish the tab order and z-order among the controls it owns. However, the most important use of the **Controls** list occurs when painting. The parent component uses the **Controls** list to instruct all owned components to paint themselves. Therefore, if a control does not exist on its parent's **Controls** list, it will not appear when the application is executed.

Recall from Chapter 6 that only TWinControl descendants can accept controls. The Panel and GroupBox are examples of components that can own other components. The **TForm** class is also a descendant of TWinControl and thus behaves like the others in that it can accept other components dropped onto it. For the purposes of testing a new component, we want to mimic the action of dropping the component on the form. Therefore, in the **FormCreate** method, the **BtnTest.Parent** property is changed to **Self**, again referencing the form.

After the **Parent** property is set, it may be necessary to modify some of the component's properties. This might include the position properties, **Left** and **Top**. If the component has a caption, it is also common to set the **Caption** property. For testing the RzButton component, setting these three properties is all that is necessary because we haven't added any other new features. For more complex components, you may be required to set additional properties and even event handlers at this time.

Any runtime accessible property can be modified in the test application. The only real restriction is that you must set the **Parent** property as described earlier before setting any other properties. This is necessary because some property changes cause the component to repaint itself, and if the component is not yet on the parent's **Controls** list, changing these properties will not have the desired effect.

Now the test application can be executed. Figure 7.3 shows the screen display of the TestBtns application. The Button1 component was dropped onto the form to illustrate that the new default values have taken effect in **BtnTest**.

 The same technique used to test a component can be used in your Delphi applications whenever you need to dynamically create a component. Again, the tricky part is setting the **Parent** property. In the component test programs, this will usually be set to **Self** to indicate that the form is responsible for painting the control. However, in an application, this could be a form, a panel, or even a notebook page.

Inserting a component into a form or panel simply involves setting the **Parent** property to the form or panel reference. However, to insert a component into a notebook (or TabbedNotebook) page, you cannot simply use the notebook reference. This is because the notebook, being a collection of page controls, cannot accept components dropped onto itself. However, each *page* of a notebook can accept components. Therefore, in order to create a component on a notebook page, the page control must be used as the parent.

The page controls are accessible through the **Objects** list of the **Pages** property. In the sample code below, a new component is placed into the current notebook page by using the **PageIndex** property to access the **Objects** list. The returned value is then typecast to **TWinControl** so that it can be assigned to the **Parent** property of the new control.

```
Idx := Notebook1.PageIndex;      { Use current page as Parent }
NewControl.Parent := TWinControl( Notebook1.Pages.Objects[ Idx ] );
```

Installing a Component on the Palette

In order to proceed to the next level of testing, the component must be installed onto the component palette. For a component to appear on the component palette, it must be linked into Delphi's component library. By default, this library resides in the DELPHI\BIN directory and is called COMPLIB.DCL. The DCL extension stands for Delphi Component Library and is a slight misnomer. While it is true that the file does represent a component library, it is actually implemented as a dynamic link library. This DLL contains all of the components that are currently installed.

Components are compiled into the component library through their component units. Whenever a new component unit is installed, the component library is rebuilt. The units that make up the current build of the library are listed in the Install Components dialog box, which is invoked by selecting the Options|Install Components menu item. Figure 7.4 shows the RzBtn unit being added to the list of installed units. Only units that contain a public **Register** procedure can be placed on the installed units list.

A Common Lib Directory

Notice that the Search Path edit field shown in Figure 7.4 includes the D:\DELPHI\LIB directory, which is the default, and the D:\RAIZE\LIB directory. I have found it to be extremely helpful to create a common lib directory that is used to hold all of the DCU files representing my components, rather than

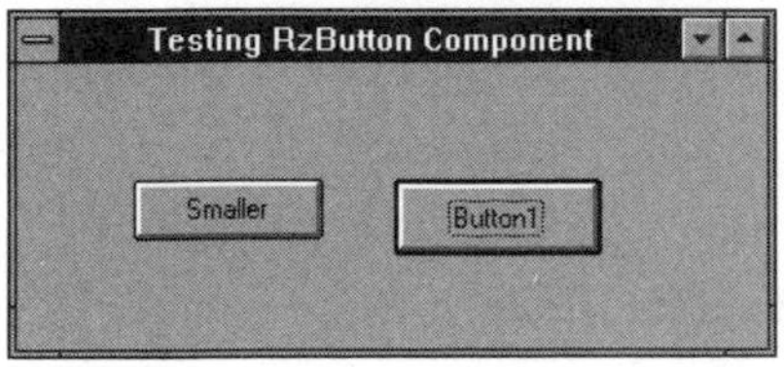

Figure 7.3

Executing the TestBtns Application.

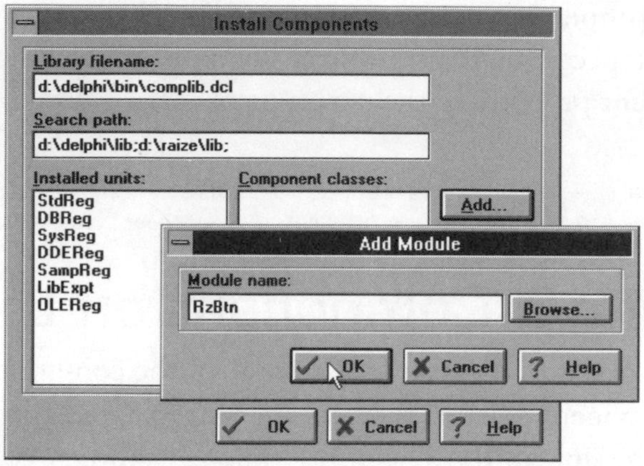

Figure 7.4

Installing a
Component.

installing directly from the development directories. Using a common directory
has two principal advantages:

First, it helps to shorten the search path used to record the location of all component units. This can be significant since the Search Path edit field is limited in
length to 127 characters. This path can get filled pretty quickly after adding just
a few custom components. Add a third-party package or two and there will be no
more room for any additional directories. Placing the *.DCU files into a common lib directory keeps the length of the search path to a minimum.

The second advantage is that it isolates the *working* set of components from the *under
development* set of components. Once you get a component to a stable state, you may
start to incorporate it into an application. Since component building is an iterative
process, you will probably go back and make changes to your component. This might
include simple maintenance or it might involve significant enhancements. In either
case, at some point in time, your component may be in an unusable state.

If you build the component library using the under development versions of
your components, this could affect the applications that were formerly using
the stable versions. That is, applications that used to work fine may begin giving you grief in peculiar ways. Keeping a separate working set of component
units gives you more control over the components that are used for ongoing
application development.

The Component Resource

There is an additional task that is performed by the install process. When a component unit is installed, Delphi searches the directories listed in the search path

for a file that has the same name as the unit but with a .DCR extension. DCR stands for Delphi Component Resource, and a DCR file is actually a Windows resource file. If a component resource file is found for a component being installed, its contents are also linked into the component library. The main purpose of the component resource file is to specify the bitmaps that are used to represent the components on the component palette.

The Image Editor that ships with Delphi can be used to create a DCR file. However, after experiencing some instabilities with this tool, I prefer to use Resource Workshop to create component resource files. Of course, any tool that can build a compiled (.RES) resource file will suffice. You could even use a text editor to create a .RC file that includes bitmaps that were created with Windows Paintbrush. The BRC resource compiler could then be used to build the .RES file. Just don't forget to change the extension of the file to .DCR.

Inside the component resource file, create a 24×24 pixel 16-color bitmap for each component defined in the corresponding unit. In order for Delphi to link each bitmap to its associated component, give each bitmap the same name as the component's class name. The only difference is that the bitmap name is in all upper case.

 The lower left pixel in the bitmap serves as the transparent color indicator. All other pixels in the bitmap with this same color will appear transparent. The BitBtn and SpeedButton components also treat bitmaps in this fashion.

If you do not create a component resource file for your new components, Delphi will use the bitmap of its ancestor if it has one, or it will use a default bitmap.

Testing the Design-Time Interface

Once the component is installed on the palette, it can be used in a Delphi application. Of course, it would be helpful to at least test its design-time behavior before doing so. Testing the design-time features of a component can become quite involved, especially for a component with a great many properties. For the RzButton component, there is not much to test because we did not add any new published properties or events that would be accessible through the Object Inspector. In this case, all we need to do is drop an instance on a form and check if

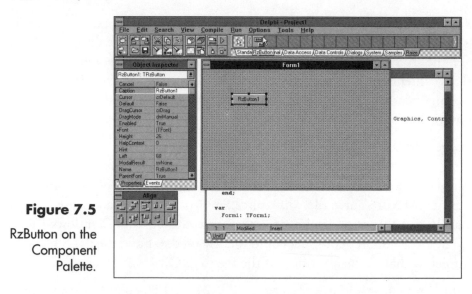

Figure 7.5

RzButton on the
Component
Palette.

it is created with the new size values in force. Figure 7.5 shows the RzButton component being used at design-time.

Adding Additional Components

Now that we have a working component, let's extend the RzBtn unit by adding two additional components, an OK button and a Cancel button. These are probably the two most-used buttons in all Windows development. Why not create a pair of components that allow us to simply drop them on a form and go? Since we want the buttons to be of a reasonable size, they will descend directly from the TRzButton class.

Adding the **TRzOKButton** and **TRzCancelButton** classes to the RzBtn unit must be done manually, because the Component Expert can only be used to create a new unit—not to enhance an existing one. Listing 7.5 shows the complete source code for the RzBtn unit that is included on the companion disk. Both additional button components override their constructors and redeclare the appropriate property values. The constructor for **TRzOKButton** sets the **Default** property (not to be confused with the **default** directive) to **True** and **ModalResult** to **mrOk**. Likewise, **TRzCancelButton**.Create sets the Cancel property to True and ModalResult to **mrCancel**.

Listing 7.5   RZBTN.PAS—A Button Hierarchy

```pascal
unit RzBtn;

interface

uses
  Classes, Controls, Forms, StdCtrls;

type
  TRzButton = class( TButton )
  public
    constructor Create( AOwner : TComponent ); override;
  published
    property Height default 26;
    property Width default 80;
  end;


  TRzOkButton = class( TRzButton )
  public
    constructor Create( AOwner : TComponent ); override;
  published
    property Default default True;
    property ModalResult default mrOK;
  end;


  TRzCancelButton = class( TRzButton )
  public
    constructor Create( AOwner : TComponent ); override;
  published
    property Cancel default True;
    property ModalResult default mrCancel;
  end;


procedure Register;

implementation

constructor TRzButton.Create( AOwner : TComponent );
begin
  inherited Create( AOwner );     { Don't Forget to Call Ancestor's Constructor }

  Width := 80;                                      { Set New Default Values }
  Height := 26;
end;


constructor TRzOkButton.Create( AOwner : TComponent );
begin
  inherited Create( AOwner );             { Inherits New Size from TRzButton }
```

```
  Caption := 'OK';
  Default := True;
  ModalResult := mrOK;
end;


constructor TRzCancelButton.Create( AOwner : TComponent );
begin
  inherited Create( AOwner );                { Inherits New Size from TRzButton }

  Caption := 'Cancel';
  Cancel := True;
  ModalResult := mrCancel;
end;



{=========================}
{== Register Procedure ==}
{=========================}

procedure Register;
begin
  RegisterComponents( 'Raize', [ TRzButton, TRzOkButton, TRzCancelButton ] );
end;

end.
```

Looking Ahead...

Now that we have an understanding of the process required to build components, the next chapter (actually, all of the remaining chapters) focuses on building different types of components and the specific techniques associated with each of them them.

Although the focus of this chapter was on the process, the components presented do represent a certain class of components that can be created. Overriding defaults is a very viable reason to create custom components. The process of overriding default values can be applied to any component by following the process outlined in this chapter. More important, however, is the fact that creating any type of component in Delphi follows this same process.

Chapter 8

Enhancing an Existing Component

Enhancing an Existing Component

The easiest way to create a custom component is to start with an existing component and "customize" it through inheritance. There's less to be done than you might imagine.

So far we've covered the rules and regulations governing the building of components in Delphi. In the remaining chapters the focus will no longer be on the principles behind building custom components, but rather the issues involved in actually implementing them. To start off, this chapter takes a closer look at enhancing existing Delphi components, with some actual examples.

In this chapter, three separate components will be created, each one descending from an existing VCL class. The new components are enhanced versions of the Panel, Label, and ListBox components. All three components are similar in that most of the processing is handled by the ancestor class. This is in fact one of the major benefits of enhancing an existing control—you can use what it already has, often without modification. However, since each component descends from a unique ancestor, different implementation issues must be handled for each component.

Fun with Panels

One of the most used components in Delphi is Panel. Because of its ability to contain other components and to automatically align itself when the size of the form changes, Panels make good toolbars and status bars. Panels are very flexible indeed. They can even be used to implement a splitter bar; Panels are used for the splitter bar itself and also for the two regions separated by the splitter.

As flexible as the Panel component is, it does have its drawbacks. First of all, it is always given a default caption. The default in Delphi is to set the caption to the name of the new component. Since panels are more commonly used as holders of other controls and thus rarely need a caption, this causes extra work. You must clear the **Caption** field using the Object Inspector. Although not a tough task, as we learned in the last chapter, it is a tedious task. It would be nice if the caption were never set in the first place.

Even at those times when a caption is needed, the Panel component does not provide many options for displaying one. A caption may be horizontally aligned either to the left or the right, or else it may be centered. But the caption always appears vertically in the center of the panel and can only be displayed on a single line.

The third drawback to the Panel component is that it does not provide much flexibility when it comes to drawing itself. For instance, you have an inner and an outer border that can appear raised or recessed, but all sides of the panel are visible. There is no way to turn off one of the sides of the panel. Recall from Chapter 1 that one of the most common reasons for creating a new component is to alter its appearance. In this first component, much of the functionality added will be to enhance how the panel draws itself.

To illustrate how the appearance of the Panel will be enhanced, Figures 8.1 and 8.2 show two forms that perform the exact same function. The form in Figure 8.1 was created using the standard Panel component. The form in Figure 8.2 was created using the RzPanel component, which we will be creating shortly. Notice that there is not much that the Panel can do to visually separate the regions of the

Figure 8.1

An Icon Viewer
Using the Standard
Panel Component

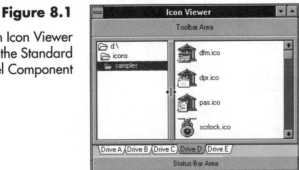

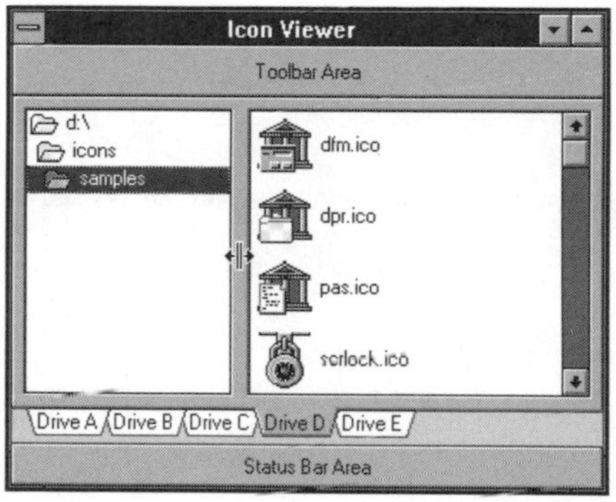

Figure 8.2

An Icon Viewer Using the RzPanel Component

form. And although a panel can be used as a splitter, it does not make a very attractive one.

In addition to demonstrating a more visually appealing toolbar, status bar, and splitter, the form on the right demonstrates additional ways that the RzPanel can be modified. Notice how there is no dark gray line above the TabSet as there is in the first form. The line is removed by using the new BevelSides property, which allows a user to toggle off any one of the four sides to the panel. The new **BorderSides** property provides the black line that visually separates the toolbar and status bar with the client area.

Figure 8.3 shows how the new panel's appearance may be further altered. When used to group controls, the **VerticalAlignment** property allows the caption of a panel to be placed in any one of nine areas on the panel. Also notice that RzPanel components can display multi-line captions. Also, the area between the inner and outer bevels can be filled with a specified color using the **BorderColor** property.

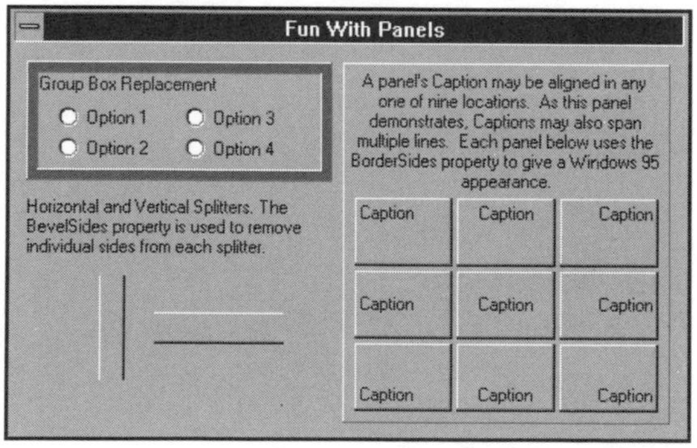

Figure 8.3

Additional Features of the RzPanel Component

Listing 8.1   RZPANEL.PAS—The RzPanel Unit

```
{=================================================================}
{= RzPanel Unit                                                  =}
{=                                                               =}
{= This unit implements an enhanced panel component which provides the =}
{= ability to toggle individual sides of the panel, display multi-line =}
{= captions, and fill in the area between bevels with a separate color. =}
{=                                                               =}
{= Building Custom Delphi Components - Ray Konopka               =}
{=================================================================}


unit RzPanel;

interface

uses
  SysUtils, WinTypes, WinProcs, Classes, Graphics, Controls, ExtCtrls, Menus,
  RzCommon;

type
  TSide = ( sdLeft, sdTop, sdRight, sdBottom );
  TSides = set of TSide;
  TVerticalAlignment = ( vaTop, vaCenter, vaBottom );

  TRzPanel = class( TCustomPanel )
  private
    FBevelSides : TSides;
    FBorderColor : TColor;
    FBorderSides : TSides;
    FVerticalAlignment : TVerticalAlignment;
    procedure SetBevelSides( Value : TSides );
    procedure SetBorderColor( Value : TColor );
    procedure SetBorderSides( Value : TSides );
    procedure SetVerticalAlignment( Value : TVerticalAlignment );
  protected
    procedure DrawSides( Rect : TRect; ULColor, LRColor : TColor;
                         Sides : TSides );
    procedure DrawBevel( var Rect : TRect; ULColor, LRColor : TColor;
                         Width : Integer; Sides : TSides );
    procedure Paint; override;
  public
    constructor Create( AOwner : TComponent ); override;
  published
    property BevelSides : TSides
      read FBevelSides
      write SetBevelSides
      default [ sdLeft, sdTop, sdRight, sdBottom ];

    property BorderColor : TColor
      read FBorderColor
      write SetBorderColor
      default clBtnFace;
```

```
    property BorderSides : TSides
      read FBorderSides
      write SetBorderSides;

    property VerticalAlignment : TVerticalAlignment
      read FVerticalAlignment
      write SetVerticalAlignment
      default vaCenter;

    { Inherited Properties & Events }
    property Align;
    property Alignment;
    property BevelInner;
    property BevelOuter;
    property BevelWidth;
(*    property BorderStyle;    Property is Not redeclared to hide it from user *)
    property BorderWidth;
    property DragCursor;
    property DragMode;
    property Enabled;
    property Caption;
    property Color;
    property Ctl3D;
    property Font;
    property Locked;
    property ParentColor;
    property ParentCtl3D;
    property ParentFont;
    property ParentShowHint;
    property PopupMenu;
    property ShowHint;
    property TabOrder;
    property TabStop;
    property Visible;

    property OnClick;
    property OnDblClick;
    property OnDragDrop;
    property OnDragOver;
    property OnEndDrag;
    property OnEnter;
    property OnExit;
    property OnMouseDown;
    property OnMouseMove;
    property OnMouseUp;
    property OnResize;
  end;


procedure Register;

implementation
```

```
{=====================}
{== TRzPanel Methods ==}
{=====================}


constructor TRzPanel.Create( AOwner : TComponent );
begin
  inherited Create( AOwner );
                              { Prevent Caption from being set to default name }
  ControlStyle := ControlStyle - [ csSetCaption, csOpaque ];
                                                  { Set Default values }
  FBevelSides := [ sdLeft, sdTop, sdRight, sdBottom ];
  FBorderColor := clBtnFace;
  FVerticalAlignment := vaCenter;
end;


procedure TRzPanel.SetBevelSides( Value : TSides );
begin
  if FBevelSides <> Value then
  begin
    FBevelSides := Value;
    Invalidate;
  end;
end;


procedure TRzPanel.SetBorderColor( Value : TColor );
begin
  if FBorderColor <> Value then
  begin
    FBorderColor := Value;
    Invalidate;
  end;
end;


procedure TRzPanel.SetBorderSides( Value : TSides );
begin
  if FBorderSides <> Value then
  begin
    FBorderSides := Value;
    Invalidate;
  end;
end;


procedure TRzPanel.SetVerticalAlignment( Value : TVerticalAlignment );
begin
  if FVerticalAlignment <> Value then
  begin
    FVerticalAlignment := Value;
    Invalidate;
  end;
end;
```

```
procedure TRzPanel.DrawSides( Rect : TRect; ULColor, LRColor : TColor;
                              Sides : TSides );
begin
  with Canvas, Rect do
  begin
    Pen.Color := ULColor;
    if sdLeft in Sides then
    begin
      MoveTo( Left, Top );
      LineTo( Left, Bottom );
    end;

    if sdTop in Sides then
    begin
      MoveTo( Left, Top );
      LineTo( Right, Top );
    end;

    Pen.Color := LRColor;
    if sdRight in Sides then
    begin
      MoveTo( Right - 1, Top );
      LineTo( Right - 1, Bottom );
    end;

    if sdBottom in Sides then
    begin
      MoveTo( Left, Bottom - 1 );
      LineTo( Right, Bottom - 1 );
    end;
  end;
end; {= TRzPanel.DrawSides =}



procedure TRzPanel.DrawBevel( var Rect : TRect; ULColor, LRColor : TColor;
                              Width : Integer; Sides : TSides );
var
  I : Integer;
begin
  Canvas.Pen.Width := 1;
  for I := 1 to Width do                        { Loop through width of bevel }
  begin
    DrawSides( Rect, ULColor, LRColor, Sides );
    InflateRect( Rect, -1, -1 );
  end;
end;



procedure TRzPanel.Paint;
var
  DrawRct, TextRct : TRect;
```

```
    TempStz     : array[ 0..255 ] of Char;
    H : Integer;
    FontHeight : Integer;
begin
  DrawRct := ClientRect;

  with Canvas, DrawRct do
  begin
    { Draw Border }

    DrawSides( DrawRct, clBlack, clBlack, FBorderSides );
    if sdLeft in FBorderSides then
      Inc( Left );
    if sdTop in FBorderSides then
      Inc( Top );
    if sdRight in FBorderSides then
      Dec( Right );
    if sdBottom in FBorderSides then
      Dec( Bottom );

    { Draw Bevels }

    if BevelOuter <> bvNone then
      DrawBevel( DrawRct, ULBevelColor[ BevelOuter ],
                 LRBevelColor[ BevelOuter ], BevelWidth, FBevelSides );

    if BorderWidth > 0 then
      DrawBevel( DrawRct, FBorderColor, FBorderColor, BorderWidth,
                 FBevelSides );

    if BevelInner <> bvNone then
      DrawBevel( DrawRct, ULBevelColor[ BevelInner ],
                 LRBevelColor[ BevelInner ], BevelWidth, FBevelSides );

    { Draw Caption }

    Brush.Color := Color;
    FillRect( DrawRct );          { Fill interior of panel to erase old caption }
    Brush.Style := bsClear;

    Font := Self.Font;
    StrPCopy( TempStz, Caption );

    TextRct := DrawRct;
    H := DrawText( Handle, TempStz, -1, TextRct,
                   dt_CalcRect or dt_WordBreak or dt_ExpandTabs or dt_VCenter or
                   TextAlignments[ Alignment ] );

    if FVerticalAlignment = vaCenter then
    begin
      Top := ( ( Bottom + Top ) - H ) shr 1;
      Bottom := Top + H;
```

```
    end
    else if FVerticalAlignment = vaBottom then
      Top := Bottom - H - 1;

    DrawText( Handle, TempStz, -1, DrawRct,
              dt_WordBreak or dt_ExpandTabs or dt_VCenter or
              TextAlignments[ Alignment ] );
  end; { with }
end; {= TRzPanel.Paint =}


{===============================}
{== Register Procedure ==}
{===============================}

procedure Register;
begin
  RegisterComponents( RaizePage, [ TRzPanel ] );
end;

end.
```

The *Custom* Classes

Let's start with the **TRzPanel** class declaration in Listing 8.1. The first thing to observe is that **TRzPanel** descends from **TCustomPanel** and not **TPanel**. **TCustomPanel** is one of several component classes in the VCL that define the properties, methods, and events necessary to implement a component, but none of the properties or events are declared as **published**. The properties and events are defined, but they are declared as either **protected** or **public**. Descendant classes, like **TPanel**, determine which properties and events appear in the Object Inspector by redeclaring them as **published**.

These *custom* classes make it possible for descendants to hide properties and events that are not applicable to the new component. More precisely, it gives descendant classes the ability to refuse to make certain properties and events visible. For example, the **TCustomPanel** class defines a **BorderStyle** property that determines whether the panel is surrounded by a solid black line or not. This feature is not needed in the RzPanel component, and in fact interferes with the **BorderSides** property. Therefore, the **TRzPanel** class does not redeclare the **BorderStyle** property, and thus it is hidden from users of the new component. All other inherited properties and events are redeclared.

The Four Sides of a Panel

The first two properties added to this component are **BevelSides** and **BorderSides**. Both are of type **TSides**, which is defined as a set of **TSide** values. **TSide** in an enumerated type containing elements representing the four sides of a rectangle. The **BevelSides** and **BorderSides** properties allow the component user to specify which sides of the panel should display a bevel or a border, respectively.

Both of these properties are implemented like most component properties. An internal data field is defined to hold the property's value. In this case, **FBevelSides** and **FBorderSides** hold their respective values. The property declaration for each property specifies the internal field in the read access clause and a private method in the write access clause.

All of the write access methods defined in **TRzPanel**, including **SetBevelSides** and **SetBorderSides**, have the same structure. Actually, most write access methods have this same format. Whenever a property alters the appearance of a component, the write access methods will typically have a format similar to the following:

```
procedure TSample.SetSomeProperty( Value : TSomeType );
begin
  if FSomeProperty <> Value then
  begin
    FSomeProperty := Value;
    Invalidate;                    { Force the component to repaint itself }
  end;
end;
```

This is a classic example of implementing a side effect using a property. First the new value is compared against the current value of the property. Only if they are different does the property get updated. If the property does need to be updated, the most common action is to invalidate the current view of the component so that it must repaint itself. The **BevelSides** and **BorderSides** properties are no different. Since changing either one effects how the panel is drawn, the **Invalidate** method is called after assigning the property a new value.

One more note regarding these two properties: Since each property is published, a default property value is specified at the end of the property declaration. For the **BevelSides** property, all sides are included in the set, whereas the **BorderSides** set property is empty. This causes the default appearance of an RzPanel to be similar to the standard Panel component.

Enhancing the Caption Property

Three enhancements have been made with respect to the **Caption** property. First of all, when a new component is dropped onto a form, the **Caption** is *not* automatically loaded with the component's name. By default, when a component is dropped onto a form, the Form Designer generates a default name for the component, for example, **RzPanel1**. If the component has a **Caption** (or **Text**) property, it is also populated with the default name. This same processing also occurs if the **Name** property is changed by the component user and the **Caption** has not been specifically set to another value. Preventing this process from occurring is accomplished by removing the **csSetCaption** style from the **ControlStyle** property in the **Create** constructor.

The second enhancement made with respect to the **Caption** is that it can now appear in any one of nine different locations on the panel. The inherited **Alignment** property allows the caption to be placed in one of three places: left, right, centered. However, as mentioned earlier, the caption always appears centered vertically. The new **VerticalAlignment** property allows the caption to be positioned at the top and bottom of the panel, in addition to the center, giving a total of nine possible positions.

The RzPanel component also wraps the **Caption** string if it is longer than the width of the panel. This is accomplished during the painting of the panel and will be explained in detail at the end of the next section.

Painting a Panel

The real work of this component is performed in the **Paint** method. The **Paint** method is a virtual method defined in the **TCustomControl** class from which **TCustomPanel** descends. It gives component writers easy access to the painting process because the **Paint** method is automatically called whenever the component needs to be repainted. More importantly, the inherited **Paint** method takes care of allocating a device context and creating the **Canvas** property.

The first task in painting our new panel is to draw the border sides. The **DrawSides** method is used to draw each segment specified in **FBorderSides**. **DrawSides** is a generic method that determines which **TSide** values are in the passed-in set, and uses the **MoveTo** and **LineTo Canvas** methods to draw each side. **DrawSides** takes two color values that represent the upper-left sides and the lower-right sides, respectively. Both color values are set to **clBlack** for the frame.

When dealing with **TRect** and **TPoint** records it is often helpful to use the **Rect** and **Point** functions from the **Classes** unit, which return the corresponding record populated with the values passed to the function. For example, the **PolyLine** method takes an array of **TPoint** records and draws a line between all of the points. Instead of creating a separate array to pass to the method, the **Point** function can be used in the method call:

```
PolyLine( [ Point( 10, 10 ), Point( 100, 10 ) ] );
```

The next step is to draw the beveling. First, the outer bevel is drawn using the **DrawBevel** method. **DrawBevel** is a wrapper around the **DrawSides** method, because the width of the bevel is controlled by the inherited **BevelWidth** property. **DrawBevel** simply calls **DrawSides** to draw a one-pixel-wide bevel, shrinks the drawing rectangle, and repeats this for the width of the bevel.

Next, the interior of the panel is filled in using the inherited **Color** property, and the **Caption** is drawn. The **DrawText** Windows API function is used to first calculate how big of a rectangle is needed to display all of the text. The height of the required rectangle is returned when the **dt_CalcRect** flag is used. The height is then used to position the text rectangle based on the **VerticalAlignment** property. The **DrawText** function is used again, this time without the **dt_CalcRect** flag, to display the actual caption. As a side effect of using the **DrawText** function, multi-line captions are supported by specifying the **dt_WordBreak** flag.

The RzCommon Unit

You may have noticed that the **TextAlignments**, **ULBevelColor**, and **LRBevelColor** arrays are not declared in the RzPanel unit. These constants and several others are declared in a separate unit that provides functionality that is shared among several components. For example, the **TextAlignments** array constant is used by the **TRzLabel** class, which will be covered later in this chapter.

The RzCommon unit is shown in Listing 8.2. All of the components presented in this book include the RzCommon unit. Minimally, each component unit uses the palette page constants defined in the RzCommon unit in each unit's **Register** procedure. We will be adding other information to this unit in future chapters.

Listing 8.2   RZCOMMON.PAS—The RzCommon Unit

```
{===============================================================================}
{= RzCommon Unit                                                              =}
{=                                                                            =}
{= This unit defines constants, types, and miscellaneous procedures and       =}
{= functions used by multiple component classes.                              =}
{=                                                                            =}
{= Building Custom Delphi Components - Ray Konopka                            =}
{===============================================================================}


unit RzCommon;

interface

uses
  WinTypes, Classes, Graphics, ExtCtrls;

type
  TFrameStyle = ( fsNone, fsFlat, fsGroove, fsBump, fsRecessed, fsRaised );

const
  ULBevelColor : array[ TPanelBevel ] of TColor = ( clWindow,
                                                    clBtnShadow,
                                                    clBtnHighlight);

  LRBevelColor : array[ TPanelBevel ] of TColor = ( clWindow,
                                                    clBtnHighlight,
                                                    clBtnShadow );

  { Frame Style Color constant arrays }

  ULFrameColor : array[ TFrameStyle ] of TColor = ( clWindow,
                                                    clWindowFrame,
                                                    clBtnShadow,
                                                    clBtnHighlight,
                                                    clBtnShadow,
                                                    clBtnHighlight );


  LRFrameColor : array[ TFrameStyle ] of TColor = ( clWindow,
                                                    clWindowFrame,
                                                    clBtnHighlight,
                                                    clBtnShadow,
                                                    clBtnHighlight,
                                                    clBtnShadow );


  TextAlignments : array[ TAlignment ] of Word = ( dt_Left,
                                                   dt_Right,
                                                   dt_Center );
```

```
const                                              { Palette Page Constants }
   RaizePage : string[ 5 ] = 'Raize';
   RaizeDBPage : string[ 8 ] = 'Raize DB';
   RaizeStatusPage : string[ 12 ] = 'Raize Status';


procedure DrawCtl3DBorder( Canvas : TCanvas; Bounds : TRect );


implementation


{=========================================}
{== Generic Draw3CtlDBorder Procedure ==}
{=========================================}

procedure DrawCtl3DBorder( Canvas : TCanvas; Bounds : TRect );
begin
  with Bounds, Canvas do
  begin
    Pen.Color := clGray;

    MoveTo( Left, Bottom - 1 );
    LineTo( Left, Top );
    LineTo( Right, Top );

    Pen.Color := clWhite;
    MoveTo( Right - 1, Top + 1 );
    LineTo( Right - 1, Bottom - 1 );
    LineTo( Left, Bottom - 1 );

    Pen.Color := clBlack;
    MoveTo( Left + 1, Bottom - 2 );
    LineTo( Left + 1, Top + 1 );
    LineTo( Right - 1, Top + 1 );

    Pen.Color := clSilver;
    MoveTo( Right - 2, Top + 2 );
    LineTo( Right - 2, Bottom - 2 );
    LineTo( Left + 1, Bottom - 2 );
  end;
end;

end.
```

A 3D Label Component

Image is everything. When it comes to designing a user interface, using the wrong control can leave your application looking flat—or random and messy. This is why it's very common to create a new component in order to enhance its appearance, as was done with the RzPanel component. In this section, we'll continue to enhance existing controls by creating a 3D label component.

So what's wrong with the standard Label component? Nothing, except that it *always* looks flat. Adding a 3D label to a form can add that extra bit of emphasis that goes a long way in creating a sharp-looking interface with an unmistakable first impression. Consider the form in Figure 8.4. The standard Label component can only display text in one style, but the RzLabel component can display text in three additional styles: *recessed*, *raised*, and *shadow*.

Listing 8.3   RZLABEL.PAS—The RzLabel Unit

```
{==========================================================================}
{= RzLabel Unit                                                          =}
{=                                                                       =}
{= Enhanced label component that can display its caption in several different =}
{= three dimensional text styles: tsNone, tsRaised, tsRecessed, tsShadow   =}
{=                                                                       =}
{= Building Custom Delphi Components - Ray Konopka                        =}
{==========================================================================}

unit RzLabel;

interface

uses
  SysUtils, WinTypes, WinProcs, Classes, Graphics, StdCtrls, RzCommon;

type
  TTextStyle = ( tsNone, tsRaised, tsRecessed, tsShadow );

  TRzLabel = class( TLabel )
  private
    FTextStyle : TTextStyle;
    FShadowColor : TColor;
    FShadowDepth : Integer;
    procedure SetTextStyle( Value : TTextStyle );
```

Figure 8.4

The RzLabel Component

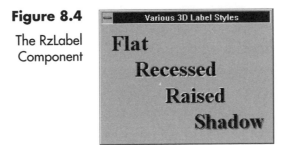

```
    procedure SetShadowColor( Value : TColor );
    procedure SetShadowDepth( Value : Integer );
    procedure Draw3DText( R : TRect; Flags : Word );
  protected
    procedure Paint; override;
  public
    constructor Create( AOwner : TComponent ); override;
  published
    property ShadowColor : TColor
      read FShadowColor
      write SetShadowColor
      default clBtnShadow;

    property ShadowDepth : Integer
      read FShadowDepth
      write SetShadowDepth
      default 2;

    property TextStyle : TTextStyle
      read FTextStyle
      write SetTextStyle
      default tsRecessed;
  end;

procedure Register;

implementation

{=====================}
{== TRzLabel Methods ==}
{=====================}

constructor TRzLabel.Create( AOwner : TComponent );
begin
  inherited Create( AOwner );
  FTextStyle := tsRecessed;
  FShadowDepth := 2;
  FShadowColor := clBtnShadow;
end;

procedure TRzLabel.SetShadowColor( Value : TColor );
begin
  if Value <> FShadowColor then
  begin
    FShadowColor := Value;
    Invalidate;
  end;
end;

procedure TRzLabel.SetShadowDepth( Value : Integer );
begin
  if Value <> FShadowDepth then
  begin
```

```
    FShadowDepth := Value;
    Invalidate;
  end;
end;


procedure TRzLabel.SetTextStyle( Value : TTextStyle );
begin
  if Value <> FTextStyle then
  begin
    FTextStyle := Value;
    Invalidate;
  end;
end;


procedure TRzLabel.Draw3DText( R : TRect; Flags : Word );
var
  CaptionStz : array[ 0..255 ] of Char;
  TempRct : TRect;
  ULColor : TColor;
  LRColor : TColor;
begin
  with Canvas do
  begin
    StrPCopy( CaptionStz, Caption );

    if WordWrap then
      Flags := Flags or dt_WordBreak;

    if not ShowAccelChar then
      Flags := Flags or dt_NoPrefix;

    Font := Self.Font;

    if FTextStyle in [ tsRecessed, tsRaised ] then
    begin
      case FTextStyle of
        tsRaised:
        begin
          ULColor := clBtnHighlight;
          LRColor := clBtnShadow;
        end;

        tsRecessed:
        begin
          ULColor := clBtnShadow;
          LRColor := clBtnHighlight;
        end;
      end;

      TempRct := R;
      OffsetRect( TempRct, 1, 1 );
```

```
      Font.Color := LRColor;
      DrawText( Handle, CaptionStz, -1, TempRct, Flags );

      TempRct := R;
      OffsetRect( TempRct, -1, -1 );
      Canvas.Font.Color := ULColor;
      DrawText( Handle, CaptionStz, -1, TempRct, Flags );
    end
    else if FTextStyle = tsShadow then
    begin
      TempRct := R;
      OffsetRect( TempRct, FShadowDepth, FShadowDepth );
      Font.Color := FShadowColor;
      DrawText( Handle, CaptionStz, -1, TempRct, Flags );
    end;

    Font.Color := Self.Font.Color;
    if not Enabled then
      Font.Color := clGrayText;
    DrawText( Handle, CaptionStz, -1, R, Flags );
  end;
end; {= TRzLabel.Draw3DText =}


procedure TRzLabel.Paint;
begin
  with Canvas do
  begin
    if not Transparent then
    begin
      Brush.Color := Self.Color;
      Brush.Style := bsSolid;
      FillRect( ClientRect );                    { Paint area behind label }
    end;
    Brush.Style := bsClear;
    Draw3DText( ClientRect, dt_ExpandTabs or TextAlignments[ Alignment ] );
  end;
end; {= TRzLabel.Paint =}


{=======================}
{== Register Procedure ==}
{=======================}

procedure Register;
begin
  RegisterComponents( RaizePage, [ TRzLabel ] );
end;

end.
```

Three Properties for 3D

Unlike **TRzPanel**, the **TRzLabel** class descends directly from **TLabel** and not **TCustomLabel** because it is not necessary to hide any functionality implemented in the ancestor class. To support drawing three-dimensional text, three additional properties are declared. The **TextStyle** property is an enumerated type specifying how the text will be drawn. The second two properties, **ShadowColor** and **ShadowDepth**, are used only if the **TextStyle** property is set to **tsShadow** and determine what color is used for the shadow and how far down and to the right the shadow will appear, respectively.

There is nothing special about the implementation of these properties. All three have an internal data field of the appropriate type, and each property declaration is structured just like the properties in the **TRzPanel** class. Even the write access methods for all three properties have the typical format described earlier.

3D Effects

Again, since we are visually enhancing the appearance of the control, the work is done in the **Paint** method. As you can see, the **Paint** method is rather short, with the real work done by the **Draw3DText** method. Let's take a closer look at this method—we'll get back to the **Paint** method shortly. To achieve 3D effects, the caption of the label is drawn three times, as demonstrated in Figure 8.5. By offsetting the caption's position and changing its color each time it is drawn, we can give the appearance that the text is three dimensional.

Welcome to the Real World

Let's go back to the **Paint** method. You may be wondering why I didn't just put the **Draw3DText** code inside the **Paint** method. This is certainly possible, but I

Figure 8.5

Drawing a 3D Label

avoided it to make a very specific point. This is not a difficult component to create, but it could have been easier if the **TCustomLabel** had been implemented a little differently. To clarify this, we need to look at the **TCustomLabel.Paint** method that appears in Listing 8.4.

Listing 8.4 The TCustomLabel.Paint Method

```
procedure TCustomLabel.Paint;
const
  Alignments: array[TAlignment] of Word = (DT_LEFT, DT_RIGHT, DT_CENTER);
var
  Rect: TRect;
begin
  with Canvas do
  begin
    if not Transparent then
    begin
      Brush.Color := Self.Color;
      Brush.Style := bsSolid;
      FillRect(ClientRect);
    end;
    Brush.Style := bsClear;
    Rect := ClientRect;
    DoDrawText(Rect, (DT_EXPANDTABS or DT_WORDBREAK) or
      Alignments[FAlignment]);
  end;
end;
```

The difficulty arises from the fact that **DoDrawText** does all the work that we are trying to override. The simple solution to enhancing the display of the label is to override the **DoDrawText** method. When the **Paint** method gets called, our new version of the **DoDrawText** method would be called.

This sounds wonderful—but the only problem is that our logic here depends on **DoDrawText** being declared as **virtual**. Unfortunately, the **DoDrawText** method is a static method. On top of this, it is also declared as **private**.

To get around this problem, we have to override the **Paint** method and provide a new **DoDrawText** method, which is what the **Draw3DText** method is. Whenever you attempt to enhance an existing component, it's quite possible to run into roadblocks like this.

Tabbing Around a List Box

Grid components have taken the visual programming industry by storm. Grids have proven to be extremely flexible and expressive components for displaying tables of data, and given the ability to turn off grid lines, they have even been used as replacements for list boxes. But the classical list box is still a very useful and powerful control. Unfortunately, much of the power of the list box control as an idea is not available in the standard ListBox component. List boxes even have some features that are not present in grids. A component that included the best of both worlds would be a very good thing to have.

Figures 8.6 and 8.7 show two forms performing the same function. The form in Figure 8.6 uses a StringGrid, whereas the form in Figure 8.7 uses the new RzTabbedListBox component. The major difference between the two is that the list box automatically supports multiple selection. Multiple rows can also be selected in the grid, but the rows must be contiguous. This is not a requirement in the list box. Figure 8.7 also shows that the RzTabbedListBox has the ability to display a horizontal scroll bar. This feature is not available in the standard ListBox component. The source code for the **TRzTabbedListBox** class is shown in Listing 8.5.

Figure 8.6

Using a Grid Component

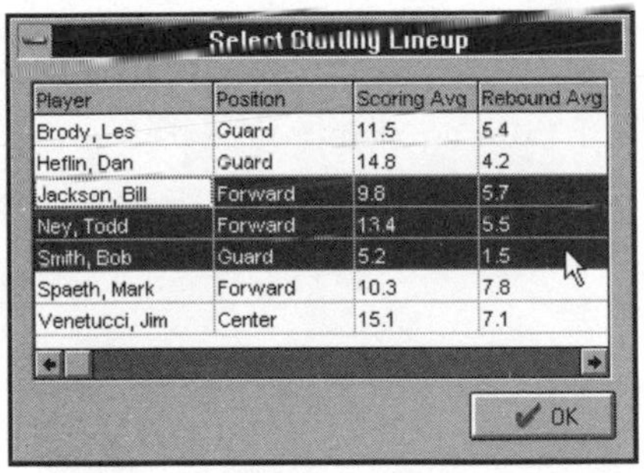

Figure 8.7

A List Box with Tab Stops

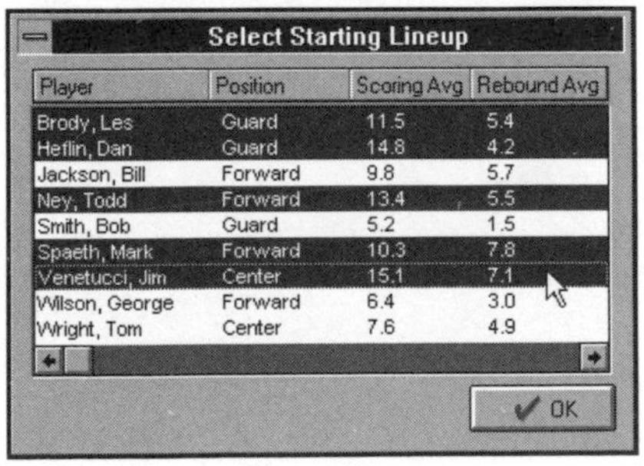

Listing 8.5 RZTABLST.PAS—The RzTabLst Unit

```
{=============================================================}
{= RzTabLst Unit                                            =}
{=                                                          =}
{= This unit implements an enhanced list box component which understands how =}
{= to process embedded tab characters to display lines in columnar format. In =}
{= addition, a horizontal scroll bar is added to the list box.               =}
{=                                                          =}
{= Building Custom Delphi Components - Ray Konopka          =}
{=============================================================}


unit RzTabLst;

interface

uses
  WinTypes, WinProcs, Classes, Graphics, Forms, StdCtrls,
  Controls, Messages, SysUtils, IntList, RzCommon;

type
  TRzTabbedListBox = class;

  TRzTabStopList = class( TIntegerList )
  private
    FListBox : TRzTabbedListBox;
  protected
    procedure SetItem( Index : Integer; Value : Longint ); override;
  public
    constructor Create;
    procedure Delete( Index : Integer ); override;
    procedure Insert( Index : Integer; Value : Longint ); override;
  end;


  TRzTabbedListBox = class( TListBox )
  private
    FHorzExtent : Word;
    FHorzScrollBar : Boolean;
    FTabStops : TRzTabStopList;
    procedure SetHorzExtent( Value : Word );
    procedure SetHorzScrollBar( Value : Boolean );
    procedure SetTabStops( Value : TRzTabStopList );
  protected
    procedure CreateParams( var Params : TCreateParams ); override;
    procedure CreateWnd; override;
  public
    constructor Create( AOwner : TComponent ); override;
    destructor Destroy; override;
    procedure UpdateTabStops;

    property TabStops : TRzTabStopList               { Read only property }
      read FTabStops
```

```
    write SetTabStops;
  published
    property HorzExtent : Word
      read FHorzExtent
      write SetHorzExtent
      default 0;

    property HorzScrollBar : Boolean
      read FHorzScrollBar
      write SetHorzScrollBar
      default False;
  end;


procedure Register;

implementation


{============================}
{== TRzTabStopList Methods ==}
{============================}

constructor TRzTabStopList.Create;
begin
  inherited Create;
  Min := 0;
  Max := MaxLongint;
end;


procedure TRzTabStopList.SetItem( Index : Integer; Value : Longint );
begin
  inherited SetItem( Index, Value );
  if FListBox <> nil then
    FListBox.UpdateTabStops;
end;


procedure TRzTabStopList.Delete( Index : Integer );
begin
  inherited Delete( Index );
  if FListBox <> nil then
    FListBox.UpdateTabStops;
end;


procedure TRzTabStopList.Insert( Index : Integer; Value : Longint );
begin
  inherited Insert( Index, Value );
  if FListBox <> nil then
    FListBox.UpdateTabStops;
end;
```

```
{=============================}
{== TRzTabbedListBox Methods ==}
{=============================}

constructor TRzTabbedListBox.Create( AOwner : TComponent );
begin
  inherited Create( AOwner );
  FTabStops := TRzTabStopList.Create;
  FTabStops.FListBox := Self;
end;


destructor TRzTabbedListBox.Destroy;
begin
  FTabStops.Free;
  inherited Destroy;
end;


procedure TRzTabbedListBox.CreateParams( var Params : TCreateParams );
begin
  inherited CreateParams( Params );          { Don't Forget to Call inhertied }
  with Params do
    Style := Style or lbs_UseTabStops or ws_HScroll or lbs_DisableNoScroll;
end;


procedure TRzTabbedListBox.CreateWnd;
begin
  inherited CreateWnd;                        { Don't Forget to Call inherited }

  { Initializing the scroll bar must occur after the Window Handle for the }
  { list box has been created }
  Perform( lb_SetHorizontalExtent, FHorzExtent, 0 );
  ShowScrollBar( Handle, sb_Horz, FHorzScrollBar );
end;


procedure TRzTabbedListBox.SetHorzExtent( Value : Word );
begin
  if Value <> FHorzExtent then
  begin
    FHorzExtent := Value;
    Perform( lb_SetHorizontalExtent, FHorzExtent, 0 );
  end;
end;


procedure TRzTabbedListBox.SetHorzScrollBar( Value : Boolean );
begin
  if Value <> FHorzScrollBar then
  begin
    FHorzScrollBar := Value;
    ShowScrollBar( Handle, sb_Horz, FHorzScrollBar );
```

```
    end;
  end;


procedure TRzTabbedListBox.SetTabStops( Value : TRzTabStopList );
begin
  FTabStops.Assign( Value );
  UpdateTabStops;
end;


{=============================================================}
{=- TRzTabbedListBox.UpdateTabStops                         =-}
{=-                                                         =-}
{=- The lb_SetTabStops message is used to set the tab stops.  The LParam  =-}
{=- parameter for this message is a pointer to an array of Word values  =-}
{=- representing the tab stops.  Therefore, the contents of the FTabStops list =-}
{=- is transferred to a temporary array.                    =-}
{=============================================================}

procedure TRzTabbedListBox.UpdateTabStops;
const
  MaxTabs = 1000;                        { 1000 Tab Stops Should be Plenty! }
var
  TabCount, I : Integer;
  TabArray : array[ 0..MaxTabs - 1 ] of Word;
begin
  TabCount := FTabStops.Count;
  if TabCount > MaxTabs then
    TabCount := MaxTabs;

  for I := 0 to TabCount - 1 do      { Copy Contents of FTabStops to Temp Array }
    TabArray[ I ] := FTabStops.Items[ I ] * 4; { Convert Chars to Dialog Units }

                                { Send message to list box to set tab stops }
  Perform( lb_SetTabStops, TabCount, Longint( @TabArray ) );
  Invalidate;
end;


{=========================}
{== Register Procedure ==}
{=========================}

procedure Register;
begin
  RegisterComponents( RaizePage, [ TRzTabbedListBox ] );
end;

end.
```

Tab Stops

Managing the list of tab stops is the job of the **TabStops** property. It functions in much the same way that the **Items** property manages the list of strings in the list box. Since each tab stop is represented by an integer value, the **TabStop** property is declared as a **TRzTabStopList**, which is a descendant of the **TIntegerList** class presented in Chapter 6. The **TabStop** property is declared as **public** because there is no property editor available that can edit an instance of the **TIntegerList** class. For now, the **TabStops** list is a run time only property.

There are four steps that must be performed in order to get the list box to display tab formatted lines. First, the **FTabStops** list must be created. This is done in the constructor of the list box. The **FTabStops** list is assigned to the return value of the **TRzTabStopList.Create** constructor. When the list is created, it does not contain any initial values. This mimics the way the **Items** property works.

The second step is to instruct the list box that it should process embedded tab characters as tab stops. All list boxes have the ability to handle tab characters (ASCII character #9) to align columns of text. However, the standard ListBox component cannot display tab-formatted lines because the correct window style is not set. To set the correct window style, the **CreateParams** method must be overridden.

The **CreateParams** method was described in Chapter 6 as a way to modify the window style of a control before the underlying control is created. For this class, the **CreateParams** method modifies the **Style** field of the **Params** parameter by adding the **lbs_UseTabStops** list box style flag. The **ws_HScroll** and **lbs_DisableNoScroll** window styles are also specified here to support adding a horizontal scroll bar to the list box.

The third step occurs at run time, with the actual setting of the tab stop values. Tab stop values are added to the list using the **Add** method. For example, the following code adds three tab stops to the list:

```
with RzTabbedListBox1 do
begin
  TabStops.Add( 15 );
  TabStops.Add( 25 );
  TabStops.Add( 40 );
end;
```

The tab stop values added to the list represent the number of characters from the left side of the list box that the tab stop should be placed. For non-fixed pitched fonts, the character width represents the average character width. Also notice that adding three tab stops to the list box creates four columns of text. The first column always appears at position zero.

Once a list of tab stops has been specified, the final step is to instruct the list box to use those values as actual tab stops. This is accomplished by calling the **UpdateTabStops** method, which sends an **lb_SetTabStops** message to the underlying list box control.

The **lb_SetTabStops** message is a standard Windows message that takes a **Word** parameter and a **Longint** parameter. The **Word** parameter is used to specify the number of tab stops being set, and the **Longint** parameter isn't a number at all but actually a pointer to an array of **Word** values representing the tab stops. Since the **TRzTabbedListBox** class manages the tab stops in an integer list, the **UpdateTabStops** method creates a temporary array that gets filled with the contents of the **FTabStops** list and is then used in the **lb_SetTabStops** message.

When the contents of the **FTabStops** list is copied to the temporary **TabArray**, the values in **FTabStops** are multiplied by four. This is necessary because the **lb_SetTabStops** message expects the tab stops to be specified in *dialog units*. A dialog unit is one-fourth the size of the average width of the system font.

Use the **Perform** method to send a message to a component. The **Perform** method can send any message to a component. If the message is a Windows message, the **Perform** method behaves similarly to the **SendMessage** API function. As an example, the following statement calculates the current line position in the **Memo1** component by sending the **em_LineFromChar** message:

```
CurrentLine := Memo1.Perform( em_LineFromChar, Memo1.SelStart, 0 );
```

Perform bypasses the Windows message queue and sends the message directly to the component's window procedure.

Smarter Tab Stops

Perhaps you're wondering, What's the purpose of the **TRzTabStopList** class? Isn't the **TIntegerList** class sufficient? The **TIntegerList** class only knows how to manage a list of numbers, which is only part of the functionality required by the tabbed list box. The principal reason for creating a new descendant of the **TIntegerList** class is so that when the list of tab stops is modified, the corresponding list box can be notified. Within the constructor of the **TRzTabbedListBox** class, after the **FTabStops** list is created, the **FListBox** field of **FTabStops** is set to reference the list box.

One of three methods is always called whenever the list of tab stops is altered: either the **SetItem**, **Insert**, or **Delete** methods. The **TRzTabStopList** overrides each of these methods so that whenever one of these methods is called, the corresponding list box can be notified. For example, the **TRzTabStopList.Insert** method calls the **inherited Insert** method to perform all the real work, and then calls the **UpdateTabStops** method of the corresponding **FListBox** field. Therefore, whenever the contents of the **TabStops** list property is altered, the ListBox component is notified of the change and updates the tab stops accordingly.

As an aside, this unit demonstrates a good example of using a *forward class reference*. The **TRzTabbedListBox** class references the **TRzTabStopList** through its **TabStops** property. Therefore, the **TRzTabStopList** must be declared before **TRzTabbedListBox**. However, the **TRzTabStopList** needs to reference the **TRzTabbedListBox** class through its **FListBox** field. To avoid a circular referencing paradox, a forward class reference is needed.

Adding a Horizontal Scroll Bar

The other two properties of **TRzTabbedListBox**, **HorzExtent** and **HorzScrollBar**, affect the behavior of the horizontal scroll bar. Like tab stops, all list boxes can display a horizontal scroll bar as long as the correct window style is set. This is the reason for specifying the **ws_HScroll** and **lbs_DisableNoScroll** style flags in the **CreateParams** method. The **ws_HScroll** style flag creates a scroll bar to be used by the control, and the **lbs_DisableNoScroll** style flag forces the scroll bar to be visible even if all of the text in the list box can be seen without scrolling to the right.

With the **HorzScrollBar** and **HorzExtent** properties, the scroll bar can be affected in two ways. First, the visibility of the scroll bar is controlled by the **HorzScrollBar Boolean** property. When this property is changed, the

ShowScrollBar API function is called to either show or hide the scroll bar. The **HorzExtent** property controls how far to the right the scroll bar can scroll. **HorzExtent** is a **Word** property representing the range of the horizontal scroll bar in pixels. If the extent is greater than the width of the list box, the scroll bar is enabled. Otherwise, the scroll bar is disabled.

The most interesting aspect of manipulating the scroll bar occurs during initialization. Since the window handle of the list box is needed to manipulate the scroll bar, initializing the scroll bar cannot occur in the **Create** constructor. Instead, scroll bar initialization occurs in the **CreateWnd** method. Recall from Chapter 6 that one of the tasks the **CreateWnd** method performs is obtaining the window handle. In this component, once the **inherited CreateWnd** method is called, the **lb_SetHorizontalExtent** message may be sent to the list box and the **ShowScrollBar** procedure may be called.

Using the RzTabbedListBox Component

The only other issue to cover regarding the RzTabbedListBox component is how to populate the **Items** list so that the strings are formatted according to the tab stops. Like the standard ListBox component, strings are added to this new component using the **Items** property either at runtime or design-time. The only difference is that you now must embed tab (ASCII #9) characters in your list items to indicate how the text should be lined up.

Using the string list editor at design-time, tab characters can be embedded by pressing Ctrl+I. For runtime tab insertion, insert the #9 character specifier into your source code at the desired locations. The following code fragment demonstrates the process:

```
with RzTabbedListBox1 do
begin
  Items.Add( 'Bob Smith' + #9 + 'Catcher' + #9 + '0.252' );
  Items.Add( 'George Wilson' + #9 + 'Outfielder' + #9 + '0.289' );
  Items.Add( 'Tom Wright' + #9 + 'Short Stop' + #9 + '0.325' );
end;
```

Looking Ahead...

In this chapter we looked at several of the issues involved in creating new components by enhancing an existing control with object-oriented techniques. In the next chapter we'll focus on creating several brand new graphical controls. In the process, we'll cover some of the finer details of the **Canvas** property, and take a closer look at property interaction as well build a hierarchy of related components.

For a far look ahead, we'll be returning to both the RzLabel and RzTabbedListBox components in Chapter 14. In that chapter, a component editor will be created for the RzLabel component, and a property editor will be created for the **TabStops** property of **TRzTabbedListBox**. With the new property editor, the **TabStops** property moves to the **published** section of the class and become available at design-time.

Part 3

Developing Components

Chapter 9

Graphical Components

Graphical Components

It's time to build an all-new component from scratch, and the best place to start is with graphical status components to display read-only data on your forms.

In the last chapter, we covered how to take an existing control and enhance its capabilities. In this chapter, we're going to start building some original controls. The most straightforward way of creating an original control is to create a graphical component. Graphical components are those that descend from the **TGraphicControl** class.

Building a new graphical component is a good way to start building custom controls, because the only real concern for the component writer is the visualization of the component and the properties that are used to manipulate that view. Graphical components do not maintain a window handle, so it is not necessary to provide the extra code needed to manage the input focus for these types of controls.

Of course, without a window handle, graphical components cannot accept other controls dropped onto them. However, from another standpoint, the lack of a window handle is a significant advantage of graphical components. By not having to allocate a window handle, graphical components do not use any of the user resource heap. This makes graphical components Windows resource friendly.

Is It Done Yet?

This is often the question users have when a process takes too long and there is no indication whether or not the process is nearing completion. To keep users at ease, it is common practice to display a progress bar that indicates in relative terms how much more work remains for a given task.

Delphi ships with a sample component that allows a developer to display such a progress bar. However, the Gauge component is not the most visually appealing progress indicator. For example, the Gauge component always appears in a flat style—there is no option for shading the control to give a 3D appearance.

As stated in the earlier chapters, one of the primary reasons for building new components is to alter the appearance of an existing control. And this is indeed the primary reason for building the RzProgressBar component, but there are some additional features added to make the component more usable. For example, the **TotalParts** and **PartsComplete** properties can be used to instruct the component to calculate the percentage value rather than setting the **Percent** property directly. These properties are quite useful during an install operation, since the component can calculate the percentage of completion from property values.

Many more properties are declared in this component than in the ones that we have covered in previous chapters, mainly because of the fact that this is the first purely custom control that we've addressed in this book. You will also notice that the properties themselves are more complex compared to those presented in earlier chapters. Their complexity stems from interactions between the properties. In the earlier chapters, the write access methods followed the standard write access method format. However, in the RzProgressBar component, many of the write access methods contain side effects that alter other property values.

Figure 9.1 shows several variations of the RzProgressBar component. The scroll bar at the top of the dialog box is used to set the **Percent** property of each

Figure 9.1

Sample Progress Bars.

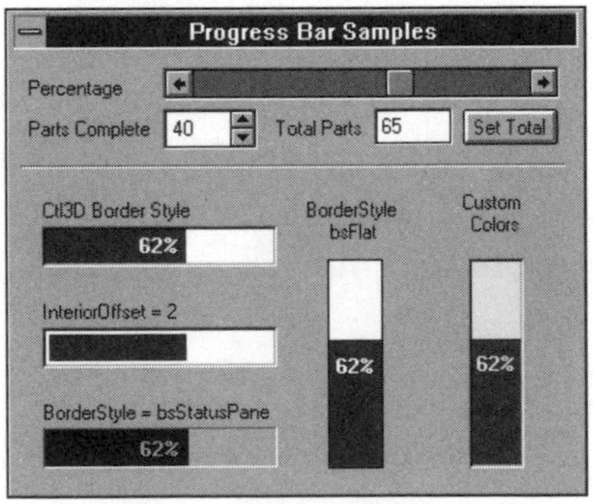

control. The **PartsComplete** and **TotalParts** properties described earlier can be modified directly using the spin button and edit field below the scroll bar. Any change to either set of controls updates the percentage values displayed in the five sample progress bars. The complete source code for the RzPrgres unit, which implements the **TRzProgressBar** class, follows in Listing 9.1.

Listing 9.1 RZPRGRES.PAS—The RzPrgres Unit

```
{=============================================================}
{= RzPrgres Unit                                            =}
{=                                                          =}
{= Custom progress bar component with several border styles (Flat, Ctl3D, and =}
{= StatusBar).  Specialized properties (PartsComplete, TotalParts) make it    =}
{= easy to control the progress bar during install processes, etc.            =}
{=                                                          =}
{= Building Custom Delphi Components - Ray Konopka           =}
{=============================================================}

unit RzPrgres;

interface

uses
  WinTypes, Classes, Graphics, Controls, Menus, ExtCtrls, RzCommon;

type
  TProgressBorderStyle = ( bsFlat, bsCtl3D, bsStatusControl );
  TProgressOrientation = ( poHorizontal, poVertical );
  TPercentRange = 0..100;
  TProgressChangeEvent = procedure(Sender: TObject; Percent: Integer) of object;

  TRzProgressBar = class( TGraphicControl )
  private
    FBackColor : TColor;
    FBarColor : TColor;
    FBorderWidth : TBorderWidth;
    FBorderStyle : TProgressBorderStyle;
    FInteriorOffset : Byte;
    FOrientation : TProgressOrientation;
    FPartsComplete : Word;
    FPercent : TPercentRange;
    FShowPercent : Boolean;
    FTotalParts : Word;
    FOnChange : TProgressChangeEvent;

    procedure SetBackColor( Value : TColor );
  procedure SetBarColor( Value : TColor );
    procedure SetBorderWidth( Value : TBorderWidth );
    procedure SetBorderStyle( Value : TProgressBorderStyle );
    function GetCtl3D : Boolean;
```

```
    procedure SetCtl3D( Value : Boolean );
    procedure SetInteriorOffset( Value : Byte );
    procedure SetOrientation( Value : TProgressOrientation );
    procedure SetPartsComplete( Value : Word );
    procedure SetPercent( Value : TPercentRange );
    procedure SetShowPercent( Value : Boolean );
    procedure SetTotalParts( Value : Word );
  protected
    procedure Paint; override;
    procedure PercentChanged; dynamic;
  public
    constructor Create( AOwner : TComponent ); override;
    procedure IncPartsByOne;
    procedure IncParts( N : Integer );
  published
    property BackColor : TColor
      read FBackColor
      write SetBackColor
      default clWhite;

    property BarColor : TColor
      read FBarColor
      write SetBarColor
      default clHighlight;

    property BorderStyle : TProgressBorderStyle
      read FBorderStyle
      write SetBorderStyle
      default bsCtl3D;

    property BorderWidth : TBorderWidth
      read FBorderWidth
      write SetBorderWidth;

    property Ctl3D : Boolean
      read GetCtl3D
      write SetCtl3D
      default True;

    property InteriorOffset : Byte
      read FInteriorOffset
      write SetInteriorOffset;

    property Orientation : TProgressOrientation
      read FOrientation
      write SetOrientation
      default poHorizontal;

    property PartsComplete : Word
      read FPartsComplete
      write SetPartsComplete;
```

```
  property Percent : TPercentRange
     read FPercent
     write SetPercent;

  property ShowPercent : Boolean
    read FShowPercent
    write SetShowPercent
    default True;

  property TotalParts : Word
    read FTotalParts
    write SetTotalParts;

  property OnChange : TProgressChangeEvent
    read FOnChange
    write FOnChange;

  { Inherited Properties & Events }
  property Align;
  property Color;
  property Font;
  property ParentFont;
  property ParentShowHint;
  property PopupMenu;
  property ShowHint;
  property Visible;
  property OnClick;
  property OnDblClick;
  property OnMouseDown;
  property OnMouseMove;
  property OnMouseUp;
end;


procedure DrawPercentBar( Canvas : TCanvas; DrawRct : TRect;
                          Offset, InteriorOffset, BorderWidth : Integer;
                          Orientation : TProgressOrientation;
                          BarColor, BackColor : TColor;
                          Percent : Integer; ShowPercent : Boolean );

procedure Register;

implementation

uses
  SysUtils, WinProcs;


{=============================}
{== TRzProgressBar Methods ==}
{=============================}
```

```
constructor TRzProgressBar.Create( AOwner : TComponent );
begin
  inherited Create( AOwner );
  ControlStyle := ControlStyle + [ csOpaque ];
  FPercent := 0;
  FShowPercent := True;
  FOrientation := poHorizontal;
  FBackColor := clWhite;
  FBarColor := clHighlight;
  FBorderWidth := 0;
  FBorderStyle := bsCtl3D;
  Width := 100;
  Height := 24;
end;


procedure TRzProgressBar.SetBackColor( Value : TColor );
begin
  if Value <> FBackColor then
  begin
    FBackColor := Value;
    Invalidate;
  end;
end;


procedure TRzProgressBar.SetBarColor( Value : TColor );
begin
  if Value <> FBarColor then
  begin
    FBarColor := Value;
    Font.Color := Value;
    Invalidate;
  end;
end;


procedure TRzProgressBar.SetBorderWidth( Value : TBorderWidth );
begin
  if Value <> FBorderWidth then
  begin
    FBorderWidth := Value;
    Invalidate;
  end;
end;


procedure TRzProgressBar.SetBorderStyle( Value : TProgressBorderStyle );
begin
  if Value <> FBorderStyle then
  begin
    FBorderStyle := Value;
```

```
      if ( FBorderStyle = bsStatusControl ) and ( FBorderWidth = 0 ) then
          FBorderWidth := 2
        else if FBorderWidth = 2 then
          FBorderWidth := 0;
        Invalidate;
      end;
    end;


function TRzProgressBar.GetCtl3D : Boolean;
begin
  Result := FBorderStyle = bsCtl3D;
end;


procedure TRzProgressBar.SetCtl3D( Value : Boolean );
begin
  if Value <> Ctl3D then
  begin
    if Value then
      FBorderStyle := bsCtl3D
    else
      FBorderStyle := bsFlat;
    Invalidate;
  end;
end;


procedure TRzProgressBar.SetInteriorOffset( Value : Byte );
begin
  if Value <> FInteriorOffset then
  begin
    FInteriorOffset := Value;
    Invalidate;
  end;
end;


procedure TRzProgressBar.SetOrientation( Value : TProgressOrientation );
begin
  if Value <> FOrientation then
  begin
    FOrientation := Value;
    Invalidate;
  end;
end;


procedure TRzProgressBar.SetPartsComplete( Value : Word );
begin
  if Value <> FPartsComplete then
  begin
```

```
    if Value > FTotalParts then
        FPartsComplete := FTotalParts
    else
        FPartsComplete := Value;

    { Setting the Percent property causes the SetPercent method to get called  }
    { which will force a repaint }
    Percent := Round( FPartsComplete / FTotalParts * 100 );
  end;
end;



procedure TRzProgressBar.SetPercent( Value : TPercentRange );
begin
  if Value <> FPercent then
  begin
    FPercent := Value;
    PercentChanged;

    { Call Repaint rather than Invalidate so that the view of the component }
    { does not get erased.  This prevents flicker. }
    Repaint;
  end;
end;



procedure TRzProgressBar.SetShowPercent( Value : Boolean );
begin
  if Value <> FShowPercent then
  begin
    FShowPercent := Value;
    Invalidate;
  end;
end;



procedure TRzProgressBar.SetTotalParts( Value : Word );
begin
  if Value <> FTotalParts then
  begin
    FTotalParts := Value;
    FPartsComplete := 0;                      { Set Internal FPartsComplete Field }
    Percent := 0;                                   { Set Percent Property }
  end;
end;



procedure TRzProgressBar.IncPartsByOne;
begin
  IncParts( 1 );
end;
```

```
procedure TRzProgressBar.IncParts( N : Integer );
begin
  PartsComplete := PartsComplete + N;
end;


procedure TRzProgressBar.PercentChanged;
begin
  if Assigned( FOnChange ) then
    FOnChange( Self, FPercent );
end;


{= DrawPercentBar                                                   =}
{=   This is an exported procedure to facilitate usage by other components   =}

procedure DrawPercentBar( Canvas : TCanvas; DrawRct : TRect;
                          Offset, InteriorOffset, BorderWidth : Integer;
                          Orientation : TProgressOrientation;
                          BarColor, BackColor : TColor;
                          Percent : Integer; ShowPercent : Boolean );
var
  PercentStr : string;
  PctRct : TRect;
  TopOffset : Integer;
begin
  with Canvas, DrawRct do
  begin
    If ShowPercent then
      PercentStr := Format( '%u%%', [ Percent ] )
    else
      PercentStr := '';

    Font.Color := BackColor;
    Brush.Color := BarColor;

    { Calculate the Size of the Left/Bottom portion of the Percentage Bar }

    if Orientation = poVertical then
    begin
      PctRct := Rect( BorderWidth + Offset,
                      ( Bottom - Offset - Offset - BorderWidth ) -
                        Round( (Longint(Bottom - Offset - Offset -BorderWidth) *
                               Percent ) / 100 ) + Offset + BorderWidth,
                      Right - Offset,
                      Bottom - Offset );
    end
    else
    begin
      PctRct := Rect( BorderWidth + Offset,
                      BorderWidth + Offset,
                      Round( ( Longint(Right - Offset - Offset - BorderWidth) *
```

```
                        Percent ) / 100 ) + Offset + BorderWidth,
                    Bottom - Offset );
    end;


    { Display the Left/Bottom portion of the Percentage Bar }

    SetTextAlign( Handle, ta_Center or ta_Top );
    TopOffset := Abs( Offset - 2 - InteriorOffset );
    TextRect( PctRct,  Right div 2, (Bottom-TextHeight('X')) div 2 + TopOffset,
            PercentStr );

    { Calculate the Size of the Right/Top portion of the Percentage Bar }

    if Orientation = poVertical then
    begin
      PctRct.Bottom := PctRct.Top;
      PctRct.Top := Top + Offset;
    end
    else
    begin
      PctRct.Left := PctRct.Right;
      PctRct.Right := Right - Offset;
    end;

    { Display the Right/Top portion of the Percentage Bar }

    Font.Color := BarColor;
    Brush.Color := BackColor;
    TextRect( PctRct,  Right div 2, (Bottom-TextHeight('X')) div 2 + TopOffset,
            PercentStr );
  end; { with }
end; {= DrawPercentBar =}


procedure TRzProgressBar.Paint;
var
  Offset : Integer;
  DrawRct : TRect;
begin
  Canvas.Font := Font;
  DrawRct := ClientRect;
  InflateRect( DrawRct, -FBorderWidth, -FBorderWidth );

  with DrawRct, Canvas do
  begin
    { Draw Border }
    { DrawCtl3DBorder and DrawBorder are defined in the RzCommon Unit }

    Offset := 1;
    case FBorderStyle of
      bsCtl3D:
      begin
        Inc( Offset );
```

```
      DrawCtl3DBorder( Canvas, DrawRct );
      end;

    bsStatusControl:
      DrawBorder( Canvas, DrawRct, clBtnShadow, clBtnHighlight );

    bsFlat:
      DrawBorder( Canvas, DrawRct, clBlack, clBlack )
  end; { case }

  { Draw Interior Offset Region }

  if FInteriorOffset > 0 then
  begin
    Brush.Style := bsClear;
    Pen.Color := Color;
    Pen.Style := psInsideFrame;
    Pen.Width := FInteriorOffset;
    Rectangle( Left + Offset, Top + Offset, Right - Offset, Bottom - Offset );
    Pen.Width := 1;                          { Be sure to restore Pen width }
    Pen.Style := psSolid;
    Brush.Style := bsSolid;
  end;
  Offset := Offset + FInteriorOffset;

  { Draw Percent Bar }

  DrawPercentBar( Canvas, DrawRct, Offset, FInteriorOffset, FBorderWidth,
                  FOrientation, FBarColor, FBackColor,
                  FPercent, FShowPercent );
  end; { with }
end; {= TRzProgressBar.Paint =}




{=========================}
{== Register Procedure ==}
{=========================}

procedure Register;
begin
  RegisterComponents( RaizePage, [ TRzProgressBar ] );
end;

end.
```

Defining a Progress Bar

The first thing that you'll notice about the **TRzProgressBar** class declaration is that it is the largest one we've encountered so far. This is because we are building a brand new custom component that does *not* inherit a user interface from an existing, predefined control. The **private** section of the class contains all the internal data fields and the read and write access methods to support all of the new properties defined in this component.

Most of the properties affect the appearance of the progress bar. For example, the **BarColor** and **BackColor** properties control the filled and unfilled colors of the bar, respectively. The **BorderStyle** property determines the type of border that surrounds the percentage bar. Valid options include **bsCtl3D**, **bsStatusControl**, and **bsFlat**.

The **BorderWidth** and **InteriorOffset** properties control the size of the progress bar independent of the normal **Left**, **Top**, **Width**, and **Height** properties. The **BorderWidth** specifies the number of pixels the border is indented from the **ClientRect** of the component. (The **ClientRect** rectangle is defined by the **Width** and **Height** properties.) The **BorderWidth** property is useful when the **BorderStyle** value is **bsStatusControl**. The **InteriorOffset** property specifies the number of pixels the outer edge of the progress percentage bar is indented from the inner edge of the border. Figure 9.1 (shown on Page 202) contains an example of a progress bar with an **InteriorOffset** set to 2.

The **Percent**, **TotalParts**, and **PartsComplete** properties are the main properties for the RzProgressBar component. These properties control how much of the progress bar is filled. The **Percent** property is defined as type **TPercentRange**. This guarantees that the **Percent** property can only accept percentages between 0 and 100. The **PartsComplete** and **TotalParts** properties are integer values, which when combined, are used to calculate a percentage based on their ratio.

Because all three of these properties control the same thing (the fill amount) they obviously must interact with one another. The next section covers just how these three properties interact, as well as investigating some other property interactions within the RzProgressBar component.

As a final note regarding the **TRzProgressBar** class declaration, take another look at the **published** section. At the very end, there are a number of redeclared properties and events. These properties and events are originally declared much higher in the ancestor class hierarchy. For example, most of them are defined in the **TControl** class, but all of them are declared as **protected** or **public** there.

When designing a new control, the component writer must determine which properties and events to publish. Graphical components generally publish the

Font and Color properties, as well as the Visible property. Most will also publish the mouse events like OnMouseDown. However, since a graphical component cannot receive the input focus, the keyboard events are not published.

Property Interaction

The primary interaction that occurs within the **TRzProgressBar** class is between the **Percent** property and the **PartsComplete** and **TotalParts** property pair. Let's start with the **SetPercent** method:

```
procedure TRzProgressBar.SetPercent( Value : TPercentRange );
begin
  if Value <> FPercent then
  begin
    FPercent := Value;
    PercentChanged;
    Repaint;
  end;
end;
```

This method is structured in much the same way the access methods were structured from the last chapter. If the new percentage value is different from the current value, the internal data field is updated and the component is repainted. For now, don't be concerned with the **PercentChanged** call; we'll come back to that shortly.

The **SetTotalParts** and **SetPartsComplete** methods are more interesting. The **SetTotalParts** method, listed below, starts out by storing the new value. However, after the new value is stored, the **FPartsComplete** field is set to zero. This is the first side effect. If the user changes the total number of parts in the process, the current value of the **PartsComplete** property becomes meaningless, so it is set to zero.

```
procedure TRzProgressBar.SetTotalParts( Value : Word );
begin
  if Value <> FTotalParts then
  begin
    FTotalParts := Value;
    FPartsComplete := 0;          { Set Internal FPartsComplete Field }
    Percent := 0;                           { Set Percent Property }
  end;
end;
```

The second side effect follows with the setting of the **Percent** *property* to zero. Take a close look at that last line again. The **Percent** property, not the **FPercent** field, is set to zero. This causes the **SetPercent** method to be called, which in turn will update the **FPercent** field *and* repaint the display.

The **SetPartsComplete** method also interacts with the other properties. Specifically, this method performs some range checking on the passed-in value. For example, it does not make sense to have more parts completed than total parts. After the range checking is done, the **Percent** property is set to the ratio of the **FPartsComplete** and **FTotalParts** fields.

```
procedure TRzProgressBar.SetPartsComplete( Value : Word );
begin
  if Value <> FPartsComplete then
  begin
    if Value > FTotalParts then
      FPartsComplete := FTotalParts
    else
      FPartsComplete := Value;

    { Setting the Percent property causes the SetPercent method to get called  }
    { which will force a repaint }
    Percent := Round( FPartsComplete / FTotalParts * 100 );
  end;
end;
```

Another example of property interaction occurs in the **SetBorderStyle** method. This method has the standard write access method structure, except for the **if-then** block in between the assignment of the new value and the call to **Invalidate**. The side effect that occurs here depends on the **BorderStyle** value selected by the user. Suppose the user selects the **bsStatusControl** border style. If the current value of the **BorderWidth** property is zero, meaning that it has not yet been modified, the **FBorderWidth** field is set to two. Setting the border width to two works well when the progress bar is dropped onto a panel and aligned to the panel's boundaries. The change in the border width keeps the edges of the recessed border away from the edges of the panel.

```
procedure TRzProgressBar.SetBorderStyle( Value : TProgressBorderStyle );
begin
  if Value <> FBorderStyle then
  begin
    FBorderStyle := Value;
    if ( FBorderStyle = bsStatusControl ) and ( FBorderWidth = 0 ) then
      FBorderWidth := 2
```

```
      else if FBorderWidth = 2 then
      FBorderWidth := 0;
      Invalidate;
   end;
end;
```

A different type of interaction occurs with the **Ctl3D** property. The separate **Ctl3D** property is provided for consistency with other Delphi components and is another variation of using side effects. Take another look at the **private** section of the class declaration. You will notice that there is no internal data field corresponding to the **Ctl3D** property. This is not a mistake. In fact, the reason for its absence is quite simple. An internal storage field is not necessary, because all of the information to determine the **Ctl3D** state is already being managed by the **BorderStyle** property.

Since there is no internal storage field for the **Ctl3D** property, we must define both a read and write access method. The **GetCtl3D** method simply returns **True** if the **BorderStyle** property is set to **bsCtl3D**, and **False** otherwise. To eliminate an **if-then-else** block, the **GetCtl3D** function utilizes the equal sign's ability to be used as comparison operator that returns a Boolean value.

```
function TRzProgressBar.GetCtl3D : Boolean;
begin
  Result := FBorderStyle = bsCtl3D;
end;
```

```
procedure TRzProgressBar.SetCtl3D( Value : Boolean );
begin
  if Value <> Ctl3D then
  begin
    if Value then
      FBorderStyle := bsCtl3D
    else
      FBorderStyle := bsFlat;
    Invalidate;
  end;
end;
```

Setting the **Ctl3D** property invokes the **SetCtl3D** method. Instead of setting an internal data field, the **BorderStyle** property is updated, depending on the new value being assigned to the **Ctl3D** property. Although there are three different types of borders for the progress bar, there are only two states for the **Ctl3D** property. Therefore, setting **Ctl3D** to **True** sets the **BorderStyle** to **bsCtl3D** and setting it to **False** sets the **BorderStyle** to **bsFlat**.

Painting the Component

Recall from Chapter 6 that the **TGraphicControl** class creates a virtual **Paint** method that gets called any time the component needs to be painted. For example, the **Invalidate** method eventually causes the component's **Paint** method to be called. In addition to providing the **Paint** method, **TGraphicControl** also declares a protected **Canvas** property. Notice that the **TRzProgressBar** class does not declare the **Canvas** property as **public** because it is not necessary to give programmers the ability to draw on the progress bar. However, the **Canvas** property is used internally by the component to draw the progress bar.

When writing a **Paint** method for a new component, you must ensure that all areas of the component are drawn. Your painting area is defined by the inherited **ClientRect** property. The **TRzProgressBar.Paint** method is broken into three steps. The first step is to draw the border. Of course, how the border is drawn depends on the state of the **BorderStyle** property. If the style is **bsCtl3D**, the **DrawCtl3DBorder** procedure is called. Recall that **DrawCtl3DBorder** is a general-purpose procedure defined in the RzCommon unit. Likewise, if the border style is **bsStatusControl** or **bsFlat**, the **DrawBorder** procedure, also defined in **RzCommon**, is used. The only difference between these two calls is that the **bsFlat** case specifies the same color for the upper-left and lower-right colors.

After drawing the border, the next step is to draw the interior offset region. The interior offset region is the area between the border and the percent bar. If this area is not drawn, anything that is behind the progress bar will show up in this area. The region is defined by a rectangle just inside the border, and its thickness is defined by the **InteriorOffset** property. As the code shows, the **Brush** and **Pen** properties of the **Canvas** are manipulated so that the **Rectangle** method can be used to fill in the area. The key statement in this step is setting the **Pen.Style** property to **psInsideFrame**. The **psInsideFrame** style is effective only when the width of the pen is greater than one. When the pen width is one, rectangles drawn appear no different either way. However, if the pen width is greater than one, the resulting rectangle is drawn inside the coordinates passed to the **Rectangle** method. Once the region is filled, the orginal values of the **Pen** and **Brush** properties are restored.

The final step in drawing the progress bar is to draw the percent bar. This task is handled by the **DrawPercentBar** procedure. Notice that **DrawPercentBar** is not declared as a method of **TRzProgressBar**. Instead, this procedure will be needed by another component defined later in this chapter, and therefore is declared as a standard procedure.

Drawing the percent bar is accomplished in two parts. The first part is to draw the filled-in region of the bar. To determine how much of the bar to fill, the current **FPercent** value is used to create the **PctRct** rectangle. The actual filling of the bar is handled by the same **Canvas** method that is responsible for displaying the percentage text.

The **TextRect** method draws text within a specified rectangle. There are three features of the **TextRect** method that are crucial for creating the desired effect. First, the area defined by the rectangle is filled with the current brush color. Second, the specified rectangle also serves as a clipping region. Text drawn outside the bounds of the rectangle is not visible. Third, the text can be drawn anywhere by specifying X and Y coordinates.

With these three effects, the percent bar is drawn twice. Figure 9.2 visually shows each step. The filled area of the percent bar is drawn by setting **Brush.Color** to the **BarColor** property, and setting **Font.Color** to **BackColor**. The **TextRect** method is called using the **PctRct** rectangle to clip part of the percent text. Next, the colors are reversed, and the **TextRect** method is called again, this time using an updated clipping rectangle.

 To prevent flicker in the display of your components, call the **Repaint** method rather than using the **Invalidate** method. **Repaint** does *not* erase the area of the component before painting like the **Invalidate** method does. For example, since the **Percent** property changes often, the **SetPercent** method calls **Repaint** directly to reflect the new percentage. The only requirement for **Repaint** to behave in this fashion is that the **ControlStyle** of the component must include **csOpaque**.

Figure 9.2

Drawing the Bar is a Two-Step Process.

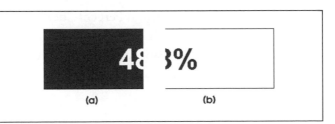

(a)   (b)

Creating a Custom Event

Not only does the **TRzProgressBar** publish inherited events, it is the first component that we have encountered that creates an event of its own. The **OnChange** event is triggered whenever the percent value is changed. Making this event available outside of the component itself gives the component user a way of responding to changes in the percent value.

An example might be an install process. The code responsible for copying files from source to destination would update the percent value of the component. As the install proceeds, the **OnChange** event could be handled in order to display feature descriptions and registration reminders. You could set it up so that a new graphic would be displayed every ten percentage points, for example. (In fairness, I should point out that most such displays are controlled by timers and are not dependent on the percentage of the task that has been completed.)

> **By Convention**
>
> If you need to provide an event that is triggered whenever the value of the component changes, name the event **OnChange**. This will keep your component consistent with other Delphi components.

Supporting this new event requires a new method pointer type, a private field to hold the method pointer value, a property declaration, and an event dispatch method. The **TProgressChangeEvent** type defines the parameters that are passed to any event handlers of this event. Like most events, the first parameter is a reference to the object that generated the event. The second parameter is the new percent value.

The **FOnChange** method pointer is defined in the **private** section, whereas the **OnChange** property is defined in the **published** section. Like all standard events, there are no access methods specified for the **OnChange** event.

The event dispatch method for this event is **PercentChanged**. This method, shown below, is quite simple. After checking that the **FOnChange** method pointer is actually assigned to a method, the associated method is executed.

```
procedure TRzProgressBar.PercentChanged;
begin
  if Assigned( FOnChange ) then
    FOnChange( Self, FPercent );
end;
```

By Convention

Event dispatch methods are declared **dynamic** because these types of methods are rarely overridden. It is more space efficient to declare these types of methods as being **dynamic** because the Dynamic Method Table (DMT) takes up less space than the Virtual Method Table (VMT).

Although all of the pieces to support the event have been specified, there is still one piece missing that prevents us from utilizing this new event. That is, how the event is generated has not yet been defined. Generating the event involves calling the event dispatch method. For this event, the appropriate place to call the **PercentChanged** method is in the **SetPercent** method. Therefore, regardless of how the user changes the percent value, the **OnChange** event will be generated.

What's the Status on That?

A well-designed user interface provides feedback to the user regarding the current state of the application. A great way to do this is through a status bar. In Delphi, status bars are as easy to create as dropping a Panel (or RzPanel) component onto the form and setting the **Align** property to **alBottom**. The difficult part lies in creating the individual panes that make up a status bar.

The individual panes are usually created by dropping more Panels within the status bar panel. However, there are two major drawbacks to this approach. First, for simple status panes, the **Caption** property of the Panel component is fine for displaying status messages, but for more complex status panes, extra code must be added to the form. The second major drawback is that since Panels can accept components dropped onto them, they allocate a window handle. For a status pane, having a window handle is not necessary (such a panel is "read-only" and never receives the focus) and wastes system resources.

A better approach is to create custom status controls that descend from **TGraphicControl** to minimize the system resources required. In addition, since the status control is built as a component, it can be reused in other applications with the click of a button. This is what component building is all about!

Figure 9.3 shows the various status controls that we will create. The three separate status bars are used to reflect different states of individual status controls. Figure 9.3 illustrates five different types of status controls. First, a standard text status

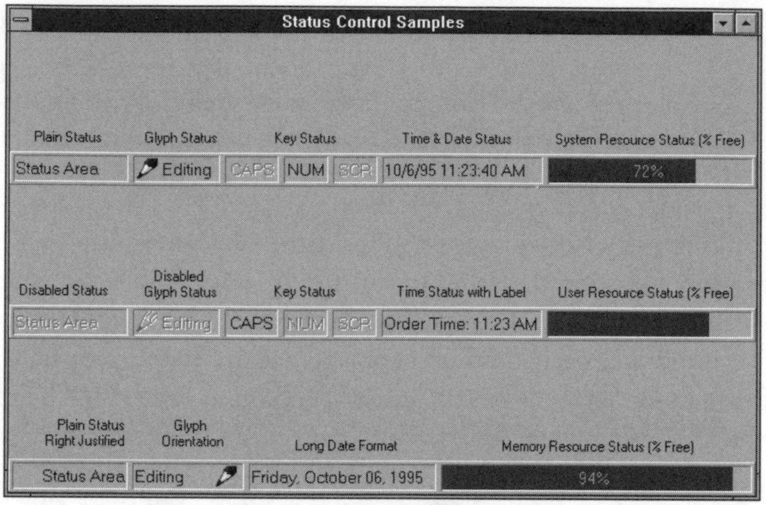

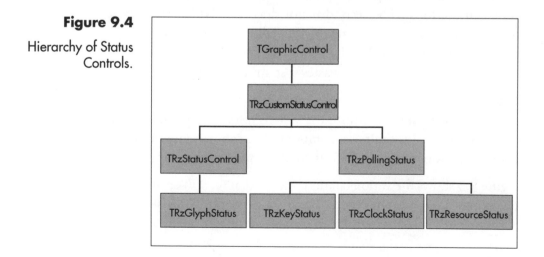

Figure 9.3

Various Status
Controls.

control provides a **Caption** property with caption alignment. The second type of status control provides the ability to display a bitmap within the status area. Next, a single keyboard status control allows users to monitor the status of different keys. The clock status control displays the current date, time, or both in a number of different formats. And finally, the resource usage of the system can be monitored using the resource status control.

All of the various status components presented in Figure 9.3 are implemented in the RzStatus unit. In fact, all of the status components are related through a

Figure 9.4

Hierarchy of Status
Controls.

common class hierarchy. Figure 9.4 illustrates the relationships among all of the status components presented in this chapter.

At the root of the hierarchy is the **TRzCustomStatusControl** class, which provides all of the basic functionality needed by all status components. This includes drawing the border and managing the **Caption** property. More on the properties of this class will be covered shortly. But first, Listing 9.2 shows the entire listing of the RzStatus unit. The following sections will take a closer look at each component defined in this unit.

Listing 9.2 RZSTATUS.PAS—The RzStatus Unit

```
{=================================================================}
{= RzStatus Unit                                                 =}
{=                                                               =}
{= This unit provide several status components, which monitor the system =}
{= clock, keyboard status, and resource usage.                   =}
{=                                                               =}
{= Building Custom Delphi Components - Ray Konopka               =}
{=================================================================}

unit RzStatus;

interface

uses
  Messages, WinTypes, Controls, Classes, Graphics, ExtCtrls, Menus,
  RzCommon, Buttons, SysUtils;

type
  TGlyphAlignment = ( gaLeft, gaRight );
  TToggleKey      = ( tkCapsLock, tkNumLock, tkScrollLock );
  TToggleState    = ( tsOn, tsOff );
  TResourceType   = ( rtSystem, rtUser, rtGDI, rtMemory );
  TDisplayStyle   = ( dsBar, dsText );

  TRzCustomStatusControl = class( TGraphicControl )
  private
    FAlignment : TAlignment;
    FBorderWidth : TBorderWidth;
    FCaptionOffset : Integer;
    FFrameStyle : TFrameStyle;

    procedure SetAlignment( Value : TAlignment );
    procedure SetBorderWidth( Value : TBorderWidth );
    procedure SetCaptionOffset( Value : Integer );
    procedure SetFrameStyle( Value : TFrameStyle );
    procedure CMTextChanged( var Msg : TMessage ); message cm_TextChanged;
  protected
    function GetCaptionRect : TRect; virtual;
    procedure DrawCaption( CaptionStr : string );
    procedure DrawStatusBorder;
```

```
      procedure Paint; override;

  property Alignment : TAlignment
    read FAlignment
      write SetAlignment
      default taLeftJustify;

    property CaptionOffset : Integer
      read FCaptionOffset
      write SetCaptionOffset
      default 0;

    { Inherited Properties }
    property Caption;
public
    constructor Create( AOwner : TComponent ); override;
    property ParentColor;
published
    property FrameStyle : TFrameStyle
      read FFrameStyle
      write SetFrameStyle
      default fsRecessed;

    property BorderWidth : TBorderWidth
      read FBorderWidth
      write SetBorderWidth
      default 2;

    { Inherited Properties }
    property Align;
    property DragCursor;
    property DragMode;
    property Font;
    property ParentFont;
    property ParentShowHint;
    property PopupMenu;
    property ShowHint;
    property Visible;
    property Enabled;
    property OnClick;
    property OnDblClick;
    property OnDragDrop;
    property OnDragOver;
    property OnEndDrag;
    property OnMouseDown;
    property OnMouseMove;
    property OnMouseUp;
end; {== TRzCustomStatusControl Class Declaration ==}


TRzStatusControl = class( TRzCustomStatusControl )
published
  property Alignment;
  property Caption;
  property CaptionOffset;
end;
```

```
TRzGlyphStatus = class( TRzStatusControl )
private
  FGlyph : TBitmap;
  FGlyphAlignment : TGlyphAlignment;
  FGlyphOffset : Integer;
  FNumGlyphs : TNumGlyphs;

  procedure SetNumGlyphs( Value : TNumGlyphs );
  procedure SetGlyph( Value : TBitmap );
  procedure SetGlyphAlignment( Value : TGlyphAlignment );
  procedure SetGlyphOffset( Value : Integer );
protected
  procedure GlyphChanged( Sender : TObject );
  function GetCaptionRect : TRect; override;
  procedure Paint; override;
public
  constructor Create( AOwner : TComponent ); override;
  destructor Destroy; override;
published
  property Glyph : TBitmap
    read FGlyph
    write SetGlyph;

  property GlyphAlignment : TGlyphAlignment
    read FGlyphAlignment
    write SetGlyphAlignment
    default gaLeft;

  property GlyphOffset : Integer
    read FGlyphOffset
    write SetGlyphOffset
    default 2;

  property NumGlyphs : TNumGlyphs
    read FNumGlyphs
    write SetNumGlyphs
    default 1;
end; {== TRzGlyphStatus Class Declaration ==}


TRzPollingStatus = class( TRzCustomStatusControl )
private
  FOnTimerExpired : TNotifyEvent;
  function GetActive : Boolean;
  procedure SetActive( Value : Boolean );
  function GetInterval : Word;
  procedure SetInterval( Value : Word );
protected
  procedure TimerExpired; dynamic;
public
  constructor Create( AOwner : TComponent ); override;
  destructor Destroy; override;
```

```
published
  property Active : Boolean
    read GetActive
    write SetActive
    default True;

  property Interval : Word
    read GetInterval
    write SetInterval
    default 500;

  property OnTimerExpired : TNotifyEvent
    read FOnTimerExpired
    write FOnTimerExpired;
end; {== TRzPollingStatus Class Declaration ==}


TRzClockStatus = class( TRzPollingStatus )
private
  FFormat : string;
  FDateTimeStr : string;
  procedure SetFormat( Value : string );
protected
  procedure TimerExpired; override;
  procedure Paint; override;
  procedure SetCurrentDateTimeStr;
public
  constructor Create( AOwner : TComponent ); override;
published
  property Format : string
    read FFormat
    write SetFormat;

  { Inherited Properties }
  property Alignment;
  property CaptionOffset;
end; {== TRzClockStatus Class Declaration ==}


TRzKeyStatus = class( TRzPollingStatus )
private
  FKey : TToggleKey;
  FState : TToggleState;

  procedure SetKey( Value : TToggleKey );
  procedure SetState( Value : TToggleState );
protected
  procedure TimerExpired; override;
  procedure Paint; override;
public
  constructor Create( AOwner : TComponent ); override;
```

```
      property State : TToggleState
        read FState;
  published
    property Key : TToggleKey
      read FKey
      write SetKey
      default tkCapsLock;
  end; {== TRzKeyStatus Class Declaration ==}


  TRzResourceStatus = class( TRzPollingStatus )
  private
    FBackColor    : TColor;
    FBarColor     : TColor;
    FFreeMemory   : Longint;
    FFreePercent  : Integer;
    FResourceType : TResourceType;
    FShowPercent  : Boolean;
    FDisplayStyle : TDisplayStyle;

    procedure SetBackColor( Value : TColor );
    procedure SetBarColor( Value : TColor );
    procedure SetDisplayStyle( Value : TDisplayStyle );
    procedure SetResourceType( Value : TResourceType );
    procedure SetShowPercent( Value : Boolean );
  protected
    procedure TimerExpired; override;
    procedure Paint; override;
  public
    constructor Create( AOwner : TComponent ); override;
    property FreeMemory : Longint
      read FFreeMemory;

    property FreePercent : Integer
      read FFreePercent;
  published
    property BackColor : TColor
      read FBackColor
      write SetBackColor;

    property BarColor : TColor
      read FBarColor
      write SetBarColor;
      default clHighlight;

    property DisplayStyle : TDisplayStyle
      read FDisplayStyle
      write SetDisplayStyle
      default dsBar;

    property ResourceType : TResourceType
      read FResourceType
```

```
      write SetResourceType
      default rtSystem;

    property ShowPercent : Boolean
      read FShowPercent
      write SetShowPercent
      default False;

    { Inherited Properties }
    property Alignment;
    property CaptionOffset;
  end; {== TRzResourceStatus Class Declaration ==}



procedure Register;


implementation

uses
  WinProcs, RzPrgres, ToolHelp;


type
  {= TRzPollingTimer Class                                             =}
  {=    Implementation specific class designed to wrap a timer component and  =}
  {=    maintain a list of polling controls.  When the internal timer fires,  =}
  {=    the TimerExpired method of each polling control in the list is called. =}

  TRzPollingTimer = class
  public
    Timer  : TTimer;
    Active : Boolean;
    PollingControls : TList;
    constructor Create;
    destructor Destroy; override;
    procedure TimerFired( Sender : TObject );
  end;

const
  VKCodes : array[ TToggleKey ] of Byte = ( vk_Capital, vk_NumLock, vk_Scroll );
  KeyStrings : array[ TToggleKey ] of string = ( 'CAPS', 'NUM', 'SCR' );

  PollingTimer : TRzPollingTimer = nil;
  ResourceStrings : array[ TResourceType ] of string = ( 'System',
                                                         'User',
                                                         'GDI',
                                                         'Memory' );


{===================================}
{== TRzCustomStatusControl Methods ==}
{===================================}
```

```pascal
constructor TRzCustomStatusControl.Create( AOwner : TComponent );
begin
  inherited Create( AOwner );
  ControlStyle := ControlStyle + [ csOpaque ];
  FFrameStyle := fsRecessed;
  FCaptionOffset := 0;
  FBorderWidth := 2;

  Width := 100;
  Height := 20;
  ParentColor := True;
end;


procedure TRzCustomStatusControl.SetAlignment( Value : TAlignment );
begin
  if Value <> FAlignment then
  begin
    FAlignment := Value;
    Invalidate;
  end;
end;


procedure TRzCustomStatusControl.SetBorderWidth( Value : TBorderWidth );
begin
  if Value <> FBorderWidth then
  begin
    FBorderWidth := Value;
    Invalidate;                      { Invalidate b/c Border position changes }
  end;
end;


procedure TRzCustomStatusControl.SetCaptionOffset( Value : Integer );
begin
  if Value <> FCaptionOffset then
  begin
    FCaptionOffset := Value;
    Invalidate;
  end;
end;


procedure TRzCustomStatusControl.SetFrameStyle( Value : TFrameStyle );
begin
  if Value <> FFrameStyle then
  begin
    FFrameStyle := Value;
    Invalidate;
  end;
end;
```

```
procedure TRzCustomStatusControl.CMTextChanged( var Msg : TMessage );
begin
  Invalidate;
end;


function TRzCustomStatusControl.GetCaptionRect : TRect;
begin
  Result := ClientRect;
  InflateRect( Result, -( BorderWidth + 2 ), -( BorderWidth + 1 ) );

  if FAlignment = taLeftJustify then
    Inc( Result.Left, FCaptionOffset )
  else if FAlignment = taRightJustify then
    Dec( Result.Right, FCaptionOffset );
end;


procedure TRzCustomStatusControl.DrawCaption( CaptionStr : string );
var
  R, TempRct : TRect;
  Stz : array[ 0..255 ] of Char;
begin
  if CaptionStr <> '' then
  begin
    Canvas.Font := Font;
    with Canvas do
    begin
      R := GetCaptionRect;

      { Set brush color so that old text in caption area gets erased }
      Brush.Color := Color;

      StrPCopy( Stz, CaptionStr );

      if not Enabled then
      begin
        TempRct := R;
        OffsetRect( TempRct, 1, 1 );
        Font.Color := clBtnHighlight;
        DrawText( Handle, Stz, StrLen( Stz ), TempRct,
                  dt_VCenter or dt_SingleLine or TextAlignments[ FAlignment ] );

        Font.Color := clBtnShadow;
        Brush.Style := bsClear;
      end;

      DrawText( Handle, Stz, StrLen( Stz ), R,
                dt_VCenter or dt_SingleLine or TextAlignments[ FAlignment ] );
    end; { with }
  end;
end; {= TRzCustomStatusControl.DrawCaption =}
```

```
procedure TRzCustomStatusControl.DrawStatusBorder;
var
  ULColor, LRColor : TColor;
  R : TRect;
begin
  with Canvas do
  begin
    Brush.Color := Color;
    FillRect( Rect( 0, 0, Width, Height ) );

    Pen.Width := 1;

    ULColor := ULFrameColor[ FFrameStyle ];
    LRColor := LRFrameColor[ FFrameStyle ];

    { Draw the Frame }
    if FFrameStyle <> fsNone then
    begin
      if ( FFrameStyle = fsGroove ) or ( FFrameStyle = fsBump ) then
      begin
        R := Rect( 1, 1, Width, Height );
        InflateRect( R, -FBorderWidth, -FBorderWidth );
        DrawBorder( Canvas, R, LRColor, LRColor );

        R := Rect( 0, 0, Width - 1, Height - 1 );
        InflateRect( R, -FBorderWidth, -FBorderWidth );
        DrawBorder( Canvas, R, ULColor, ULColor );
      end
      else
      begin
        R := ClientRect;
        InflateRect( R, -FBorderWidth, -FBorderWidth );
        DrawBorder( Canvas, R, ULColor, LRColor );
      end;
    end;
  end; { with Canvas ... }
end; {= TRzCustomStatusControl.DrawStatusBorder =}


procedure TRzCustomStatusControl.Paint;
begin
  DrawStatusBorder;
  DrawCaption( Caption );
end;



{==============================}
{== TRzGlyphStatus Methods ==}
{==============================}

constructor TRzGlyphStatus.Create( AOwner : TComponent );
begin
```

```
    inherited Create( AOwner );
    FGlyph := TBitmap.Create;
    FGlyph.OnChange := GlyphChanged;
    FNumGlyphs := 1;
    FGlyphAlignment := gaLeft;
end;


destructor TRzGlyphStatus.Destroy;
begin
  FGlyph.Free;
  inherited Destroy;
end;


procedure TRzGlyphStatus.SetGlyphAlignment( Value : TGlyphAlignment );
begin
  if Value <> FGlyphAlignment then
  begin
    FGlyphAlignment := Value;
    Invalidate;
  end;
end;


procedure TRzGlyphStatus.SetGlyphOffset( Value : Integer );
begin
  if Value <> FGlyphOffset then
  begin
    FGlyphOffset := Value;
    Invalidate;
  end;
end;


procedure TRzGlyphStatus.SetNumGlyphs( Value : TNumGlyphs );
begin
  if Value <> FNumGlyphs then
  begin
    FNumGlyphs := Value;
    Invalidate;
  end;
end;


procedure TRzGlyphStatus.GlyphChanged( Sender : TObject );
var
  N : Integer;
begin
  if FGlyph.Width mod FGlyph.Height = 0 then
  begin
```

```
    N := FGlyph.Width div FGlyph.Height;
   if N > 4 then
       N := 1;
     SetNumGlyphs( N );
   end;
   Invalidate;
end;


procedure TRzGlyphStatus.SetGlyph( Value : TBitmap );
begin
  FGlyph.Assign( Value );
end;


function TRzGlyphStatus.GetCaptionRect : TRect;
begin
  Result := inherited GetCaptionRect;

  if FGlyphAlignment = gaLeft then
    Inc( Result.Left, FGlyphOffset + FGlyph.Width div FNumGlyphs )
  else
    Dec( Result.Right, FGlyphOffset  + FGlyph.Width div FNumGlyphs );
end;


procedure TRzGlyphStatus.Paint;
var
  DestRct, DrawRct, SrcRct, CaptionRct : TRect;
  DestBmp : TBitmap;
  W, H, X, TopOffset : Integer;
  S : array[ 0..255 ] of Char;
begin
  inherited Paint;

  Canvas.Font := Font;
  with Canvas do
  begin
    CaptionRct := GetCaptionRect;
    Brush.Color := Color;

    W := FGlyph.Width div FNumGlyphs;
    if ( CaptionRct.Bottom - CaptionRct.Top ) < FGlyph.Height then
      H := CaptionRct.Bottom - CaptionRct.Top
    else
      H := FGlyph.Height;

    DestRct := Rect( 0, 0, W, H );
    if ( FNumGlyphs > 1 ) and not Enabled then
      SrcRct := Rect( W, 0, W + W, H )
    else
      SrcRct := Rect( 0, 0, W, H );
```

```
    if FGlyphAlignment = gaLeft then
    X := FGlyphOffset
    else
      X := Width - ( W + FGlyphOffset + BorderWidth + 2 );

    DrawRct := Rect( X, 0, X + W, H );
    TopOffset := Abs( ( Height - H - BorderWidth - 1) ) div 2;
    OffsetRect( DrawRct, 0, BorderWidth + TopOffset );

    { The DestBmp holds the desired region of the FGlyph bitmap }

    DestBmp := TBitmap.Create;
    try
      { Don't Forget to Set the Width and Height of Destination Bitmap }
      DestBmp.Width := W;
      DestBmp.Height := H;
      DestBmp.Canvas.CopyRect( DestRct, FGlyph.Canvas, SrcRct );
      Draw( DrawRct.Left, DrawRct.Top, DestBmp );
    finally
      DestBmp.Free;
    end;
  end; { with }
end; {= TRzGlyphStatus.Paint =}


{=============================}
{== TRzPollingTimer Methods ==}
{=============================}

constructor TRzPollingTimer.Create;
begin
  inherited Create;
  Timer := TTimer.Create( nil );
  Timer.Enabled := True;
  Timer.OnTimer := TimerFired;
  Timer.Interval := 500;

  PollingControls := TList.Create;
end;


destructor TRzPollingTimer.Destroy;
begin
  Timer.Free;
  PollingControls.Free;
  inherited Destroy;
end;


procedure TRzPollingTimer.TimerFired( Sender : TObject );
var
  I : Integer;
```

```
begin
  for I := 0 to PollingControls.Count - 1 do
    TRzPollingStatus( PollingControls.Items[ I ] ).TimerExpired;
end;



{==============================}
{== TRzPollingStatus Methods ==}
{==============================}

constructor TRzPollingStatus.Create( AOwner : TComponent );
begin
  inherited Create( AOwner );

  { If the PollingTimer object has not already been created, then create it }
  if PollingTimer = nil then
    PollingTimer := TRzPollingTimer.Create;
  PollingTimer.PollingControls.Add( Self );
end;


destructor TRzPollingStatus.Destroy;
begin
  { Delete current Polling Control from PollingControls list }
  with PollingTimer.PollingControls do
    Delete( IndexOf( Self ) );

  if PollingTimer.PollingControls.Count = 0 then
  begin
    { If no more polling controls are left, destroy PollingTimer }
    PollingTimer.Free;
    PollingTimer := nil;
  end;
  inherited Destroy;
end;


function TRzPollingStatus.GetActive : Boolean;
begin
  Result := PollingTimer.Timer.Enabled;
end;


procedure TRzPollingStatus.SetActive( Value : Boolean );
begin
  if Value <> PollingTimer.Timer.Enabled then
    PollingTimer.Timer.Enabled := Value;
end;


function TRzPollingStatus.GetInterval : Word;
begin
```

```
    Result := PollingTimer.Timer.Interval;
end;


procedure TRzPollingStatus.SetInterval( Value : Word );
begin
  if Value <> PollingTimer.Timer.Interval then
    PollingTimer.Timer.Interval := Value;
end;


procedure TRzPollingStatus.TimerExpired;
begin
  if Assigned( FOnTimerExpired ) then
    FOnTimerExpired( Self );
end;

{==============================}
{-- TRzClockStatus Methods --}
{==============================}

constructor TRzClockStatus.Create( AOwner : TComponent );
begin
  inherited Create( AOwner );
  Width := 150;
  FFormat := '';
  FDateTimeStr := '';
end;


procedure TRzClockStatus.SetCurrentDateTimeStr;
begin
  if FFormat <> '' then
    FDateTimeStr := FormatDateTime( FFormat, Now )
  else
    FDateTimeStr := DateTimeToStr( Now );
end;


procedure TRzClockStatus.TimerExpired;
begin
  SetCurrentDateTimeStr;
  if Caption = '' then
    Caption := FDateTimeStr
  else
    DrawCaption( FDateTimeStr );
  inherited TimerExpired;
end;



procedure TRzClockStatus.Paint;
begin
```

```
    Caption := FDateTimeStr;
   inherited Paint;
end;


procedure TRzClockStatus.SetFormat( Value : string );
begin
  if Value <> FFormat then
  begin
    FFormat := Value;
    SetCurrentDateTimeStr;
    Invalidate;
  end;
end;



{============================}
{== TRzKeyStatus Methods ==}
{============================}

constructor TRzKeyStatus.Create( AOwner : TComponent );
begin
  inherited Create( AOwner );
  Width := 45;
  Alignment := taCenter;
end;


procedure TRzKeyStatus.SetKey( Value : TToggleKey );
begin
  if Value <> FKey then
  begin
    FKey := Value;
    Invalidate;
  end;
end;


procedure TRzKeyStatus.SetState( Value : TToggleState );
begin
  if Value <> FState then
  begin
    FState := Value;
    Invalidate;
  end;
end;


procedure TRzKeyStatus.TimerExpired;
begin
  { If the low-order bit is 1, the key is active (or On) }
  if ( GetKeyState( VKCodes[ FKey ] ) and $1 ) = $1 then
```

```
      SetState( tsOn )
  else
      SetState( tsOff );
    inherited TimerExpired;
end;


procedure TRzKeyStatus.Paint;
begin
  Enabled := FState = tsOn;
  Caption := KeyStrings[ FKey ];
  inherited Paint;
end;


{==============================}
{== TRzResourceStatus Methods ==}
{==============================}

constructor TRzResourceStatus.Create( AOwner : TComponent );
begin
  inherited Create( AOwner );
  FResourceType := rtSystem;
  FBackColor := clWindow;
  FBarColor := clHighlight;
  FFreeMemory := 0;
  FFreePercent := 0;
  FShowPercent := False;
  ShowHint := True;
end;


procedure TRzResourceStatus.SetBackColor( Value : TColor );
begin
  if Value <> FBackColor then
  begin
    FBackColor := Value;
    Invalidate;
  end;
end;


procedure TRzResourceStatus.SetBarColor( Value : TColor );
begin
  if Value <> FBarColor then
  begin
    FBarColor := Value;
    Invalidate;
  end;
end;
```

```
procedure TRzResourceStatus.SetDisplayStyle( Value : TDisplayStyle );
begin
  if Value <> FDisplayStyle then
  begin
    FDisplayStyle := Value;
    Invalidate;
  end;
end;


procedure TRzResourceStatus.SetResourceType( Value : TResourceType );
begin
  if Value <> FResourceType then
  begin
    FResourceType := Value;
    TimerExpired;
  end;
end;


procedure TRzResourceStatus.SetShowPercent( Value : Boolean );
begin
  if Value <> FShowPercent then
  begin
    FShowPercent := Value;
    Invalidate;
  end;
end;


function GetTotalMemory : Longint;
var
  MemInfo : TMemManInfo;
  WinFlags : Longint;

  {= GlobalHeapSize                                                       =}
  {=   This function uses the GlobalFirst/GlobalNext functions in ToolHelp to =}
  {=   cycle through all global blocks and sum up their size.             =}

  function GlobalHeapSize : Longint;
  var
    GE : TGlobalEntry;
    MoreData : Boolean;
  begin
    Result := 0;
    GE.dwSize := SizeOf( GE );
    MoreData := GlobalFirst( @GE, global_All );
    while MoreData do
    begin
      Result := Result + GE.dwBlockSize;
      MoreData := GlobalNext( @GE, global_All );
    end;
```

```
      if Result <> 0 then
        Result := Result div 1024;  { Convert to Kb }
      end;

begin {= GetTotalMemory =}
  MemInfo.dwSize := SizeOf( MemInfo );
  MemManInfo( @MemInfo );

  { Calculating the Total amount of memory depends on the system }
  with MemInfo do
  begin
    WinFlags := GetWinFlags;
    if WinFlags and wf_Enhanced <> 0 then
    begin
      { Running Windows in Enhanced Mode }
      Result := ( dwTotalPages + dwSwapFilePages ) * wPageSize div 1024;
    end
    else if WinFlags and wf_Cpu286 <> 0 then
    begin
      { Running Windows in Standard Mode on a 286 }
      Result := dwFreePages * wPageSize div 1024 + GlobalHeapSize;
    end
    else
    begin
      { Running Windows in Standard Mode on a 386 or Better }
      Result := GlobalHeapSize;
    end;
  end; { with }
end; {= GetTotalMemory =}


procedure TRzResourceStatus.TimerExpired;
var
  TotalMemory : Longint;
  OldPercent  : Integer;
begin
  FFreeMemory := 0;
  OldPercent := FFreePercent;
  case FResourceType of
    rtSystem:
      FFreePercent := GetFreeSystemResources( gfsr_SystemResources );

    rtUser:
      FFreePercent := GetFreeSystemResources( gfsr_UserResources );

    rtGDI:
      FFreePercent := GetFreeSystemResources( gfsr_GDIResources );

    rtMemory:
    begin
      FFreeMemory := Round( GetFreeSpace( 0 ) / 1024 );
      TotalMemory := GetTotalMemory;
```

```
        FFreePercent := Round( FFreeMemory / TotalMemory * 100 );
    end;
    end; { case }

    if FFreePercent <> OldPercent then
    begin
      Hint := Format('%s: %d%%', [ ResourceStrings[FResourceType], FFreePercent]);
      Invalidate;
    end;
    inherited TimerExpired;
end; {= TRzResourceStatus.TimerExpired =}


procedure TRzResourceStatus.Paint;
var
  DrawRct : TRect;
begin
  if FDisplayStyle = dsText then
  begin
    if FResourceType = rtMemory then
      Caption := FloatToStrF( FFreeMemory, ffNumber, 10, 0 ) + ' KB'
    else
      Caption := Format( '%u%%', [ FFreePercent ] );
    inherited Paint;
  end
  else
  begin
    DrawStatusBorder;
    Canvas.Font := Font;
    DrawRct := ClientRect;
    InflateRect( DrawRct, -FBorderWidth, -FBorderWidth );

    { Use DrawPercentBar procedure from RzPrgres Unit }

    DrawPercentBar( Canvas, DrawRct, 1, 0, FBorderWidth, poHorizontal,
                    FBarColor, FBackColor, FFreePercent, FShowPercent );
  end;
end; {= TRzResourceStatus.Paint =}


{=======================}
{== Register Procedure ==}
{=======================}

procedure Register;
begin
  RegisterComponents( RaizeStatusPage,
                      [ TRzStatusControl, TRzClockStatus, TRzKeyStatus,
                        TRzGlyphStatus, TRzResourceStatus ] );

end;


end.
```

The Custom Status Component

Since we are creating a hierarchy of components, the base status component class follows the structure used quite often in the VCL under these circumstances. That is, the **TRzCustomStatusControl** class is defined as a *custom* component class. Rather than publish all available properties, many are declared as **protected**, and it is up to a descendent class to publish the necessary properties.

The **TRzCustomStatusControl** class defines several properties and events, many of which are inherited from ancestor classes. Only two of the newly defined properties are published in this base class: **FrameStyle** and **BorderWidth**. The caption-oriented properties **Alignment** and **CaptionOffset** are not published because not all descendent components need to provide access to these properties.

The properties in this class are quite simple and all use the standard write access method structure we have seen so many times before. The interesting aspects of this base class come from its methods. To start, the **DrawStatusBorder** method is responsible for drawing the border around the status control. Since this method is inherited by all status components, this code is written only once. Drawing the actual border is simplified by using the **DrawBorder** procedure defined in the RzCommon unit.

The **DrawCaption** method looks more complicated than it really is. This method is responsible for drawing the passed-in **CaptionStr** string within the caption area. The caption area is defined by the rectangle returned from the virtual method **GetCaptionRect**. This function is defined in the **TRzCustomStatusControl** class to return a rectangle slightly smaller than the component's client area. This offset accounts for the width of the border. The **GetCaptionRect** method also utilizes the **CaptionOffset** property to adjust the rectangle.

Once the **DrawCaption** method obtains the caption bounds, the **DrawText** API procedure is used to display the text. This is the same technique that was used to draw the caption of the RzLabel component. Even the 3D effects are carried over into this component. If the status control is disabled, the caption is drawn twice, once using the **clBtnHighight** color and then again using the **clBtnShadow** color. This gives a recessed appearance to the text of a disabled status pane.

The last major method in the **TRzCustomStatusControl** class is the **CMTextChanged** message handling method. This method only has one line, but it is quite significant. It responds to an internal component message that is sent to a component whenever its **Text** (or **Caption**) property has been changed. Let's take a closer look at component messages, and then we will return to the significance of the **CMTextChanged** method.

Component Messages

Delphi defines a number of *component messages* that are passed between components. The messages are used to indicate changes in the state of a component. Many of them correspond to Windows messages.

Most of the messages are generated by the **TControl** class. That is, when a component receives a Windows message, the **TControl** ancestor class handles the message and often needs to propagate that message down to all of the components owned by the component receiving the message. Since an owned component does not need to be a component possessing a window handle, Delphi avoids resending the original Windows message, and instead sends the component message.

Table 9.1 lists all of the standard component messages. The message constants are declared in the VCL **Controls** unit and the values of these constants are defined in a range not used by Windows. Under this architecture, it is possible to create user-defined component messages by defining new constants using the **cm_Base** value and offsets greater than 39. (I would not use any value smaller than 100 to allow room for the VCL to add other standard messages in future versions.) To generate the message, use the **Perform** method. For example,

```
const
  cm_UserDefinedMsg = cm_Base + 101;
. . .
  Perform( cm_UserDefinedMsg, 0, 1 );
```

While it is possible to create a user defined component message, it is not common to do so. Instead, it is more common to respond to one of these component messages in a descendent class using a message-handling method. (Message-handling methods covered in Chapter 2.)

Since message-handling methods are always invoked as a result of a message being sent to the component, component message handlers do not need to be visible to a component user. And as such, they are always declared **private** or **protected**. Component message handlers allow component writers to intercept a component message and perform some action.

Table 9.1 Delphi's Component Messages

Message Constant	Value	Description
cm_Base	$0f00;	Base constant used by all other component messages.
cm_Activate	cm_Base + 0;	Specific to forms. Sent when form first displayed and whenever focus changes to different modeless form within the same application.
cm_Deactivate	cm_Base + 1;	Specific to forms. Always sent before a cm_Activate message to the form losing the focus.
cm_GotFocus	cm_Base + 2;	No longer used.
cm_LostFocus	cm_Base + 3;	No longer used.
cm_CancelMode	cm_Base + 4;	Sent to a focused control providing opportunity to cancel any internal modes before losing focus, such as capturing mouse input.
cm_DialogKey	cm_Base + 5;	A key was pressed that has special meaning in a dialog box. (For example, Tab, Enter, the Arrow keys, and so on.)
cm_DialogChar	cm_Base + 6;	Sent to the form when characters are pressed and a component that does not accept keyboard input has the focus.
cm_FocusChanged	cm_Base + 7;	Sent to the form indicating which control now has the focus.
cm_ParentFontChanged	cm_Base + 8;	Sent when the ParentFont property for the control has changed.
cm_ParentColorChanged	cm_Base + 9;	Sent when the ParentColor property for the control has changed.
cm_HitTest	cm_Base + 10;	Sent when a control needs to determine if a given point is to be considered on the component.
cm_VisibleChanged	cm_Base + 11;	The Visible property has changed.
cm_EnabledChanged	cm_Base + 12;	The Enabled property has changed.
cm_ColorChanged	cm_Base + 13;	The Color property has changed.
cm_FontChanged	cm_Base + 14;	The Font property has changed.
cm_CursorChanged	cm_Base + 15;	The Cursor property has changed.
cm_Ctl3dChanged	cm_Base + 16;	The Ctl3D property has changed.
cm_ParentCtl3dChanged	cm_Base + 17;	The ParentCtl3D property has changed.
cm_TextChanged	cm_Base + 18;	The Text or Caption property has changed.
cm_MouseEnter	cm_Base + 19;	Sent when the mouse pointer becomes positioned over the component.
cm_MouseLeave	cm_Base + 20;	Sent when the mouse pointer is moved outside of the bounds of the component.
cm_MenuChanged	cm_Base + 21;	Sent to the form when a menu item has changed.
cm_AppKeyDown	cm_Base + 22;	Used to transmit menu shortcut key events trapped by the Application object and forwarded to the main form.
cm_AppSysCommand	cm_Base + 23;	Used to transmit wm_SysCommand messages from the Application object to the main form.
cm_ButtonPressed	cm_Base + 24;	A SpeedButton was pressed.

Table 9.1 Delphi's Component Messages (continued)		
Message Constant	**Value**	**Description**
cm_ShowingChanged	cm_Base + 25;	The Showing property has changed.
cm_Enter	cm_Base + 26;	Sent when a component receives the input focus.
cm_Exit	cm_Base + 27;	Sent when a component loses the input focus.
cm_DesignHitTest	cm_Base + 28;	Sent when the mouse pointer moved over a component while in design-mode.
cm_IconChanged	cm_Base + 29;	The Icon property has changed.
cm_WantSpecialKey	cm_Base + 30;	Sent to a component when a special key (such as Tab, Enter, or the Arrow keys) is pressed. Allows a component to handle special keys in a particular way.
cm_InvokeHelp	cm_Base + 31;	Sent by a DLL's Application object to the main Application object using the DLL when online help needs to be activated.
cm_WindowHook	cm_Base + 32;	Sent by a DLL's Application object to the main Application object using the DLL to establish a window hook.
cm_Release	cm_Base + 33;	Sent by a form to itself indicating that the form should be destroyed.
cm_ShowHintChanged	cm_Base + 34;	The ShowHint property has changed.
cm_ParentShowHintChanged	cm_Base + 35;	The ParentShowHint property has changed.
cm_SysColorChange	cm_Base + 36;	The system colors have been altered.
cm_WinIniChange	cm_Base + 37;	A change has been made to the WIN.INI file.
cm_FontChange	cm_Base + 38;	The Font property has changed.
cm_TimeChange	cm_Base + 39;	The system time has changed.

When the Caption Changes

The **TRzCustomStatusControl** demonstrates handling a component message by providing a **CMTextChange** message-handling method that responds to the **cm_TextChange** message. As noted in Table 9.1, the **cm_TextChange** message is sent whenever the **Text** or **Caption** property of a component is altered.

Why does the **TRzCustomStatusControl** need to handle this message? It does so in order to update the display as the user types text into the Object Inspector. The **CMTextChange** method is listed again below and shows that the control is invalidated whenever this message is received.

```
procedure TRzCustomStatusControl.CMTextChanged( var Msg : TMessage );
begin
  Invalidate;
end;
```

If this message were not handled, the caption of the status control would not be updated until the user does something to cause the status control to repaint itself, such as changing its **Width** property.

> **By Convention**
>
> Message-handling methods are given the same name as the message to which they are responding without the underscore. For example, the message-handling method for the **wm_Paint** message would be **WMPaint**.

As a final note, to create a normal status control, the **TRzCustomStatusControl** class is not used. Instead, the **TRzStatusControl** class, which descends from the base class (and publishes the **Alignment**, **Caption**, and **CaptionOffset** properties) is provided for this purpose.

Using a Bitmap Property

The **RzGlyphStatus** component descends from **TRzStatusControl**. It differs from a normal status control in that it is able to display a bitmap. Using bitmaps in status panes has become quite popular in newer applications. For example, Microsoft Word uses a bitmap of a printer to indicate background printing tasks.

Incorporating a bitmap property into a component is relatively straightforward, thanks to the **TBitmap** class defined in the Graphics unit. The first step is to provide an internal storage field to hold the bitmap. The **TRzGlyphStatus** class defines the **FGlyph** property for this purpose. The term "glyph" is used to be consistent with the **TBitBtn** and **TSpeedButton** components, which both have a **Glyph** property. This new property is not called **Picture** because, unlike the Image component, the RzGlyphStatus component accepts *only* bitmaps.

The next step is to create the bitmap object. This is accomplished in the **Create** constructor. Creating the bitmap object is no different from creating any other type of VCL object. For example, the **FGlyph** bitmap is created with the following line:

```
FGlyph := TBitmap.Create;
```

Because we are creating a bitmap object, it is necessary in this class to provide a destructor to guarantee that the bitmap object is released when the status component is destroyed. As the following code shows, the destructor simply calls the **Free** method of the **FGlyph** object before calling the inherited destructor.

```
destructor TRzGlyphStatus.Destroy;
begin
  FGlyph.Free;
  inherited Destroy;
end;
```

When the bitmap object is created, it does not contain an image. Getting an image into the object is handled by setting the **Glyph** property directly to an existing bitmap object, or by using the **LoadFromFile** method to load a bitmap file. **LoadFromFile** is a method of the **TBitmap** class, and is accessible through the **Glyph** property. If the **Glyph** property is set to an existing bitmap, the **SetGlyph** method uses the **TBitmap's Assign** method to make a copy of the passed-in bitmap. Note that since the **Assign** method always makes a copy of the bitmap, there is no need to compare the current glyph to the new one.

The **GetCaptionRect** method is overridden in this class in order to provide room for the glyph. In particular, when the **TRzStatusControl.DrawCaption** method is called, the rectangle returned from **GetCaptionRect** will prevent the text from appearing on top of the bitmap.

Once the desired bitmap object is selected, it is up to the **Paint** method to display it in the status area. Since the inherited **Paint** method knows how to paint the border and draw the caption, the **TRzGlyphStatus.Paint** method only needs to display the bitmap. Displaying a bitmap is a simple matter of calling the **Draw** method of the **Canvas** property. However, this **Paint** method is more complicated because it adds code to display only one glyph at a time rather than the entire bitmap. In addition, the **Paint** method is smart enough to use the second glyph if the control is disabled. This is the same functionality provided by the BitBtn and SpeedButton components.

To extract a portion of a bitmap, the **CopyRect** method is used. **CopyRect** is actually a method of the **TCanvas** class, but since **TBitmap** contains a **Canvas** property, this method is available. For the RzGlyphStatus component, the **FGlyph** bitmap holds the main bitmap, which contains one or more glyphs. The **Paint** method copies a region of the **FGlyph** bitmap to a temporary bitmap, which is then drawn in the status control. The code to do this is as follows:

```
DestBmp := TBitmap.Create;
try
  DestBmp.Width := W;
  DestBmp.Height := H;
  DestBmp.Canvas.CopyRect( DestRct, FGlyph.Canvas, SrcRct );
  Draw( DrawRct.Left, DrawRct.Top, DestBmp );
finally
  DestBmp.Free;
end;
```

The **SrcRct** rectangle is set to surround the desired glyph in the **FGlyph** bitmap, whereas the **DestRct** rectangle determines where the source image is drawn in the destination bitmap.

 The most common mistake that occurs when copying an image from one canvas to another is forgetting to set the size of the destination canvas image. In the **TRzGlyphStatus.Paint** method, before the **CopyRect** method is called, the **DestBmp** object's **Width** and **Height** must be set to nonzero values.

Notice the usage of the **try...finally** block in the previous example. Whenever you need to create a object, you should use the exception handling features of Delphi to protect the allocated resource. As shown above, the **DestBmp** bitmap object is guaranteed to be freed even in the event of an exception.

The last method of interest in the **TRzGlyphStatus** component is the **GlyphChanged** method. This method checks the width and height of the new bitmap to determine the number of glyphs embedded in the bitmap. A glyph is defined as a square region of a bitmap. For example, a bitmap that has a width and height equal to 20 contains one glyph. A bitmap 40 pixels wide and 20 pixels high contains two glyphs.

The significance of the **GlyphChanged** method is that it is called any time the bitmap referenced by **FGlyph** is changed. This is accomplished by assigning the **FGlyph.OnChange** event to the **GlyphChanged** method in the constructor. The **GlyphChanged** method is defined with a single **TObject** parameter so it is compatible with the **OnChange** event.

At first, you may be tempted to place this code in the **SetGlyph** method. The problem with this approach is that it will work only if you set the **Glyph** property to a bitmap object. If you use the **LoadFromFile** method of **TBitmap**, the number of glyphs is not calculated correctly because the **SetGlyph** method never gets called. By pointing the **FGlyph.OnChange** event to the **GlyphChanged** method, we are guaranteed to find out about any the bitmap changes.

Polling Controls

The remaining status components are all similar in that they must poll the system to determine what to display. Polling suggests a timer, and the Delphi **TTimer** class is well suited to handle this task. Unfortunately, timers are a limited resource in Windows, so it does not make sense to embed a **TTimer** reference in each class. If this were done, each status component created would have its own, separate timer object.

A better approach is to have all instances of polling controls use a single timer object. This is the exact purpose of the **TRzPollingStatus** and **TRzPollingTimer** classes. These two classes work together to allow all polling status controls to share a single timer object. The **TRzPollingTimer** class is an implementation-specific class and as such is located in the implementation section of the RzStatus unit.

The **TRzPollingTimer** class is a wrapper for a **TTimer** instance and a **TList** instance. Access to these two fields are through the **Timer** and **PollingControls** fields, respectively. The **TRzPollingStatus** class uses the **PollingTimer** variable (which is of type **TRzPollingTimer**) to manage all of the polling controls in the current application.

The **TRzPollingStatus** component ensures that the management of the **PollingTimer** object is handled transparently, without the need for user involvement. For example, when a new polling control is created, the constructor of **TRzPollingStatus** (shown below) checks to see if the **PollingTimer** variable has been created, and creates it if it has not. Next, the new polling control instance is added to the **PollingControls** list.

```
constructor TRzPollingStatus.Create( AOwner : TComponent );
begin
  inherited Create( AOwner );

  { If the PollingTimer object has not already been created, then create it }
  if PollingTimer = nil then
    PollingTimer := TRzPollingTimer.Create;
  PollingTimer.PollingControls.Add( Self );
end;
```

The destructor for **TRzPollingStatus**, shown below, is responsible for cleaning up the **PollingTimer** variable. When a polling control is destroyed, the **TRzPollingStatus.Destroy** destructor is called, which first removes the current polling control instance from the **PollingControls** list. After this, if there are no more controls in the **PollingControls** list, the **PollingTimer** object is destroyed.

```
destructor TRzPollingStatus.Destroy;
begin
  { Delete current Polling Control from PollingControls list }
  with PollingTimer.PollingControls do
    Delete( IndexOf( Self ) );

  if PollingTimer.PollingControls.Count = 0 then
  begin
    { If no more polling controls are left, destroy PollingTimer }
    PollingTimer.Free;
    PollingTimer := nil;
  end;
  inherited Destroy;
end;
```

The **TRzPollingStatus** component also provides properties that expose the properties specific to the embedded Timer component of **TRzPollingTimer**. This allows descendent classes to access the **Active** and **Interval** properties. There are both read and write access methods for each of these properties because the data for each property is stored in the **PollingTimer** variable and not in the class itself.

The relationship between the **TRzPollingStatus** and the **TRzPollingTimer** classes is based on the **OnTimerExpired** event defined in the **TRzPollingStatus** class. When the timer owned by **PollingTimer** is triggered, the **TimerFired** method is called. This method loops through each control in the **PollingControls** list and calls its **TimerExpired** event dispatch method. Like the **PercentChanged** method for the **TRzProgressBar**, the **TimerExpired** event simply executes the associated method pointer for the **FOnTimerExpired** event. It is through the **TimerExpired** method that descendent classes have access to a polling mechanism. As you will see, the remaining status controls all focus on the **TimerExpired** method.

What Time Is It?

The **TRzClockStatus** class defines a component that will display the current date, time, or both in a status pane. The format of the date and time displayed is controlled by the **Format** property. This property can be set to any string acceptable to the **FormatDateTime** function. For example, the format string of 'm/d/yy h:mm' creates displays like '10/7/95 8:30'. There are even special symbols that are associated with certain formats. For example, the format string of 'dddddd' produces a display like 'Saturday, October 10, 1995.'

The **TimerExpired** method, shown below, simply sets the **FDateTimeStr** field to the current date and time value returned by the standard **Now** function:

```
procedure TRzClockStatus.TimerExpired;
begin
  SetCurrentDateTimeStr;
  if Caption = '' then
    Caption := FDateTimeStr
  else
    DrawCaption( FDateTimeStr );
  inherited TimerExpired;
end;
```

If the **Caption** value is not empty, the inherited **DrawCaption** method is called to display the new clock status. You may wonder about the purpose of using the separate **FDateTimeStr** field. Why didn't I just use the **Caption** property?

Although all the status controls presented in this chapter have access to the **Caption** property, none of these components has direct access to the **FCaption** data field. Normally this would not be a problem, but since setting the **Caption** property causes the entire control to repaint itself, it does pose a potential problem with the clock status component. If the clock displays seconds, the display is updated at least once a second. If the **Caption** property were set to the new time, the border of the corresponding status control would also be drawn every time the time display is updated. By using the internal **FDateTimeStr** field, only the text representing the current clock status is affected.

Keyboard Status

The **TRzKeyStatus** component class displays the current toggle state of either the CapsLock, ScrLock, or NumLock keys. The desired key is selected using the **Key** property. The **TimerExpired** method uses the **GetKeyState** API function to determine the current toggle state of the selected key. If the state of the key changes, the display is updated. A text string representing the key is displayed in the caption area. The caption appears enabled or disabled depending upon the state of the respective key. The read-only **State** property indicates the current state of the key.

System Status

The last component that we'll be covering in this chapter is the RzResourceStatus component. Like the RzClockStatus and the RzKeyStatus, this component must poll the system to determine what to display. This component can display any one of four possible system resource values. The four values include the free system resources for either the User or GDI heaps, the system-wide free resources, and the amount of free memory. Each of these values can be displayed as a text string or a percentage bar.

Because of the ability to display free resources as a percentage bar, the **TRzResourceStatus** class has many properties similar to those found in the RzProgressBar component. For example, the **ShowPercent**, **BarColor**, and **BackColor** properties are all carried over from the **TRzProgressBar** class. And it doesn't stop there. In the **Paint** method, the **DrawPercentBar** method defined in the **RzPrgres** unit is used to fill in the status area.

Being a descendant of **TRzPollingStatus**, the real work of this class occurs in the **TimerExpired** method. Using the **GetFreeSystemResources** API function, the System, User, and GDI percentages can be obtained. Calculating the amount of free memory is much more complicated. The amount of free memory is obtained from the **GetFreeSpace** API function. The difficult challenge is determining the total amount of memory available in Windows in order to calculate the percentage.

After some rigorous research, I found out that calculating the total amount of memory depends on the type of computer you are using and whether or not the system is running in enhanced mode. The result of my research is the **GetTotalMemory** function, which takes all of these quirks into consideration to return the total amount of memory available in Windows.

Looking Ahead...

In the next chapter we will continue to discuss creating new custom components. But instead of building graphical controls that do not receive the input focus, the components presented in the next chapter demonstrate how to utilize a component's window handle to control such things as the input focus. We will also look into the steps necessary to build components that are comprised of multiple sub-components.

Chapter 10

Custom
Components
from Scratch

Custom Components from Scratch

Sometimes there's no convenient control ancestor to subclass. Sometimes you have to do it all yourself. It's not as hard as you might think.

In the last chapter, we built our first set of custom components, which included the RzProgressBar component and a number of status panes. All of these components are descendants of the **TGraphicControl** class, and as graphical controls they do not suffer from the extra overhead of managing a window handle. However, without a window handle, graphical components are limited as to how they interact with the user.

For example, although the **TForm** class forwards mouse events to graphical controls, it is not possible for a component to respond to keyboard events and focus changes without having a window handle. In fact, you will recall from Chapter 6 that this is the primary criterion used to determine from which class, **TGraphicControl** or **TWinControl**, a component should descend.

This chapter covers the details involved in creating *windowed* components; that is, components that descend from the **TWinControl** class. The chapter is broken into three sections, with each section focusing on a different aspect of building custom components.

The first section demonstrates how to provide complete mouse and keyboard support in your components. In this section, the **TCustomControl** class is used to create a track bar component. More visually effective than a scroll bar, this control demonstrates several important aspects of custom component development including managing the focus, owner-draw support, and bitmap manipulation.

The second section takes you step by step through the process of using the **TWinControl** class to create component wrappers for your external custom controls. In the exercise, component wrappers are created for the check box and radio button controls in Borland's Windows Custom Controls (BWCC) library.

And finally, the third section concludes this chapter with a demonstration of how to create a component that is made up of multiple sub-components. In this section, a mailing address component is created that encapsulates several data-aware edit fields representing a standard layout for a U.S. mailing address. And since the sub-components are data-aware, the component can be linked to a DataSource component and used to edit the address fields of a database table.

Sliding around in Delphi

Windows 95's new user interface offers several new controls that are not available in Windows 3.1. One of these new controls is the TrackBar. The TrackBar is similar to a scroll bar, but with a more effective visual interface. The control's thumb rides along on a track, which is partitioned into specific positions. The TrackBar control is used quite extensively in Windows 95. For example, this control is used to adjust the volume setting for the system's sound card and to change the resolution of the desktop.

Figure 10.1 shows several variations of the RzTrackBar component that will be constructed in this section. RzTrackBar is a Delphi component that provides all

Figure 10.1

Sample
RzTrackBar
Components.

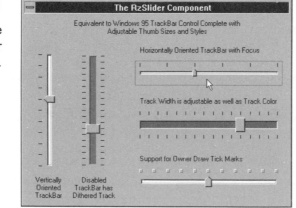

of the functionality of the Windows 95 TrackBar control, but *without* the new user interface. This allows the RzTrackBar component to be used in Windows 3.X applications.

Building the RzTrackBar component relies on the techniques introduced in the last chapter, such as providing complete visualization of the component. This is important because, although similar to a scroll bar, the **TRzTrackBar** class does not descend from any existing control, and is therefore responsible for its own visualization.

In addition, the RzTrackBar component demonstrates how to provide complete mouse and keyboard support to a custom control. The user can interact with this component using either the mouse or the keyboard. Using the mouse, the user can drag the thumb to a new position, or click inside the track to move the thumb in the direction of the mouse click. Likewise, the keyboard can be used to manipulate the control. The thumb can be moved using the arrow keys, including Home, End, PgUp, and PgDn.

Of course, in order to accept keyboard input, the component must have the focus, and this affects the appearance of the control. Several different techniques are used to create the visual interface of the RzTrackBar component. For example, the thumb is not drawn by hand. Instead, the thumb is actually a bitmap that is drawn on the component. Becausee there are several different styles of thumbs, a resource file is used to manage all of the bitmaps.

Related to the issue of drawing the control is the fact that the RzTrackBar component supports owner-draw tick marks. This gives users the ability to provide their own style of tick marks. Figure 10.1 shows an example where the tick marks are replaced with raised boxes. The owner-draw mechanism provided by this component gives the users complete freedom to come up with elaborate tick marks of their own creation.

As you can see from Figure 10.1, the RzTrackBar component can be configured in many different ways. In fact, the **TRzTrackBar** class is one of the more complex components presented in this book. Listing 10.1 shows the complete source code for the RzTrkBar unit. The **TRzTrackBar** class has more properties, events, and methods than any other component covered so far.

Listing 10.1 RZTRKBAR.PAS—The RzTrkBar Unit

```
{==============================================================================}
{= RzTrkBar Unit                                                              =}
{=                                                                            =}
{= The TRzTrackBar component is a slider control that mimics the behavior of  =}
{= the Windows 95 TrackBar control. This control works with mouse -and-       =}
{= keyboard input.                                                            =}
{=                                                                            =}
{= Building Custom Delphi Components - Ray Konopka                            =}
{==============================================================================}

unit RzTrkBar;

interface

uses
  Messages, WinTypes, WinProcs, Classes, Graphics, Controls, Menus,
  ExtCtrls, RzCommon;

type
  TTrackOrientation = ( toHorizontal, toVertical );
  TThumbSize = ( tsSmall, tsMedium, tsLarge );
  TThumbStyle = ( tsBox, tsPointer );
  TTickStyle = ( tkStandard, tkOwnerDraw );

  TRzTrackBar = class;                            { Forward class reference }

  TDrawTickEvent = procedure ( TrackBar : TRzTrackBar; Canvas : TCanvas;
                               Location : TPoint; Index : Integer ) of object;

  TRzTrackBar = class( TCustomControl )
  private
    FBorderWidth : Integer;
    FMax : Integer;
    FMin : Integer;
    FOrientation : TTrackOrientation;
    FPageSize : Word;
    FPosition : Integer;
    FTickStyle : TTickStyle;
    FShowTicks : Boolean;
    FSliding : Boolean;

    FThumbHeight : Integer;
    FThumbRct : TRect;
    FThumbSize : TThumbSize;
    FThumbStyle : TThumbStyle;
    FThumbWidth : Integer;
    FHalfWidth : Integer;

    FTrackColor : TColor;                         { Attributes for track }
    FTrackRct : TRect;
    FTrackWidth : Word;
```

```
      FDitherBmp : TBitmap;
      FThumbBmp : TBitmap;
      FMaskBmp : TBitmap;
      FBackgroundBmp : TBitmap;

      FOnChange : TNotifyEvent;                              { Custom events }
      FOnDrawTick : TDrawTickEvent;

      procedure SetMax( Value : Integer );
      procedure SetMin( Value : Integer );
      procedure SetOrientation( Value : TTrackOrientation );
      procedure SetPosition( Value : Integer );
      procedure SetShowTicks( Value : Boolean );
      procedure SetThumbSize( Value : TThumbSize );
      procedure SetThumbStyle( Value : TThumbStyle );
      procedure SetTickStyle( Value : TTickStyle );
      procedure SetTrackWidth( Value : Word );
      procedure SetTrackColor( Value : TColor );
      procedure LoadThumbBitmaps;
      procedure UpdateDitherBitmap;
      procedure WMGetDlgCode( var Msg : TWMGetDlgCode ); message wm_GetDlgCode;
      procedure WMSize( var Msg : TWMSize); message wm_Size;
      procedure CMEnabledChanged( var Msg : TMessage ); message cm_EnabledChanged;
  protected
    procedure DrawTrack; virtual;
    procedure DrawTicks; virtual;
    procedure DrawThumb; virtual;
    procedure Paint; override;

    procedure Change; dynamic;
    procedure DrawTick( Canvas : TCanvas; Location : TPoint;
                        Index : Integer ); dynamic;
    procedure DoEnter; override;
    procedure DoExit; override;
    procedure KeyDown( var Key : Word; Shift : TShiftState ); override;
    procedure MouseDown( Button : TMouseButton; Shift : TShiftState;
                         X, Y : Integer ); override;
    procedure MouseMove( Shift : TShiftState; X, Y : Integer ); override;
    procedure MouseUp( Button : TMouseButton; Shift : TShiftState;
                       X, Y : Integer ); override;
  public
    constructor Create( AOwner : TComponent ); override;
    destructor Destroy; override;
  published
    property Max : Integer
      read FMax
      write SetMax
      default 10;

    property Min : Integer
      read FMin
      write SetMin
      default 0;
```

```
property Orientation : TTrackOrientation
  read FOrientation
  write SetOrientation
  default toHorizontal;

property PageSize : Word
  read FPageSize
  write FPageSize
  default 1;

property Position : Integer
  read FPosition
  write SetPosition;

property ShowTicks : Boolean
  read FShowTicks
  write SetShowTicks
  default True;

property ThumbSize : TThumbSize
  read FThumbSize
  write SetThumbSize
  default tsMedium;

property ThumbStyle : TThumbStyle
  read FThumbStyle
  write SetThumbStyle
  default tsPointer;

property TickStyle : TTickStyle
  read FTickStyle
  write SetTickStyle
  default tkStandard;

property TrackColor : TColor
  read FTrackColor
  write SetTrackColor
  default clWhite;

property TrackWidth : Word
  read FTrackWidth
  write SetTrackWidth
  default 8;

property OnChange : TNotifyEvent
  read FOnChange
  write FOnChange;

property OnDrawTick : TDrawTickEvent
  read FOnDrawTick
  write FOnDrawTick;
```

```pascal
    { Inherited Properties & Events }
    property Color;
    property DragCursor;
    property DragMode;
    property Enabled;
    property HelpContext;
    property Hint;
    property ParentShowHint;
    property PopupMenu;
    property ShowHint;
    property TabOrder;
    property TabStop default True;
    property Visible;

    property OnClick;
    property OnDragDrop;
    property OnDragOver;
    property OnEndDrag;
    property OnEnter;
    property OnExit;
    property OnKeyDown;
    property OnKeyPress;
    property OnKeyUp;
    property OnMouseDown;
    property OnMouseMove;
    property OnMouseUp;
  end;


procedure Register;

implementation

{$R RZTRKBAR.RES}                               { Access to bitmaps for thumbs }

{========================}
{== TRzTrackBar Methods ==}
{========================}

constructor TRzTrackBar.Create( AOwner : TComponent );
begin
  inherited Create( AOwner );
  Width := 200;
  Height := 50;
  FTrackWidth := 8;
  FOrientation := toHorizontal;
  FTrackColor := clWhite;
  FMin := 0;
  FMax := 10;
  FPosition := 0;
  FBorderWidth := 4;
  FPageSize := 1;
```

```
    TabStop := True;
    FShowTicks := True;
    FSliding := False;

    FThumbBmp := TBitmap.Create;                    { Create internal bitmap objects }
    FMaskBmp := TBitmap.Create;
    FBackgroundBmp := TBitmap.Create;
    FThumbStyle := tsPointer;
    FThumbSize := tsMedium;
    FDitherBmp := TBitmap.Create;
    FDitherBmp.Width := 8;
    FDitherBmp.Height := 8;
    UpdateDitherBitmap;
    LoadThumbBitmaps;
end;


destructor TRzTrackBar.Destroy;
begin
  FDitherBmp.Free;                 { Be sure to free internally allocated objects }
  FThumbBmp.Free;
  FMaskBmp.Free;
  FBackgroundBmp.Free;

  inherited Destroy;
end;


procedure TRzTrackBar.SetMax( Value : Integer );
begin
  if Value <> FMax then
  begin
    FMax := Value;
    if FPosition > FMax then      { If new max is less than current Position... }
      Position := FMax;                          { Update the Position property }
    Invalidate;
  end;
end;


procedure TRzTrackBar.SetMin( Value : Integer );
begin
  if Value <> FMin then
  begin
    FMin := Value;
    if FPosition < FMin then   { If new min is greater than current Position... }
      Position := FMin;                          { Update the Position property }
    Invalidate;
  end;
end;
```

```
procedure TRzTrackBar.SetOrientation( Value : TTrackOrientation );
begin
  if Value <> FOrientation then
  begin
    FOrientation := Value;
    LoadThumbBitmaps;                   { Get new bitmaps if Orientation changes }
    Invalidate;
  end;
end;


procedure TRzTrackBar.SetPosition( Value : Integer );
begin
  if Value <> FPosition then
  begin
    if Value < FMin then                                { Range Checking }
      Value := FMin
    else if Value > FMax then
      Value := FMax;

    FPosition := Value;

    { No need to be fancy in Design-mode.  Simply invalidate the control.    }
    { Besides, it is not appropriate to call the Change event at design-time. }

    if csDesigning in ComponentState then
      Invalidate
    else
    begin
                          { Erase old thumb image by drawing background bitmap }
      Canvas.Draw( FThumbRct.Left, FThumbRct.Top, FBackgroundBmp );

      DrawThumb;                                   { Draw thumb at new location }
      Change;                                        { Trigger Change event }
    end;
  end;
end; {= TRzTrackBar.SetPosition =}


procedure TRzTrackBar.SetShowTicks( Value : Boolean );
begin
  if Value <> FShowTicks then
  begin
    FShowTicks := Value;
    Invalidate;
  end;
end;


procedure TRzTrackBar.SetThumbSize( Value : TThumbSize );
begin
  if Value <> FThumbSize then
```

```
    begin
      FThumbSize := Value;
      LoadThumbBitmaps;                    { Reload bitmaps if thumb size changes }
      Invalidate;
    end;
end;


procedure TRzTrackBar.SetThumbStyle( Value : TThumbStyle );
begin
  if Value <> FThumbStyle then
  begin
    FThumbStyle := Value;
    LoadThumbBitmaps;                      { Reload bitmaps if thumb style changes }
    Invalidate;
  end;
end;


procedure TRzTrackBar.SetTickStyle( Value : TTickStyle );
begin
  if Value <> FTickStyle then
  begin
    FTickStyle := Value;
    Invalidate;
  end;
end;


procedure TRzTrackBar.SetTrackColor( Value : TColor );
begin
  if Value <> FTrackColor then
  begin
    FTrackColor := Value;
    UpdateDitherBitmap;
    Invalidate;
  end;
end;


procedure TRzTrackBar.SetTrackWidth( Value : Word );
begin
  if FTrackWidth <> Value then
  begin
    FTrackWidth := Value;
    if FTrackWidth < 6 then
      FTrackWidth := 6;
    Invalidate;
  end;
end;
```

```
{ Array Constants hold all bitmap resource names for easy access }

const
  ThumbBitmapNames : array[ TTrackOrientation, TThumbSize ] of PChar =
    ( ( 'SmHorzThumb', 'MedHorzThumb', 'LgHorzThumb' ),
      ( 'SmVertThumb', 'MedVertThumb', 'LgVertThumb' ) );
  MaskBitmapNames : array[ TTrackOrientation, TThumbSize ] of PChar =
    ( ( 'SmHorzThumbMask', 'MedHorzThumbMask', 'LgHorzThumbMask' ),
      ( 'SmVertThumbMask', 'MedVertThumbMask', 'LgVertThumbMask' ) );
  BoxBitmapNames : array[ TTrackOrientation, TThumbSize ] of PChar =
    ( ( 'SmHorzBox', 'MedHorzBox', 'LgHorzBox' ),
      ( 'SmVertBox', 'MedVertBox', 'LgVertBox' ) );


procedure TRzTrackBar.LoadThumbBitmaps;
begin
  if FThumbStyle = tsPointer then
  begin
    FThumbBmp.Handle := LoadBitmap( HInstance,
                             ThumbBitmapNames[ FOrientation, FThumbSize ]);
    FMaskBmp.Handle := LoadBitmap( HInstance,
                             MaskBitmapNames[ FOrientation, FThumbSize ] );
  end
  else
  begin
    FThumbBmp.Handle := LoadBitmap( HInstance,
                             BoxBitmapNames[ FOrientation, FThumbSize ]);
  end;

  if FOrientation = toVertical then
  begin
    FThumbHeight := FThumbBmp.Width;
    FThumbWidth := FThumbBmp.Height;
  end
  else
  begin
    FThumbHeight := FThumbBmp.Height;
    FThumbWidth := FThumbBmp.Width;
  end;
  FHalfWidth := FThumbWidth div 2;
end; {= TRzTrackBar.LoadThumbBitmaps =}


procedure TRzTrackBar.UpdateDitherBitmap;
var
  C : TColor;
  I, J : Integer;
begin
  C := clSilver;
  if ColorToRGB( FTrackColor) = clSilver then
    C := clGray;
```

```
    with FDitherBmp.Canvas do
    begin
      Brush.Color := FTrackColor;
      FillRect( Rect( 0, 0, FDitherBmp.Width, FDitherBmp.Height ) );
      for I := 0 to 7 do
        for J := 0 to 7 do
          if ( I + J ) mod 2 <> 0 then
            Pixels[ I, J ] := C;
    end;
end; {= TRzTrackBar.UpdateDitherBitmap =}


procedure TRzTrackBar.DrawTrack;
begin
  { Calculate the Size of the Track }
  if FOrientation = toVertical then
  begin
    FTrackRct.Top := FHalfWidth + FBorderWidth;
    FTrackRct.Bottom := Height - FBorderWidth - FHalfWidth;
    FTrackRct.Left := ( Width - FTrackWidth ) div 2;
    FTrackRct.Right := FTrackRct.Left + FTrackWidth;
  end
  else
  begin
    FTrackRct.Top := ( Height - FTrackWidth ) div 2;
    FTrackRct.Bottom := FTrackRct.Top + FTrackWidth;
    FTrackRct.Left := FHalfWidth + FBorderWidth;
    FTrackRct.Right := Width - FBorderWidth - FHalfWidth;
  end;

  { Draw the Track }
  Canvas.Brush.Color := FTrackColor;

  if not Enabled then
    Canvas.Brush.Bitmap := FDitherBmp;

  Canvas.FillRect( FTrackRct );
  DrawCtl3DBorder( Canvas, FTrackRct );                    { From RzCommon unit }
end; {= TRzTrackBar.DrawTrack =}


procedure TRzTrackBar.DrawTicks;
var
  Delta : Real;
  I, X, Y : Integer;
begin
  Canvas.Pen.Color := clBlack;
  with FTrackRct do
  begin
    if FOrientation = toVertical then
    begin
                                       { Delta is spacing between tick marks }
      Delta := ( Height - FThumbWidth - 2 * FBorderWidth ) / ( FMax - FMin );
```

```
        for I := FMin to FMax do
        begin
          Y := Trunc( Delta * ( I - FMin ) ) + FBorderWidth;

          if FTickStyle = tkStandard then
          begin
            Canvas.MoveTo( FBorderWidth, Y + FHalfWidth );
            Canvas.LineTo( 10, Y + FHalfWidth );
            if FThumbStyle = tsBox then              { Draw Ticks on Other Side }
            begin
              Canvas.MoveTo( Width - 10, Y + FHalfWidth );
              Canvas.LineTo( Width - FBorderWidth, Y + FHalfWidth );
            end;
          end
          else                                    { Provide hook to owner draw ticks }
            DrawTick( Canvas, Point( 0, Y + FHalfWidth ), I );
        end;
      end
      else
      begin
        Delta := ( Width - FThumbWidth - 2 * FBorderWidth ) / ( FMax - FMin );

        for I := FMin to FMax do
        begin
          X := Trunc( Delta * ( I - FMin ) ) + FBorderWidth;

          if FTickStyle = tkStandard then
          begin
            Canvas.MoveTo( X + FHalfWidth, FBorderWidth );
            Canvas.LineTo( X + FHalfWidth, 10 );
            if FThumbStyle = tsBox then              { Draw Ticks on Other Side }
            begin
              Canvas.MoveTo( X + FHalfWidth, Height - 10 );
              Canvas.LineTo( X + FHalfWidth, Height - FBorderWidth );
            end;
          end
          else                                    { Provide hook to owner draw ticks }
            DrawTick( Canvas, Point( X + FHalfWidth, 0 ), I );
        end;
      end;
    end;
  end;
end; {= TRzTrackBar.DrawTicks =}


procedure TRzTrackBar.DrawThumb;
var
  Offset : Longint;
  WorkBmp : TBitmap;
  WorkRct : TRect;
begin
  { Calculate new location of thumb based on Position }
  if FOrientation = toVertical then
```

```
begin
  Offset := ( Longint( Height ) - FThumbWidth - 2 * FBorderWidth ) *
            ( FPosition - FMin ) div ( FMax - FMin );
  FThumbRct.Left := ( Width - FThumbHeight ) div 2;
  FThumbRct.Right := FThumbRct.Left + FThumbHeight;
  FThumbRct.Bottom := Height - Offset - FBorderWidth;
  FThumbRct.Top := FThumbRct.Bottom - FThumbWidth;
end
else
begin
  Offset := ( Longint( Width ) - FThumbWidth - 2 * FBorderWidth ) *
            ( FPosition - FMin ) div ( FMax - FMin );
  FThumbRct.Left := Offset + FBorderWidth;
  FThumbRct.Right := FThumbRct.Left + FThumbWidth;
  FThumbRct.Top := ( Height - FThumbHeight ) div 2;
  FThumbRct.Bottom := FThumbRct.Top + FThumbHeight;
end;

{ Save background image of new thumb location }
FBackgroundBmp.Width := FThumbBmp.Width;
FBackgroundBmp.Height := FThumbBmp.Height;
FBackgroundBmp.Canvas.CopyRect( Rect(0, 0, FThumbBmp.Width, FThumbBmp.Height),
                                Canvas, FThumbRct );

{ Draw the thumb by displaying the thumb bitmap }

{ WorkBmp is used to combine the Thumb bitmap and the background so that the }
{ background of the track appears in the corners of the Thumb image. }

{ If ThumbStyle is tsBox, there is no need to mask out the background, so }
{ just copy the thumb image to the control canvas. }

WorkBmp := TBitmap.Create;
try
  { Don't forget to set working bitmap size to that of thumb bitmap }
  WorkBmp.Height := FThumbBmp.Height;
  WorkBmp.Width := FThumbBmp.Width;

  { WorkRct specifies the Width and Height of the region we are dealing with }
  WorkRct := Rect( 0, 0, FThumbBmp.Width, FThumbBmp.Height );

  if FThumbStyle = tsPointer then
  begin
    { Copy the FBackgroundBmp image to WorkBmp }

    WorkBmp.Canvas.CopyMode := cmSrcCopy;
    WorkBmp.Canvas.CopyRect( WorkRct, FBackgroundBmp.Canvas, WorkRct );

    { Combine the FBackgroundBmp and the FMaskBmp images using the cmSrcAnd }
    { CopyMode. White pixels in mask have no effect. Background shows through. }
```

```
      WorkBmp.Canvas.CopyMode := cmSrcAnd;
      WorkBmp.Canvas.CopyRect( WorkRct, FMaskBmp.Canvas, WorkRct );

      { Copy the Thumb bitmap onto the Working bitmap using the cmSrcPaint }
      { mode. Black pixels in Thumb bitmap let background show through. }

      WorkBmp.Canvas.CopyMode := cmSrcPaint
    end
    else
      WorkBmp.Canvas.CopyMode := cmSrcCopy;

    WorkBmp.Canvas.CopyRect( WorkRct, FThumbBmp.Canvas, WorkRct );

    if not Enabled then
    begin
      { If control is disabled, dither the thumb as well as the track }
      WorkBmp.Canvas.Brush.Bitmap := FDitherBmp;
      WorkBmp.Canvas.FloodFill( WorkRct.Right - 3, WorkRct.Bottom - 3,
                                clSilver, fsSurface );
    end;

    { Copy the working bitmap onto the control's Canvas at thumb position }
    Canvas.CopyRect( FThumbRct, WorkBmp.Canvas, WorkRct );
  finally
    WorkBmp.Free;
  end;
end; {= TRzTrackBar.DrawThumb =}


procedure TRzTrackBar.Paint;
begin
  with Canvas do
  begin
    if Focused then        { Indicate focus by drawing dotted box around control }
      DrawFocusRect( ClientRect );
    DrawTrack;
    if FShowTicks then
      DrawTicks;
    DrawThumb;
  end;
end;


procedure TRzTrackBar.Change;
begin
  if Assigned( FOnChange ) then
    FOnChange( Self );
end;


{= TRzTrackBar.DrawTick
{=   This method is the event dispatch method for the OnDrawTick event.     =}
```

```
{=    The parameters are:                                            =}
{=      Canvas - The Canvas for the TrackBar Control                 =}
{=      Location - Point record indicating X or Y coordinates of tick mark  =}
{=      Index - Position index of tick mark to be drawn              =}

procedure TRzTrackBar.DrawTick( Canvas : TCanvas; Location : TPoint;
                                Index : Integer );
begin
  if Assigned( FOnDrawTick ) then              { Allow user to draw custom ticks }
    FOnDrawTick( Self, Canvas, Location, Index );
end;


procedure TRzTrackBar.DoEnter;
begin
  inherited DoEnter;
  Refresh;      { When control gets focus, update display to show focus border }
end;


procedure TRzTrackBar.DoExit;
begin
  inherited DoExit;
  Refresh;   { When control loses focus, update display to remove focus border }
end;


procedure TRzTrackBar.KeyDown( var Key : Word; Shift : TShiftState );
begin
  inherited KeyDown( Key, Shift );

  case Key of
    vk_Prior:                                { PgUp Key - increases Position }
      Position := FPosition + FPageSize;

    vk_Next:                                 { PgDn Key - decreases Position }
      Position := FPosition - FPageSize;

    vk_End:
      if FOrientation = toVertical then      { End is at Right for horizontal }
        Position := FMin                 { TrackBar, Bottom for vertical TrackBar }
      else
        Position := FMax;

    vk_Home:
      if FOrientation = toVertical then      { Home is at Left for horizontal }
        Position := FMax                 { TrackBar, Top for vertical TrackBar }
      else
        Position := FMin;

    vk_Left:                                        { Decrease Position }
      if FPosition > FMin then
        Position := FPosition - 1;
```

```
      vk_Up:                                              { Increase Position }
        if FPosition < FMax then
          Position := FPosition + 1;

      vk_Right:                                           { Increase Position }
        if FPosition < FMax then
          Position := FPosition + 1;

      vk_Down:                                            { Decrease Position }
        if FPosition > FMin then
          Position := FPosition - 1;
    end; { case }
end; {= TRzTrackBar.KeyDown =}


procedure TRzTrackBar.MouseDown( Button : TMouseButton; Shift : TShiftState;
                                 X, Y : Integer );
var
  PtX, PtY : Integer;
  Delta : Real;
begin
  inherited MouseDown( Button, Shift, X, Y );
  SetFocus;                                       { Move focus to TrackBar }

  if ( Button = mbLeft ) and PtInRect( FThumbRct, Point( X, Y ) ) then
  begin
    { User pressed the left mouse button while on the thumb }
    FSliding := True;
  end
  else if ( Button = mbLeft ) and PtInRect( FTrackRct, Point( X, Y ) ) then
  begin
    { User pressed left mouse button inside the track on either side of thumb. }
    { Determine which side of thumb user clicked, and then update position     }

    if FOrientation = toVertical then
    begin
      Delta := ( Height - FThumbWidth - 2 * FBorderWidth ) / ( FMax - FMin );
      PtY := Trunc( Delta * ( ( FMax - FPosition ) - FMin ) ) + FBorderWidth;
      if Y < PtY then
        Position := FPosition + FPageSize
      else
        Position := FPosition - FPageSize;
    end
    else
    begin
      Delta := ( Width - FThumbWidth - 2 * FBorderWidth ) / ( FMax - FMin );
      PtX := Trunc( Delta * ( FPosition - FMin ) ) + FBorderWidth;
      if X < PtX then
        Position := FPosition - FPageSize
      else
        Position := FPosition + FPageSize;
    end;
```

```
    end;
end; {= TRzTrackBar.MouseDown =}


procedure TRzTrackBar.MouseMove( Shift : TShiftState; X, Y : Integer );
var
  P, W, H : Integer;
begin
  inherited MouseMove( Shift, X, Y );

  { If mouse is over thumb, then change cursor to either crSizeNS or crSizeWE  }
  { depending on whether the orientation is vertical or horizontal.            }

  if PtInRect( FThumbRct, Point( X, Y ) ) then
  begin
    if FOrientation = toVertical then
      Cursor := crSizeNS
    else
      Cursor := crSizeWE;
  end
  else
    Cursor := crDefault;

  { If in Sliding state, then move the thumb to the closest tick mark. }
  if FSliding then
  begin
    if FOrientation = toVertical then
    begin
      H := Height - FHalfWidth;
      P := Round( ( ( H - Y ) / H ) * ( FMax - FMin ) + FMin );
    end
    else
    begin
      W := Width - FHalfWidth;
      P := Round( ( ( X - FHalfWidth ) / W ) * ( FMax - FMin ) + FMin  );
    end;

    if P > FMax then
      P := FMax;
    if P < FMin then
      P := FMin;
    Position := P;
  end;
end; {= TRzTrackBar.MouseMove =}


procedure TRzTrackBar.MouseUp( Button : TMouseButton; Shift : TShiftState;
                               X, Y : Integer );
begin
  inherited MouseUp( Button, Shift, X, Y );

  if ( Button = mbLeft ) then
    FSliding := False;
end;
```

```
procedure TRzTrackBar.WMGetDlgCode( var Msg : TWMGetDlgCode );
begin
  inherited;
  Msg.Result := dlgc_WantArrows;            { So TrackBar can process arrow keys }
end;


procedure TRzTrackBar.WMSize( var Msg : TWMSize );
begin
  inherited;
  if Height > Width then
    Orientation := toVertical
  else
    Orientation := toHorizontal;
end;


procedure TRzTrackBar.CMEnabledChanged( var Msg : TMessage );
begin
  inherited;
  Invalidate;
end;



{=======================}
{== Register Procedure ==}
{=======================}

procedure Register;
begin
  RegisterComponents( RaizePage, [ TRzTrackBar ] );
end;

end.
```

The TRzTrackBar Class

Since the RzTrackBar component is responsible for painting itself, I chose to create the **TRzTrackBar** class as a descendant of the **TCustomControl** class rather than the **TWinControl** class. (Although **TRzTrackBar** does not descend from any existing component, like all Delphi objects, it must descend from an existing VCL *class*.) Recall from Chapter 6 that **TCustomControl** is a direct descendant of **TWinControl**. So **TCustomControl** has all of the same features as **TWinControl**. The only difference between the two classes is that **TCustomControl** provides a **Canvas** property and a virtual **Paint** method.

Like most components, much of the **TRzTrackBar** class declaration is involved with the specification of the component's properties. Table 10.1 summarizes these properties and specifies the type of each property and its default value.

Table 10.1	Properties and Events for TRzTrackBar		
Property	**Type**	**Default Value**	**Description**
Max	Integer	10	Specifies the maximum positional value.
Min	Integer	0	Specifies the minimum positional value.
Orientation	TTrackOrientation	toHorizontal	Thumb moves left-to-right or top-to-bottom.
PageSize	Word	1	Number of ticks to move when using PgUp/PgDn keys or clicking mouse inside track.
Position	Integer	0	Current positional value.
ShowTicks	Boolean	True	Specifies whether or not tick marks are shown.
ThumbSize	TThumbSize	tsMedium	Small, Medium, and Large size thumbs available.
ThumbStyle	TThumbStyle	tsPointer	Thumb can be a pointer or a box. If the tsBox style is chosen, tick marks are drawn on both sides of the track.
TickStyle	TTickStyle	tkStandard	Set to tkOwnerDraw to draw your own tick marks.
TrackColor	TColor	clWhite	Specifies the fill color used for the track.
TrackWidth	Word	8	Specifies the width of the track in pixels.
OnChange	TNotifyEvent	n/a	Event triggered when positional value changes.
OnDrawTick	TDrawTickEvent	n/a	Event triggered when a tick mark needs to be drawn. TickStyle must be set to tkOwnerDraw.

Although this class declares a lot of properties, the significance of the class lies in its methods. There are four basic categories of methods used in the **TRzTrackBar** class. First, the **KeyDown** and **WMGetDlgCode** methods provide support for keyboard manipulation. The **MouseDown**, **MouseMove**, and **MouseUp** methods obviously support moving the thumb with the mouse. The next category of methods are those involved in responding to changes in the input focus. This includes the **DoEnter** and **DoExit** methods. And the final category are those methods involved in giving the RzTrackBar component its appearance. The methods in this group include **Paint**, **DrawTrack**, **DrawTicks**, **DrawTick**, and **DrawThumb**.

Before diving into these four categories, I would first like to make a few comments on the constructor and destructor of this class. First of all, there are four **TBitmap** objects defined in this class. The **FThumbBmp**, **FMaskBmp**, and **FBackgroundBmp** objects are used to support drawing the thumb. The **FDitherBmp** object is used to dither the track area and thumb (that is, "gray them out") when the control is disabled. These objects must be created in the constructor. From the source listing, you can see that this simply involves calling the **Create** constructor for each bitmap object. Immediately upon creation, the bitmap objects are empty, and so the **LoadThumbBitmaps** method is called to populate the bitmap objects with bitmap images from the resource file. Since the bitmap objects are created by the component, the **TRzTrackBar.Destroy** destructor first frees the bitmap objects and then calls its inherited destructor.

Handling Keyboard Events

Providing keyboard support for a component is accomplished by overriding one or more of the keyboard event dispatch methods. These methods are **KeyDown**, **KeyUp**, and **KeyPress**. These three methods correspond to the **wm_KeyDown**, **wm_KeyUp**, and **wm_Char** Windows messages, respectively.

For the **TRzTrackBar** class, the **KeyDown** method is overridden in order to allow the user to move the thumb using the arrow keys, including Home, End, PgUp, and PgDn. A **case** statement on the **Key** value is used to determine which key was pressed. Depending on the key pressed, the **Position** property is altered appropriately.

 List case constants in *ascending* order. This allows the compiler to optimize the **case** statement into a series of jumps as opposed to a sequence of independent (and slower) calculations. For example, In the **TRzTrackBar.KeyDown** method, the virtual key codes are listed in numeric order.

So why handle **KeyDown** and not **KeyPress**? There are two reasons. First, the **KeyDown** method has access to the virtual key code value of the key pressed and not just its character value. This allows us to compare the **Key** value to constants such as **vk_Left**. Second, the **KeyDown** event repeats if the user continues to hold down the key. For this component, it makes sense to continue to move the thumb as long as one of the arrow keys is held down.

Before the **KeyDown** method will have any effect on the control, there is one more step that must be performed. We must provide a message handling method to respond to the **wm_GetDlgCode** message. Normally, Windows handles certain keystrokes like the Tab and arrow keys. The **wm_GetDlgCode** message allows a window to handle the keystrokes in whatever way it sees fit.

For example, Windows normally processes the arrow keys by moving the focus from one control to another. To prevent this default behavior, the **WMGetDlgCode** method, shown below, sets the **Msg.Result** value to **dlgc_WantArrows**. Now, the arrow keys can be used to alter the **Position** property instead.

```
procedure TRzTrackBar.WMGetDlgCode( var Msg : TWMGetDlgCode );
begin
  inherited;
  Msg.Result := dlgc_WantArrows;              { So TrackBar can process arrow keys }
end;
```

Handling Mouse Events

One of the requirements for the RzTrackBar component is to allow the user to manipulate the thumb position using the mouse. To provide the desired mouse support, three methods are overridden: **MouseDown**, **MouseMove**, and **MouseUp**.

The **MouseDown** method is called whenever a mouse button is pressed while the mouse pointer is positioned over the component. The first task performed by **MouseDown** is to change the focus to the selected track bar by calling **SetFocus**. By default, clicking on a control does not automatically set its focus.

 When overriding an event dispatch method like **Click** or **MouseDown**, be sure to call the inherited method so that the corresponding event gets triggered. Without this call, users of your components will not be able to add custom code to the event.

The second task performed depends on the location of the mouse event and which button is pressed. If the left mouse button is pressed while positioned over the thumb, indicating that the user wants to slide the thumb along the track, the **FSliding** flag is set to **True**. The **FSliding** flag is used in the **MouseMove** method to determine if the user is trying to slide the thumb.

If the left mouse button is pressed and the mouse pointer is positioned within the track, but not on the thumb, the thumb is moved in the direction toward the mouse pointer. The number of positions the thumb moves is determined by the **PageSize** property.

The **MouseMove** method is called whenever the mouse is moved over the component. **MouseMove** first checks to see if the mouse is positioned over the thumb using the **PtInRect** API function. If it is, the cursor is changed to reflect the way in which the thumb can be moved along the track. When the mouse moves off the thumb, the cursor is restored to its default value. Changing the cursor like this gives the user visual feedback as to the operation of this control.

As mentioned earlier, the **MouseMove** method handles sliding the thumb to different positions along the track. If the **FSliding** flag is set, the closest tick position is calculated using the current mouse position, and then the **Position** property is updated to move the thumb to that position.

By default, components that are derived from **TControl** have the **csCaptureMouse** style flag included in the **ControlStyle** property. Having this flag set causes the component to continue to receive mouse move events even if the mouse is moved outside the bounds of the component. The component receives the events as long as the mouse button remains down. This is called *capturing* the mouse.

Capturing the mouse is particularly useful for the RzTrackBar component because it allows the thumb to be moved without requiring that the mouse remain positioned over the control. Furthermore, with mouse capturing enabled, not only are mouse move events sent to the component, but the final mouse-up event is guaranteed to be sent to the control. This is important because the **MouseUp** method is responsible for turning off the **FSliding** flag, and thus taking the track bar out of sliding mode.

Handling the Input Focus

Since we created the **TRzTrackBar** class as a descendant of **TCustomControl**, which is a descendant of **TWinControl**, our component can receive the focus. Fortunately, we do not have to do anything special in order for this to happen. It is a service provided by the operating system.

However, our component needs to respond to focus *changes*. All components that can be focused need to provide some way of visually identifying that it has the focus. Most standard controls use a dotted line or box somewhere within the control to indicate focus. For example, the caption of a focused check box is surrounded by a dotted line.

There are two methods that are important for managing the focus. They are **DoEnter** and **DoExit**. Both of these methods are event dispatch methods that are called internally in the VCL in response to **wm_SetFocus** and **wm_KillFocus** messages, respectively. The **TRzTrackBar** class overrides these two methods in order to instruct the component to repaint itself. The **Paint** method described in the next section alters the appearance of the control if it has the focus.

Also associated with the focus are the **TabStop** and **TabOrder** properties, which are defined in the **TWinControl** class. By default, the **TabStop** property is **False**. To override this, we simply specify a new default value when it is published in the **TRzTrackBar** class. But don't forget to set the new value in the constructor.

Painting the TrackBar

The virtual **Paint** method is automatically called whenever the component's view needs to be updated. This is no different from how the **Paint** method behaved in the graphical controls presented in the last chapter. The **TRzTrackBar.Paint** method is divided into four steps. The first step is to determine if the control needs to reflect that it has the focus. To do this, the inherited **Focused** property is checked. If it is **True**, the **DrawFocusRect** method is called, passing it the rectangle representing the client area of the control. The top horizontal track bar in Figure 10.1 (page 254) shows the effect of this call.

The second step involves drawing the track. This is handled by the **DrawTrack** method, which first calculates the dimensions of the track using the current **Width** and **Height** of the component and the specified **TrackWidth**. The track is always centered within the client area regardless of orientation. The track is shortened by half the width of the thumb at each end. This allows the *center* of the thumb to go to the *ends* of the track.

Once the dimensions of the track are calculated, the interior of the track is filled using the **TrackColor** property. If the control happens to be disabled, then the track's interior is dithered by assigning the **FDitherBmp** to the **Canvas.Brush.Bitmap** property. The **FDitherBmp** is an 8 x 8 bitmap that is created within the **TRzTrackBar** class. Since the bitmap is affected by changes in the **TrackColor** value, the bitmap is updated whenever the **TrackColor** changes. Figure 10.2 illustrates what the **FDitherBmp** bitmap looks like when the **TrackColor** is **clWhite**. Finally, the border of the track is drawn using the **DrawCtl3DBorder** procedure from the RzCommon unit.

Figure 10.2

The FDitherBmp
Pattern.

Drawing the Ticks

The third step in painting the RzTrackBar component is to draw the tick marks. This process is handled by the **DrawTicks** method. (Don't confuse this with the **DrawTick** method, which will be described shortly.) Most of the code in **DrawTicks** is used to determine where the tick marks will be drawn. Since the calculations to determine this depend on the orientation of the track bar, the method first checks the **Orientation** property.

Regardless of the control's orientation, the process is the same. First, the number of pixels between tick marks is calculated. Next, all positions between **FMin** and **FMax**, inclusive, are iterated over. For each position, the appropriate coordinate of where the tick mark is to be located is calculated, and finally the tick mark is drawn. By default, tick marks are drawn above the track for horizontal track bars and to the left of the track for vertical ones. If the **ThumbStyle** property is set to **tsBox**, the tick marks are drawn on both sides of the track.

The tick marks themselves are drawn at every position and are represented as simple black lines six pixels long. However, the RzTrackBar component adds quite a bit of flexibility when it comes to displaying tick marks. By using Delphi events, the **DrawTicks** method provides a way for a component user to override how the ticks are drawn.

If the **TickStyle** property is set to **tkOwnerDraw**, the **DrawTicks** method bypasses its own drawing of tick marks and calls the **DrawTick** event dispatch method instead. The **DrawTick** method generates the **OnDrawTick** event whenever a single tick mark needs to be drawn. **OnDrawTick** is of type **TDrawTickEvent**, which is defined as

```
TDrawTickEvent = procedure ( TrackBar : TRzTrackBar; Canvas : TCanvas;
                             Location : TPoint; Index : Integer ) of object;
```

Therefore, event handlers for this event receive four parameters. The first parameter is a reference to the track bar generating the event. Use this reference to determine the dimensions and orientation of the track bar. The second parameter is a reference to the track bar's **Canvas** property. This provides direct access for drawing custom tick marks.

The third parameter is a **TPoint** record populated with either the X or Y coordinate of the tick mark. For a horizontal track bar, the X coordinate is filled in, while a vertical track bar specifies a Y coordinate value. Use this record to draw the tick marks at the correct locations.

The final parameter is an index representing the position value of the tick mark to be drawn. Use this index to skip certain marks or to provide other interesting effects. Figure 10.3 illustrates several examples of owner-draw track bars. The source code for the this form is shown in Listing 10.2.

Listing 10.2   TICKFORM.PAS—Handling the OnDrawTick Event

```
unit TickForm;

interface

uses
  SysUtils, WinTypes, WinProcs, Messages, Classes, Graphics, Controls,
  Forms, Dialogs, ExtCtrls, RzTrkBar;

type
  TForm1 = class(TForm)
    RzTrackBar1: TRzTrackBar;
    RzTrackBar2: TRzTrackBar;
    RzTrackBar4: TRzTrackBar;
    RzTrackBar3: TRzTrackBar;
    Image1: TImage;
    Image2: TImage;
    procedure RzTrackBar1DrawTick(TrackBar: TRzTrackBar; Canvas: TCanvas;
      Location: TPoint; Index : Integer );
    procedure RzTrackBar2DrawTick(TrackBar: TRzTrackBar; Canvas: TCanvas;
      Location: TPoint; Index : Integer );
    procedure RzTrackBar3DrawTick(TrackBar: TRzTrackBar; Canvas: TCanvas;
      Location: TPoint; Index : Integer );
    procedure RzTrackBar4DrawTick(TrackBar: TRzTrackBar; Canvas: TCanvas;
      Location: TPoint; Index: Integer);
  private
    { Private declarations }
  public
    { Public declarations }
  end;

var
  Form1: TForm1;

implementation
```

```
{$R *.DFM}

uses
  RzCommon;

procedure TForm1.RzTrackBar1DrawTick( TrackBar: TRzTrackBar; Canvas: TCanvas;
                                      Location: TPoint; Index : Integer );
begin
  Canvas.Draw( Location.X - 4, 4, Image1.Picture.Bitmap );
end;

procedure TForm1.RzTrackBar2DrawTick( TrackBar: TRzTrackBar; Canvas: TCanvas;
                                      Location: TPoint; Index : Integer );
begin
  DrawBorder( Canvas, Rect( Location.X - 3, 4, Location.X + 3, 10 ),
              clBtnHighlight, clBtnShadow );
  DrawBorder( Canvas, Rect( Location.X - 3, TrackBar.Height - 10,
                            Location.X + 3, TrackBar.Height - 4 ),
              clBtnHighlight, clBtnShadow );
end;

procedure TForm1.RzTrackBar3DrawTick( TrackBar: TRzTrackBar; Canvas: TCanvas;
                                      Location: TPoint; Index : Integer);
var
  W : Integer;
begin
  with Canvas, Location do
  begin
    if Index mod 2 = 0 then
      W := 16
    else
      W := 8;
    Pen.Color := clBtnShadow;
    MoveTo( 20 - W, Y - 1 );
    LineTo( 20, Y - 1 );
    MoveTo( TrackBar.Width - 20, Y - 1 );
    LineTo( TrackBar.Width - 20 + W, Y - 1 );

    Pen.Color := clBtnHighlight;
    MoveTo( 20 - W, Y );
    LineTo( 20, Y );
    MoveTo( TrackBar.Width - 20, Y );
    LineTo( TrackBar.Width - 20 + W, Y );
  end;
end;

procedure TForm1.RzTrackBar4DrawTick( TrackBar: TRzTrackBar; Canvas: TCanvas;
                                      Location: TPoint; Index: Integer);
begin
  Canvas.Draw( 4, Location.Y - 4, Image2.Picture.Bitmap );
end;

end.
```

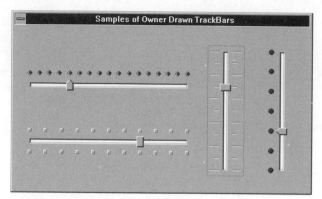

Figure 10.3

Drawing Tick
Marks by Hand.

Notice how the third track bar uses the **Index** parameter to alternate the lengths
of successive tick marks. Another interesting effect is achieved by using a hidden
Image component. In the first and fourth track bars, the bitmap stored in the
Image component is drawn at each tick mark location.

Setting the Position

Before continuing with the final step in painting the RzTrackBar, let's turn our
attention for a moment to the **SetPosition** write access method for the **Position**
property. Although not directly related to drawing the component, the **Position**
property does determine where the thumb is placed. With respect to this, whenever the **Position** value is changed, the thumb needs to be moved, and thus the
view of the component needs to be updated. As such, the **SetPosition** method
could be written as follows:

```
procedure TRzTrackBar.SetPosition( Value : Integer );
begin
  if Value <> FPosition then
  begin
    if Value < FMin then                               { Range Checking }
      Value := FMin
    else if Value > FMax then
      Value := FMax;

    FPosition := Value;
    Invalidate;                                { Repaint the entire control }
  end;
end;
```

The problem with writing the method this way is that whenever the position is
changed, the entire control is invalidated. This has the unfortunate side effect of

causing the control to flicker as the thumb is moved— not to mention causing extra work to repaint the track and tick marks that are unaffected by the position change.

A better solution is to keep track of the image behind the thumb. When the thumb is moved to a new location, the old background image is drawn at the previous thumb position. This restores the track view without having to repaint the entire track. Next, the image at the new position value is stored in the background bitmap, and finally, the thumb image is displayed at the current position. This is a summary of the process provided by the **DrawThumb** method.

Drawing the Thumb

As alluded to in the previous section on **SetPosition**, the thumb is displayed using a set of bitmaps; three bitmaps to be exact. The first bitmap represents the image of the thumb. Since the thumb is not necessarily rectangular, pixels that are to be transparent are colored black. The second bitmap required holds a mask that is used to isolate the actual thumb image. The mask bitmap contains only black and white pixels. Black pixels are used to represent those pixels in the thumb bitmap that should be displayed. White pixels in the mask designate transparent regions. Figure 10.4 shows what these two bitmaps look like for the medium, horizontal thumb. The third bitmap is used to record the background image behind the thumb. All three bitmaps are the same size.

These three bitmaps are used to display the thumb without completely covering what is behind the thumb. If the thumb were rectangular, this would not be a concern. But since several of the thumbs have a point at one end, the areas to

Figure 10.4

Thumb and Mask Bitmaps.

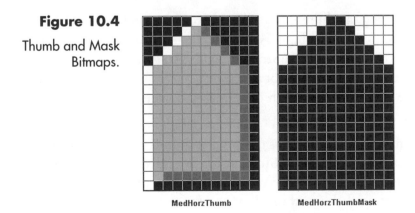

MedHorzThumb   MedHorzThumbMask

either side of the point should be transparent. That is, the background, such as the track or tick marks, should appear in these transparent regions.

The **DrawThumb** method first calculates the location of the thumb using the current **Position**. Once this rectangle is determined, it is used to designate the area of the component that will represent the background of the new thumb position. The **FBackgroundBmp** is then populated with this image using the **CopyRect** method described in the last chapter. This background bitmap will be used when the thumb is moved. Before the new position is set, the background bitmap is displayed at the current thumb position. This has the visual effect of erasing the thumb.

Because the thumb bitmap may contain regions designed to appear transparent, a temporary working bitmap is used to combine the background bitmap, the mask bitmap, and the thumb. Each bitmap is copied to the working bitmap using the **CopyRect** method.

However, to create the desired effect, the **CopyMode** property needs to be altered as each bitmap is copied to the working copy. The **CopyMode** property affects how the pixels in the source and destination bitmaps are combined. Its default value is **cmSrcCopy**, which means that the source image overwrites the preexisting image on the destination canvas. Table 10.2 summarizes the possible values for **CopyMode**.

Seasoned Windows programmers will notice that **CopyMode** represents the *raster operation* codes that are used for GDI functions like **BitBlt** and **StretchBlt**. In fact, the cmXXXX constants map directly to those Windows GDI constants.

Let's get back to drawing the thumb. First, the **cmSrcCopy** mode is used to copy the background image to the working version. Second, the mask bitmap is copied onto the working bitmap using the **cmSrcAnd** mode. Using this mode, any pixels that are white in the mask bitmap do not affect the working bitmap. This has the effect of letting the background show through the mask wherever the mask contains a white pixel.

After copying the mask, the third step is to copy the thumb bitmap to the working bitmap. For this operation, the **cmSrcPaint** mode is used. Under this mode, any pixels that are black in the thumb bitmap do not affect the working bitmap. Therefore, the background shows through at the corners on either side of the thumb point.

Table 10.2	CopyMode Values
Value	**Effect**
cmBlackness	Turns all pixels in destination canvas to black.
cmDstInvert	Inverts the destination canvas.
cmMergeCopy	Combines a pattern and the source canvas using the Boolean AND operator.
cmMergePaint	Combines the inverted source canvas with the destination canvas using the Boolean OR operator.
cmNotSrcCopy	Copies the inverted source canvas to the destination canvas.
cmNotSrcErase	Inverts the result of combining the destination canvas and source canvas using the Boolean OR operator.
cmPatCopy	Copies a pattern to the destination canvas.
cmPatInvert	Combines the destination canvas with a pattern using the Boolean XOR operator.
cmPatPaint	Combines the inverted source canvas with a pattern using the Boolean OR operator. Combines the result of this operation with the destination canvas using the Boolean OR operator.
cmSrcAnd	Combines pixels from the destination canvas and source canvas using the Boolean AND operator.
cmSrcCopy	Copies the source canvas to the destination canvas.
cmSrcErase	Inverts the destination canvas and combines the result with the source canvas using the Boolean AND operator.
cmSrcInvert	Combines pixels from the destination canvas and source canvas using the Boolean XOR operator.
cmSrcPaint	Combines pixels from the destination canvas and source canvas using the Boolean OR operator.
cmWhiteness	Turns all pixels in destination canvas to white.

Figure 10.5 emphasizes this process by showing the effects of the second and third steps individually. The **TrackWidth** has been increased so that the thumb point intersects with the side of the track. Notice how the track side is allowed to show through the thumb even though the thumb bitmap is rectangular. The final step is to copy the working bitmap onto the component's canvas. This causes the thumb to appear at its new position.

New and Improved SetPosition

Since the **DrawThumb** method manages drawing the thumb without having to repaint the entire control, this method can be used in the **SetPosition** method to

Figure 10.5

Drawing the
RzTrackBar's
Thumb.

avoid flicker and unnecessary work. The modified version of **SetPosition** incorporating **DrawThumb** is shown in Listing 10.3. Notice how the old background is restored before drawing the thumb.

Listing 10.3 The Improved SetPosition Method

```
procedure TRzTrackBar.SetPosition( Value : Integer );
begin
  if Value <> FPosition then
  begin
    if Value < FMin then                                  { Range Checking }
      Value := FMin
    else if Value > FMax then
      Value := FMax;

    FPosition := Value;

    { No need to be fancy in Design-mode.  Simply invalidate the control.    }
    { Besides, it is not appropriate to call the Change event at design-time. }

    if csDesigning in ComponentState then
      Invalidate
    else
    begin
                        { Erase old thumb image by drawing background bitmap }
      Canvas.Draw( FThumbRct.Left, FThumbRct.Top, FBackgroundBmp );

      DrawThumb;                                  { Draw thumb at new location }
      Change;                                        { Trigger Change event }
    end;
  end;
end; {= TRzTrackBar.SetPosition =}
```

As an aside, notice the **ComponentState** test. If the **ComponentState** property contains the **csDesigning** flag, the component is being used within the Form Designer. At design-time, it is sufficient to simply invalidate the control if the position value is changed. Besides, the **Change** event does not need to be generated at design-time.

Using Bitmaps from a Resource File

The **DrawThumb** method described earlier depends on a series of bitmaps representing the different styles and sizes of thumbs that can be used in the RzTrackBar component. Eighteen bitmaps are stored in the RZTRKBAR.RES binary resource file.

Two of these bitmaps are shown in Figure 10.4. The **MedHorzThumb** and **MedHorzThumbMask** bitmaps are used when displaying the thumb for a track bar that has its **Orientation** property set to **toHorizontal**, **ThumbStyle** set to **tsPointer**, and **ThumbSize** set to **tsMedium**. The remaining bitmaps in the RES file are used for the other combinations of these three properties.

Using the bitmaps in a component requires two steps. First, the resource file must be included in the component unit. The $R compiler directive is used to specify the name of the resource file to include. For the RzTrkBar unit, the following line includes the bitmap resource file:

```
{$R RZTRKBAR.RES}
```

Once the bitmaps are included, they need to be loaded into **TBitmap** objects so that they can be used. This is accomplished by using the **LoadBitmap** API function. Since this function returns a handle to a Windows bitmap object, **LoadBitmap** is used in the following way:

```
var
  SampleBmp : TBitmap;
. . .
  SampleBmp.Handle := LoadBitmap( HInstance, 'MedHorzThumb' );
```

The return value of **LoadBitmap** is assigned to the **Handle** property of the **TBitmap** object. The **HInstance** parameter is defined internally by Delphi and represents the current instance of the application. Since the bitmap resource file is linked into the application, this parameter allows the **LoadBitmap** function to find the appropriate bitmap.

Creating a Wrapper Component

The **TWinControl** class provides more than just support for the input focus. While this is a major advantage of the class, **TWinControl** also provides support for a number of other messages that are not available to graphical controls. Most important is the ability to manage the window handle. The **TWinControl** class also provides the functionality necessary to support using traditional Windows custom controls within Delphi.

Delphi supports the use of traditional Windows custom controls (that is, DLL-based controls) by creating component wrappers that interface between the Delphi environment and the control's DLL. To demonstrate this process, we will be constructing component wrappers for the check box and radio button controls found in Borland's Windows Custom Controls (BWCC) library.

Why not just build a new native VCL component? There are several reasons that you may opt to create a component wrapper rather than build an entirely new control. First, you may have an existing custom control library that you wish to continue using in Delphi. This is especially important if the library contains stable, well-tested controls.

Another reason for creating component wrappers is to support development in multiple languages. Windows custom controls are not product-bound in the same way that Delphi's VCL components are. If you need to develop applications in different programming languages, creating a component wrapper to enable using the custom control in Delphi may be a viable solution.

Another reason is that it may not be worth the effort to rebuild the control as a Delphi component. Because building a component wrapper for a control is significantly less complicated than building a entirely new control from scratch (especially for ambitious controls like grids or charts), creating a component wrapper provides a quick way of incorporating a custom control into your Delphi applications.

The RzBwcc Components

Those of you who have experience with any Borland product are probably familiar with the BWCC-style controls. (These contain stylish glyphs for message boxes and the "chiseled steel" look in various places.) Figure 10.6 shows the BWCC style check box and radio button controls at work in a Delphi application. Listing 10.4 contains the source code for the RzBwcc unit, which implements the **TRzBwccCheckBox** and **TRzBwccRadioButton** component classes.

For more examples of creating component wrappers, look at the **StdCtrls** unit, which contains the Delphi components for all of the standard controls provided by Windows. Because the standard controls are implemented in custom control libraries, the principles described here are the same as those used in the **StdCtrls** unit.

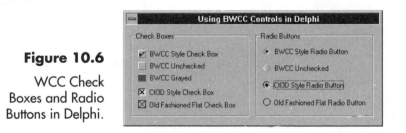

Figure 10.6

WCC Check
Boxes and Radio
Buttons in Delphi.

Listing 10.4   RZBWCC.PAS—The RzBwcc Unit

```
{==============================================================}
{= RzBwcc Unit                                                =}
{=                                                            =}
{= The components in this unit (TRzBwccCheckBox and TRzBwccRadioButton) are =}
{= component wrappers for the corresponding Borland Style controls found in =}
{= the BWCC custom control library (BWCC.DLL).                 =}
{=                                                            =}
{= Building Custom Delphi Components - Ray Konopka             =}
{==============================================================}

unit RzBwcc;

interface

uses
  Messages, Classes, Graphics, Controls, StdCtrls, Menus, RzCommon;

type
  TRzBwccCheckBox = class( TWinControl )
  private
    FAlignment : TLeftRight;
    FAllowGrayed : Boolean;
    FState : TCheckBoxState;
    procedure SetAlignment( Value : TLeftRight );
    function GetChecked: Boolean;
    procedure SetChecked( Value : Boolean );
    procedure SetState( Value : TCheckBoxState );
    procedure CMDialogChar( var Msg : TCMDialogChar ); message cm_DialogChar;
    procedure CNCommand( var Msg : TWMCommand ); message cn_Command;
  protected
    procedure ToggleState; virtual;
    procedure CreateParams( var Params : TCreateParams ); override;
    procedure CreateWnd; override;
  public
    constructor Create( AOwner : TComponent ); override;
  published
    property Alignment: TLeftRight
      read FAlignment
      write SetAlignment
      default taRightJustify;
```

```
      property AllowGrayed: Boolean
        read FAllowGrayed
        write FAllowGrayed
        default False;

      property Checked: Boolean
        read GetChecked
        write SetChecked
        stored False;

      property State: TCheckBoxState
        read FState
        write SetState
        default cbUnchecked;

      { Inherited Properties and Events }
      property Caption;
      property Color;
      property DragCursor;
      property DragMode;
      property Enabled;
      property Font;
      property ParentColor;
      property ParentFont;
      property ParentShowHint;
      property PopupMenu;
      property ShowHint;
      property TabOrder;
      property TabStop default True;
      property Visible;
      property OnClick;
      property OnDragDrop;
      property OnDragOver;
      property OnEndDrag;
      property OnEnter;
      property OnExit;
      property OnKeyDown;
      property OnKeyPress;
      property OnKeyUp;
      property OnMouseDown;
      property OnMouseMove;
      property OnMouseUp;
    end;


  TRzBwccRadioButton = class( TButtonControl )
  private
    FAlignment: TLeftRight;
    FChecked: Boolean;
    procedure SetAlignment( Value : TLeftRight );
    procedure SetChecked( Value : Boolean );
    procedure CMDialogChar( var Msg : TCMDialogChar ); message cm_DialogChar;
```

```
    procedure CNCommand( var Msg : TWMCommand ); message cn_Command;
  protected
    procedure CreateParams( var Params : TCreateParams ); override;
    procedure CreateWnd; override;
  public
    constructor Create( AOwner : TComponent ); override;
  published
    property Alignment : TLeftRight
      read FAlignment
      write SetAlignment
      default laRightJustify;

    property Checked : Boolean
      read FChecked
      write SetChecked
      default False;

    { Inherited Properties and Events }
    property Caption;
    property Color;
    property Ctl3D;
    property DragCursor;
    property DragMode;
    property Enabled;
    property Font;
    property ParentColor;
    property ParentCtl3D;
    property ParentFont;
    property ParentShowHint;
    property PopupMenu;
    property ShowHint;
    property TabOrder;
    property TabStop default True;
    property Visible;
    property OnClick;
    property OnDblClick;
    property OnDragDrop;
    property OnDragOver;
    property OnEndDrag;
    property OnEnter;
    property OnExit;
    property OnKeyDown;
    property OnKeyPress;
    property OnKeyUp;
    property OnMouseDown;
    property OnMouseMove;
    property OnMouseUp;
  end;


procedure Register;

implementation
```

```
uses
  WinTypes, WinProcs, SysUtils, Forms;

const
  SLoadLibraryError = 'Failed to load %s for %s. '#13 +
                       'LoadLibrary error code %d.';
  LibName = 'BWCC.DLL';

var
  BwccHandle : THandle;                    { Handle for BWCC Dynamic Link Library }


{===============================}
{== TRzBwccCheckBox Methods ==}
{===============================}

constructor TRzBwccCheckBox.Create( AOwner : TComponent );
begin
  if BwccHandle < 32 then              { If BWCC not loaded, raise an exception }
    raise EComponentError.CreateFmt( SLoadLibraryError, [ LibName,
                                                         'TRzBwccCheckBox',
                                                         BwccHandle ] );

  inherited Create( AOwner );
  ControlStyle := [ csSetCaption, csDoubleClicks ];
  FAlignment := taRightJustify;        { Default Caption on right of check box }
  Height := 17;
  Width := 140;
  TabStop := True;
end;


procedure TRzBwccCheckBox.CreateParams( var Params : TCreateParams );
begin
  inherited CreateParams( Params );
  CreateSubClass( Params, 'BorCheck' );  { Specify BWCC Class Name for Control }

  with Params do
  begin
    { Use the bs_3State style and not bs_Auto3State, so that we can control }
    { the display of the Grayed state using the AllowGrayed property.      }

    Style := Style or bs_3State;
    if FAlignment = taLeftJustify then
      Style := Style or bs_LeftText;          { Add style flag if Left aligned }
  end;
end;


procedure TRzBwccCheckBox.CreateWnd;
begin
  inherited CreateWnd;
  Perform( bm_SetCheck, Cardinal( FState ), 0 );
end;
```

```pascal
procedure TRzBwccCheckBox.ToggleState;
begin
  { Cycle through states:  [Grayed ->] Checked -> Unchecked -> }
  case FState of
    cbUnchecked:
    begin
      if AllowGrayed then
        State := cbGrayed
      else
        State := cbChecked;
    end;

    cbChecked:
      State := cbUnchecked;

    cbGrayed:
      State := cbChecked;
  end; { case }
end;


procedure TRzBwccCheckBox.SetAlignment( Value : TLeftRight );
begin
  if Value <> FAlignment then
  begin
    FAlignment := Value;
    RecreateWnd;                    { Recreate the window handle with new style }
  end;
end;


function TRzBwccCheckBox.GetChecked : Boolean;
begin
  Result := Perform( bm_GetCheck, 0, 0 ) = Ord( cbChecked );
end;


procedure TRzBwccCheckBox.SetChecked( Value : Boolean );
begin
  if Value then
    State := cbChecked
  else
    State := cbUnchecked;
end;


procedure TRzBwccCheckBox.SetState( Value : TCheckBoxState );
begin
  if Value <> State then
  begin
    FState := Value;
    if HandleAllocated then
```

```
      Perform( bm_SetCheck, Cardinal( FState ), 0 );
    Click;                                      { Trigger OnClick event }
  end;
end;



{= TRzBwccCheckBox.CMDialogChar                                     =}
{=   The cmDialogChar component message is handled so that if the user presses =}
{=   the Access key for the control (e.g. Alt+C), the component will gain the =}
{=   focus and toggle its state.                                    =}

procedure TRzBwccCheckBox.CMDialogChar( var Msg : TCMDialogChar );
begin
  with Msg do
  begin
    if IsAccel( CharCode, Caption ) and CanFocus then
    begin
      SetFocus;
      if Focused then
        ToggleState;              { If able to change focus, toggle its state }
      Result := 1;      { Setting to 1 indicates that message has been handled }
    end
    else
      inherited;
  end;
end;



{= TRzBwccCheckBox.CNCommand                                        =}
{=   This component notification message is used to indicate when the user =}
{=   clicked on the component.  This method is responsible for changing the =}
{=   state of the check box.                                        =}

procedure TRzBwccCheckBox.CNCommand( var Msg : TWMCommand );
begin
  if Msg.NotifyCode = bn_Clicked then
    ToggleState;
end;




{===============================}
{-- TRzBwccRadioButton Methods --}
{===============================}

constructor TRzBwccRadioButton.Create( AOwner : TComponent );
begin
  if BwccHandle < 32 then              { If Bwcc not loaded, raise an exception }
    raise EComponentError.CreateFmt( SLoadLibraryError, [ LibName,
                                              'TRzBwccRadioButton',
                                              BwccHandle ] );
```

```
    inherited Create( AOwner );
    ControlStyle := [ csSetCaption, csDoubleClicks ];
    FAlignment := taRightJustify;          { Default Caption on right of check box }
    Height := 17;
    Width := 140;
    TabStop := True;
end;


procedure TRzBwccRadioButton.CreateParams( var Params : TCreateParams );
begin
  inherited CreateParams( Params );
  CreateSubClass( Params, 'BorRadio' );  { Specify BWCC class name for control }


  with Params do
  begin
    Style := Style or bs_AutoRadioButton;
    if FAlignment = taLeftJustify then
      Style := Style or bs_LeftText;         { Add style flag if Left aligned }
  end;
end;


procedure TRzBwccRadioButton.CreateWnd;
begin
  inherited CreateWnd;
  Perform( bm_SetCheck, Cardinal( FChecked ), 0 );
end;


procedure TRzBwccRadioButton.SetAlignment( Value : TLeftRight );
begin
  if Value <> FAlignment then
  begin
    FAlignment := Value;
    RecreateWnd;                    { Recreate the window handle with new style }
  end;
end;


procedure TRzBwccRadioButton.SetChecked( Value : Boolean );

  procedure TurnOffSiblings;
  var
    I : Integer;
    Sibling : TControl;
  begin
    if Parent <> nil then
    begin
      for I := 0 to Parent.ControlCount - 1 do
      begin
```

```
          Sibling := Parent.Controls[ I ];
          if ( Sibling <> Self ) and ( Sibling is TRzBwccRadioButton ) then
            TRzBwccRadioButton( Sibling ).SetChecked( False );
      end;
    end;
  end; {= TurnOffSiblings =}

begin   {= TRzBwccRadioButton.SetChecked =}
  if Value <> FChecked then
  begin
    FChecked := Value;
    TabStop := Value;
    if HandleAllocated then
      Perform( bm_SetCheck, Cardinal( FChecked ), 0 );

    if FChecked then
    begin
      TurnOffSiblings;
      Click;                                   { Trigger OnClick event }
    end;
  end;
end; {= TRzBwccRadioButton.SetChecked =}


procedure TRzBwccRadioButton.CMDialogChar( var Msg : TCMDialogChar );
begin
  with Msg do
  begin
    if IsAccel( CharCode, Caption ) and CanFocus then
    begin
      SetFocus;
      Result := 1;     { Setting to 1 indicates that message has been handled }
    end
    else
      inherited;
  end;
end;


procedure TRzBwccRadioButton.CNCommand( var Msg : TWMCommand );
begin
  case Msg.NotifyCode of
    bn_Clicked:
      SetChecked( True );

    bn_DoubleClicked :
      DblClick;
  end;
end;


{=====================}
{== Register Procedure ==}
{=====================}
```

```
procedure Register;
begin
  RegisterComponents( RaizePage, [ TRzBwccCheckBox, TRzBwccRadioButton ] );
end;
```

```
{=================================}
{== RzBwccExitProc Procedure ==}
{=================================}
```

```
var
  ErrorMode : Cardinal;
```

```
procedure FreeBwccDLL; far;
begin
  if BwccHandle >= 32 then                { If DLL was successfully loaded... }
    FreeLibrary( BwccHandle );                                   { Free it }
end;
```

```
initialization
      { Prevent generic Windows Error Message if Windows Cannot Find the DLL }
  ErrorMode := SetErrorMode( sem_NoOpenFileErrorBox );
  BwccHandle := LoadLibrary( LibName );              { Load BWCC control DLL }
  SetErrorMode( ErrorMode );

                      { Add exit procedure to guarantee BWCC.DLL gets freed }
  AddExitProc( FreeBwccDLL );
end.
```

Initialization and Cleanup

The Borland custom controls are located in the BWCC.DLL file. In order to use these component wrappers, the RzBwcc unit must ensure that the BWCC.DLL is loaded before the control is accessed. This is handled by adding code to the **initialization** section of the RzBwcc unit as shown in Listing 10.5.

Listing 10.5   Initializing the RzBwcc Unit

```
const
  LibName = 'BWCC.DLL';

var
  BwccHandle : THandle;               { Handle for BWCC Dynamic Link Library }
  ErrorMode : Cardinal;


procedure FreeBwccDLL; far;
begin
```

```
   if BwccHandle >= 32 then                    { If DLL was successfully loaded... }
     FreeLibrary( BwccHandle );                                     { Free it }
end;


initialization
       { Prevent generic Windows Error Message if Windows Cannot Find the DLL }
   ErrorMode := SetErrorMode( sem_NoOpenFileErrorBox );
   BwccHandle := LoadLibrary( LibName );                 { Load BWCC control DLL }
   SetErrorMode( ErrorMode );

                          { Add exit procedure to guarantee BWCC.DLL gets freed }
   AddExitProc( FreeBwccDLL );
end.
```

The DLL is explicitly loaded using the **LoadLibrary** API function. **LoadLibrary** returns a module handle that is used to reference the DLL. This handle is stored in a unit variable for future reference. The call to **LoadLibrary** is wrapped with calls to **SetErrorMode**. By default, if Windows cannot find the DLL file specified in the call to **LoadLibrary**, an error message is displayed. This process can be overridden by passing **sem_NoOpenFileErrorBox** flag to the **SetErrorMode** function. Of course, after the call to **LoadLibrary**, the original error mode is restored.

The last step performed by the initialization code is to add an exit procedure to Delphi's exit procedure chain. The **AddExitProc** procedure from the SysUtils unit is used to specify a **far** procedure that is guaranteed to be called when the application terminates. It is through this exit procedure that the BWCC library is freed.

The TRzBwccCheckBox Class

Although the RzBwcc unit implements both the **TRzBwccCheckBox** and **TRzBwccRadioButton** classes, the principles involved in creating both components are roughly equivalent. Only the check box control will be covered here.

The **TRzBwccCheckBox** class is a direct descendant of the **TWinControl** class. **TWinControl** is used as the ancestor rather than **TCustomControl** because the underlying custom control already knows how to paint itself. Thus, our Delphi counterpart does not need to be concerned with painting.

In order to interface to the underlying custom control, the Delphi component wrapper needs to override the **Create** constructor and the **CreateParams** method. The constructor for a component wrapper, like native VCL components, is responsible for setting initial values for the underlying control.

A good practice to follow in the constructor for component wrappers is to test to see if the desired DLL was successfully loaded. In the **TRzBwccCheckBox.Create** constructor, if the **BwccHandle** variable is less than 32, the BWCC.DLL library was not successfully loaded. In this event, an exception is raised indicating the error and the construction is aborted.

The most important method in a component wrapper is the **CreateParams** method. Within this method, Windows is instructed to treat this component as a subclass of the underlying custom control. This is accomplished by using the **CreateSubClass** method. **CreateSubClass** accepts two parameters: the **Params** object, and the name of a window class. The window class corresponds to the class name used by the underlying control. For the controls in RzBwcc, the class names are **BorCheck** and **BorRadio**.

CreateSubClass should be called immediately following the call to the inherited **CreateParams** method. After calling **CreateSubClass**, the **Style** field of the **Params** object can be set to alter the style of the custom control. For example, in the **TRzBwccCheckBox** class, the **Params.Style** field is set to include the **bs_3State** style.

Using Messages to Interact with the Control

Once the component is subclassed as the underlying control, it can be installed and dropped onto a Delphi form. However, although the control will appear to be working, it will not be very usable. That is, we have not yet defined any properties to allow the user to manipulate the component.

The **TRzBwccCheckBox** class mimicks the **TCustomCheckBox** class in the StdCtrls unit. This was done so that the new BWCC style check box could be manipulated in much the same way as the standard check box component. To this end, **TRzBwccCheckBox** declares four properties:

The **Alignment** property determines where the **Caption** appears. The default setting is **taRightJustify**. (Speaking of the **Caption**, you will note that the **TWinControl** class does provide automatic support for several properties and events including **Caption**, **Font**, **OnClick**, and **OnKeyPress**.) The second property, **AllowGrayed**, is used to control whether or not the check box can display a third, *grayed*, state.

The **Checked** and **State** properties are related to each other. The **Checked** property is a Boolean value that is set to **True** if the check box has a check in it. The

State property is an enumerated value that contains either **cbUncheck**, **chChecked**, or **cbGrayed**. Like **Checked**, the value of **State** also depends on what is displayed in the check box.

The access methods for these properties are what is of interest. To start with, the **SetAlignment** method looks like a standard write access method except that instead of calling **Invalidate**, **RecreateWnd** is called. **RecreateWnd**, like its name suggests, re-creates the underlying window and allocates a new window handle. So, why is this necessary? When the alignment is changed, the control window must be re-created because the alignment is controlled through a window style and not through a window message. Therefore, by calling **RecreateWnd**, the **CreateParams** method will get called again, and the window style can be adjusted according to the **FAlignment** field.

The **Checked** value, on the other hand, is obtained through a message. The **GetChecked** method sends the **bm_GetCheck** message to the underlying window using the **Perform** method. (The actual messages that must be sent will vary from control to control. Consult the control's vendor to find out what messages are available.) The **bm_GetCheck** message returns either 0, 1, or 2 to represent unchecked, checked, or grayed, respectively.

The **SetState** method uses the **bm_SetCheck** message to instruct the underlying control to display a particular state. An interesting aspect of the **State** property is that although its value can be retrieved using the **bm_GetCheck** message, an internal **FState** field is maintained for the **TRzBwccCheckBox** class. The **FState** field is needed in the event the control window needs to be re-created. When the underlying BWCC check box is re-created, its state is reset to unchecked—the state it had just before being re-created is lost. The **FState** field makes the **State** property persistent.

However, just providing the **FState** field is not enough. When the control is re-created, the state of the control still gets cleared. In order to re-establish the state of the check box, we need to override the **CreateWnd** method. Recall from Chapter 6 that the **CreateWnd** method is called whenever the underlying window needs to be created. For the **TRzBwccCheckBox** class, the **CreateWnd** method first calls its inherited method, then sends a **bm_SetCheck** message to the newly created window to re-establish the previous check box state.

Component Notification Messages

Another method of interest in the **TRzBwccCheckBox** class is the **CNCommand** method. **CNCommand** is a message handling method that responds to the **cn_Command** *component notification* message. Component notifications are sent to a component when the component's underlying window receives a corresponding Windows message. For example, the **cn_Command** message is sent when the control window receives a **wm_Command** message. Table 10.3 lists all of the available notification messages.

So why does the RzBwccCheckBox component need to be notified of **wm_Command** messages? Since the style of the check box was set to **bs_3State** and not **bs_Auto3State**, the component is responsible for changing the state of the check box when the control is clicked. By trapping the **cn_Command** notification message, the RzBwccCheckBox component is notified whenever the control is clicked. In the event of such a notification, the **ToggleState** method is called to update the state of the control.

Table 10.3 Delphi's Component Notification Messages

Notification Message	Sent when Following Windows Message Is Received Constant
cn_CharToItem	wm_CharToItem
cn_Command	wm_Command
cn_CompareItem	wm_CompareItem
cn_CtlColor	wm_CtlColor
cn_DeleteItem	wm_DeleteItem
cn_DrawItem	wm_DrawItem
cn_HScroll	wm_HScroll
cn_MeasureItem	wm_MeasureItem
cn_ParentNotify	wm_ParentNotify
cn_VKeyToItem	wm_VKeyToItem
cn_VScroll	wm_VScroll
cn_KeyDown	wm_KeyDown
cn_KeyUp	wm_KeyUp
cn_Char	wm_Char
cn_SysKeyDown	wm_SysKeyDown
cn_SysChar	wm_SysChar

Encapsulating Multiple Controls

All of the components that we have encountered so far have one thing in common: They all encapsulate a single control. While this is certainly the norm, it is by no means a restriction. The VCL is indeed sufficiently rich to support encapsulating multiple controls within a single larger control. To illustrate the issues involved in encapsulating multiple controls, we'll build a data-aware mailing address component.

The RzAddress component is a single component that consists of separate subcomponents representing the different fields in a typical U.S. address. The component is made up of five DBEdit components, one DBComboBox, and six Label components. The layout of these components is illustrated in Figure 10.7, which shows the RzAddress component being used in an application.

Before getting into the details of the **TRzAddress** class, you may be wondering why anyone would want to build a component like this. Aside from the ever-popular answer, "Because you can," there are two principle reasons for encapsulating multiple controls in a single component. The first is to promote *reusability*, and the second is to promote *consistency*.

For data-entry applications, entering an address is a very common task. Unfortunately, the forms used to enter address information generally capture additional information not relevant to the address. This extra information prevents the form from being reused in other applications. However, a component like RzAddress forces you to think about reusing a *portion* of the form rather than the entire form.

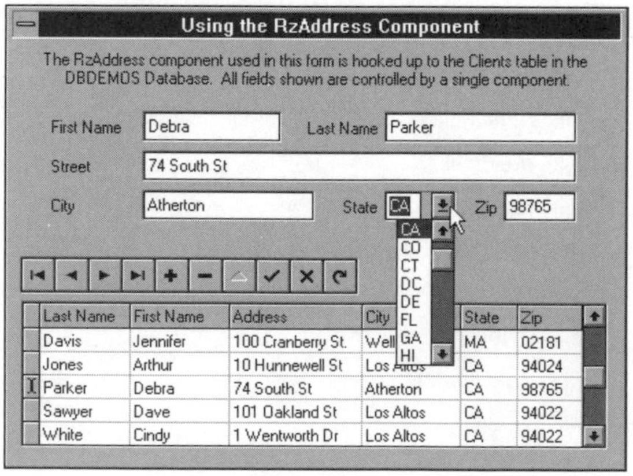

Figure 10.7

Editing an
Address the
Easy Way!

The second benefit, *consistency*, is more of an issue with end users. Let's continue with the address example here. Without a reusable component, every application that provides fields for entering an address will have slight variations between them. The length of the last name field may be shorter in one application than another. The state field may be represented by an edit field in one program and by a combo box in another. By creating a single component to represent the group of controls, consistency can be maintained among applications.

The TRzAddress Class

The RzAddress component is implemented in the RzAddr unit, which is shown in Listing 10.6. The **TRzAddress** class descends from **TWinControl** because it essentially needs to be able to contain other controls within itself, and by now we know that a window handle is needed to support this feature. **TWinControl** is not your only option. If you would like a border around the controls, the **TPanel** or **TGroupBox** classes could serve as ancestors equally well.

Listing 10.6   RZADDR.PAS—The RzAddr Unit

```
{==============================================================}
{= RzAddr Unit                                               =}
{=                                                           =}
{= This unit implements the RzAddress component which is comprised of the  =}
{= the following edit fields: First Name, Last Name, Street, City, and Zip.  =}
{= The State field is actually a combo box which is populated with the 50  =}
{= states and the District of Columbia. The edit fields are data-aware,  =}
{= and thus this component can be hooked up to a DataSource.  =}
{=                                                           =}
{= Building Custom Delphi Components - Ray Konopka           =}
{==============================================================}

unit RzAddr;

interface

uses
  Classes, Controls, StdCtrls, DB, DBCtrls, Graphics, ExtCtrls, RzCommon;

type
  TEditField = ( efFirstName, efLastName, efStreet, efCity, efZip );
  TEditChangeEvent = procedure ( Field : TEditField; Text : string ) of object;

  TRzAddress = class( TWinControl )
  private
    FEdtFirstName : TDBEdit;
    FEdtLastName : TDBEdit;
```

```
    FEdtStreet : TDBEdit;
    FEdtCity : TDBEdit;
    FCbxState : TDBComboBox;
    FEdtZip : TDBEdit;
    FStateList : TStringList;        { Internal List of State Abbreviations }
    FOnChange : TEditChangeEvent;    { Common Change Event for all Edit Fields }

    function GetCharCase : TEditCharCase;
    procedure SetCharCase( Value : TEditCharCase );
    function GetDataSource : TDataSource;
    procedure SetDataSource( Value : TDataSource );
    function GetField( Index : Integer ) : string;
    procedure SetField( Index : Integer; Value : string );

    function CreateEdit : TDBEdit;
    function CreateLabel( S : string ) : TLabel;
    function CreateCombo : TDBComboBox;
    procedure CreateStateList;
    procedure DoChange( Sender : TObject );
  protected
    procedure Change( Field : TEditField; Text : string ); dynamic;
    procedure CreateWnd; override;
  public
    constructor Create( AOwner : TComponent ); override;
    destructor Destroy; override;

    property EdtFirstName : TDBEdit
      read FEdtFirstName;

  published
    property CharCase : TEditCharCase
      read GetCharCase
      write SetCharCase;

    property DataSource : TDataSource
      read GetDataSource
      write SetDataSource;

    property FirstNameField : string
      index 1
      read GetField
      write SetField;

    property LastNameField : string
      index 2
      read GetField
      write SetField;

    property StreetField : string
      index 3
      read GetField
      write SetField;
```

```
    property CityField : string
      index 4
      read GetField
      write SetField;

    property StateField : string
      index 5
      read GetField
      write SetField;

    property ZipField : string
      index 6
      read GetField
      write SetField;

    property OnChange : TEditChangeEvent
      read FOnChange
      write FOnChange;

    property Font;
    property ParentFont;
  end;

procedure Register;

implementation

uses
  DsgnIntf;

{=======================}
{== TRzAddress Methods ==}
{=======================}


constructor TRzAddress.Create( AOwner : TComponent );
var
  TempLbl : TLabel;
begin
  inherited Create( AOwner );

  { All labels are created using the TempLbl component because we do not need  }
  { to reference these controls elsewhere.  Cleanup is handled when the         }
  { TComponent ancestor class frees all components on the Components list.       }

  TempLbl := CreateLabel( 'First Name' );
  TempLbl.SetBounds( 0, 8, 50, 13 );
  FEdtFirstName := CreateEdit;
  FEdtFirstName.SetBounds( 67, 4, 97, 20 );

  TempLbl := CreateLabel( 'Last Name' );
  TempLbl.SetBounds( 182, 8, 52, 13 );
```

```
  TempLbl.Alignment := taRightJustify;
  FEdtLastName := CreateEdit;
  FEdtLastName.SetBounds( 240, 4, 137, 20 );

  TempLbl := CreateLabel( 'Street' );
  TempLbl.SetBounds( 0, 36, 28, 13 );
  FEdtStreet := CreateEdit;
  FEdtStreet.SetBounds( 67, 32, 310, 20 );

  TempLbl := CreateLabel( 'City' );
  TempLbl.SetBounds( 0, 64, 17, 13 );
  FEdtCity := CreateEdit;
  FEdtCity.SetBounds( 67, 60, 121, 20 );

  TempLbl := CreateLabel( 'State' );
  TempLbl.SetBounds( 200, 64, 34, 13 );
  TempLbl.Alignment := taRightJustify;
  FCbxState := CreateCombo;
  FCbxState.SetBounds( 240, 60, 50, 20 );

  TempLbl := CreateLabel( 'Zip' );
  TempLbl.SetBounds( 300, 64, 20, 13 );
  TempLbl.Alignment := taRightJustify;
  FEdtZip := CreateEdit;
  FEdtZip.SetBounds( 326, 60, 51, 20 );

  CreateStateList;

  Width := 382;
  Height := 86;
end; {= TRzAddress.Create =}


destructor TRzAddress.Destroy;
begin
  FStateList.Free;
  inherited Destroy;
end;


function TRzAddress.CreateLabel( S : string ) : TLabel;
begin
  Result := TLabel.Create( Self );
  Result.Parent := Self;
  Result.Visible := True;
  Result.Caption := S;
end;


function TRzAddress.CreateEdit : TDBEdit;
begin
  Result := TDBEdit.Create( Self );
```

```
    Result.Parent := Self;
    Result.Visible := True;
    Result.OnChange := DoChange;        { Assign OnChange event of each Edit field }
                                        { to point to TRzAddress.DoChange method   }
end;


function TRzAddress.CreateCombo : TDBComboBox;
begin
  Result := TDBComboBox.Create( Self );
  Result.Parent := Self;
  Result.Visible := True;
  Result.Sorted := True;
end;


procedure TRzAddress.CreateWnd;
begin
  inherited CreateWnd;
  { When CreateWnd is called, the Items list of FCbxState is cleared. }
  { Therefore, the contents of the FStateList are copied back into FCbxState }

  FCbxState.Items.Assign( FStateList );
end;


procedure TRzAddress.CreateStateList;
begin
  FStateList := TStringList.Create;
  FStateList.Add( 'AK' );
  FStateList.Add( 'AL' );
  FStateList.Add( 'AR' );
  FStateList.Add( 'AZ' );
  FStateList.Add( 'CA' );
  FStateList.Add( 'CO' );
  FStateList.Add( 'CT' );
  FStateList.Add( 'DC' );
  FStateList.Add( 'DE' );
  FStateList.Add( 'FL' );
  FStateList.Add( 'GA' );
  FStateList.Add( 'HI' );
  FStateList.Add( 'IA' );
  FStateList.Add( 'ID' );
  FStateList.Add( 'IL' );
  FStateList.Add( 'IN' );
  FStateList.Add( 'KS' );
  FStateList.Add( 'KY' );
  FStateList.Add( 'LA' );
  FStateList.Add( 'MA' );
  FStateList.Add( 'MD' );
  FStateList.Add( 'ME' );
  FStateList.Add( 'MI' );
```

```
  FStateList.Add( 'MN' );
  FStateList.Add( 'MO' );
  FStateList.Add( 'MS' );
  FStateList.Add( 'MT' );
  FStateList.Add( 'NC' );
  FStateList.Add( 'ND' );
  FStateList.Add( 'NE' );
  FStateList.Add( 'NH' );
  FStateList.Add( 'NJ' );
  FStateList.Add( 'NM' );
  FStateList.Add( 'NV' );
  FStateList.Add( 'NY' );
  FStateList.Add( 'OH' );
  FStateList.Add( 'OK' );
  FStateList.Add( 'OR' );
  FStateList.Add( 'PA' );
  FStateList.Add( 'RI' );
  FStateList.Add( 'SC' );
  FStateList.Add( 'SD' );
  FStateList.Add( 'TN' );
  FStateList.Add( 'TX' );
  FStateList.Add( 'UT' );
  FStateList.Add( 'VA' );
  FStateList.Add( 'VT' );
  FStateList.Add( 'WA' );
  FStateList.Add( 'WI' );
  FStateList.Add( 'WV' );
  FStateList.Add( 'WY' );
end; {= TRzAddress.CreateStateList =}


procedure TRzAddress.Change( Field : TEditField; Text : string );
begin
  if Assigned( FOnChange ) then
    FOnChange( Field, Text );
end;


{= TRzAddress.DoChange                                                =}
{=    This method gets called if the OnChange event occurs for any of the edit =}
{=    fields contained in this component.  The Change event dispatch method is =}
{=    called to surface those events to the user.                     =}

procedure TRzAddress.DoChange( Sender : TObject );
var
  Field : TEditField;
begin
  if Sender = FEdtFirstName then
    Field := efFirstName
  else if Sender = FEdtLastName then
    Field := efLastName
  else if Sender = FEdtStreet then
```

```
      Field := efStreet
   else if Sender = FEdtCity then
      Field := efCity
   else
      Field := efZip;
   Change( Field, TDBEdit( Sender ).Text );
end;


function TRzAddress.GetCharCase : TEditCharCase;
begin
   Result := FEdtFirstName.CharCase;
end;


procedure TRzAddress.SetCharCase( Value : TEditCharCase );
begin
   if Value <> FEdtFirstName.CharCase then
   begin
      FEdtFirstName.CharCase := Value;
      FEdtLastName.CharCase := Value;
      FEdtStreet.CharCase := Value;
      FEdtCity.CharCase := Value;
      FEdtZip.CharCase := Value;
   end;
end;


function TRzAddress.GetDataSource : TDataSource;
begin
   { Use FEdtFirstName to Get Current DataSource }
   Result := FEdtFirstName.DataSource;
end;


procedure TRzAddress.SetDataSource( Value : TDataSource );
begin
   if Value <> FEdtFirstName.DataSource then
   begin
      { Assign All Internal Controls to Same DataSource }
      FEdtFirstName.DataSource := Value;
      FEdtLastName.DataSource := Value;
      FEdtStreet.DataSource := Value;
      FEdtCity.DataSource := Value;
      FCbxState.DataSource := Value;
      FEdtZip.DataSource := Value;
   end;
end;


function TRzAddress.GetField( Index : Integer ) : string;
begin
   case Index of
```

```
   1: Result := FEdtFirstName.DataField;
   2: Result := FEdtLastName.DataField;
   3: Result := FEdtStreet.DataField;
   4: Result := FEdtCity.DataField;
   5: Result := FCbxState.DataField;
   6: Result := FEdtZip.DataField;
  end;

end;


procedure TRzAddress.SetField( Index : Integer; Value : string );
begin
  case Index of
    1: FEdtFirstName.DataField := Value;
    2: FEdtLastName.DataField := Value;
    3: FEdtStreet.DataField := Value;
    4: FEdtCity.DataField := Value;
    5: FCbxState.DataField := Value;
    6: FEdtZip.DataField := Value;
  end;
end;




{=========================}
{== Register Procedure ==}
{=========================}


procedure Register;
begin
  RegisterComponents( RaizePage, [ TRzAddress ] );

  { The following RegisterPropertyEditor calls instruct the Object Inspector   }
  { to hold off accepting the text entered into the specified fields until the }
  { Enter key is pressed.                                                       }

  RegisterPropertyEditor( TypeInfo( string ), TRzAddress,
                          'FirstNameField', TStringProperty );
  RegisterPropertyEditor( TypeInfo( string ), TRzAddress,
                          'LastNameField', TStringProperty );
  RegisterPropertyEditor( TypeInfo( string ), TRzAddress,
                          'StreetField', TStringProperty );
  RegisterPropertyEditor( TypeInfo( string ), TRzAddress,
                          'CityField', TStringProperty );
  RegisterPropertyEditor( TypeInfo( string ), TRzAddress,
                          'StateField', TStringProperty );
  RegisterPropertyEditor( TypeInfo( string ), TRzAddress,
                          'ZipField', TStringProperty );
end;

end.
```

The **private** section of this class contains an object field for each sub-component. The sub-components are created in the **Create** constructor. One by one, each sub-component is dynamically created and positioned within the RzAddress component. Note that the coordinates passed to the **SetBounds** method are relative to the main component's client area.

A few supporting methods are provided to make it easier to construct the sub-components. These include **CreateLabel**, **CreateCombo**, and **CreateEdit**. Each of these methods creates an object of the appropriate type and then sets the **Parent** and **Visible** properties. The **CreateLabel** method then sets the caption of the label, while the **CreateCombo** method sets the **Sorted** property to **True**. The **CreateEdit** method finishes up by assigning the **OnChange** event of the sub-component to point to the **TRzAddress.DoChange** method. We'll come back to the importance of this shortly.

After all of the sub-components are created, the internal **FStateList** is populated. **FStateList** is a string list object that is used to populate the state combo box. The combo box itself cannot be used to store the strings because it is dynamically created and therefore does not provide persistent storage. We could expose a **StateList** property of **TRzAddress**, but there is no real need to give the user direct access to this list.

Since we create the string list within the component, we provide a destructor so that we may free the memory used by the string list. Speaking of destructors, who's responsible for destroying the sub-components? Well, actually we are. What I mean is that the component writer is responsible for making sure the sub-components are released when the main component is destroyed. You may have already noticed that there is no code that specifically frees the sub-components.

When each sub-component is created, **Self** is passed to the **Create** constructor. This causes the sub-component to be placed onto the **TRzAddress.Components** list. The **Components** list, you will recall, is defined in the **TComponent** class. Therefore, when the main component is destroyed, the inherited destructor from **TComponent** takes care of freeing all of the components on the **Components** list. So, as long as a valid owner is passed to the constructor for each sub-component, we do not have to worry about cleaning up the sub-components.

Accessing Sub-Components through Properties

There are three basic ways of accessing a sub-component through the main component. All three involve properties, and each provides a different level of control. The first way is to provide a generic property for the main component that gets mapped to each sub-component. The **DataSource** property is an example of this type of access. Note that the **TRzAddress** class does not maintain an internal field for holding the **DataSource** value. Instead, the sub-components themselves are used to manage the property. As you can see from the **SetDataSource** method, when the **TRzAddress.DataSource** is changed, the **DataSource** properties for all sub-components are updated with the new value.

The second way of providing access to sub-components is to provide individual properties that correspond to properties in each sub-component. The **FirstNameField**, **LastNameField**, and **CityField** are examples of this type of access. Each one of these *field* properties corresponds to the **DataField** property of one of the sub-components. Unlike the **DataSource** property, these field names cannot be shared among the sub-components. Figure 10.8 shows the **FirstNameField** property being edited to link the corresponding sub-component to the appropriate table column. (As an aside, the field properties also provide a good example of using indexed properties. All six properties are supported by the same access methods: **GetField** and **SetField**.)

Figure 10.8

Editing the
FirstNameField
Property.

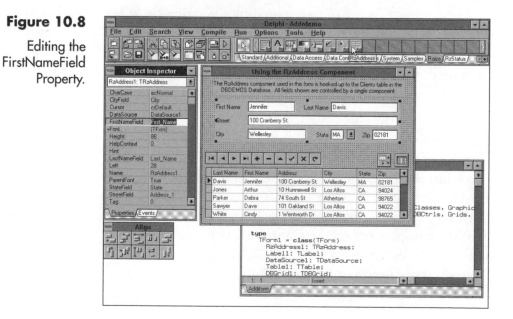

The third way of providing access to sub-components is to expose a reference to the sub-component. Because this gives complete access to the sub-component, it is generally not wise to do this. As an example, the **EdtFirstName** property provides a reference to the **FEdtFirstName** edit field. With this reference, the end user has access to the properties of **FEdtFirstName**, and therefore, could affect the way the entire RzAddress component behaves. For example, the edit control could be moved or resized. More dramatic is the problem of setting the **DataSource** property of the **FEdtFirstName** field directly. The moral is that a sub-component reference can be used to bypass all other types of access.

Exposing Events that Occur in Sub-Components

Earlier, I mentioned that each edit field created gets its **OnChange** event assigned to the **DoChange** method. Like properties, events can be exposed individually or shared. But because of the event architecture, a hybrid between the two can be achieved. When a change event occurs in one of the edit fields, the **DoChange** method is called. Since the **Sender** parameter identifies which component generated the message, this information can be passed on to the end user's event handler for the main component's **OnChange** event.

The **OnChange** event for the RzAddress component receives two parameters. The first parameter is an enumerated value indicating the sub-component that generated the event. For example, if the change event occurred in the **FEdtCity** edit field, the first parameter would have a value of **efCity**. The second parameter contains the current contents of the edit field. Using these two parameters, a user can create a single event handler to handle all of the **OnChange** events that occur within the sub-components.

Looking Ahead...

In the next chapter, we'll be taking a slight detour from the visual components presented in this and the previous chapter. Chapter 11 starts by focusing on the issues involved in constructing non-visual components. Of course, our detour will not last very long. After covering non-visual control, we quickly get back into the visual nature of component building and investigate how to construct dialog box components.

Chapter 11

Dialogs and Nonvisual Components

Dialogs and Nonvisual Components

How you look is sometimes less important than what you do—especially for Delphi VCL components.

W hy are dialog box components and nonvisual components grouped into the same chapter? Clearly dialog components, like OpenDialog, are visual in nature. This is true, but the underlying component class for both dialogs and nonvisual components are very similar. Both types descend directly from **TComponent** and thus appear in the Delphi Form Designer as icons showing the same image that appears in the component palette. The most distinguishing feature between these types of components and the ones covered in earlier chapters is that neither dialog components nor nonvisual components take up any real estate on the form where they are placed.

Both types of components have fewer published properties because there are generally fewer attributes that can be modified at design-time for these two types of components. Most published properties control some visual aspect of a component. Without a visual interface, these types of properties are not needed.

By design, dialog components encapsulate an external module (a form) into a component. Many nonvisual components also encapsulate an external module within a component framework. However, instead of a form, an application programming interface (API) or even a single function may be the external module being encapsulated. In this respect, nonvisual and dialog components serve as component wrappers around an existing code base, much like the component wrappers presented in Chapter 10.

No matter what is actually being encapsulated, there are two main reasons for creating a nonvisual or dialog component. The first one also happens to be one of the primary reasons for creating components in general, that is, the ability to define properties for attributes that can be set at design-time.

The second reason is to provide an easier way to use the functionality being encapsulated. For example, this chapter's first component is the RzLauncher, which is used to launch applications. It provides a component wrapper around the **ShellExecute** Windows API function. Yes, this function could be called directly, but the component provides several benefits. For example, being a Win API function, the string parameters passed to **ShellExecute** must be null-terminated strings. These are not the same type of strings used by default in Delphi (that is, Pascal strings). Therefore, the component automatically handles the string type conversion. This makes the component much easier to use that simply calling the function.

Aside from a few additional features, the RzLauncher component maps directly to the underlying **ShellExecute** function. The RzMail component, on the other hand, is a nonvisual component that encapsulates several of the functions that make up the Simple Messaging API (MAPI). Of course, the individual MAPI functions could be called directly, but these functions are even more complex than **ShellExecute**. Instead, the RzMail component provides a uniquely Delphi interface to sending mail messages.

However, nothing captures ease of use like a dialog component—an entire form complete with all of its functionality encapsulated into a component. The third component that I'll be presenting is RzLookupDialog. This dialog component is a component wrapper around a form that provides a generic way of quickly searching a database table. It is generic in the sense that the application using the component provides the data. This allows the RzLookupDialog to be used in any database application.

Remember that by using the techniques covered in this chapter, virtually *any* piece of Object Pascal code can be transfigured into a component.

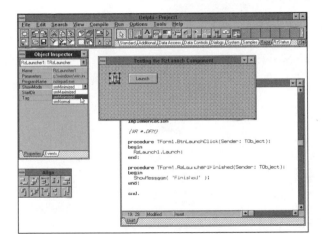

Figure 11.1

The RzLauncher
Component.

Mission Control

As mentioned earlier, the first nonvisual component we will build is the RzLauncher
component. An instance of this component is shown in Figure 11.1. This component is used to launch other programs from within a Delphi application. The
source code for the **TRzLauncher** class is found in the RzLaunch unit, shown in
Listing 11.1.

Listing 11.1   RZLAUNCH.PAS—The RzLaunch Unit

```
{==============================================================}
{= RzLaunch Unit                                             =}
{=                                                           =}
{= This unit implements the TRzLauncher component. This component is used to  =}
{= launch an application from within a Delphi application. To actually run    =}
{= the desired program, the ShellExecute function is used.   =}
{=                                                           =}
{= Building Custom Delphi Components - Ray Konopka           =}
{==============================================================}

unit RzLaunch;

interface

uses
  SysUtils, WinTypes, WinProcs, Messages, Classes, Graphics, Controls,
  Forms, Dialogs, ExtCtrls, RzCommon;

type
  ELaunchError = class( Exception )                  { Custom Exception Class }
    ErrorCode : Integer;
  end;
```

```
      TShowMode = ( smNormal, smMaximized, smMinimized );

const
    ShowWindowModes : array[ TShowMode ] of Integer =
      ( sw_Normal, sw_ShowMaximized, sw_ShowMinimized );

type
    TRzLauncher = class(TComponent)
    private
      FHInstance : THandle;
      FProgramName : string;
      FParameters : string;
      FShowMode : TShowMode;
      FStartDir : string;
      FTimer : TTimer;
      FOnFinished : TNotifyEvent;
    protected
      procedure Finished; dynamic;
      procedure TimerExpired( Sender : TObject );
    public
      constructor Create( AOwner : TComponent ); override;
      destructor Destroy; override;
      procedure Launch;

      property HInstance : THandle                            { Read Only Property }
        read FHInstance;
    published
      property ProgramName : string
        read FProgramName
        write FProgramName;

      property Parameters : string
        read FParameters
        write FParameters;

      property ShowMode : TShowMode
        read FShowMode
        write FShowMode
        default smNormal;

      property StartDir : string
        read FStartDir
        write FStartDir;

      property OnFinished : TNotifyEvent
        read FOnFinished
        write FOnFinished;
    end;

procedure Register;

implementation
```

```
uses
  ShellApi;

function CreateLaunchError( ErrCode : Integer ) : ELaunchError;
var
  ErrMsg : string;
begin
  case ErrCode of
    0, 8 : ErrMsg := 'Out of Memory';
    2 : ErrMsg := 'File Not Found';
    3 : ErrMsg := 'Path Not Found';
    5 : ErrMsg := 'Sharing Violation';
    6 : ErrMsg := 'Library/Segment Error';
    10 : ErrMsg := 'Incorrect Version of Windows';
    11 : ErrMsg := 'Invalid File';
    12, 13 : ErrMsg := 'Invalid DOS Version';
    14, 31 : ErrMsg := 'File Type has No Association';
    15 : ErrMsg := 'Cannot Load a Real-Mode Application';
    16 : ErrMsg := 'Invalid Attempt to Launch Second Instance';
    19 : ErrMsg := 'Cannot Load a Compressed Executable File';
    20 : ErrMsg := 'Invalid Dynamic Link Library';
    21 : ErrMsg := 'Application Requires Win32';
    else
      ErrMsg := 'Unknown Error';
  end;
  Result := ELaunchError.Create( ErrMsg );
  Result.ErrorCode := ErrCode;
end;


{============================}
{== TRzLauncher Methods ==}
{============================}

constructor TRzLauncher.Create( AOwner : TComponent );
begin
  inherited Create( AOwner );
  FShowMode := smNormal;
  FTimer := TTimer.Create( Self );
  FTimer.Enabled := False;
  FTimer.OnTimer := TimerExpired;
  FHInstance := 0;
end;



destructor TRzLauncher.Destroy;
begin
  FTimer.Enabled := False;                               { Turn Off Timer }
  inherited Destroy;
end;



procedure TRzLauncher.Finished;
begin
```

```
    if Assigned( FOnFinished ) then
      FOnFinished( Self );
end;


procedure TRzLauncher.TimerExpired( Sender : TObject );
begin
  { This is not the most reliable way of determining if the app }
  { is still running, but it works under most circumstances. }
  if GetModuleUsage( FHInstance ) = 0 then
  begin
    FHInstance := 0;
    FTimer.Enabled := False;
    Finished;
  end;
end;


procedure TRzLauncher.Launch;
var
  PgmStz : array[ 0..255 ] of Char;
  ParamStz : array[ 0..255 ] of Char;
  DirStz : array[ 0..255 ] of Char;
  E : EInOutError;
  Hnd : THandle;
begin
  FHInstance := 0;
  StrPCopy( PgmStz, FProgramName );
  StrPCopy( ParamStz, FParameters );
  StrPCopy( DirStz, FStartDir );

  Hnd := ShellExecute( HWnd_Desktop, 'open', PgmStz, ParamStz, DirStz,
                       ShowWindowModes[ FShowMode ] );
  if Hnd <= 32 then
    raise CreateLaunchError( Hnd )
  else
  begin
    FHInstance := Hnd;
    FTimer.Enabled := True;                                   { Start Timer }
  end;
end; {= TRzLauncher.Launch =}


{=======================}
{== Register Procedure ==}
{=======================}

procedure Register;
begin
  RegisterComponents( RaizePage, [ TRzLauncher ] );
end;


end.
```

The properties that are defined for this component correspond to four of the parameters passed to the **ShellExecute** function. In particular, **ProgramName** specifies the name and path of the program to be launched. Any command-line arguments are specified in the **Parameters** property. A starting directory can be set using the **StartDir** property. And finally, the **ShowMode** property determines the initial state of the launched program's main window. Initial states include normal, maximized, and minimized. The additional parameters to **ShellExecute** are handled internally by the component.

The **ProgramName**, **Parameters**, and **StartDir** properties are simple string properties while the **ShowMode** property is an enumerated value representing one of the standard Windows show mode constants. One interesting aspect regarding all of these properties is that none of them uses any access methods. That is, the properties simply reference internal fields.

In general, nonvisual components use a lot fewer access methods. Recall that most of the access methods that we have encountered use the standard format of testing the current value against the new value. If they differ, the new value is stored and the control is invalidated. But since we are dealing with a nonvisual component, there is no visual interface to invalidate, and thus, no need to have a write access method.

We Have Lift-Off

To launch the program specified by the component's properties, the **Launch** method is used. First, the string property values are converted to null-terminated string equivalents using the **StrPCopy** function. Once converted, the strings are passed to the **ShellExecute** function.

ShellExecute provides much more flexibility and functionality than the outdated **WinExec** function. For example, with **ShellExecute**, you can also specify a file name whose extension is associated with an application. **ShellExecute** will execute the application associated with the data file.

 The array of characters must start with a 0 index.

Arrays of characters can be used anywhere a **PChar** parameter is required. This makes it easier to allocate memory for null-terminated strings. For example, the following two procedures are equivalent:

```
procedure TForm1.Button1Click(Sender: TObject);
var
  Msg : PChar;
begin
  Msg := StrAlloc( 255 );
  StrPCopy( Msg, Edit1.Text );
  MessageBox( Handle, Msg, 'Tip', mb_OK );
  StrDispose( Msg );
end;

procedure TForm1.Button2Click(Sender: TObject);
var
  Msg : array[ 0..255 ] of Char;
begin
  StrPCopy( Msg, Edit1.Text );
  MessageBox( Handle, Msg, 'Tip', mb_OK );
end;
```

If the call is successful, the return value is a handle to the new application's instance, which is stored in the **HInstance** property. If the call is unsuccessful, the return value is an error code, which is then used to raise a custom exception.

Houston, We Have a Problem

If a problem occurs and the desired program cannot be launched, **ShellExecute** returns an error code. This value could be propagated to the user by way of a function result. However, the **TRzLauncher** class raises an exception instead—and not just any exception. The RzLaunch unit declares a new exception class called **ELaunchError**, which is derived from **Exception**. The **ELaunchError** exception is further augmented by the addition of an **ErrorCode** field.

The **CreateLaunchError** procedure takes care of the details of creating the exception object. The majority of the code in this procedure determines which string message will be passed the exception's **Create** constructor. The string used is determined by the error code returned from **ShellExecute**. The **CreateLaunchError** procedure finishes up by setting the **ErrorCode** field to the passed-in **ErrCode** value.

With the **CreateLaunchError** procedure in place, if an error occurs, an **ELaunchError** exception is created with the correct error code. The following code fragment shows how a **try...except** block is used to handle potential launch problems:

```
try
  RzLauncher1.Launch;
except
  on E : ELaunchError do
  begin
    if E.ErrorCode = 2 then
      ShowMessage( 'Program Not Found.  Try Again.' )
    else
      raise;                                    { Re-raise the Exception }
  end;
end;
```

The Eagle Has Landed

There is one more interesting feature of the **TRzLaunch** class. The **OnFinished** event allows users to be notified when the launched application has been terminated. In order to determine when the application in question is no longer running, the **HInstance** property is periodically checked. This, of course, suggests a timer. The **FTimer** private object is created in the **TRzLauncher** constructor, and its **OnTimer** event is assigned to the **TRzLauncher.TimerExpired** method.

If the application is successfully launched, the internal timer is enabled, or started. This causes the **TimerExpired** method to be executed roughly once every second. In it, the **GetModuleUsage** function is called to return the usage count of the **HInstance** module. As long as the usage count is greater than zero, the application is still running. If the usage count drops to zero, the timer is stopped, and the **Finished** event dispatch method is called to generate the **OnFinished** event.

I must point out that using the **GetModuleUsage** function in this way (to determine if an application is still running) is not the most reliable way of doing this. Potential problems can arise because Windows will reuse instance handles. For this example, however, the solution works quite well.

Sending Mail in Delphi

Everybody loves getting mail (especially electronic mail, because bills are not sent via email). In recent years, email has become an integral part of corporate computing—so much so that Microsoft's requirements for Windows 95 logo certification include requirements for email support. Specifically, an application must support sending data and product-specific files from within the application. (Of course, this only makes sense if the application is document-driven.)

For example, a memory optimizing utility doesn't really have a need to support email. However, an argument could be made stating that the results of the optimizations could be sent electronically to a system administrator. Yes, it's weak argument, but the point is that many, many applications are beginning to take advantage of email, and so should your own Delphi applications.

This is the driving force behind the construction of the RzMailMessage component. The goal of this nonvisual component is to provide an easy way to give a Delphi application email support. The keyword in that last sentence is *easy*. Providing access to basic mail functions is relatively straightforward, but providing easy access requires more work.

Providing email support is accomplished by using the *Messaging Application Programming Interface* (MAPI). There are two flavors of MAPI: Simple and Extended. *Extended* MAPI supports the entire MAPI specification while *Simple* MAPI is a set of twelve Extended MAPI functions providing basic support for sending and receiving messages. The RzMailMessage component utilizes the Simple MAPI functions.

Figure 11.2 illustrates how the RzMailMessage component is used in an application. This component allows a user to specify all of the elements of a typical mail message using properties. There are properties to support a subject line and the

Figure 11.2

Using the RzMailMessage Component.

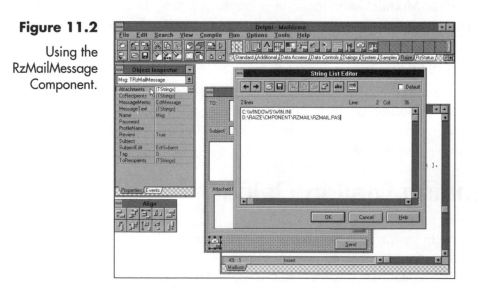

message text. Messages are addressed by adding names to the **ToRecipients** and **CcRecipients** properties. Files can even be attached to a message using the **Attachments** property as shown in the figure.

When all of the properties describing the message have been specified, the message is sent using the **Send** method. The **Send** method packages all of the information specified by the properties into a format that can be used by the MAPI functions. Before the message is sent, the user can review the message by setting the **Review** property to **True**. Setting this flag causes the underlying messaging system to display a common compose dialog containing the new message. The user then has the opportunity to make changes to the message or even cancel it.

The TRzMailMessage Class

Listing 11.2 shows the source code for the RzMail unit, which contains the class declaration for the **TRzMailMessage** class. The first thing to note about this class is that the **MessageText**, **ToRecipients**, **CcRecipients**, and **Attachments** properties are string lists. The **MessageText** property is obviously a string list to support multiple lines of text. The other three properties are lists so that they can support multiple entries. As a result, the RzMailMessage component can be used to send a message to virtually an unlimited number of recipients and attach an unlimited number of files. (NOTE: Although there are no limits imposed by the component, the underlying messaging system may impose restrictions on the number of recipients and attached files.)

Listing 11.2   RZMAIL.PAS—The RzMail Unit

```
{==============================================================================}
{= RzMail Unit                                                              =}
{=                                                                          =}
{= This unit implements the RzMailMessage component which uses the Simple   =}
{= Messaging API (MAPI) functions from MAPI.DLL to send mail messages.      =}
{= This component supports multiple TO and CC recipients and multiple       =}
{= attached files.                                                          =}
{=                                                                          =}
{= Building Custom Delphi Components - Ray Konopka                          =}
{==============================================================================}

unit RzMail;

interface

uses
  SysUtils, WinTypes, WinProcs, Messages, Classes, Graphics, Controls,
  Forms, Dialogs, StdCtrls;
```

```
type
  EMapiUserAbort = class( EAbort );                        { Silent Exception }
  EMapiError = class( Exception )
    ErrorCode : Integer;
  end;


  TRzMailMessage = class( TComponent )
  private
    FAttachments : TStrings;
    FToRecipients : TStrings;
    FCcRecipients : TStrings;
    FMessageMemo : TCustomMemo;
    FMessageText : TStrings;
    FPassword : string;
    FProfileName : string;
    FReview : Boolean;
    FSession : Longint;
    FSubject : string;
    FSubjectEdit : TCustomEdit;
    procedure SetAttachments( Value : TStrings );
    procedure SetToRecipients( Value : TStrings );
    procedure SetCcRecipients( Value : TStrings );
    procedure SetMailMessage( Value : TStrings );
  protected
    procedure Notification( AComponent : TComponent;
                            Operation : TOperation ); override;
  public
    constructor Create( AOwner : TComponent ); override;
    destructor Destroy; override;

    procedure Logon;
    procedure Logoff;
    procedure Send;
  published
    property Attachments : TStrings
      read FAttachments
      write SetAttachments;

    property CcRecipients : TStrings
      read FCcRecipients
      write SetCcRecipients;

    property MessageMemo : TCustomMemo
      read FMessageMemo
      write FMessageMemo;

    property MessageText : TStrings
      read FMessageText
      write SetMailMessage;

    property ProfileName : string
      read FProfileName
      write FProfileName;
```

```
    property Password : string
      read FPassword
      write FPassword;

    property Review : Boolean
      read FReview
      write FReview
      default True;

    property ToRecipients : TStrings
      read FToRecipients
      write SetToRecipients;

    property Subject : string
      read FSubject
      write FSubject;

    property SubjectEdit : TCustomEdit
      read FSubjectEdit
      write FSubjectEdit;
  end;


procedure Register;

implementation

uses
  RzCommon, SmplMapi;

const
  MapiErrMsgs : array[ mapi_User_Abort..mapi_E_Not_Supported ] of string[ 24 ] =
    ( 'User Abort',
      'Failure',
      'Login Failure',
      'Disk Full',
      'Insufficient Memory',
      'Access Denied',
      '',
      'Too Many Sessions',
      'Too Many Files',
      'Too Many Recipients',
      'Attachment Not Found',
      'Attachment Open Failure',
      'Attachment Write Failure',
      'Unknown Recipient',
      'Bad RecipType',
      'No Messages',
      'Invalid Message',
      'Text Too Large',
      'Invalid Session',
      'Type Not Supported',
```

```
                   'Ambiguous Recipient',
                   'Message In Use',
                   'Network Failure',
                   'Invalid EditFields',
                   'Invalid Recips',
                   'Not Supported' );


function CreateMapiError( ErrCode : Integer ) : Exception;
begin
  if ErrCode = mapi_User_Abort then     { If user abort, raise silent exception }
  begin
    Result := EMapiUserAbort.Create( 'MAPI: Process Aborted by User' );
  end
  else
  begin
    Result := EMapiError.CreateFmt( 'MAPI: %s. ErrorCode = %d',
                                    [ MapiErrMsgs[ ErrCode ], ErrCode ] );
    EMapiError( Result ).ErrorCode := ErrCode;
  end;
end;



{===========================}
{== TRzMailMessage Methods ==}
{===========================}



constructor TRzMailMessage.Create( AOwner : TComponent );
begin
  inherited Create( AOwner );
  FAttachments := TStringList.Create;
  FToRecipients := TStringList.Create;
  FCcRecipients := TStringList.Create;
  FMessageText := TStringList.Create;
  FReview := True;
end;



destructor TRzMailMessage.Destroy;
begin
  FAttachments.Free;
  FToRecipients.Free;
  FCcRecipients.Free;
  FMessageText.Free;
  inherited Destroy;
end;



{= TRzMailMessage.Notification                                          =}
{=   This method is overridden to ensure that FMemo is set to nil if the  =}
{=   corresponding Memo component is deleted from the form. This method    =}
```

```
{=   should be used whenever a component contains a reference to another component.      =}

procedure TRzMailMessage.Notification( AComponent : TComponent;
                                       Operation : TOperation );
begin
  inherited Notification( AComponent, Operation );

  if Operation = opRemove then
  begin
    if AComponent = FMessageMemo then
      FMessageMemo := nil
    else if AComponent = FSubjectEdit then
      FSubjectEdit := nil;
  end;
end;


procedure TRzMailMessage.SetAttachments( Value : TStrings );
begin
  FAttachments.Assign( Value );
end;


procedure TRzMailMessage.SetToRecipients( Value : TStrings );
begin
  FToRecipients.Assign( Value );
end;


procedure TRzMailMessage.SetCcRecipients( Value : TStrings );
begin
  FCcRecipients.Assign( Value );
end;


procedure TRzMailMessage.SetMailMessage( Value : TStrings );
begin
  FMessageText.Assign( Value );
end;


procedure TRzMailMessage.Logon;
var
  ProfileStz : array[ 0..255 ] of Char;
  PasswordStz : array[ 0..255 ] of Char;
  RetCode : Integer;
begin
  StrPCopy( ProfileStz, FProfileName );
  StrPCopy( PasswordStz, FPassword );
  RetCode := MapiLogon( 0, ProfileStz, PasswordStz, mapi_Logon_UI + mapi_Dialog,
                        0, FSession );
  if RetCode > 0 then
```

```
      raise CreateMapiError( RetCode );
end;


procedure TRzMailMessage.Logoff;
var
  RetCode : Integer;
begin
  if FSession = 0 then
    Exit;

  RetCode := MapiLogoff( FSession, 0, 0, 0 );
  if RetCode > 0 then
    raise CreateMapiError( RetCode );
  FSession := 0;
end;


{ Supporting Constants and Types used to cast generic pointers }
const
  MaxNumFiles = 65520 div SizeOf( TMapiFileDesc );
  MaxNumRecips = 65520 div SizeOf( TMapiRecipDesc );

type
  TFileArray = array[ 0..MaxNumFiles - 1 ] of TMapiFileDesc;
  TRecipArray = array[ 0..MaxNumRecips - 1 ] of TMapiRecipDesc;
  TRecipBufArray = array[ 0..MaxNumRecips - 1 ] of PMapiRecipDesc;


procedure TRzMailMessage.Send;
var
  AttachmentPositions : string;
  Files : Pointer;
  FilesMemSize : Word;
  FullPath : string;
  TempStz : array[ 0..255 ] of Char;
  RecipClass : Longint;
  Recips : Pointer;
  RecipsMemSize : Word;
  RecipBuffer : Pointer;
  RecipBufMemSize : Word;
  RecipName : array[ 0..255 ] of Char;
  Msg : TMapiMessage;
  RetCode : Longint;
  SubjectStz : array[ 0..255 ] of Char;
  I, J, MessageLen : Integer;
  SendFlags : Longint;
begin
  Screen.Cursor := crHourGlass;
  try
    FillChar( Msg, SizeOf( TMapiMessage ), 0 );        { Clear out Msg structure }
```

```
if FMessageMemo <> nil then                    { If component linked to memo... }
  FMessageText.Assign( FMessageMemo.Lines );             { use memo contents }

{ Attached files replace characters in the message body.  The following   }
{ code adds blank spaces at the end of the message so that any attached    }
{ files will have a place to be inserted into the message, without over-   }
{ writing any portion of the message text.                                 }

AttachmentPositions := '';
for I := 1 to FAttachments.Count do
  AttachmentPositions := AttachmentPositions + ' ';
if AttachmentPositions <> '' then
  FMessageText.Add( AttachmentPositions );

Msg.lpszNoteText := FMessageText.GetText;              { Populate message body }
MessageLen := StrLen( FMessageText.GetText );

if FSubjectEdit <> nil then
  StrPCopy( SubjectStz, FSubjectEdit.Text )
else
  StrPCopy( SubjectStz, FSubject );
Msg.lpszSubject := SubjectStz;

{ Add Recipients to Message }
                                        { Specify the number of recipients }
Msg.nRecipCount := FToRecipients.Count + FCcRecipients.Count;

RecipsMemSize := SizeOf( TMapiRecipDesc ) *
                  ( FToRecipients.Count + FCcRecipients.Count );
GetMem( Recips, RecipsMemSize );          { Allocate Memory for Recips Array }
FillChar( Recips^, RecipsMemSize, 0 );

RecipBufMemSize := SizeOf( PMapiRecipDesc ) *
                    ( FToRecipients.Count + FCcRecipients.Count );
GetMem( RecipBuffer, RecipBufMemSize );  { Allocate Memory for RecipBuffer }

for I := 0 to FToRecipients.Count + FCcRecipients.Count - 1 do
begin
  if I < FToRecipients.Count then
  begin
    StrPCopy( RecipName, FToRecipients[ I ] );
    RecipClass := mapi_TO;
  end
  else
  begin
    StrPCopy( RecipName, FCcRecipients[ I - FToRecipients.Count ] );
    RecipClass := mapi_CC;
  end;

  { Call MapiResolveName to get the Address for the RecipName recipient }
  RetCode := MapiResolveName( FSession, 0, RecipName,
                              mapi_Logon_UI + mapi_Dialog, 0,
```

```
                                    TRecipBufArray( RecipBuffer^ )[ I ] );
      if RetCode > 0 then
      begin
        for J := 0 to I - 1 do
          MapiFreeBuffer( TRecipBufArray( RecipBuffer^ )[ J ] );
        raise CreateMapiError( RetCode );
      end;

      { Populate Recips array with data retrieved in RecipBuffer }

      TRecipArray( Recips^ )[ I ].ulRecipClass := RecipClass;

      TRecipArray( Recips^ )[ I ].lpszName :=
        TRecipBufArray( RecipBuffer^ )[ I ]^.lpszName;

      TRecipArray( Recips^ )[ I ].lpszAddress :=
        TRecipBufArray( RecipBuffer^ )[ I ]^.lpszAddress;
    end;
    Msg.lpRecips := Recips;

    { Add Attachments to Message }

    Msg.nFileCount := FAttachments.Count;  { Specify the number of attachments }

    FilesMemSize := SizeOf( TMapiFileDesc ) * FAttachments.Count;
    GetMem( Files,  FilesMemSize );
    FillChar( Files^, FilesMemSize, 0 );

    for I := 0 to FAttachments.Count - 1 do
    begin
      FullPath := ExpandFileName( FAttachments[ I ] );
      TFileArray(Files^)[ I ].lpszPathName :=StrNew(StrPCopy(TempStz,FullPath));

      { Place each attachment at one of the spaces added to the end of the msg }
      TFileArray( Files^ )[ I ].nPosition := MessageLen - 3 - I;
    end;
    Msg.lpFiles := Files;

    { Send the Message }
    try
      if FReview or ( FToRecipients.Count = 0 ) then
        SendFlags := mapi_Logon_UI + mapi_Dialog    { Show the compose dialog }
      else
        SendFlags := mapi_Logon_UI;

      { MapiSendMail will attempt to use the session established by MapiLogon }
      { or if FSession is 0, it will use a shared session, and if one is not  }
      { available, a new session is started.                                  }

      RetCode := MapiSendMail( FSession, 0, Msg, SendFlags, 0 );
      if RetCode > 0 then
        raise CreateMapiError( RetCode );
```

```
    finally
      { Clean Up:  Lots of dynamic memory to free up }

      for I := 0 to FToRecipients.Count + FCcRecipients.Count - 1 do
        MapiFreeBuffer( TRecipBufArray( RecipBuffer^ )[ I ] );
      FreeMem( Recips, RecipsMemSize );
      FreeMem( RecipBuffer, RecipBufMemSize );

      for I := 0 to FAttachments.Count - 1 do
        StrDispose( TFileArray( Files^ )[ I ].lpszPathName );
      FreeMem( Files, FilesMemSize );
    end;
  finally
    Screen.Cursor := crDefault;
  end;
end;


{=======================}
{== Register Procedure ==}
{=======================}

procedure Register;
begin
  RegisterComponents( RaizePage, [ TRzMailMessage ] );
end;

end.
```

A significant portion of the **TRzMailMessage** class exists to support the string list properties. First, in the **private** section of the class declaration, each list has a field object. It is important to notice that each of these fields, as well as the corresponding properties, are declared as **TStrings** objects and not **TStringList**.

Recall from the discussion on string lists in Chapter 6 that **TStringList** is a descendant of **TStrings**, and that **TStrings** is an abstract class that defines all of the functions necessary to manipulate a list of strings. However, the **TStrings** class does not provide any storage for the strings. Storage must be provided by descendent classes such as **TStringList**.

Declaring these properties as **TStrings** allows users of this component to assign any other **TString's** descendent object to the property. For example, if an application has a list box filled with file names to be attached to the message, the contents of the list can be moved into the **Attachments** list using the following code:

```
RzMailMessage1.Attachments := ListBox1.Items;
```

On the other hand, if the **Attachments** property was specifically declared as a **TStringList**, users could only assign other **TStringList** objects to the property. This is because the **Items** property in a list box is of type **TListBoxStrings**.

Declaring the properties as **TStrings** ensures type compatibility with any string list type, but this component must also provide internal storage for the strings, because each list can be edited at design-time using the Object Inspector. Providing internal storage for each list is handled in the component's **Create** constructor. Instead of creating an instance of **TStrings** for each property, a **TStringList** object is created. The assignment is valid because **TStringList** is a descendant of **TStrings**.

 Never create a **TStrings** object *instance*, because **TStrings** is an abstract class. This means that some of its methods are declared but not defined. Calling one of these undefined methods results in an exception. It is the responsibility of descendent classes to override these methods with "real" methods that turn the abstract **TStrings** class into something useful.

Since this component needs to maintain storage for each of its property lists, a little extra work is required. Specifically, a write access method must be defined for each property. Each access method is responsible for copying the list of strings referenced by the **Value** parameter into the property's internal string list. Copying strings from one list to another is accomplished by calling the **Assign** method. The **SetAttachments** method is shown below to illustrate the process:

```
procedure TRzMailMessage.SetAttachments( Value : TStrings );
begin
  FAttachments.Assign( Value );
end;
```

Component References

The RzMailMessage component also provides two properties to facilitate the construction of a mail application. Specifically, the **TRzMailMessage** class provides two component reference properties: **SubjectEdit** and **MessageMemo**. When the **Send** method is called, the contents of the edit field referenced by **SubjectEdit** are used to populate the subject line. Likewise, **MessageText** is populated with the contents of the memo control referenced by **MessageMemo**.   Figure 11.3 shows how these two properties are used to link two controls to the RzMailMessage component.

Take a close look at the Object Inspector in Figure 11.3, specifically, the MessageMemo property.   The Object Inspector is displaying all of the memo components currently on the form.   This capability is provided automatically by the Object Inspector.   It is a result of declaring the **MessageMemo** property to be of type **TCustomMemo**.   **TCustomMemo** is the base class for all memo components.   The Object Inspector uses the class of the component reference property to determine which components appear in the list.   In the same way, the **SubjectEdit** property can be linked to any **TCustomEdit** control.

Pick the most appropriate class for component references.   For example, the **MessageMemo** property could be declared as a **TMemo** reference, but then the property could only be assigned to **TMemo** controls. DBMemo components, which descend from **TCustomMemo**, could not be linked to the **MessageMemo** property.

The **TRzMailMessage** class does not define any access methods for these two properties.   However, it does define a **Notification** method.   Recall from Chapter 6 that a component's **Notification** method is called whenever a component

Figure 11.3

Linking to
RzMailMessage.

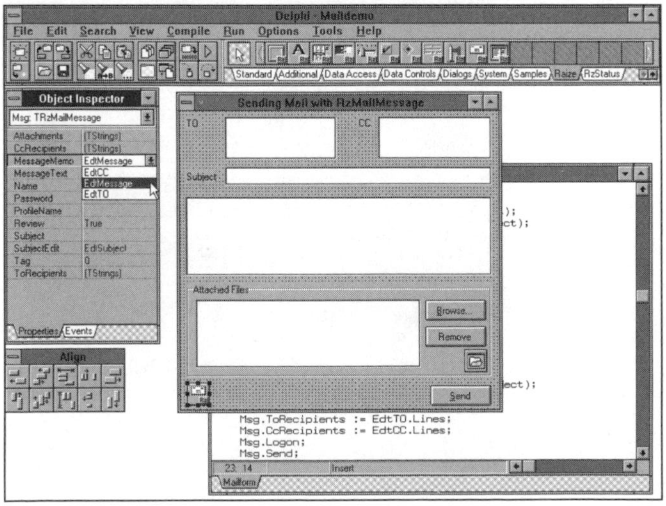

is inserted into or removed from the owner's **Components** list. The **Notification** method helps to ensure that the component references remain valid. If a component has published component references, it is imperative to override the **Notification** method.

Consider the form shown in Figure 11.4. The **SubjectEdit** property is assigned to **Edit1**. The Object Inspector displays the value of **SubjectEdit** by referencing the **FSubjectEdit.Name** property. Figure 11.5 shows what happens when Edit1 is deleted from the form. Without a **Notification** method, the RzMailMessage

Figure 11.4

Linked to an
Edit Field.

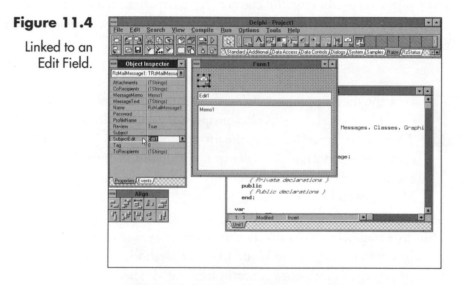

Figure 11.5

No More
Edit1.

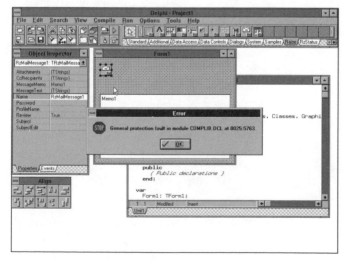

component has no way of knowing that the **FSubjectEdit** reference is no longer valid. When the Object Inspector attempts to access the **FSubjectEdit.Name**, a GPF occurs.

This problem can be prevented by overriding the **Notification** method. The **Notification** method receives two parameters: a reference to a component and the type of operation performed on that component. The operation parameter will be **opInsert** or **opRemove**. For the **TRzMailMessage** class, we are only concerned when components are removed. If the component being removed is the same one referenced by the **MessageMemo** property, the reference is cleared by setting the property to **nil**. The same is done for the **SubjectEdit** property.

Sending the Message

The **Send** method is responsible for taking all of the data specified in the component's properties and packaging it into a format that can be used by the MAPI functions. The format is defined by the **TMapiMessage** record. This record, in addition to several other types and function declarations, is defined in the SmplMapi unit, which is shown in Listing 11.3. The SmplMapi unit is a translation of the MAPI.H file from the MAPI SDK for use in Delphi applications. The **Send** method uses several of the functions and types defined in this unit.

Listing 11.3   SMPLMAPI.PAS—The SmplMapi Unit

```
{=============================================================================}
{= SmplMapi Unit                                                            =}
{=                                                                          =}
{= This is an interface unit to the constants, types, procedures, and       =}
{= functions defined for the Simple Messaging API. (i.e. MAPI.DLL)          =}
{=                                                                          =}
{= Building Custom Delphi Components - Ray Konopka                           =}
{=============================================================================}

unit SmplMapi;

interface

uses
  WinTypes;

const
  mapi_MessageId_Length = 64;

type
```

```
  PMapiFileDesc = ^TMapiFileDesc;
  TMapiFileDesc = record
    ulReserved : Longint;                               { Reserved - must be 0 }
    flFlags : Longint;                                               { Flags }
    nPosition : Longint;           { Character in text to be replaced by attachment }
    lpszPathName : PChar;                          { Full path name of attachment file }
    lpszFileName : PChar;                           { Original file name (Optional) }
    lpFileType : PChar;                          { Attachment file type (Optional) }
  end;

const
  mapi_Ole        = $00000001;
  mapi_Ole_Static = $00000002;

type
  PMapiRecipDesc = ^TMapiRecipDesc;
  TMapiRecipDesc = record
    ulReserved : Longint;
    ulRecipClass : Longint;                                  { Recipient class }
                                   { mapi_Orig, mapi_TO, mapi_CC, mapi_BCC }
    lpszName : PChar;                                          { Recipient name }
    lpszAddress : PChar;                          { Recipient address (Optional) }
    ulEIDSize : Longint;                    { Count in bytes of size of pEntryID }
    lpEntryID : PChar;                    { System-specific recipient reference }
  end;

const
  mapi_Orig = 0;                                            { Message originator }
  mapi_TO   = 1;                                             { Primary recipient }
  mapi_CC   = 2;                                                { Copy recipient }
  mapi_BCC  = 3;                                          { Blind copy recipient }

type
  PMapiMessage = ^TMapiMessage;
  TMapiMessage = record
    ulReserved : Longint;                               { Reserved - must be 0 }
    lpszSubject : PChar;                                     { Message subject }
    lpszNoteText : PChar;                                       { Message text }
    lpszMessageType : PChar;                                   { Message class }
    lpszDateReceived : PChar;       { Received date in YYYY/MM/DD HH:MM format }
    lpszConversationID : PChar;                      { Conversation thread ID }
    flFlags : Longint;                            { Unread, return receipt }
    lpOriginator : PMapiRecipDesc;                { Originator descriptor }
    nRecipCount : Longint;                         { Number of recipients }
    lpRecips : PMapiRecipDesc;                    { Recipient descriptors }
    nFileCount : Longint;                     { Number of file attachments }
    lpFiles : PMapiFileDesc;                      { Attachment descriptors }
  end;

const
  mapi_Unread           = $00000001;
  mapi_Receipt_Requested = $00000002;
  mapi_Sent             = $00000004;
```

```
    mapi_Logon_UI           = $00000001;                        { Display logon UI }
    mapi_New_Session        = $00000002;                        { Do not use default }
    mapi_Dialog             = $00000008;                        { Display a send note UI }
    mapi_Unread_Only        = $00000020;                        { Only unread messages }
    mapi_Envelope_Only      = $00000040;                        { Only header information }
    mapi_Peek               = $00000080;                        { Do not mark as read }
    mapi_Guarantee_Fifo     = $00000100;                        { Use date order }
    mapi_Body_As_File       = $00000200;
    mapi_AB_NoModify        = $00000400;            { Do not allow mods of AB entries }
    mapi_Suppress_Attach    = $00000800;                    { Header + body, no files }
    mapi_Force_Download     = $00001000;            { Download new mail during Logon }


{== The 12 Simple MAPI Functions ==}

function MapiLogon( WndParent : Longint; Name, Password : PChar;
                    Flags, Reserved : Longint;
                    var Session : Longint ) : Longint;

function MapiLogoff( Session, WndParent,
                     flFlags, ulReserved : Longint ) : Longint;

function MapiSendMail( Session, WndParent : Longint;
                    var Msg : TMapiMessage;
                    Flags, Reserved : Longint ) : Longint;

function MapiSendDocuments( WndParent : Longint;
                        DelimChar, FullPaths, FileNames : PChar;
                        Reserved : Longint ) : Longint;

function MapiFindNext( Session, WndParent : Longint;
                    MessageType, SeedMessageID : PChar;
                    Flags, Reserved : Longint; MessageID : PChar ) : Longint;

function MapiReadMail( Session, WndParent : Longint;
                    MessageID : PChar; Flags, Reserved : Longint;
                    var MessageOut : PMapiMessage ) : Longint;

function MapiSaveMail( Session, WndParent : Longint;
                    var Msg : TMapiMessage; Flags, Reserved : Longint;
                    MessageID : PChar ) : Longint;

function MapiDeleteMail( Session, WndParent : Longint;
                        MessageID : PChar;
                        Flags, Reserved : Longint ) : Longint;

function MapiFreeBuffer( Memory : Pointer ) : Longint;

function MapiAddress( Session, WndParent : Longint;
                        Caption : PChar; EditFields : Longint;
                        Labels : PChar; RecipsCount : Longint;
                        var Recips : PMapiRecipDesc; Flags, Reserved : Longint;
                        NewRecipsCount : Pointer;
                        var NewRecips : PMapiRecipDesc ) : Longint;
```

```
function MapiDetails( Session, WndParent : Longint;
                      var Recip : PMapiRecipDesc;
                      Flags, Reserved : Longint ) : Longint;

function MapiResolveName( Session, WndParent : Longint;
                          Name : PChar; Flags, Reserved : Longint;
                          var Recip : PMapiRecipDesc ) : Longint;

const
  Success_Success              = 0;
  mapi_User_Abort              = 1;
  mapi_E_Failure               = 2;
  mapi_E_Login_Failure         = 3;
  mapi_E_Disk_Full             = 4;
  mapi_E_Insufficient_Memory   = 5;
  mapi_E_Access_Denied         = 6;
  mapi_E_Too_Many_Sessions     = 8;
  mapi_E_Too_Many_Files        = 9;
  mapi_E_Too_Many_Recipients   = 10;
  mapi_E_Attachment_Not_Found  = 11;
  mapi_E_Attachment_Open_Failure  = 12;
  mapi_E_Attachment_Write_Failure = 13;
  mapi_E_Unknown_Recipient     = 14;
  mapi_E_Bad_RecipType         = 15;
  mapi_E_No_Messages           = 16;
  mapi_E_Invalid_Message       = 17;
  mapi_E_Text_Too_Large        = 18;
  mapi_E_Invalid_Session       = 19;
  mapi_E_Type_Not_Supported    = 20;
  mapi_E_Ambiguous_Recipient   = 21;
  mapi_E_Message_In_Use        = 22;
  mapi_E_Network_Failure       = 23;
  mapi_E_Invalid_EditFields    = 24;
  mapi_E_Invalid_Recips        = 25;
  mapi_E_Not_Supported         = 26;

implementation

function MapiLogon;         external 'MAPI' index 209;
function MAPILogoff;        external 'MAPI' index 210;
function MAPISendMail;      external 'MAPI' index 211;
function MAPISendDocuments; external 'MAPI' index 208;
function MAPIFindNext;      external 'MAPI' index 214;
function MAPIReadMail;      external 'MAPI' index 213;
function MAPISaveMail;      external 'MAPI' index 212;
function MAPIDeleteMail;    external 'MAPI' index 215;
function MAPIFreeBuffer;    external 'MAPI' index 17;
function MAPIAddress;       external 'MAPI' index 217;
function MAPIDetails;       external 'MAPI' index 218;
function MAPIResolveName;   external 'MAPI' index 219;

end.
```

The first step is to clear out the **Msg** record using the standard **FillChar** procedure. Several of the fields in the **TMapiMessage** record must be set to zero, so **FillChar** is used to initialize the entire record. Next, if the **MessageMemo** property references a control, the control's contents are copied to the **MessageText** string list. (Yes, this will overwrite any data already in the **MessageText** list.)

After populating the **MessageText** list, spaces are added to the end of the text. One space is added for each attached file. MAPI requires that an attached file occupy a position in the message body. The spaces serve as placeholders for the attached files.

Once the message text has been adjusted, the **lpszNoteText** field of the **Msg** record is populated with the text. Since **lpszNoteText** is of type **PChar**, the **GetText** method is used to return a pointer to the entire message contained in **FMessageText**.

After the **Msg.lbszSubject** field is populated, the recipients stored in the **ToRecipients** and **CcRecipients** properties must be translated into an array of **TMapiRecipDesc** records. However, since the number of recipients can vary, the memory for the array is allocated dynamically. What makes this code especially tricky is that the **TMapiRecipDesc** record also has references to null-terminated strings that must also be allocated memory.

For each recipient in either list, the **MapiResolveName** function is called to determine the email address corresponding to the name of the recipient. **MapiResolveName** uses the current user's address book to resolve the name. If the name cannot be resolved, a common MAPI dialog box is displayed allowing the user to select the correct address. The resolved address is then stored in the **Recips** array. When all of the recipients have been processed, the **Msg.lpRecips** field is assigned to the **Recips** array. A similar process then occurs for the file attachments, which must be formatted into an array of **TMapiFileDesc** records.

Once the **Msg** record has been formatted, the **MapiSendMail** function is called to send the message. If the **Review** flag is set or no **ToRecipients** are specified, the common compose dialog box is displayed before the message is actually sent. The **MapiSendMail** function returns an error code if the call was unsuccessful, much like the **ShellExecute** function. In the event of an error, a custom exception is raised. This process is similar to the one used in the **RzLauncher** component except that if the error resulted from the user aborting the process, a silent exception is raised.

Finally, once the message has been sent, all of the dynamic memory allocated in the process is released. All of this code is wrapped in a **try...finally** block to ensure the memory gets released even if the **MapiSendMail** call fails.

Using RzMailMessage

Since the RzMailMessage component utilizes the Simple MAPI specification, this component requires a MAPI-compliant messaging system such as the one used in Windows for Workgroups, Windows NT, or Windows 95. Figure 11.6 gives a final look at the RzMailMessage component in action under Windows 95.

Dialog Boxes as Components

Dialog components are nonvisual components that provide a wrapper around a Delphi form. Dialog components by themselves are useless, because the main purpose of a dialog component is to provide persistent data for a dialog box. Without a dialog box, a dialog component does not have much value.

Because of a dialog component's dependency on a form, you may be tempted to just reuse the form, and bypass creating a component wrapper. Although tempting, there are three main advantages that dialog components have over regular forms, and all three are based on the persistent data maintained by the component class. First, dialog components can be customized to some extent in each

Figure 11.6

Sending Mail in Windows 95.

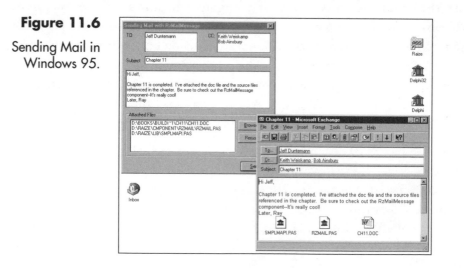

application without affecting the underlying form file. This is possible because the changes are stored in the component and not in the form file.

Second, a dialog component provides an interface between the application and the form. This interface is generally much easier than dealing with the form directly. Furthermore, changes in the underlying form have minimal impact on the application as long as the interface remains unchanged.

The third advantage is that dialog components dynamically create the underlying form only when necessary. And once the form is closed, the dialog component destroys the form. Aside from removing this burden from the component user, this helps to minimize the amount of system resources used by the application.

Picking a Dialog Box

Before we can build a dialog component, we need a dialog box. We will use the **TRzLookupForm** shown in Figure 11.7. This form is a dialog box used to perform a quick lookup on a database table. Although similar in concept to a **DBLookupCombo**, this form has several additional features. For example, the **TRzLookupForm** provides keyboard searching and grid navigation. However, the most important feature of this form is that it can be used with both tables and queries.

The form is actually quite simple. The grid is connected to a DataSource component, which must be assigned to a table or query at runtime because there are no Dataset components on this form. The edit field at the top of the form is where the user enters characters to perform keyboard searching. Virtually all of the methods defined for the **TRzLookupForm** class are related to this searching process.

Figure 11.7

The
TRzLookupForm
Dialog Box.

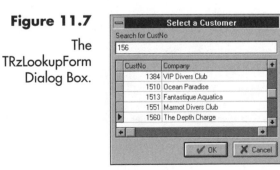

Use panels to automatically align controls on a form. For example, the **TRzLookupForm** uses four panels: One to surround the edit field set to **alTop**; one around the grid set to **alClient**; one at the bottom set to **alBottom**; and one around the buttons inside the panel at the bottom. This nested panel is set to **alRight**. As the form's size changes, the grid fills up the form, and the buttons stay aligned to the right.

Listing 11.4 shows the source code for the unit file corresponding to the **TRzLookupForm** form. In it, the **EdtSearchChange** event handler is responsible for updating the current record of the dataset referenced by the **SrcLookup** data source. As the user enters characters into the edit field, the database cursor is moved to the record where the **SearchField** contents most closely match the value entered by the user. Since the grid is tied to the dataset through the data source, its position is updated as each key is pressed.

Which brings us to the **EdtSearchKeyPress** method: On each keypress, this event handler uses the **NumbersOnly** flag to determine if only numeric characters can be entered in the edit field. As an example, if the **NumbersOnly** flag is **True**, and the user presses an "A," the character will be discarded and a beep will sound.

Listing 11.4   RZLOOKFM.PAS—The RzLookFm Unit

```
{==============================================================================}
{= RzLookFm Unit                                                             =}
{=                                                                           =}
{= This is the form unit for the TRzFrmLookup form.  This form is displayed  =}
{= by the TRzLookupDialog component when its Execute method is called. This  =}
{= dialog box form contains an edit field and a database grid. The edit field =}
{= is used to enter keyboard searches on a particular column.                =}
{=                                                                           =}
{= Building Custom Delphi Components - Ray Konopka                           =}
{==============================================================================}

unit RzLookFm;

interface

uses
  SysUtils, WinTypes, WinProcs, Messages, Classes, Graphics, Controls,
  Forms, Dialogs, StdCtrls, Grids, DBGrids, DB, Buttons, ExtCtrls;

type
  TRzLookupForm = class(TForm)
```

```
      SrcLookup: TDataSource;
      PnlPrompt: TPanel;
      PnlLookup: TPanel;
      PnlButtons: TPanel;
      PnlButtonOffset: TPanel;
      BtnOK: TBitBtn;
      BtnCancel: TBitBtn;
      GrdLookup: TDBGrid;
      EdtSearch: TEdit;
      LblPrompt: TLabel;
      procedure EdtSearchChange(Sender: TObject);
      procedure FormShow(Sender: TObject);
      procedure FormResize(Sender: TObject);
      procedure EdtSearchKeyPress(Sender: TObject; var Key: Char);
    private
    public
      SearchField : string;
      NumbersOnly : Boolean;
    end;

var
  RzLookupForm: TRzLookupForm;

implementation

{$R *.DFM}

uses
  DBTables;


{==========================}
{== TRzFrmLookup Methods ==}
{==========================}

{= TRzFrmLookup.EdtSearchChange                                        =}
{=   This method is called whenever the contents of the EdtSearch edit field =}
{=   changes.  As the user enters characters, this method performs a simple  =}
{=   linear search looking for a match.                                =}
{=                                                                     =}
{= Comments: T
{=   The FindNearest method is not used because it is limited to working only =}
{=   with TTables. Plus, FindNearest is fine for searching for string values, =}
{=   but it does not work well for searching for numbers.              =}
{=
{=   The dataset must be sorted on the column being searched.          =}

procedure TRzLookupForm.EdtSearchChange(Sender: TObject);
begin
  with SrcLookup.Dataset do
  begin
    DisableControls;                 { Disable controls so grid does not flicker }
```

```
    try
      First;
      while not EOF and
        ( UpperCase( FieldByName(SearchField).AsString ) < EdtSearch.Text ) do
      begin
        Next;
      end;
    finally
      EnableControls;                          { Be sure to enable the controls }
    end;
  end; { with }
end;


procedure TRzLookupForm.FormShow(Sender: TObject);
begin
  EdtSearch.SetFocus;                { Reset the focus if dialog redisplayed }
  SrcLookup.Dataset.First;           { Move cursor to first record in grid }
end;


procedure TRzLookupForm.FormResize(Sender: TObject);
begin
  EdtSearch.Width := GrdLookup.Width;                    { Resize the edit field }
end;


procedure TRzLookupForm.EdtSearchKeyPress(Sender: TObject; var Key: Char);
begin
  if NumbersOnly and
     ( Key in [ #32..#255 ] ) and
     not ( Key in [ '-', '+', '0'..'9' ] ) then
  begin
    MessageBeep( 0 );
    Key := #0;
  end;
end;

end.
```

Wrapping the Dialog in a Component

Now that we have a dialog box, we can start building the RzLookupDialog component. As mentioned before, dialog components define properties that can be manipulated at design-time to affect how the dialog box is displayed. The RzLookupDialog component defines several such properties.

Many of the properties defined in the **TRzLookupDialog** class, shown in Listing 11.5, affect the appearance of the underlying form. The properties in this set include **BorderStyle, Caption, Height, Width,** and **Font.** The remaining properties define attributes of the search process.

The **SearchField** string property is used to specify the column in the table that will be used for keyboard searching. The **NumbersOnly** property controls whether or not alphabetic characters can be entered into the search edit field. However, the most important property is **Dataset**. This property is set to the **TTable** or **TQuery** component that will provide the data that fills the form's grid.

Listing 11.5 RZLOOKUP.PAS—The RzLookup Unit

```
{==================================================================}
{= RzLookup Unit                                                 =}
{=                                                               =}
{= This unit implements the TRzLookupDialog component. This component is used =}
{= to display the contents of a dataset, from which the user can select a    =}
{= record in that dataset.  The dialog also provides keyboard searching.     =}
{=                                                               =}
{= Building Custom Delphi Components - Ray Konopka               =}
{==================================================================}


unit RzLookup;

interface

uses
  Classes, Graphics, Forms, DB, RzCommon;

type
  TRzLookupDialog = class( TComponent )
  private
    FBorderStyle : TFormBorderStyle;
    FCaption : string;
    FDataset : TDataset;
    FHeight : Integer;
    FFont : TFont;
    FNumbersOnly : Boolean;
    FSearchField : string;
    FWidth : Integer;
    procedure SetFont( Value : TFont );
  protected
    procedure Notification( AComponent : TComponent;
                            Operation : TOperation ); override;
  public
    constructor Create( AOwner : TComponent ); override;
    destructor Destroy; override;
    function Execute : Boolean;
  published
    property BorderStyle : TFormBorderStyle
      read FBorderStyle
      write FBorderStyle
      default bsSizeable;
```

```
      property Caption : string
        read FCaption
        write FCaption;

      property Dataset : TDataset
        read FDataset
        write FDataset;

      property Font : TFont
        read FFont
        write SetFont;

      property Height : Integer
        read FHeight
        write FHeight
        default 300;

      property NumbersOnly : Boolean
        read FNumbersOnly
        write FNumbersOnly;

      property SearchField : string
        read FSearchField
        write FSearchField;

      property Width : Integer
        read FWidth
        write FWidth
        default 350;
  end;


procedure Register;

implementation

uses
  WinTypes, Controls, RzLookFm;



{===============================}
{== TRzLookupDialog Methods ==}
{===============================}

constructor TRzLookupDialog.Create( AOwner : TComponent );
begin
  inherited Create( AOwner );
  FHeight := 300;
  FWidth := 350;
  FBorderStyle := bsSizeable;
  FFont := TFont.Create;
  if Owner is TForm then                              { If Owner is a form... }
```

```
      FFont.Assign( TForm( Owner ).Font );        { Use the form's font by default }
end;


destructor TRzLookupDialog.Destroy;
begin
  FFont.Free;
  inherited Destroy;
end;


procedure TRzLookupDialog.Notification( AComponent : TComponent;
                                        Operation : TOperation);
begin
  inherited Notification( AComponent, Operation );

  { If FDataset gets removed, clear the reference to avoid GPF! }
  if ( Operation = opRemove ) and ( AComponent = FDataset ) then
    FDataset := nil;
end;


procedure TRzLookupDialog.SetFont( Value : TFont );
begin
  FFont.Assign( Value );
end;


function TRzLookupDialog.Execute : Boolean;
begin
  { Dynamically create the Lookup form }
  { RzLookupForm declared in the RzLookFm unit }
  RzLookupForm := TRzLookupForm.Create( Application );
  try
    { Initialize properties of lookup form }
    RzLookupForm.BorderStyle := FBorderStyle;
    RzLookupForm.Width := FWidth;
    RzLookupForm.Height := FHeight;
    RzLookupForm.Font := FFont;
    RzLookupForm.Caption := FCaption;
    RzLookupForm.NumbersOnly := FNumbersOnly;
    RzLookupForm.LblPrompt.Caption := 'Search for ' + FSearchField;
                            { Set the field to be used for keyboard searching }
    RzLookupForm.SearchField := FSearchField;
                                        { Set dataset used to populate the grid }
    RzLookupForm.SrcLookup.Dataset := FDataset;

    Result := RzLookupForm.ShowModal = idOK;          { Display the dialog box }
  finally
    RzLookupForm.Free;                            { Don't forget to free the form }
  end;
end;
```

```
{===========================}
{== Register Procedure ==}
{===========================}

procedure Register;
begin
  RegisterComponents( RaizePage, [ TRzLookupDialog ] );
end;

end.
```

No matter how many customizable properties are provided, unless there is a way to display the dialog box, the component is worthless. This is the task handled by the **Execute** method. All dialog box components have a method similar to **Execute**. The responsibilities of this method include creating an instance of the underlying form, initializing the form, displaying the form in a modal state, and finally destroying the form when it is closed.

> **By Convention**
> The function used to display the underlying form is named **Execute**, and returns **True** if the OK button pressed, and **False** otherwise.

All of these requirements are handled by the **TRzLookupDialog.Execute** function. First, an instance of the **TRzLookupForm** class is created. (By the way, notice the use of the **RzLookupForm** variable that is defined in the **RzLookFm** unit.) Next, the component's properties are used to initialize the form's properties. After this, the form is displayed by calling the form's **ShowModal** method, and when the dialog is closed, the **RzLookupForm** variable is destroyed.

Using the RzLookupDialog

Figure 11.8 shows how the RzLookupDialog component is used in an application. The figure shows a simple data entry form used to edit the **Orders** table located in the DBDEMOS database that ships with Delphi. The RzLookupDialog component is used to help the user select a customer for the order.

All of the data controls on the main form are connected to the **TblOrders** table via **SrcOrders**. However, the **DlgLookup** component is connected directly to the **TblCustomer** table. When the Search button is pressed, the **Execute** method connects the SrcLookup component on the dialog form to the TblCustomer table

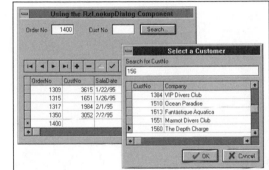

Figure 11.8

Selecting a
Customer.

on the main form. Therefore, the grid will display all of the records in the customer table.

The following method is taken from the sample program shown in the figure and demonstrates how this new component is used to pick a customer. The **Execute** function is called to launch the dialog box and returns when the dialog box is closed. If the return value is **True**, meaning the OK button was pressed, the CustNo column of the current record in the **Orders** table is updated with the CustNo value from the current record in the Customer table.

```
procedure TForm1.BtnSearchClick(Sender: TObject);
begin
  if DlgLookup.Execute then
  begin
    TblOrders.Edit;
    TblOrdersCustNo.Value := TblCustomerCustNo.Value;
  end;
end;
```

That's it. This is all of the code necessary to perform the lookup.

Looking Ahead...

At this point, we have built over a dozen components, and in the process have covered nearly every aspect of component building in Delphi. However, there is still a lot more to learn. Two important topics need to be discussed: data-aware components and property editors. Building data-aware components will be covered next in Chapter 12, while property editors will have to wait until Chapter 14.

Chapter 12

Data-Aware Components

12
Data-Aware Components

Delphi's data-aware components engage in a very important dialog with the underlying database. Here's how to get your components in on the conversation.

In the past several chapters, we've covered a variety of component types including graphical components, custom controls, and nonvisual components. There is only one more category left to cover: *data-aware components.* In this chapter, we'll be taking an in-depth look at the steps required to create a component that establishes a link to a database.

Data-aware components are nothing more than components that can be connected to part of a database. They may be connected to a single field, like the DBEdit component, or they may be connected to the entire table, like a DBGrid. The majority of data-aware components are single-field type controls.

Surprisingly, creating a data-aware component is not a very complex task. In general, the most difficult aspect of the process is coming up with the base component to make data-aware. Unlike the previous categories of components discussed in this book, data-aware components do not descend from any particular class. Instead, creating a data-aware component is more accurately described as a conversion process.

Once you have a non-data-aware component selected, converting it into a data-aware version is relatively straightforward: To become data-aware, an object field and a few methods must be defined in order to support the data connection between the component and the dataset.

As with any type of connection, a data-aware component follows a protocol that defines how data is passed between the component and the associated dataset. However, unlike most connection types, this protocol specification is undocumented. Well, actually some documentation does exist, but its coverage is limited to only the simplest form of data awareness.

Data Awareness

There are two basic forms of data-awareness: *data-browsing* and *data-editing*. Providing data-browsing (that is, read-only) awareness is the easier of the two. The component is simply responsible for reflecting the current value in the database field. Providing data-editing awareness is more difficult because in addition to reflecting the current value, that value can be modified by the user by manipulating the component.

In this chapter, I'll demonstrate both types of data awareness through the construction of two data-aware components. First, a data-aware version of the RzStatusControl from Chapter 9 will guide us through the steps necessary to provide data-browsing awareness. To demonstrate data-editing awareness, a data-aware version of Borland's SpinEdit sample component that ships with Delphi will be created.

Data Browsing

The first data-aware component that we will create in this chapter is the RzDBStatusControl component. This component is simply a status control that can be connected to a database field. Figure 12.1 shows the RzDBStatusControl being used to display the ItemsTotal column of the Orders table from the DBDEMOS database.

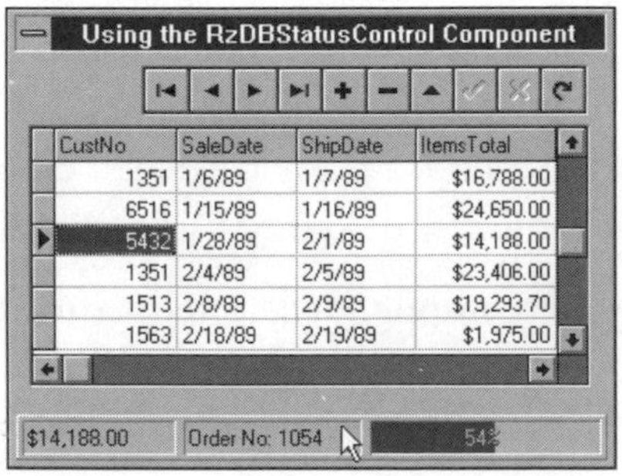

Figure 12.1

Data-Aware
Status Controls.

Figure 12.1 also shows how a field label can be specified for an RzDBStatusControl to aid in identifying the contents of the status pane. The **FieldLabel** property is set to 'Order No: ' in the second status control displaying the order number. (Note: There is no OrderNo column in the table because its corresponding field object has its **Visible** property set to **False**.)

There are either two or three steps involved in creating a data-browsing component; the actual number of steps depends on the type of component being used. The first step is to add the code necessary to prevent the user from altering the data represented by the component. This is necessary because, as a data-browsing component, any changes made will not update the database field value. If the component serving as the base is read-only by default, like a status control, this step is "already done" and can be skipped.

The last two steps in creating a data-browsing component are always required. Each one is covered in detail in the following sections.

The Data Link and Its Properties

Once you have a component that provides read-only capabilities, the next step is to create the data link and its associated properties. The data link is an object whose purpose is to provide a communication channel between the component and the data source. Figure 12.2 illustrates this by showing the relationships between a data-aware control, a data source, a dataset, and a data link.

Figure 12.2

The Data Link Communication Channel.

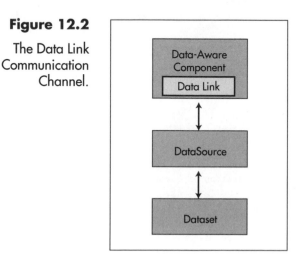

The data link object is owned by the data-aware component, common for all data-aware controls. That is, the component is responsible for the construction and destruction of its data link object. The RzDBStatusControl component is no exception.

Listing 12.1 contains a partial listing of the **RzStatus** unit, first presented in Chapter 9. The **TRzDBStatusControl** is added into this same unit, but rather than show all of the other classes again, only the code associated with this new component is listed.

Listing 12.1 RZSTATUS.PAS—The RzStatus Unit (Part 2)

```
{==============================================================}
{= RzStatus Unit                                             =}
{=                                                           =}
{= This is a partial listing of the RzStatus unit. This portion of the unit =}
{= contains the class declaration for the TRzDBStatusControl component class. =}
{=                                                           =}
{= Building Custom Delphi Components - Ray Konopka           =}
{==============================================================}

unit RzStatus;

interface

uses
  Messages, WinTypes, Controls, Classes, Graphics, ExtCtrls, Menus,
  RzCommon, Buttons, SysUtils, DBTables, DB;


  TRzDBStatusControl = class( TRzCustomStatusControl )
  private
    FDataLink : TFieldDataLink;
    FFieldLabel : string;

    function GetDataField : string;
    procedure SetDataField( const Value : string );
    function GetDataSource : TDataSource;
    procedure SetDataSource( Value : TDataSource );

    procedure SetFieldLabel( const Value : string );
    procedure DataChange( Sender : TObject );
  protected
    procedure Notification( AComponent : TComponent;
                            Operation : TOperation ); override;
  public
    constructor Create( AOwner : TComponent ); override;
    destructor Destroy; override;
  published
    property DataField : string
      read GetDataField
      write SetDataField;
```

```
    property DataSource : TDataSource
      read GetDataSource
      write SetDataSource;

    property FieldLabel : string
      read FFieldLabel
      write SetFieldLabel;

    { Inherited Properties }
    property Alignment;            { No Need to surface Caption property b/c the }
    property CaptionOffset;          { DataSource will supply the display string }
  end; {== TRzDBStatusControl Class Declaration ==}


procedure Register;


implementation

uses
  WinProcs, RzPrgres, ToolHelp;


{== Other Methods Here ==}


{================================}
{== TRzDBStatusControl Methods ==}
{================================}

constructor TRzDBStatusControl.Create( AOwner : TComponent );
begin
  inherited Create( AOwner );
  FFieldLabel := '';

  FDataLink := TFieldDataLink.Create;                        { Create DataLink }
  FDataLink.OnDataChange := DataChange;                { Assign Event Handler }
end;


destructor TRzDBStatusControl.Destroy;
begin
  FDataLink.Free;
  FDataLink := nil;
  inherited Destroy;
end;


procedure TRzDBStatusControl.Notification( AComponent : TComponent;
                                           Operation : TOperation );
begin
  inherited Notification( AComponent, Operation );
```

```
    if ( Operation = opRemove ) and
       ( FDataLink <> nil ) and
       ( AComponent = DataSource ) then
      DataSource := nil;
  end;



function TRzDBStatusControl.GetDataField : string;
begin
  Result := FDataLink.FieldName;
end;



procedure TRzDBStatusControl.SetDataField( const Value : string );
begin
  FDataLink.FieldName := Value;
end;



function TRzDBStatusControl.GetDataSource : TDataSource;
begin
  Result := FDataLink.DataSource;
end;



procedure TRzDBStatusControl.SetDataSource( Value : TDataSource );
begin
  FDataLink.DataSource := Value;
end;



{= TRzDBStatusControl.DataChange                                       =}
{=  This method gets called as a result of a number of different events: =}
{=                                                                     =}
{=    1. The underlying field value changes.  Occurs when changing the value =}
{=       of the column tied to this control and then move to a new column or a =}
{=       new record.                                                   =}
{=    2. The corresponding Dataset goes into Edit mode.                =}
{=    3. The corresponding Dataset referenced by DataSource changes.   =}
{=    4. The current cursor is scrolled to a new record in the table.  =}
{=    5. The record is reset through a Cancel call.                    =}
{=    6. The DataField property changes to reference another column.   =}

procedure TRzDBStatusControl.DataChange( Sender : TObject );
begin
  if FDataLink.Field = nil then
    Caption := ''
  else
    Caption := FFieldLabel + FDataLink.Field.DisplayText;
end;
```

```
procedure TRzDBStatusControl.SetFieldLabel( const Value : string );
begin
  if Value <> FFieldLabel then
  begin
    FFieldLabel := Value;
    DataChange( Self );                        { Repaint with new FieldLabel }
  end;
end;


{=====================}
{== Register Procedure ==}
{=====================}

procedure Register;
begin
  RegisterComponents( RaizeStatusPage,
                      [ TRzStatusControl, TRzClockStatus, TRzKeyStatus,
                        TRzGlyphStatus, TRzResourceStatus ] );

  RegisterComponents( RaizeStatusPage, [ TRzDBStatusControl ] );
end;


end.
```

The **TRzDBStatusControl** class descends from **TRzStatusControl**, so it inherits the functionality necessary to behave as a status control. This descendent class only needs to be concerned with providing the database capabilities. To this end, the **TRzDBStatusControl** class declares a private object, **FDataLink**, of type **TFieldDataLink**. The **TFieldDataLink** class is used whenever the component is to be connected to a single field in the database.

> **By Convention**
>
> Data-aware component classes are named using the *DB* prefix. The prefix follows the leading *T* and the group identifier, if specified. Some examples include: **TDBEdit**, **TDBListBox**, and **TRzDBStatusControl**.

In addition to the **FDataLink** object, the **TRzDBStatusControl** class defines two published properties. The **DataField** and **DataSource** properties are common to anyone who has written a database application in Delphi. These two properties allow the component user to specify the other end of the communications channel. All data-aware components must provide at least a **DataSource** property. Controls that map to a single database field must also provide the **DataField** property.

Interestingly, neither of these properties has its value maintained by the component class. Instead, these values are managed by the data link object. The corresponding access methods for these two properties are provided so that the component user can access them through the **FDataLink** object. The **GetDataField** and **GetDataSource** read access methods simply return the value of the corresponding property of the **FDataLink** object. Likewise, the **SetDataField** and **SetDataSource** write access methods assign the specified value to the corresponding property of the **FDataLink** object.

Although managed by the data link object, the **DataSource** property is still a component reference for the **TRzDBStatusControl** class. Therefore, a **Notification** method is provided. Notice that in the **Notification** method, the **FDataLink** object is tested for a **nil** value. This is necessary because the **DataSource** property reference in the following line uses the **FDataLink** object to get its value.

Since the **FDataLink** object is referenced in the access methods for the **DataField** and **DataSource** properties, it needs to be created before accessing either one of these properties. The best place to create the **FDataLink** object is in the component's constructor, as the **TRzDBStatusControl** class demonstrates. Also, don't forget to free the data link in the component's destructor.

Responding to Data Changes

The final step in creating a data-browsing component is to add the code to respond to changes in the data as the current record in the dataset moves up and down the table. So far, we have established a communication path between the component and the data source, but we have not specified how the component will interpret the data provided by the data source.

From the component's viewpoint, it is only necessary to get the value to be displayed when the value changes. Fortunately, the **TFieldDataLink** class defines the **OnDataChange** event, which is triggered by a number of different actions. Table 12.1 lists each action that generates the **OnDataChange** event. In short, the event is generated any time the underlying field object's value changes.

Table 12.1 OnDataChange Triggers
Actions that Trigger the OnDataChange Event
The underlying field value changes. Occurs when changing the value of the column tied to this control and then moving to a new column or a new record.
The corresponding dataset goes into Edit mode.
The corresponding dataset referenced by DataSource changes.
The current cursor is scrolled to a new record in the table.
The record is reset through a Cancel call.
The DataField property changes to reference another column.

In order to respond to this event, an event handler must be provided. The **TRzDBStatusControl** class defines the **DataChange** method for this purpose. However, before the **DataChange** method will respond to **OnDataChange** events, we must instruct the data link object to send this event to the **DataChange** method. This is performed in the constructor, where the **FDataLink.OnDataChange** event is assigned to the **DataChange** method.

Typically, assigning an event handler in code is discouraged because it can lead to problems if the user assigns a new handler using the Object Inspector. However, this is not a problem in this instance because the **FDataLink** object is a private object and the component user has no way to alter the event handlers of this object. In fact, for data-aware components, this is the only way of being notified that the data has changed.

Since we are building a component, the Object Inspector cannot be used to generate the event handler procedure block. The **DataChange** method must therefore be created manually. The **DataChange** method must be declared as a procedure with a single **TObject** parameter because the **OnDataChange** event is defined as a **TNotifyEvent**.

The **DataChange** method is where the component determines what to display based on the data stored in the current database field. The current value is retrieved by using the **Field** property of the **FDataLink** object. The **Field** property is of type **TField**, and as such can be used to return the current value in a number of formats. For example, **FDataLink.Field.AsInteger** returns the current value in an integer format. This might be useful if we were making a data-aware progress bar.

Before accessing the field object, it's good practice to make sure that the field has been assigned some value. The field object is only assigned when the **DataSource** and **DataField** property both contain valid entries. If the **DataField** property is blank, the **DataChange** event will still get executed, but the field object will be **nil**.

If the field object is not available, then a default, or invalid, value is usually displayed. For the RzDBStatusControl component, an empty string is displayed. If the field object is available, its properties are used to obtain the data to display. For this component, the **DisplayText** property of the field object is prefixed with the **FieldLabel** string specified by the user.

The **DisplayText** property is used instead of the **Text** property so that the status control displays the formatted value. The **Text** property always contains the unformatted value. For example, if a field represents a currency value, the **DisplayText** property returns a value such as "$1,572.38" while the **Text** property returns "1572.38."

Now that we have finished constructing a data-browsing component, it's time to move on to the next level of awareness, and build a data-editing component.

Data Editing

Building a data-editing component is actually an extension of building a data-browsing component. To demonstrate the process of adding support for data-editing, the RzDBSpinEdit component will be created. RzDBSpinEdit is a data-aware version of the SpinEdit sample component that ships with Delphi. Figure 12.3 shows the RzDBSpinEdit component being used to edit the Qty field of the Items tables in the DBDEMOS database.

The RzDBSpinEdit component, like all data-editing components, provides both data-browsing and data-editing features. For example, like a data-browser, as the

Figure 12.3

Using the RzDBSpinEdit Component.

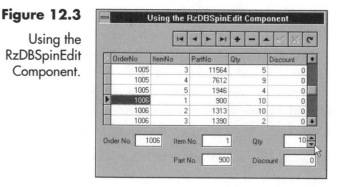

user scrolls through the records in the table, the component is updated to reflect the current field value. But unlike a data-browser, any change made to this value is reflected back into the database.

Listing 12.2 contains the source code for the RzDBSpin unit that defines the **TRzDBSpinEdit** class. This component class inherits its spin edit capabilities from the **TSpinEdit** class and therefore only needs to provide the data-editing features. As you can see from the class declaration, creating a data-editing component is much more involved than creating a data-browsing component. However, because data-editing controls must also behave as data-browsers, there is some duplication of functionality. In fact, building a data-editing component starts with the same steps required to build a data-browsing component.

Listing 12.2   RZDBSPIN.PAS—The RzDBSpin Unit

```
{=============================================================}
{= RzDBSpin Unit                                            =}
{=                                                          =}
{= This unit implements the TRzDBSpinEdit component which is a data-aware =}
{= version of the TSpinEdit Sample component provided with Delphi.        =}
{=                                                          =}
{= Building Custom Delphi Components - Ray Konopka           =}
{=============================================================}

unit RzDBSpin;

interface

uses
  SysUtils, WinTypes, WinProcs, Messages, Classes, Graphics, Controls,
  Forms, StdCtrls, Spin, DB, DBTables, RzCommon;

type
  EInvalidFieldType = class( Exception );

  TRzDBSpinEdit = class( TSpinEdit )
  private
    FAlignment : TAlignment;
    FDataLink : TFieldDataLink;
    FFocused : Boolean;
    FDisplayText : string;
    FCanvas : TControlCanvas;

    function GetDataField : string;
    procedure SetDataField( const Value : string );
    function GetDataSource : TDataSource;
    procedure SetDataSource( Value : TDataSource );
    function GetReadOnly : Boolean;
```

```
    procedure SetReadOnly( Value : Boolean );
    procedure CheckFieldType( const Value : string );

    procedure DataChange( Sender : TObject );
    procedure EditingChange( Sender : TObject );
    procedure UpdateData( Sender : TObject );
    procedure ActiveChange( Sender : TObject );

    procedure WMCut( var Msg : TMessage ); message wm_Cut;
    procedure WMPaste( var Msg : TMessage ); message wm_Paste;
    procedure WMPaint( var Msg : TWMPaint ); message wm_Paint;
    procedure UpdateFocus( Value : Boolean );
    procedure CMEnter( var Msg : TCMEnter ); message cm_Enter;
    procedure CMExit( var Msg : TCMExit ); message cm_Exit;
  protected
    procedure Notification( AComponent : TComponent;
                            Operation : TOperation ); override;
    procedure Change; override;
    procedure KeyDown( var Key : Word; Shift : TShiftState ); override;
    procedure KeyPress( var Key : Char ); override;
    procedure UpClick( Sender : TObject ); override;
    procedure DownClick( Sender : TObject ); override;
  public
    constructor Create( AOwner : TComponent ); override;
    destructor Destroy; override;
  published
    property DataField : string
      read GetDataField
      write SetDataField;

    property DataSource : TDataSource
      read GetDataSource
      write SetDataSource;

    property ReadOnly : Boolean          { This property controls the ReadOnly }
      read GetReadOnly                            { State of the DataLink }
      write SetReadOnly
      default False;

    { Inherited Properties }
    property BorderStyle;
    property Width default 50;
  end;

procedure Register;

implementation


{==========================}
{-- TRzDBSpinEdit Methods --}
{==========================}
```

```
constructor TRzDBSpinEdit.Create( AOwner : TComponent );
begin
  inherited Create( AOwner );
  Width := 50;

  inherited ReadOnly := True;            { Sets the edit control to be read-only }

  FDataLink := TFieldDataLink.Create;

  { To support the TField.FocusControl method, set the FDataLink.Control      }
  { property to point to the spin button.  The Control property requires a    }
  { TWinControl component.                                                    }
  FDataLink.Control := Self;

  FDataLink.OnDataChange := DataChange;              { Assign Event Handlers }
  FDataLink.OnUpdateData := UpdateData;
  FDataLink.OnEditingChange := EditingChange;
  FDataLink.OnActiveChange := ActiveChange;
end;


destructor TRzDBSpinEdit.Destroy;
begin
  FDataLink.Free;
  FDataLink := nil;
  FCanvas.Free;
  inherited Destroy;
end;


procedure TRzDBSpinEdit.Notification( AComponent : TComponent;
                                      Operation : TOperation );
begin
  inherited Notification( AComponent, Operation );
  if ( Operation = opRemove ) and
     ( FDataLink <> nil ) and
     ( AComponent = DataSource ) then
    DataSource := nil;
end;


function TRzDBSpinEdit.GetDataField : string;
begin
  Result := FDataLink.FieldName;
end;


procedure TRzDBSpinEdit.SetDataField( const Value : string );
begin
  CheckFieldType( Value );                    { Check that field type is Integer }
  FDataLink.FieldName := Value;
end;
```

```
function TRzDBSpinEdit.GetDataSource : TDataSource;
begin
  Result := FDataLink.DataSource;
end;


procedure TRzDBSpinEdit.SetDataSource( Value : TDataSource );
begin
  FDataLink.DataSource := Value;
end;


function TRzDBSpinEdit.GetReadOnly : Boolean;
begin
  Result := FDataLink.ReadOnly;
end;


procedure TRzDBSpinEdit.SetReadOnly( Value : Boolean );
begin
  FDataLink.ReadOnly := Value;
end;


{= TRzDBSpinEdit.CheckFieldType                                      =}
{=   This method checks to make sure the field type corresponding to the  =}
{=   column referenced by Value is either ftInteger, ftSmallInt, or ftWord.  =}
{=   If it is not, then an EInvalidFieldType exception is raised.         =}

procedure TRzDBSpinEdit.CheckFieldType( const Value : string );
var
  FieldType : TFieldType;
begin
  if ( Value <> '' ) and
     ( FDataLink <> nil ) and
     ( FDataLink.Dataset <> nil ) and
     ( FDataLink.Dataset.Active ) then
  begin
    FieldType := FDataLink.Dataset.FieldByName( Value ).DataType;
    if ( FieldType <> ftInteger ) and
       ( FieldType <> ftSmallInt ) and
       ( FieldType <> ftWord ) then
    begin
      raise EInvalidFieldType.Create( 'RzDBSpinEdit.DataField can only be ' +
                                      'connected to columns of type Integer' );
    end;
  end;
end;


procedure TRzDBSpinEdit.Change;
begin
```

```
    if FDataLink <> nil then
      FDataLink.Modified;              { Tell the FDataLink that the data has changed }
    inherited Change;
end;


procedure TRzDBSpinEdit.KeyDown( var Key : Word; Shift : TShiftState );
begin
  inherited KeyDown( Key, Shift );

  { Need to handle Old-Fashioned Cut, Paste, and Delete keystrokes }
  if ( Key = vk_Delete ) or
     ( ( Key = vk_Insert ) and ( ssShift in Shift ) ) then
    FDataLink.Edit;
end;


procedure TRzDBSpinEdit.KeyPress( var Key : Char );
begin
  inherited KeyPress( Key );

  { The field object referenced by FDataLink will tell us which keys are valid }

  if ( Key in [ #32..#255 ] ) and
     ( FDataLink.Field <> nil ) and
     not FDataLink.Field.IsValidChar( Key ) then
  begin
    MessageBeep( 0 );
    Key := #0;                                   { Invalid keys are discarded }
  end;

  case Key of
    ^H, ^V, ^X, #32..#255:
      FDataLink.Edit;                   { Put corresponding Dataset into Edit mode }

    #27:                                              { Escape key pressed }
    begin
      FDataLink.Reset;
      SelectAll;
      Key := #0;
    end;
  end;
end;


procedure TRzDBSpinEdit.UpClick( Sender : TObject );
begin
  if ReadOnly then
    MessageBeep( 0 )                { Prevent change if FDataLink is ReadOnly }
  else
  begin
    if FDataLink.Edit then           { Put corresponding Dataset into Edit mode }
```

```
      Value := Value + Increment;
  end;
end;


procedure TRzDBSpinEdit.DownClick( Sender : TObject );
begin
  if ReadOnly then
    MessageBeep( 0 )                    { Prevent change if FDataLink is ReadOnly }
  else
  begin
    if FDataLink.Edit then           { Put corresponding Dataset into Edit mode }
      Value := Value - Increment;
  end;
end;



{= TRzDBSpinEdit.DataChange                                             =}
{=   This method gets called as a result of a number of different events: =}
{=                                                                       =}
{=   1. The underlying field value changes.  Occurs when changing the value =}
{=      of the column tied to this control and then move to a new column or a =}
{=      new record.                                                      =}
{=   2. The corresponding Dataset goes into Edit mode.                   =}
{=   3. The corresponding Dataset referenced by DataSource changes.      =}
{=   4. The current cursor is scrolled to a new record in the table.     =}
{=   5. The record is reset through a Cancel call.                       =}
{=   6. The DataField property changes to reference another column.      =}

procedure TRzDBSpinEdit.DataChange( Sender : TObject );
begin
  if FDataLink.Field <> nil then
  begin
    if FAlignment <> FDataLink.Field.Alignment then
    begin
      Text := '';        { Forces the Text assignment below to cause a Repaint }
      FAlignment := FDataLink.Field.Alignment;
    end;

    Text := FDataLink.Field.Text;
    if FFocused and FDataLink.CanModify then
      FDisplayText := Text
    else
      FDisplayText := FDataLink.Field.DisplayText;
  end
  else                                          { There is no field assignment }
  begin
    FAlignment := taLeftJustify;
    if csDesigning in ComponentState then
      Text := Name                    { In design-mode, show Name of component }
    else
      Text := '';
```

```
  end;
end; {= TRzDBSpinEdit.DataChange =}


{= TRzDBSpinEdit.UpdateData                                              =}
{=   This method gets called when the corresponding field value and the  =}
{=   contents of the SpinEdit need to be synchronized.  Note that this method =}
{=   only gets called if this control was responsible for altering the data. =}

procedure TRzDBSpinEdit.UpdateData(Sender: TObject);
begin
  { You can cancel the Update process by raising an exception in this method.}

  FDataLink.Field.Text := Text;
end;


{= TRzDBSpinEdit.EditingChange                                           =}
{=   This method gets called when the State of the attached Dataset (via the =}
{=   DataSource) changes between an Editing state and a Non-Editing state.  =}
{=   The different states are described below:                            =}
{=                                                                        =}
{=   Editing States        Non-Editing States                            =}
{=   ───────               ──────────                                     =}
{=   dsEdit                dsInactive                                     =}
{=   dsInsert              dsBrowse                                       =}
{=   dsSetKey              dsCalcFields                                   =}
{=                                                                        =}
{= NOTE: This method only gets called if the DataLink is not ReadOnly.    =}

procedure TRzDBSpinEdit.EditingChange(Sender: TObject);
begin
  { The ReadOnly property of the underlying edit control is toggled according }
  { to the state of the DataSource.                                          }

  inherited ReadOnly := not FDataLink.Editing;
end;


{= TRzDBSpinEdit.ActiveChange                                            =}
{=   This method gets called whenever the Active property of the attached =}
{=   Dataset changes.                                                     =}
{=                                                                        =}
{=   NOTE: You can use the FDataLink.Active property to determine the *new* =}
{=         state of the Dataset.                                          =}

procedure TRzDBSpinEdit.ActiveChange( Sender : TObject );
begin
  { If the Dataset is becoming Active, then check to make sure the field type }
  { of the DataField property is an Integer type.                            }
```

```
    if ( FDataLink <> nil ) and FDataLink.Active then
      CheckFieldType( DataField );
end;



{= Both the WMPaste and WMCut methods had to be copied from the TSpinEdit   =}
{= class because placing the Dataset into Edit mode must come before altering =}
{= the text, but after checking for ReadOnly.                               =}

procedure TRzDBSpinEdit.WMPaste( var Msg : TMessage );
begin
  if not EditorEnabled or ReadOnly then   { EditorEnabled defined in TSpinEdit }
    Exit;
  FDataLink.Edit;
  inherited;
end;



procedure TRzDBSpinEdit.WMCut( var Msg : TMessage );
begin
  if not EditorEnabled or ReadOnly then
    Exit;
  FDataLink.Edit;
  inherited;
end;



{= TRzDBSpinEdit.WMPaint
{=    This method takes a trick provided in the DBCtrls unit for handling the  =}
{=    display of right-justified text into an edit field.  If the text needs  =}
{=    to be drawn right-justified, then the text is drawn manually. Otherwise, =}
{=    the default message handler handles it.  The contents are always drawn  =}
{=    left-justified when the control has the focus.                          =}

procedure TRzDBSpinEdit.WMPaint( var Msg : TWMPaint );
var
  Width, Margin, X, I : Integer;
  EditRct, TempRct : TRect;
  DC : HDC;
  PS : TPaintStruct;
begin
  if ( FAlignment = taLeftJustify ) or FFocused then
  begin
    inherited;
    Exit;
  end;

  if FCanvas = nil then
  begin
    FCanvas := TControlCanvas.Create;            { Need something to draw on }
    FCanvas.Control := Self;                     { Create a Control Canvas }
  end;
```

```
  DC := Msg.DC;
  if DC = 0 then
    DC := BeginPaint( Handle, PS );                          { Set up Windows for painting }
  FCanvas.Handle := DC;                               { Connect Canvas to device context }

  try
    FCanvas.Font := Font;
    with FCanvas do
    begin
      { Because the SpinButton is inside the edit field, the entire client area }
      { is not used for drawing text.  Send the em_GetRect method to get the    }
      { rect to use.  Adjust the right side to avoid drawing under spin button  }
      EditRct := ClientRect;
      Perform( em_GetRect, 0, LongInt( @TempRct ) );

      if BorderStyle = bsSingle then
      begin
        EditRct.Right := TempRct.Right + 7;
        if NewStyleControls then
          Dec( EditRct.Right, 2 );
        Brush.Color := clWindowFrame;
        FrameRect( EditRct );                                        { Draw the Border }
        InflateRect( EditRct, -1, -1 );
      end
      else
        EditRct.Right := TempRct.Right;

      Brush.Color := Color;
      Width := TextWidth( FDisplayText );
      if BorderStyle = bsNone then
        Margin := 0
      else
        Margin := 2;
      if FAlignment = taRightJustify then
        X := EditRct.Right - Width - Margin
      else                                                  { Handle Center Alignment }
        X := ( EditRct.Left + EditRct.Right - Width ) div 2;
      TextRect( EditRct, X, Margin, FDisplayText );                   { Draw the Text }
    end;
  finally
    FCanvas.Handle := 0;
    if Msg.DC = 0 then
      EndPaint( Handle, PS );
  end;

end;


procedure TRzDBSpinEdit.UpdateFocus( Value : Boolean );
begin
  { Because Alignment automatically reverts back to taLeftJustify when control }
  { gets the focus, the control must be repainted, when the focus changes.     }
```

```
    if FFocused <> Value then
    begin
      FFocused := Value;
      if FAlignment <> taLeftJustify then
        Invalidate;
      FDataLink.Reset;
    end;
  end;


procedure TRzDBSpinEdit.CMEnter( var Msg : TCMEnter );
begin
  UpdateFocus( True );
  inherited;
end;


procedure TRzDBSpinEdit.CMExit( var Msg : TCMExit );
begin
  try                    { Attempt to Update the record if focus leaves the spin edit }
    FDataLink.UpdateRecord;
  except
    SelectAll;
    SetFocus;                      { Keep the focus on the control if Update fails }
    raise;                                        { Re-raise the exception }
  end;

  UpdateFocus( False );
  inherited;
end;




{==========================}
{== Register Procedure ==}
{==========================}

procedure Register;
begin
  RegisterComponents( RaizePage, [ TRzDBSpinEdit ] );
end;

end.
```

The Data Link Revisited

Like data-browsing components, data-editing controls need to create a data link object in order to access the data in the database. Therefore, the **TRzDBSpinEdit** class declares an **FDataLink** private object and the corresponding **DataSource** and **DataField** properties. As was done in the **TRzDBStatusControl** class, the **FDataLink** object is created in the component's constructor and destroyed in the destructor.

The access methods for the **DataSource** and **DataField** properties are identical to those defined in **TRzDBStatusControl** with the exception of the **SetDataField** method. Before assigning a new field name to the **FDataLink.FieldName** property, the new name is passed to the **CheckFieldType** method. This method checks the data type of the specified field to make sure that it references an integer type field. This check is necessary because the inherited spin edit control can only handle integer values. Check the type to ensure that the component cannot be connected to a non-integer field.

When the user specifies a new **DataField**, the **CheckFieldType** method uses the **FDataLink** object to access the associated dataset to retrieve the **DataType** value of the new field name. If the **DataType** is not one of the integer types (that is, **ftInteger**, **ftSmallInt**, and **ftWord**), an exception is raised. In this event, the exception causes control to jump out of the **SetDataField** method and skip assigning the field name. Raising an exception like this is especially useful at design-time. If the user attempts to select a non-integer **DataField**, the exception prevents the assignment and causes the Delphi IDE to display an error message.

Read Only

In addition to the **DataSource** and **DataField** properties, data-editing components will generally declare a **ReadOnly** property. This property provides component users with access to the **ReadOnly** property of the data link object. Specifically, this property indicates whether or not the underlying field object allows editing. For example, even if the component allows editing, any changes made in the component will *not* be reflected in the database unless the field object also allows editing. Therefore, it makes sense to prevent the user from editing the data if the **FDataLink.ReadOnly** property is **True**.

Unfortunately, adding this property can be quite confusing because some components already define a **ReadOnly** property. Examples include **TEdit**, **TMemo**, and **TSpinEdit**. All of these components define a **ReadOnly** property that, when **True**, prevents the user from altering the data in the control.

In situations like this, it is not possible to use the inherited **ReadOnly** property because there is no way to synchronize the inherited **ReadOnly** property with the **ReadOnly** property of the underlying field object. For example, even though a data-aware control and its underlying field object are connected via the data link, the data-aware control is not notified of changes made to the field object's properties. In particular, if the field object's **ReadOnly** value is changed, the data-aware control is not made aware of the change.

The **TRzDBSpinEdit** class handles this problem by overriding the inherited **ReadOnly** property. The new property functions as an access point to the **FDataLink.ReadOnly** property. Whenever the **ReadOnly** state of the control is needed, the new property is used. For example, the **UpClick** and **DownClick** methods, which are called when the user presses one of the spin buttons, checks the new **ReadOnly** property to determine if the control can be updated. If **ReadOnly** is set to **True**, a beep is sounded and the value is unchanged.

What happens to the inherited **ReadOnly** property? It is still accessible by using the **inherited** keyword before the property name. This is demonstrated by the **TRzDBSpinEdit** class, which uses the inherited **ReadOnly** flag to prevent users from entering data into the control unless it is connected to a data source and a data field. In the constructor, the component is placed into **ReadOnly** mode with the following statement:

```
inherited ReadOnly := True;
```

But if the control is set to be read-only, how does the user ever enter data? Although the component is not notified of changes in the data link's read-only state, it can be notified of several other events. One of them will be used to turn off the inherited **ReadOnly** property when the component needs to allow editing.

DataChange Revisited

Recall from the RzDBStatusControl component that the data link object triggers an **OnDataChange** event whenever the field value changes. In order to be notified of the event, the RzDBStatusControl component defined the **DataChange** event handler. Likewise, the RzDBSpinEdit component needs to be notified when it is appropriate to update the display. As a result, the **TRzDBSpinEdit** class defines a **DataChange** event handler.

Although this component's version is more complicated, it essentially performs the same task; that is, to query the field object for the correct value to display. As usual, the **TRzDBSpinEdit.DataChange** method first checks to make sure the **Field** object is not **nil**. If it is, a **DataField** has *not* been specified for the component. In this circumstance, the **Text** property of the component is set to either the component name if in design-mode or to an empty string if not.

If a field object has been assigned, the **DataChange** method first updates the **FAlignment** field. This private field is used when the component paints itself. If the control has the focus, the text in the edit portion is always drawn left-justified. However, if the control does not have the focus, the text is drawn using the alignment value specified by the field object. This will usually be **taRightJustify** because the RzDBSpinEdit component can only be connected to integer type fields and these fields use **taRightJustify** by default. (NOTE: The actual painting process is described in the source code.)

The next step is to populate the component's **Text** property with the value stored in the corresponding field's **Text** property. This ensures the correct value is displayed. The assignments to **FDisplayText** that follow are provided to support displaying formatted numbers. The separate **FDisplayText** variable is used because the formatted output is only displayed when the control does not have the focus. Furthermore, it is not possible to set the component's **Text** property to the field's **DisplayText** because the inherited **TSpinEdit** class converts the **Text** string into an integer value in order to increment and decrement the value. If the **Text** property contains formatting characters like commas, the conversion will fail.

More Data Events

In addition to the **OnDataChange** event, all data-editing components must provide an event handler for the data link's **OnUpdateData** event. This event is triggered when the corresponding field object's value needs to be synchronized to the value represented by the component. In other words, this event is the opposite of **OnDataChange**. Instead of retrieving the current value from the database, this event is used to *set* the current value.

The **TRzDBSpinEdit** class defines the **UpdateData** method to handle the **OnUpdateData** event. This method updates the database by assigning the F**DataLink.Field.Text** property to the current string stored in the component.

There are additional events triggered by the data link that can be very useful to data-editing components. One such event is the **OnActiveChange** event. This event occurs whenever the **Active** property of the attached dataset changes; that is, when the dataset opens or closes.

The **TRzDBSpinEdit** class defines the **ActiveChange** event handler for this event to verify the field type of the **DataField** property. When the dataset is being opened, which is determined by checking the **FDataLink.Active** property, the **CheckFieldType** method is called. This verification is necessary because opening a dataset does not cause the **SetDataField** method to be called. Therefore, it is possible that **DataField** specifies a field name that does not exist in the new table. More importantly, the field may exist, but it could be of the wrong type. If the field type is not an integer, the exception that is raised will prevent the dataset from opening. This further ensures that the RzDBSpinEdit component can only be connected to valid fields.

So what about the **ReadOnly** problem? It was stated earlier that the inherited **ReadOnly** property is set to **True** in the constructor to prevent the user from entering data unless the component is connected to a valid data field. Therefore, the problem is that in order to edit the data, the inherited **ReadOnly** property must be turned off.

The solution is to write an event handler for the data link object's **OnEditingChange** event. This event occurs when the **State** property of the attached dataset changes between an editing state and a non-editing state. Table 12.2 describes the two categories of database states.

The **TRzDBSpinEdit.EditingChange** method handles this event by setting the inherited **ReadOnly** property to the opposite value of the data link's **Editing** property. This results in the inherited **ReadOnly** property being turned off when the dataset enters one of the editing states. Likewise, when the dataset returns to a non-editing state, the component reverts to being read-only.

AutoEdit

Consider a form containing a dataset, a data source, and several data-aware components. Further suppose that all of the components are connected appropriately. By default, if the user makes a change in any of the data-aware controls, the dataset is automatically placed into edit mode. This feature is controlled by the **AutoEdit** property of the DataSource component, but the real work is performed by the data-aware components.

Table 12.2 Dataset States

Editing States	Non-Editing States
dsEdit	dsInactive
dsInsert	dsBrowse
dsSetKey	dsCalcFields

To support these automatic edit features, the data-editing control is responsible for determining when to jump into edit mode. Providing this capability requires trapping every process that can alter the data contents of the control. This will be different depending on the type of control. For the RzDBSpinEdit component, there are several ways in which the text can be modified. The user can press keys on the keyboard, use the clipboard to cut and paste text, or press either the up or down spin buttons.

The various extra methods of **TRzDBSpinEdit** are provided to trap for the above conditions. No matter what the circumstances of the change, if the contents of the spin edit control changes, the **FDataLink.Edit** method is called. This method places the associated dataset into edit mode. This **Edit** method is defined as a function that returns **True** if the dataset was indeed placed into edit mode.

Focus Changes

When creating a data-editing component, you must also be aware of focus changes, particularly if the component *loses* focus. In this event, the component should force the **OnUpdateData** event to be generated. This is accomplished by calling the data link's **UpdateRecord** method. The **CMExit** message handling method for the **TRzDBSpinEdit** class wraps the call inside a **try...except** block. If the update fails, the focus is returned to the control.

For more examples of data-aware controls, take a look at the source code for the **DBCtrls** unit. This unit defines all of the standard data-aware controls, and contains quite a bit of useful information. For example, the data-aware features of the **TRzDBSpinEdit** component parallel the methods demonstrated in the **TDBEdit** component class.

The Final Step

The final task in creating a data-editing component is to override the **Change** event dispatch method. Within this method, and before calling the inherited method, set the data link's **Modified** property to **True**. This instructs the data link that the record will need to be updated before moving on to a new record. Without setting the **Modified** flag, it would be possible for changes made using the component to be discarded. Setting the **Modified** property prevents this from happening.

As you can see, creating a fully functional data-editing component is quite a bit more involved that creating a simple read-only data browser. However, once the protocol is understood, creating new data-editing components becomes more tedious than complex.

Looking Ahead...

The key to writing data-aware components is the data link. But, surprisingly, the data link is only a small portion of the Delphi database architecture. The field objects that have been casually mentioned in this chapter are much more crucial to the overall architecture. In the next chapter, we'll learn more about these field objects and see how they can be used to create data-aware business components. This new type of component gives Delphi applications a way of adopting a three-tiered approached to database programming that is highly appropriate for business-oriented applications.

Part 4

Advanced Techniques

Chapter 13

Data-Aware Business Components

Data-Aware Business Components

Delphi components present some unique advantages for the embodiment of business rules in exterprise-wide database applications.

In the last chapter, we covered the steps necessary to create data-aware controls. In the process, we found that data-aware controls utilize a data link object to maintain a communication channel between the control and the data source. While the data link is a crucial element in supporting data-aware controls, the real workhorses in Delphi's database architecture are the field objects.

Field objects control the attributes of each column in a database table or result set. They are also responsible for supplying the data to the data source, which in turn uses the data link to transfer the data to the data-aware controls. In this chapter, we'll be covering field objects in more detail. This is necessary because the *data-aware business components* introduced in this chapter are highly dependent on field objects.

Field objects are responsible for giving a data-aware business component its data-awareness. As we shall see, business components are indeed data-aware, but they are unlike data-aware controls in that they do not provide a user interface element. Instead, they are nonvisual components that serve to encapsulate the business rules associated with an object whose data is stored in a database table.

What Are Business Components?

Before diving into the technical details on how to build a business component, it would make sense to know what it is we're actually going to build. It also wouldn't hurt to know why we might want to build something like this. This section addresses both of these concerns.

With a steady increase in demand for client/server programming, there has been growing emphasis placed on dividing an application into three distinct layers. These layers typically include the *user interface layer*, the *data access layer*, and the *business rules layer*. Each layer is isolated from the others. This means that none of the layers needs to be concerned with how the other layers perform their respective functions. This philosophy is commonly called the *three-tiered approach* to database application development.

The user interface layer and the data access layer are fairly easy to separate. Delphi does a good job of this through the dataset and data source components. The user interface, isolated in the form file, does not need to know how or where the data is accessed. This arrangement makes creating database applications very simple. However, when business rules need to be incorporated into the application, they are typically embodied in methods of the form class. The problem with this is that the form is actually part of the user interface layer. This violation of the three-tiered approach does not promote reusability.

The reason is that database tables are rarely dedicated to a single application, let alone a single form. Placing the business rules associated with a table inside a form's methods works for that particular form only. Another programmer might misunderstand the business rules and implement them in a slightly different way in another form or another program, with resulting data consistency bugs that are often extremely hard to detect and fix.

To demonstrate the potential problems, consider the following: You're developing an application that needs to determine the number of vacation days an employee has earned for the current year. You could write the code to calculate this number in one of the form's methods; for example, a button click event handler. However, if you need to perform this same calculation in another program, or even on another form, you would have to duplicate the code—and make sure you really do duplicate the code.

In practice, this scenario is usually avoided by wrapping the calculation code inside a function that resides in a separate Delphi unit that can then be used by any application that needs to perform that function. This certainly increases the ability to reuse the calculation code, but requires extra parameters defining the values needed for the calculation. This can get quite long for complex business rules. Furthermore, this particular function is only applicable to employees. This suggests that an object-oriented solution would be far more appropriate in circumstances like this.

A better approach would be to construct an employee class that encapsulates the data associated with an employee and knows how to perform the necessary related business functions, such as calculating the number of vacation days earned. This function would be defined as a method of the employee class. In this same way, any business rules associated with an employee can be defined in the class. Another example might be a rule that specifies that an employee's salary cannot exceed some salary cap.

The only problem with this approach is in how it fits in with the way Delphi works. That is, how does an employee object interact with the Delphi database architecture? For example, a typical Delphi database application uses data-aware controls connected to a data source, which is then connected to a dataset. In this arrangement, the data-aware controls directly edit the record referenced by the dataset.

The problem lies in getting the data into and out of the employee object. Any time a change is made in any one of the data-aware controls, the employee object has to be updated. This requires handling events, which unfortunately requires writing code in the form file, which was in fact the original problem we've been trying to avoid! Even if we can keep the employee object in synch with the controls, there is still the problem of posting the record to the database. The posting process would have to be interrupted so that the data could be moved from the employee object to the underlying field objects. Again, this would require more code in the form file.

As an alternative, you could adopt the employee object approach, but avoid using the data-aware controls. Although this solution does eliminate some of the synchronization code needed, it is no better than the previous approach because the advanced features of the data-aware controls (for example, auto-editing) are sacrificed.

The Best of Both Worlds

The data-aware business component architecture presented in this chapter provides a framework for building classes that encapsulate data and business rules without sacrificing the data-aware controls. Furthermore, implemented as Delphi components, business components are easily reused in separate applications. Simply drop the appropriate business component on the form and connect it to a dataset. All of the business rules associated with that object are available through the component's properties and methods.

What makes business components data-aware? The term "data-aware" is used to denote the similarity between these components and the data-aware controls. As we saw in the last chapter, data-aware controls are linked to a dataset, usually to a single column or field, and the value displayed is based on the current cursor position in the dataset. In the same way, data-aware business components are also linked to a dataset. But instead of being linked to a single column like a DBEdit component, the business component can reference any of the columns, much like a DBGrid. Furthermore, the data referenced by the component is always based on the current record in the dataset.

The similarities between these two types of components are attributed to the fact that both are influenced by field objects. This common influence is also the primary reason data-aware business components work cooperatively with data-aware controls. That is, field objects ensure that changes made in a data-aware control are reflected in the business component and vice-versa. The remarkable aspect of this solution is that this synchronization is performed automatically without any intervention from the component user.

This all means that field objects have a significant role in the architecture for data-aware business components. As a result, before describing the details of the business component architecture, the next section presents an in-depth look at field objects and their capabilities.

Field Objects

Field objects are perhaps the most underrated (and poorly understood) feature in Delphi's entire database architecture. Field objects correspond to columns in a database table or result set, and are implemented as nonvisual components. Each data type that may be used in a column is represented by a field component class.

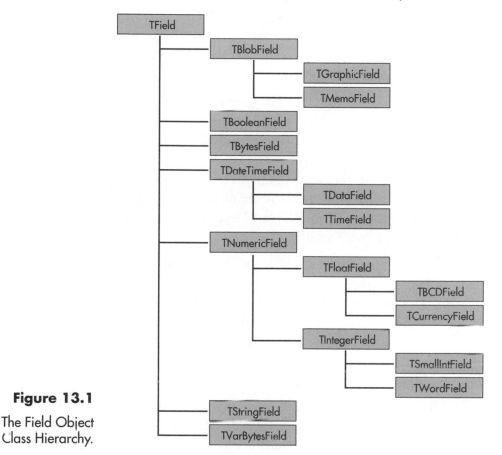

Figure 13.1

The Field Object
Class Hierarchy.

Examples include **TStringField**, **TDataField**, and **TCurrencyField**. Figure 13.1
shows that all field classes descend from a common **TField** class.

Field objects are very powerful components. Their obscurity is mainly due to the
fact that they are not represented visually. That is, they do not appear on the
component palette, and therefore are not dropped onto a form. Instead, field
objects are created implicitly whenever a dataset is opened, or else explicitly by
the user using the Fields Editor.

How field objects are accessed depends on how they were created. If the field
objects are created implicitly by the dataset, they can be accessed only at runtime
using either the **Fields** array property or the **FieldByName** method, as shown in
the following code fragment. (**TblEmployee** is a **TTable** component referencing
the Employee table in the DBDEMOS database.)

```
TblEmployee.Fields[ 4 ].AsDateTime := Now;

TblEmployee.FieldByName( 'HireDate' ).AsDateTime := Now;
```

Both of the above statements set the **HireDate** field object to the current date using the **Now** function. Since the **Fields** array and **FieldByName** method return a reference to a **TField** object and *not* one of the descendent classes, the **AsDateTime** conversion property must be used. The **TField** class defines several such conversion properties, which enable users to treat the data stored in the field object in a number of different ways. For example, to treat the value stored in a field object as a string value, the **AsString** conversion property is used. Likewise, since the **Now** function returns a **TDateTime** value, the **AsDataTime** property is used to ensure type compatibility.

When field objects are created explicitly, they can be accessed directly without having to reference them through a dataset. There are many advantages to this approach. The most important is that when field objects are created explicitly, they are available at design-time. But before we can access the field objects, they must first be created using the Fields Editor.

The Fields Editor

The Fields Editor gives application developers the ability to create, delete, and define field objects for a dataset. The Fields Editor is invoked at design-time by double-clicking on a dataset component, or by selecting the "Fields editor..." menu item from the dataset's popup menu. Figure 13.2 shows the Fields Editor being used in the EmpEdtr1 application, the first version of an employee editor.

Unlike the **Fields** array and **FieldByName** methods, which are only available at runtime, explicitly created field objects are available at design-time. This is because field objects created by the Fields Editor are *owned* by the form rather than by the dataset. Implicitly created field objects are owned by the dataset, and the dataset only surfaces the field objects through the **Fields** array and **FieldByName** method. Explicitly created field objects, on the other hand, are surfaced by the form class as individual components. They appear in the form's class declaration just like any other component dropped onto the form.

Regardless of how the field objects are created, the dataset the objects are associated with always maintains a reference to the field objects. In fact, the dataset always ensures that its associated field objects are destroyed when necessary. Since

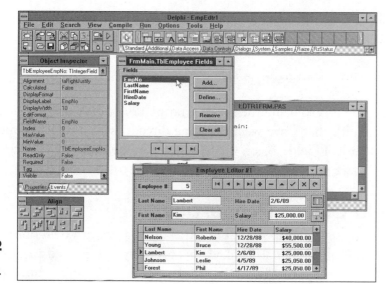

Figure 13.2

The Fields Editor.

the dataset maintains a reference to all field objects, even those owned by a form, the **Fields** array and **FieldByName** method can always be used to access a field object at runtime.

Another important aspect of field objects is that they are indeed components with properties and events that can be modified at design-time. Of course, this means that the field objects must be explicitly created using the Fields Editor so that they can appear in the Object Inspector. But once created, selecting any of the fields in the Fields Editor causes the corresponding field object to appear in the Object Inspector.

When the Fields Editor creates a field object, it names the object by concatenating the dataset name and the column name. This is demonstrated in Figure 13.2, where the field object corresponding to the EmpNo column is named **TblEmployeeEmpNo**. Note that the field objects are also accessible through the component combo box of the Object Inspector.

Perhaps the strongest argument for creating field objects using the Fields Editor is that explicitly created field objects have the same data type as the database column to which they are mapped. For example, the **TblEmployeeHireDate** field object is declared as a **TDateTimeField**. As a result, accessing the field object's data is more efficient and more concise. Consider the following statement, which again sets the HireDate column to the current date, but this time using the **TblEmployeeHireDate** field object:

```
TblEmployeeHireDate.Value := Now;
```

Compare this to using the **Fields** array and **FieldByName** method shown earlier. Also notice that since we are dealing directly with a **TDateTimeField**, and not just a basic **TField** object, we can use the **Value** property to access the data in its native data type. That is, there is no need to convert the data.

Field Object Properties

There are several important properties associated with field objects. For example, each field object has a **DisplayLabel** property that is used to specify the column heading that appears in a DBGrid. In Figure 13.2, notice how spaces have been added to the LastName, FirstName, and HireDate column headings.

In addition to **DisplayLabel**, the **DisplayWidth** and **Index** properties also affect how the columns appear in a grid. **DisplayWidth** is used to control the size of a column, and **Index** determines the column ordering. The **Visible** property is also very useful for fields that are to appear in a grid—you don't always need every field in a table to be on display. Notice that the DBGrid in Figure 13.2 does not display the EmpNo column. This is because the **Visible** property for the **TblEmployeeEmpNo** field object has been set to **False**. This removes the column from the grid, but does not prevent individual controls from accessing the data.

The properties of field objects provide much more functionality than simply altering a grid's display. For example, the **Currency** property of **TblEmployeeSalary** is set to **True**. This causes Delphi to automatically format the floating-point number stored in the Salary column using the currency settings stored in the Control Panel. Any data-aware control linked to this field will display the salary as a monetary value. This is also demonstrated in Figure 13.2 where both the grid and **EdtSalary** edit field display formatted values.

Another useful property is **EditMask**. As with the **Currency** property, when specified in a field object the **EditMask** is used by all controls linked to that field object. In the **EmpEdtr1** application, a date mask is specified for **TblEmployeeHireDate**.

Calculated Fields

One of the most important uses of field objects is in the creation of calculated fields. Calculated fields look like any other column to the end user, except that they cannot be modified. The data being displayed is calculated at runtime using values from other columns. For example, Figure 13.3 shows the second version of the employee editor, **EmpEdtr2**, which creates a calculated field called MonthlySal. This new column will display the result of dividing the Salary by twelve.

Using calculated fields requires two steps. First, the field must be defined using the Fields Editor. To do this, press the Define button in the Fields Editor and specify a name and type for the new field. You may also be required to specify a size of the field, if the data type of the field may vary in size. For example, if you define a **TStringField**, you will need to specify the size of the string.

The second step involves writing an event handler for the dataset's **OnCalcFields** event. This event occurs every time a record in a dataset needs to be displayed. In the event handler, set the calculated field's **Value** to the result of the desired calculation. The **OnCalcFields** event handler for the **TblEmployee** dataset in **EmpEdtr2** looks like the following:

```
procedure TFrmMain.TblEmployeeCalcFields( Dataset : TDataset );
begin
  TblEmployeeMonthlySal.Value := TblEmployeeSalary.Value / 12;
end;
```

Figure 13.3

Creating a
Calculated
Field.

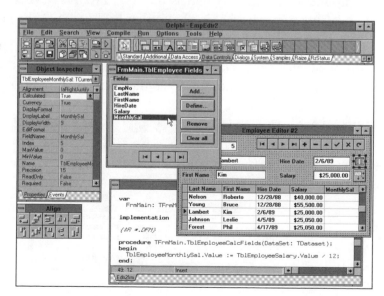

Notice that calculated fields are accessed using a field object. The Fields Editor created the **TblEmployeeMonthlySal** field object when the MonthlySal calculated field was defined. In this example, the field object is declared as a **TCurrencyField**.

By the way, the **OnCalcFields** event only occurs at runtime. The MonthlySal column in the grid in Figure 13.3 is not populated. Figure 13.4 shows how the above event handler correctly populates the MonthlySal column at runtime.

The Business Component Framework

Given that detailed look at the field objects, we're now ready to cover the details surrounding the business component framework. The entire business component framework is defined by a single class, **TRzBusinessComponent**. Actual business components are defined as descendants of this base class.

The basic principle behind the business component architecture is that a business component maintains a set of field object references that are linked to a particular dataset. Whenever the business component needs to access data, it uses the field objects. By using the field objects, the business component is automatically aware of any changes to data made by data-aware controls, including grids.

Simply having a business object use field objects is not that difficult a task. As we have seen, field objects can be accessed through a dataset. What makes the business component concept different is that the **TRzBusinessComponent** class is able to *explicitly* create field objects, without having to use the Fields Editor.

Every business component inherits a **Dataset** property from the **TRzBusinessComponent** class. This property is linked to the desired dataset either at design-time or at runtime. When the business component is connected to

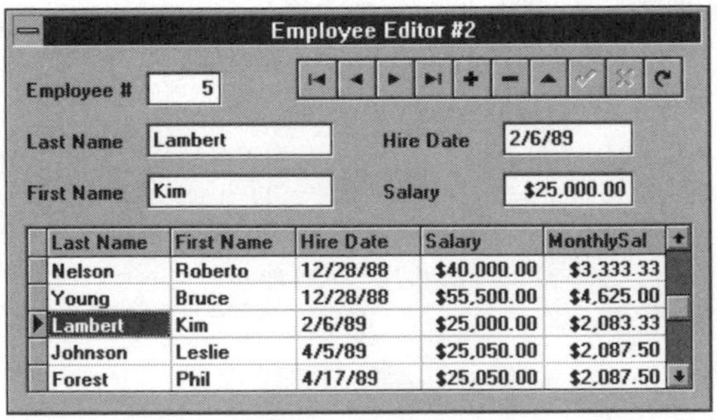
Employee Editor #2
Employee #
5
Last Name
Lambert
Hire Date
2/6/89
First Name
Kim
Salary
$25,000.00
Last Name
First Name
Hire Date
Salary
MonthlySal
Nelson
Roberto
12/28/88
$40,000.00
$3,333.33
Young
Bruce
12/28/88
$55,500.00
$4,625.00
Lambert
Kim
2/6/89
$25,000.00
$2,083.33
Johnson
Leslie
4/5/89
$25,050.00
$2,087.50
Forest
Phil
4/17/89
$25,050.00
$2,087.50

Figure 13.4

Creating a Calculated Field.

a dataset at design-time, the business component explicitly creates the desired field objects using the same mechanism used by the Fields Editor. This even results in field objects appearing in the form's class declaration. More importantly, the business component itself obtains a reference to each of the field objects, which it can then use to support business rules and functions.

The Base Class

Let's take a look at some code. Listing 13.1 shows the source code for the **RzBizCmp** unit, which contains the **TRzBusinessComponent** class. First, notice that this class descends from **TComponent**. Therefore, business objects are implemented as components that can be installed on the component palette and dropped onto forms. Furthermore, this allows descendent classes to define published properties to appear in the Object Inspector, allowing attributes to be specified at design-time.

Listing 13.1   RZBIZCMP.PAS—The RzBizCmp Unit

```
{=============================================================}
{= RzBizCmp Unit                                             =}
{=                                                           =}
{= This unit implements the TRzBusinessComponent class.  This class     =}
{= represents an abstract class which is used as the base class for building =}
{= data-aware business components.                           =}
{=                                                           =}
{= Building Custom Delphi Components - Ray Konopka            =}
{=============================================================}


unit RzBizCmp;

interface

uses
  Classes, DB, DBTables;

type
  TRzBusinessComponent = class( TComponent )
  private
    FDataset : TDataset;
  protected
    procedure Notification( AComponent : TComponent;
                            Operation : TOperation ); override;
    procedure SetDataset( Value : TDataset ); virtual;

    procedure SetupFields; virtual;
    procedure CreateFields; virtual; abstract;
    function CreateField( const FieldName : string ) : TField;
```

```
      function CreateCalcField( const FieldName : string;
                                FieldClass : TFieldClass;
                                Size : Word ) : TField;
  published
    property Dataset : TDataset
      read FDataset
      write SetDataset;
  end;



implementation

uses
  DBConsts, Dialogs;



{==================================}
{== TRzBusinessComponent Methods ==}
{==================================}


{= TRzBusinessComponent.Notification                                  =}
{=   This method is overridden to ensure that FDataset is set to nil if the =}
{=   corresponding Dataset is deleted from the form. This method should be  =}
{=   used whenever a component contains a reference to another component.    =}

procedure TRzBusinessComponent.Notification( AComponent : TComponent;
                                             Operation : TOperation );
begin
  inherited Notification( AComponent, Operation );
  if ( Operation = opRemove ) and ( AComponent = FDataset ) then
    FDataset := nil;
end;



{= TRzBusinessComponent.SetDataset                                    =}
{=   After setting the Dataset, you must call SetupFields to ensure that the =}
{=   field objects get created.                                       =}

procedure TRzBusinessComponent.SetDataset( Value : TDataset );
begin
  if Value <> FDataset then
  begin
    FDataset := Value;
    try
      SetupFields;
    except
      on EDBEngineError do
      begin
        MessageDlg( 'To connect to a Dataset, the Dataset must be able to ' +
                    'generate a result set.', mtError, [ mbOk ], 0 );
        FDataset := nil;
      end;
```

```
    on EDatabaseError do
    begin
      FDataset := nil;
      raise;
    end;
  end;
end;
end;


{= TRzBusinessComponent.SetupFields                              =}
{=   This method is responsible for making sure the appropriate functions are =}
{=   called when the field objects are created. More precisely, there are pre-=}
{=   and post- operations that must be performed.                 =}
{=                                                                =}
{=   Pre-Operations   Dataset must be closed                      =}
{=                    Dataset's FieldDefs must be updated         =}
{=                                                                =}
{=   Post-Operations  Re-establish original Dataset state         =}
{=                    Send DataEvent message to Dataset.Designer  =}

procedure TRzBusinessComponent.SetupFields;
var
  ActiveState : Boolean;
begin
  if FDataset = nil then
    Exit;                                { No need to set up if Dataset is nil }

  { Dataset must be closed in order to create new field objects }
  ActiveState := FDataset.Active;               { Save current state }
  if ActiveState then
    FDataset.Active := False;

  { Must call Update to gain Access to All Field Defs }
  FDataset.FieldDefs.Update;

  CreateFields;                  { Call to Descendant's CreateFields method }

  FDataset.Active := ActiveState;

  { If the developer has not yet invoked the Field Editor, then the Dataset   }
  { Designer does not exist. If the designer doesn't exist, it is not         }
  { necessary to call DataEvent.  Besides if you do, it will cause a GPF      }

  if FDataset.Designer <> nil then
    FDataset.Designer.DataEvent( deFieldListChange, 0 );
end; {= TRzBusinessComponent.SetupFields =}


{= TRzBusinessComponent.CreateField                              =}
{=   This method simplifies the process of creating fields.  First, the      =}
{=   Dataset is searched for a matching FieldName. If one exists, then that   =}
```

```
{=   one is used.  If not, then a  new field is created from the FieldDef     =}
{=   object corresponding to the desired field name.                          =}

function TRzBusinessComponent.CreateField( const FieldName : string ) : TField;
begin
  { First, try to find an existing field object.  FindField is the same as    }
  { FieldByName, but doesn't raise an exception if the field cannot be found.  }
  Result := FDataset.FindField( FieldName );

  if Result = nil then
  begin
    { If cannot find an existing field object... }
    { Instruct the FieldDefs object create a Field Object }

    Result := FDataset.FieldDefs.Find( FieldName ).CreateField( Owner );

    { We need to give the new field object a name so that it can appear in }
    { the Object Inspector. Use the default naming convention. }

    Result.Name := FDataset.Name + FieldName;
  end;
end; {= TRzBusinessComponent.CreateField =}


{= TRzBusinessComponent.CreateCalcField                                      =}
{=   This method simplifies the process of creating calculated fields. First, =}
{=   the Dataset is searched for a matching FieldName. If one exists, then     =}
{=   that one is used.  If not, then a new field is created from the passed    =}
{=   FieldClass parameter.                                                     =}

function TRzBusinessComponent.CreateCalcField( const FieldName : string;
                                               FieldClass : TFieldClass;
                                               Size : Word ) : TField;
begin
  Result := FDataset.FindField( FieldName );
  if Result = nil then
  begin
    if FieldClass = nil then
      DBErrorFmt( SUnknownFieldType, [ FieldName ] );

    { Create Desired Field Object using a Class Reference Variable }
    Result := FieldClass.Create( Owner );
    try
      Result.FieldName := FieldName;

      { Size is only necessary if new field is one of the following types }
      if ( Result is TStringField ) or
         ( Result is TBCDField ) or
         ( Result is TBlobField ) or
         ( Result is TBytesField ) or
         ( Result is TVarBytesField ) then
      begin
```

```
      Result.Size := Size;
    end;
    Result.Calculated := True;
    Result.Dataset := FDataset;
    Result.Name := FDataset.Name + FieldName;
  except
    Result.Free;                    { If error occurs, be sure to release memory }
    raise;
  end;
 end;
end; {= TRzBusinessComponent.CreateCalcField =}


end.
```

The only data the **TRzBusinessComponent** class contains is a reference to a dataset. The private **FDataset** object is used to support the **Dataset** property. This property is used to connect the business component to a particular dataset. This reference is necessary because it is the dataset that knows which fields are defined. More precisely, every dataset maintains a list of field definitions that describe the attributes of each field in the dataset. The attributes include the field type and size, and even the order in which it appears in the result set. As we will soon see, the business component uses the dataset to access the field definitions in order to create the appropriate field objects.

Since the **Dataset** property is a component reference, the **TRzBusinessComponent** class defines a **Notification** method. Recall that the **Notification** method ensures that **FDataset** does not reference a non-existent dataset.

Assigning the Dataset

The first interesting method of this class is the **SetDataset** method, which is the write access method for the **Dataset** property. When a dataset is assigned to this property, this method starts a chain of events that results in the construction of the field objects.

The **SetDataset** method is fairly straightforward. First, it behaves like a standard write access method by comparing the new dataset with the current dataset. If they are the same, the method exits without further action. If they are different, the new dataset is assigned to the **FDataset** object. After the assignment, the **SetupFields** method is called. This method will be described in detail in the next section, but for now simply understand that it is basically responsible for preparing the dataset for creating field objects.

The **SetupFields** call is surrounded by a **try...except** block, because it is possible that the field objects cannot be created. This usually happens when the dataset does not specify enough information to generate a result set. For example, a Table component must specify values for the **DatabaseName** and **TableName** properties before a result set can be generated. Likewise, the Query component requires the **DatabaseName** and **SQL** properties to be specified. If the field objects cannot be created, the assignment is aborted and the **FDataset** object is set to **nil**.

Setting Up the Fields

The **SetupFields** method performs the necessary pre- and post-setup operations that enable field objects created by descendent classes to be visible to the form and, more importantly, to the Fields Editor. It is important to notice that the **TRzBusinessComponent** class does *not* specify the field objects to be created. It simply provides the means for doing so. The specification of which field objects are to be created is the responsibility of the descendent class.

After the **SetupFields** method checks that the **FDataset** object is not **nil**, the dataset is closed. In order to create field objects, the dataset must be closed. The current state of the dataset is stored so that it may be re-established, if necessary, at the end of the process.

Next, **SetupFields** instructs the dataset to update its field definitions list. This is necessary so that all possible field definitions become available to the descendent class. In order to create a field object, there must exist a corresponding field definition. The call to **FDataset.FieldDefs.Update** ensures that all possible field definitions are available.

Once these two pre-creation steps have been performed, the **CreateFields** method is called. **CreateFields** is an abstract method that must be defined in a descendent class. As we will see shortly, a descendent class uses this method to specify which field objects are to be created.

After the call to **CreateFields**, the dataset is reopened if necessary and the Dataset Designer is updated. The Dataset Designer is just another name for the Fields Editor. Updating the Designer ensures that if the Fields Editor is invoked after the business component creates the field objects, those fields objects will appear correctly in the Fields Editor.

This is a significant step. Since the field objects are created using the same mechanism used by the Fields Editor, business components interact seamlessly with the Delphi design environment. Therefore, developers still have access to all of the design-time features of field objects. They just happen to be created by the business component. Furthermore, any changes made to the field objects using the Object Inspector are also reflected in the business component. This allows a business component to be *customized* for a given application.

Creating the Field Objects

CreateField and **CreateCalcField** are support methods that are designed to be called from within the **CreateFields** method of a descendent class. Both of these methods are responsible for instructing the dataset to create a field object.

Let's begin with the **CreateField** method. This method takes a single parameter that represents the name of the field to create. The field name must match a column name in the result set. Before attempting to create a new field object, the method tries to find an existing field object using the **FDataset.FindField** method. If a field object is found, that field object is used, and the function exits.

If a field object is not found, the dataset's **FieldDefs** list is searched to find the field definition corresponding to the desired field name. Since the **FieldDefs.Find** method returns a reference to the appropriate **TFieldDef**, an immediate call to the **TFieldDef.CreateField** method is made. This is the statement that actually creates the field object. As with all components, the constructor for field objects requires an owner. Therefore, the owner of the business component is passed to the **CreateField** method. Typically, the owner of the business component will be a form. When it is, the field object will also appear in the form's class declaration.

For completeness, the new field object is given a name following the naming convention used by the Fields Editor. That is, the name is the concatenation of the dataset name and the data field name. Naming the component is mandatory if the field object is to appear in the Object Inspector.

The **CreateCalcField** method also creates a new field object, but instead of using the dataset's field definitions to construct the object, the defining attributes for the field object are passed to the method. In particular, the **CreateCalcField** method accepts three parameters: a field name, a field class, and a size. This mimics the information required by the Fields Editor when defining a calculated field.

The field name defines the name of the calculated field. This name will also serve as the default **DisplayLabel** for the field object. The **FieldClass** parameter is used to specify which type of field to create. This is a classic example of using a *class reference* variable. The **TFieldClass** type is declared as:

```
TFieldClass = class of TField;
```

Therefore, the **FieldClass** parameter can be assigned to any of the **TField** descendent classes. And since the **TField** hierarchy is designed with a virtual constructor, the appropriate field object will be created.

The **Size** parameter is only applicable when the **FieldClass** parameter specifies a field type that requires a size. For example, if the **FieldClass** is set to **TStringField**, the **Size** parameter defines the size of the string. Notice how the **is** operator is used to avoid setting the **Size** property unless required by the field type.

Like the **CreateField** method, if an existing calculated field exists, a new field object is not created. And if a new field object is created, it is given a default name following the same naming convention. As a precautionary measure, the code setting up the calculated field is surrounded by the **try...except** block. This is to ensure that if an exception occurs, the new field object is destroyed.

Building a Business Component

At this point, we have the framework in place for building a business component. However, it is not apparently obvious how this framework will help encapsulate business rules into a component, which is, after all, the ultimate goal. In this section, we'll use this framework to build an employee business component.

This component will define methods to determine how long the employee has been employed by the company and the number of vacation days that have been earned for the current year. In addition, a business rule will be implemented that prevents the employee's salary from exceeding a user defined salary cap.

Let's get to work. There are three major steps involved in building a business component:

1. Define the Descendent Class

2. Write the CreateFields Method

3. Define any Business Rules or Methods

The Class Declaration

Listing 13.2 shows the RzDBEmp unit, which contains the **TRzDBEmployee** class definition. Objects of this class represent employee records stored in the same Employee table that has been used in the earlier examples. The class declaration is responsible for declaring the field objects that will be used in the component. The field objects are stored as private elements of the class. Each field object supports a property providing access to the field object.

Listing 13.2   RZDBEMP.PAS—The RzDBEmp Unit

```
{========================================================================}
{= RzDBEmp Unit                                                        =}
{=                                                                     =}
{= This unit implements the TRzDBEmployee class.  This class represents an =}
{= abstract class which is used as the base class for building data-aware =}
{= business object components.                                         =}
{=                                                                     =}
{= Building Custom Delphi Components - Ray Konopka                     =}
{========================================================================}


unit RzDBEmp;

interface

uses
  Classes, DB, DBTables, SysUtils, RzBizCmp, RzCommon;

type
  EExceedSalaryCap = class( Exception );

  TRzDBEmployee = class( TRzBusinessComponent )
  private
    { Field Objects }
    FEmpNo : TIntegerField;
    FLastName : TStringField;
    FFirstName : TStringField;
    FHireDate : TDateTimeField;
    FSalary : TFloatField;
    { Calculated Field Object }
    FMonthlySal : TFloatField;
    { Business Property }
    FSalaryCap : Single;
  protected
    procedure CreateFields; override;
  public
    { Methods Implementing Business Rules }
    function FullName : string;
```

```
    function YearsOfService : Single;
    function TotalVacationDays : Integer;
    procedure ValidateSalary( Sender : TField );

    { Specify properties to enforce read-only attribute }
    property EmpNo : TIntegerField
      read FEmpNo;

    property LastName : TStringField
      read FLastName;

    property FirstName : TStringField
      read FFirstName;

    property HireDate : TDateTimeField
      read FHireDate;

    property Salary : TFloatField
      read FSalary;

    property MonthlySal: TFloatField
      read FMonthlySal;

  published
    property SalaryCap : Single
      read FSalaryCap
      write FSalaryCap;
  end;


procedure Register;


implementation

uses
  Dialogs;


{============================}
{== TRzDBEmployee Methods ==}
{============================}


{= TRzDBEmployee.CreateFields                                         =}
{=   This method specifies the Field Objects that are to be used by the   =}
{=   Employee Business Component.                                     =}

procedure TRzDBEmployee.CreateFields;
begin
  FEmpNo := CreateField( 'EmpNo' ) as TIntegerField;
```

```
    FLastName := CreateField( 'LastName' ) as TStringField;
    FLastName.DisplayLabel := 'Last Name';

    FFirstName := CreateField( 'FirstName' ) as TStringField;
    FFirstName.DisplayLabel := 'First Name';

    FHireDate := CreateField( 'HireDate' ) as TDateTimeField;
    FHireDate.DisplayLabel := 'Hire Date';
    FHireDate.EditMask := '!99/99/00;1;_';

    FSalary := CreateField( 'Salary' ) as TFloatField;
    FSalary.Currency := True;
    FSalary.OnValidate := ValidateSalary;

    FMonthlySal := CreateCalcField( 'MonthlySal', TFloatField, 0 ) as TFloatField;
    FMonthlySal.DisplayLabel := 'Monthly Salary';
    FMonthlySal.Currency := True;
end; {= TRzDBEmployeeObject.CreateFields =}


function TRzDBEmployee.FullName : string;
begin
  Result := FirstName.Value + ' ' + LastName.Value;
end;


function TRzDBEmployee.YearsOfService : Single;
begin
  Result := Trunc( Now - HireDate.Value ) / 365;
end;


{= TRzDBEmployee.TotalVacationDays                                          =}
{=    This method calculates the number of vacation days available for the  =}
{=    current year.  The number is based on how long the employee has been  =}
{=    with the company.  The number is scaled according to the employee's   =}
{=    years of service.  The scale is as follows:                           =}
{=                                                                          =}
{=    Less than 6 months = 0 days                                           =}
{=    Less than 5 years  = 10 days (2 Weeks)                                =}
{=    5 to 9 years       = 15 days (3 Weeks)                                =}
{=    10 to 14 years     = 20 days (4 Weeks)                                =}
{=    15 to 19 years     = 25 days (5 Weeks)                                =}
{=    ...                                                                    =}

function TRzDBEmployee.TotalVacationDays : Integer;
var
  YOS : Real;
begin
  YOS := YearsOfService;
  if YOS < 0.5 then
    Result := 0
```

```
    else
      Result := ( Trunc( YOS ) div 5 + 2 ) * 5;
end;


{= TRzDBEmployee.ValidateSalary                                      =}
{=   This method gets called whenever the Salary column in the table is  =}
{=   updated.  If the Salary exceeds the salary cap, an exception is raised  =}
{=   to abort the current process.  For example, if the salary cap is set to  =}
{=   70,000 and the user enters 85,000 and then tries to Post the change, the =}
{=   exception will cause the Post to fail.                           =}
{=                                                                    =}
{= WARNING:                                                           =}
{=   This method relies on the assignment of the OnValidate event to this  =}
{=   method in the CreateFields method.  While this does work, it can cause  =}
{=   a conflict if the user specifies an OnValidate event handler for the  =}
{=   same event using the Object Inspector.                           =}

procedure TRzDBEmployee.ValidateSalary( Sender : TField );
begin
  if ( FSalaryCap <> 0 ) and ( Salary.Value > FSalaryCap ) then
    raise EExceedSalaryCap.CreateFmt( 'Salary cannot exceed %m',
                                      [ FSalaryCap ] );
end;



{=======================}
{== Register Procedure ==}
{=======================}

procedure Register;
begin
  RegisterComponents( RaizePage, [ TRzDBEmployee ] );
end;


end.
```

The first five properties declared in this class represent field objects that are mapped to five of the six possible columns in the Employee table. The PhoneExt column is not used. This shows that a business component can operate on a subset of columns in a table. Of course, the Fields Editor could be invoked and a **PhoneExt** field object could be created. In this case, the **PhoneExt** field object could be used by the form, but the employee component would know nothing about it.

The **MonthlySal** property is for a calculated field object. All of these properties are declared as read-only. This does not prevent the user from changing the underlying table data, but simply prevents the user from altering or deleting the field object.

When declaring the field objects, it is imperative that the data type used for each object match the corresponding column type. For example, **FSalary** must be declared as **TFloatField**, and **FHireDate** must be declared as **TDateTimeField**.

Sometimes the correct field type is not always obvious. For example, it very common for columns that appear to contain integer values to be defined as floating point columns. The easiest way to determine the field types used by a dataset is to create a new project in Delphi and drop a table component on the form. Next, specify the **DatabaseName** and **TableName** of the desired table. Finally, use the Fields Editor to create all of the field objects. You can then look at the form's declaration or the Object Inspector to get the field types for each column.

In addition to declaring the field object properties, the **TRzDBEmployee** class also declares a number of business methods and a published property. The **SalaryCap** property is used to specify the maximum annual salary that can be earned by any one employee. The employee component will prevent any salary from exceeding this limit.

When you wish to create a floating point property, as in the **SalaryCap** property for the **TRzDBEmployee** class, do not use the **Real** type. Instead, use **Single**, **Double**, or **Extended**. The reason for this is that the default property editor for floating point numbers does not correctly handle **Real** type values.

Writing the CreateFields Method

The most important method of any business component is the **CreateFields** method. Recall that **CreateFields** gets called in the middle of the **SetupFields** method inherited from the base class. It is the responsibility of this method to create the desired field objects. It is also where the initial settings for the objects are specified. Creating each object is relatively easy thanks to the **CreateField** method inherited from **TRzBusinessComponent**. The only tricky aspect is that since **CreateField** returns a **TField**, the return value must be casted to the appropriate type before being assigned to the private variable. For example, the following statement shows how the **as** operator is used to cast the **TField** object returned from **CreateField** into a **TStringField**:

```
FFirstName := CreateField( 'FirstName' ) as TStringField;
```

Once the individual field objects are created, any of the object's properties can be modified. For example, the **DisplayLabel** property is commonly altered to create more appropriate labels by adding spaces and removing abbreviations. In addition, the **Currency** property for the **FSalary** field object is set to **True** so that salary values always appear formatted.

Events handlers can also be specified within this method. For example, the **OnValidate** event of the **FSalary** field object is set to the **ValidateSalary** method. By assigning a handler to this event, any time the value in the **FSalary** field object needs to be validated, the **ValidateSalary** method will be called. The **ValidateSalary** method, in turn, uses the **SalaryCap** property to ensure that the salary value does not exceed the specified limit.

Defining Business Rules and Methods

The other methods defined in the **TRzDBEmployee** class represent business functions. The methods are fairly simple, but they do illustrate how the field objects are used to perform such calculations. For example, the **YearsOfService** method uses the **HireDate** field object to retrieve the starting date of the current employee in the corresponding dataset.

The **TotalVacationDays** method is an example of another business function. In the **TRzDBEmployee** class, this method uses a linear scale based on how long the employee has been with the company. Although this is a simple approach to determine vacation days, the calculation requires several steps. First, the years of service must be determined. Next, the six month ineligibility period must be accounted for, and finally, the actual number of days must be computed.

Of course, this method would have to be modified to reflect a particular company's vacation policy. Unfortunately, the rules defining this method will never be this simple. Based on my experience with the vacation accrual methods of various companies, I expect this method to be quite lengthy indeed!

The last method defined in the **TRzDBEmployee** class is the event handler for validating salary values. The **ValidateSalary** method simply compares the value of the **Salary** field object with the current setting of the **SalaryCap** property. If the **SalaryCap** is not zero, and the new salary exceeds the salary cap, an **EExceedSalaryCap** custom exception is raised.

Raising an exception works very well in this circumstance. The exception causes the current process that requested the validation to be aborted. For example, if the salary cap is set to $70,000 and the user enters $80,000 for an employee, and then attempts to post the change, the validation will fail, and the exception will cancel the post.

Registration

In a sense, there are actually four steps involved in building a business component, not three as I previously stated. The last step is to define a **Register** procedure. Like all components, in order to use the employee business component at design-time, it must be registered and installed onto the Component Palette. Therefore, the RzDBEmp unit also defines a **Register** procedure.

Using a Business Component

Once installed on the palette, the **RzDBEmployee** business component can be used in an application. Using a business component simply requires dropping one on a form and connecting to a dataset.

The Connection

Figure 13.5 shows an RzDBEmployee component on a form along with a Table, a DataSource, and a DBGrid. The grid is connected to the DataSource, which is connected to the Table. The grid shows that the Table component is set to the Employee table.

The RzDBEmployee component is currently selected and appears in the Object Inspector. At this point, the component has just been dropped on the form, and has not yet been connected to the Table component.

Figure 13.6 shows the same form after the **RzDBEmployee1.Dataset** property is set to Table1. When the assignment is made, all of the field objects defined in the **TRzDBEmployee** class are created. The effects of the assignment are apparent in the **TForm1** class declaration in the code editor window. Notice all of the new field objects that have been created.

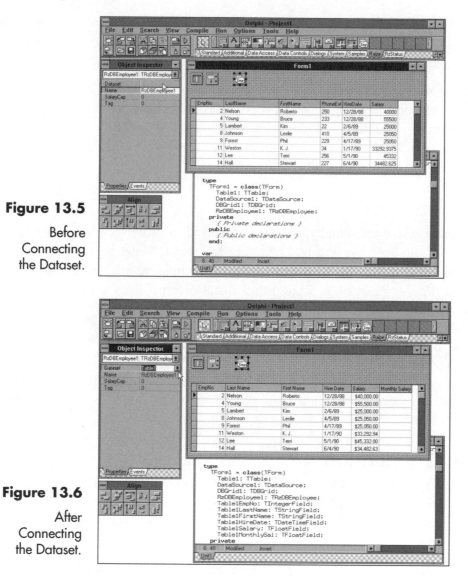

Figure 13.5

Before Connecting the Dataset.

Figure 13.6

After Connecting the Dataset.

The presence of the field objects is also apparent in the grid. Notice how the PhoneExt column is no longer displayed, and that all of the labels have been changed. But the most obvious change is the addition of the MonthlySalary column. This corresponds to the **MonthlySal** calculated field created by the business component.

Figures 13.5 and 13.6 demonstrate what happens when a business component is connected to a dataset that specifies enough information to generate a result set.

In fact, in this example, the table was already opened. What happens if a business component is connected to a dataset that is not fully defined? The result of this is shown in Figure 13.7.

This figure shows what happens when the **Dataset** property of the **RzDBEmployee1** component is assigned to a table that does not have values assigned to the **DatabaseName** and **TableName** properties. Recall that the **SetDataset** method of the **TRzBusinessComponent** class wraps the call to **SetupFields** inside a **try...except** block. In the example shown in Figure 13.7, an **EDBEngineError** exception is raised by the **FDataset.FieldDefs.Update** call in the **SetupFields** method. The default message for this exception is "Invalid Parameter." In order to display a more appropriate message to the user, the exception is handled and a new message is displayed

The Employee Editor (Revisited)

As a final demonstration of the employee business component, the employee editor program that has been used throughout this chapter is redesigned using this new component. Figure 13.8 shows that the new editor is structured in much the same way as the earlier versions, but now all of the columns in the grid are populated with calculated fields. This is done to demonstrate how to access the business functions of the business component from within an application.

Figure 13.7

Connecting to
an Invalid
Dataset.

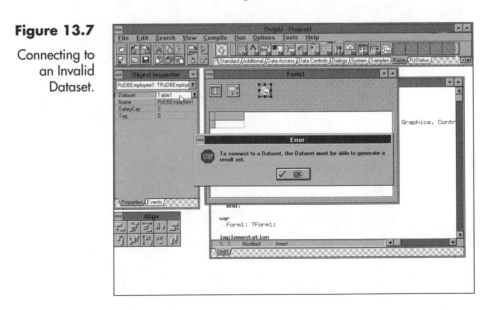

Figure 13.8 shows that an RzDBEmployee component, called **BizEmployee**, has been dropped onto the form. Once the **BizEmployee** object is connected to the **TblEmployee** table, completing the editor requires only a few additional steps. First, additional calculated fields **FullName**, **YearsOfService**, and **VacationDays** are created using the Fields Editor. Recall that **MonthlySal** is automatically created by the business component. Next, the **Visible** property for both the **FirstName** and **LastName** field objects is set to **False**. And finally, an event handler is written to populate the four calculated fields.

Figure 13.9 shows this final version of the employee editor running. Notice that the entire grid is populated using only four lines of code in the **TblEmployeeCalcFields** method. The simplicity of this method is a consequence of the power of the **BizEmployee** object.

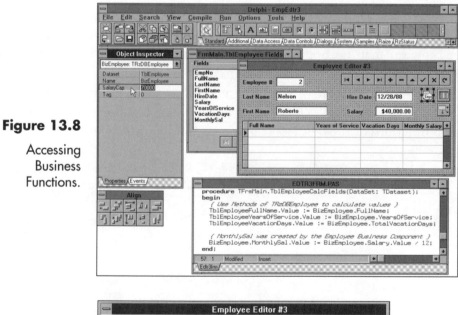

Figure 13.8

Accessing Business Functions.

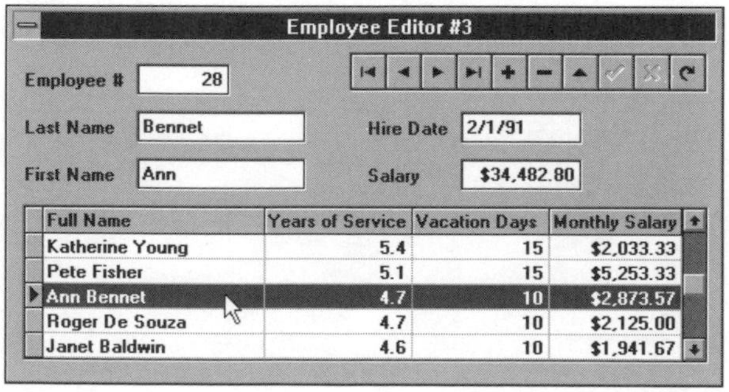

Figure 13.9

The RzDBEmployee Component at Work.

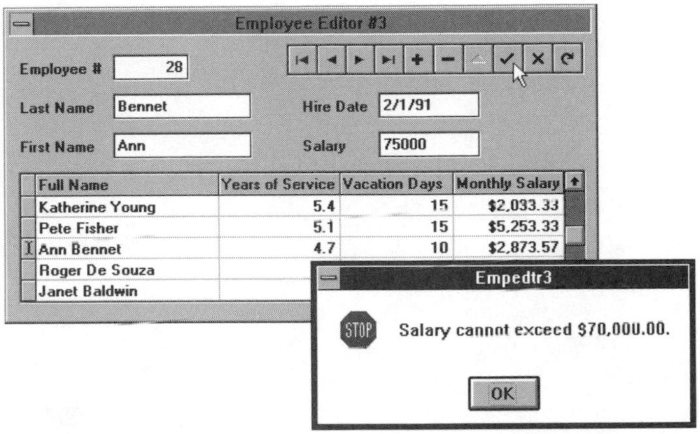

Figure 13.10

Exceeding the
Salary Cap.

Figure 13.10 shows how the RzDBEmployee component prevents the user from specifying a salary that exceeds the salary cap. In this example, the salary cap is set to $70,000 and the user attempts to give Ann Bennet a $75,000 salary. When the user attempts to post the change, the validation rule is checked. Since the validation fails, an exception is raised, causing the message box to be displayed, and the post to fail.

Looking Ahead...

At this point in the book, we've reached a plateau. In essence, we've covered all of the different types of components that can be created in Delphi. But our work is not yet done. In the next chapter, we'll be focusing on how to enhance a component with property editors and component editors. Incorporating these design-time editors into a component can dramatically change how a component is used.

Chapter 14

Property Editors and Component Editors

Property Editors and Component Editors

Components are objects—and when you tell an object, "Go edit yourself," you also have to provide the machinery that lets it do your bidding.

Since Chapter 7, twenty-two different components have been built demonstrating virtually every type of component that can be created in Delphi. At this point, it's time to change our focus from building components to enhancing them after they have been constructed. In particular, over the next three chapters we'll discover how to enhance the design-time features of a component through the use of property editors and component editors, how to create robust components through the use of advanced debugging techniques, and how to make components easier to use through online help support, plus much more.

The Design-Time Environment

This chapter begins this change of focus by investigating how components interact with the Delphi design environment; specifically, how components interact with the Object Inspector and the Form Designer. From the user's perspective, the Object Inspector is responsible for editing individual properties of a component, while the Form Designer is responsible for manipulating the component as a whole.

Behind the scenes, each design tool uses a set of editors to perform the actual work. The Object Inspector relies on *property editors* to define the editing capabilities associated with a property as well as to control how the property value appears in the Object Inspector. The Form Designer depends on *component editors* to determine which menu items appear in the context menu, and what action occurs when the component is double-clicked.

At design time, when a component is selected on a form, the Object Inspector creates instances of the property editors needed for the properties defined in the selected component. Likewise, the Form Designer creates an instance of the component editor registered for that component.

Delphi comes with a set of default design-time editors that handle a wide variety of editing tasks. Usually, one of the default editors will be sufficient for a component. However, there are times when a default editor is not adequate for a particular property or component. In these situations, the component writer may opt to modify an existing editor or create an entirely new one.

The task of creating a new property or component editor is simplified by the object-oriented nature of both types of editors. As with components, there are class hierarchies defined in Delphi that provide the basic behavior of both types of editors. Creating a new editor is a simple matter of creating a new descendent class and registering it with Delphi.

Once registered, the new editor operates seamlessly within the design environment. This environment also supports registering an editor that replaces an already registered editor. This ability provides the basis for a significant feature of property editors and component editors. That is, properties and components are not aware of the editors used by the design-time environment.

To demonstrate how to build custom property and component editors, two property editors and one component editor will be created in this chapter. The first property editor is for the **Format** property of the RzClockStatus component from Chapter 9. This new editor makes it easier for the user to set the date and time format used in the status control.

The second property editor is for the **TabStops** property of the RzTabbedListBox component from Chapter 8. This is an example of where a custom property editor is built so that a formerly **public** property can be moved to the **published** section. Therefore, with the new property editor, the tab stops for an RzTabbedListBox can be set at design-time.

The component editor presented at the end of this chapter provides a more visual way of editing the attributes of the RzLabel component from Chapter 8. The new component editor is also responsible for adding additional menu items to the component's context menu.

Property Editors

In Chapter 5, we took a brief look at property editors from the user's perspective. In particular, we focused on how the different editors appear in the Object Inspector. How does the Object Inspector know how to edit a particular property? The Object Inspector determines this by using a property editor. For every property displayed in the Object Inspector, a property editor is created that specifies how the property value can be modified.

Property editors are responsible for two primary tasks. First and foremost, the editor is responsible for defining how the property can be edited. There are two basic ways in which this can be performed. First, the value can be modified within the Object Inspector itself—for example, entering a new number or selecting an item from a combo box. The second way involves displaying a dialog box that provides specialized editing features.

The second task property editors must perform is converting the value of the property between its native format and a string value. This is necessary because the Object Inspector only knows how to display string data. It's up to each property editor to provide the Object Inspector with a string representation of its current value.

Standard Property Editors

As mentioned earlier, Delphi provides a number of standard property editors that handle the editing tasks associated with most types of properties. The standard property editors are defined in the **DsgnIntf** unit. This unit also contains the class declaration for the **TPropertyEditor** class, which is the base class for all property editors.

Figure 14.1 shows the hierarchical relationships among all of the standard property editors, while Table 14.1 summarizes the editing capabilities supported by

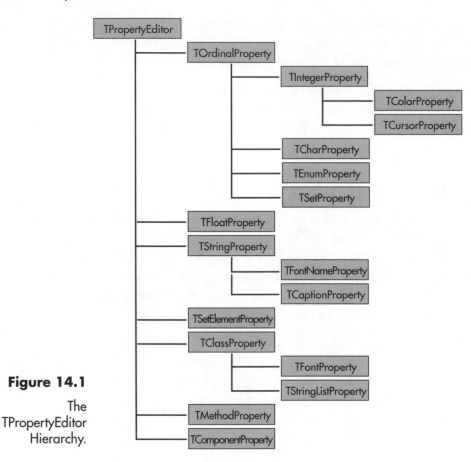

Figure 14.1

The TPropertyEditor Hierarchy.

each of these editors. There are many other property editors defined in Delphi, but they are specialized versions designed for specific properties and are generally not used as ancestors for custom property editors.

Building a Property Editor

To build a new property editor, begin by creating a new class that is derived from the **TPropertyEditor** class or one of its descendants. Customizing a property editor is accomplished by overriding a few key methods. Fortunately, the **TPropertyEditor** class also provides a number of supporting methods that makes this task relatively painless.

As mentioned earlier, one of the primary tasks that a property editor must perform is translating a property's value from its native type into a string value. When

Table 14.1   Editing Capabilities of the Standard Property Editors

Property Editor	Editing Capabilities
TPropertyEditor	Base class for all property editors.
TOrdinalProperty	The base class of all ordinal property editors. Responsible for determining if all components selected display the same value.
TIntegerProperty	Default editor for all Longint type properties and all subtypes of the Longint type (for example, Integer, Word, 1..10). This editor prevents the user from entering values outside the legal range for the particular integer type.
TColorProperty	Customized integer editor for TColor properties. This editor provides three editing features. First, the current color value is displayed using a predefined color constant or its hexadecimal equivalent. Second, a drop-down list containing the predefined color constants is created. Finally, if the user double-clicks in the value column of the Object Inspector, the color-selection dialog box is displayed.
TCursorProperty	Customized integer editor for Cursor properties. This editor displays a drop-down list of all the cursors available.
TCharProperty	Default editor for Char properties including sub-types of Char (for example, Char, 'A'..'Z').
TEnumProperty	Default editor for any enumerated type. Responsible for displaying a drop-down list containing each element of the enumeration.
TSetProperty	Default property editor for all set properties. This editor does not edit the set directly but displays sub-properties for each element of the set.
TFloatProperty	Default property editor for all floating point numbers.
TStringProperty	Default property editor for all string properties including strings of restricted length (for example, string[40]).
TFontNameProperty	Customized string editor for the TFont.Name property. This editor displays a drop-down list of all the font names known by Windows.
TCaptionProperty	Customized string editor for Caption and Text properties. This editor updates the value of the property after each keypress rather than only after the Enter key is pressed.
TSetElementProperty	Default property editor for individual set elements. This editor is responsible for displaying the element name in the property name column in the Object Inspector. In addition, the value of each set element is shown as a Boolean value.
TClassProperty	Default property editor for all object types. This editor displays the class name of the object and displays the object's properties as sub-properties. The sub-property values can be modified.
TFontProperty	Customized class property editor for Font properties. Shows each property of the TFont class as sub-properties, but also displays the Font selection dialog box.
TStringListProperty	Customized class property editor for string list properties. This editor displays the contents of the string list in a memo field that is part of a dialog box.
TMethodProperty	Default property editor for method pointer properties. This is editor used for events.
TComponentProperty	Default editor for component reference properties. This editor displays a drop-down list of components located on the current form that have a compatible type with the selected property.

the Object Inspector needs to display the value of a property, it accesses the **Value** property of the property editor defined for that property. The **TPropertyEditor** class defines two virtual access methods that are used to support the **Value** property. Descendent classes override these methods to specify how the data is to be translated.

The **GetValue** method returns the string representation of a property value. In the **TPropertyEditor** class, this method returns "(unknown)," but in a descendent class, this method returns an equivalent string value for the property. For example, the **GetValue** method for the **TIntegerProperty** editor is defined as:

```
function TIntegerProperty.GetValue : string;
begin
  Result := IntToStr( GetOrdValue );
end;
```

The **GetOrdValue** method is one of the supporting methods mentioned earlier. This method returns the value stored in the corresponding property. Because the native data type for an integer property is an ordinal value, the **GetOrdValue** method is used. The **TPropertyEditor** class also defines the **GetFloatValue**, **GetStrValue**, and **GetMethodValue** methods for accessing other types of property data. With these four methods, any type of property can be accessed.

When the user enters a new value for a property using the Object Inspector and then presses the Enter key, the **SetValue** method of the property editor is called. This method must perform the opposite translation defined in the **GetValue** method. That is, the new string value for the property is passed to the **SetValue** method, which must then be converted into the appropriate data type and finally stored in the corresponding property. Again, the supporting methods of **TPropertyEditor** make this relatively straightforward.

For example, the **SetValue** method for the **TFloatProperty** editor, shown below, converts the string value parameter to an equivalent floating point number, which it then passes to the **SetFloatValue** method. Note that the **TPropertyEditor** class provides matching **SetX*xx*Value** methods for each of the supporting **GetX*xx*Value** methods described earlier.

```
procedure TFloatProperty.SetValue( const Value : string );
begin
  SetFloatValue( StrToFloat( Value ) );
end;
```

Of course, not all **GetValue** and **SetValue** methods are this simple. It's often necessary to provide some validation in these methods. For example, if the string entered for a floating point property is not a valid number, the **StrToFloat** method raises an exception that prevents the assignment from taking place. Likewise, the **TIntegerProperty.SetValue** method performs range checking before calling **SetOrdValue**.

Defining the Editing Capabilities

Overriding the **GetValue** and **SetValue** methods accomplishes the first part of defining a property editor. The second task is to define the editing capabilities. This task is also accomplished by overriding various methods to produce the desired effects.

Virtually every custom property editor will override the **GetAttributes** method. This method is used by the Object Inspector to determine which editing tools should be used for this property. The **GetAttributes** method is a function that returns a set of type **TPropertyAttributes**. The possible elements of this set are listed in Table 14.2. The table also describes the effect each attribute has on the Object Inspector.

Table 14.2 Property Attribute Flags

Property Attribute	Description
paValueList	This attribute is specified for editors that require a list of items to be displayed in a drop-down list. If this attribute is set, the GetValues method is called to populate the list.
paSortList	This attribute instructs the Object Inspector to sort the list of items displayed in the drop-down list. Only valid if paValueList is also set.
paSubProperties	This attribute indicates that the property editor defines sub-properties that are to be displayed indented and below the current property. If this attribute is set, the GetProperties method is called to generate the list of properties.
paDialog	This attribute is set for property editors that display a dialog box in its Edit method. This attribute must be set in order to have the ellipsis button appear to the right of the property in the Object Inspector.
paMultiSelect	When this attribute is set, the property is displayed when multiple components are selected.
paAutoUpdate	This attribute instructs the Object Inspector to call the SetValue method after each change made to the property value. If this attribute is not specified, the SetValue is only called when the user presses the Enter key or moves off the current property.
paReadOnly	This attribute is set to prevent the user from modifying the property value.

The **Edit** method is called whenever the ellipsis button is pressed or the value column in the Object Inspector is double-clicked. The **Edit** method is primarily used to display a dialog box that will be used to edit the property. There are two common reasons for providing a dialog box editor. First, the dialog box can provide a more visual way of setting the property, which cannot be achieved through text methods.

Second, the property may be an object. Yes, the **TClassProperty** (see Table 14.1) class could be used for this property, but again, the resulting editor is text-based. It's common to provide a dialog box that allows all of the properties of the object to be manipulated at the same time. For example, the standard **TFontProperty** editor defines an **Edit** method that displays the font selection dialog box.

Note that it is not a requirement that the **Edit** method display a dialog box. The **TMethodProperty** class, for example, does not set the **paDialog** attribute in the GetAttributes method, but does define an **Edit** method. This method is called whenever the user double-clicks in the value column of an event property. The **Edit** method is responsible for instructing Delphi to generate the event handler code in the appropriate form file.

When a property editor wishes to display a list of items in a drop-down list, the **GetValues** method must be overridden. The **GetValues** method is called by the Object Inspector when the user presses the drop-down button next to the property value. The button is displayed as a result of specifying the **paValueList** attribute in the **GetAttributes** method.

The **GetValues** method receives a single parameter, which is a reference to a procedure. This procedure is called for each item that is to appear on the list. This procedure requires a string parameter representing the string value that will be displayed in the list. When the user selects an item from the list, the Object Inspector calls the property editor's **SetValue** method with the selected string value. The following example shows how the **TFontNameProperty** editor instructs the Object Inspector to display all of the screen fonts:

```
procedure TFontNameProperty.GetValues( Proc : TGetStrProc );
var
  I : Integer;
begin
  for I := 0 to Screen.Fonts.Count - 1 do
    Proc( Screen.Fonts[ I ] );
end;
```

If you are going to create a property editor that supports multiple selection (that is, the **GetAttributes** method specifies the **paMultiSelect** attribute), it will be necessary to override the **AllEqual** method. This method is called to determine if the Object Inspector displays a value for the property when multiple components are selected.

The **AllEqual** method is a Boolean function that should return **True** only if all of the property values are indeed equal. To facilitate the comparison of all of the selected values, the **TPropertyEditor** class provides several **GetX*xx*ValueAt** methods that return the property value of one of the selected components. For example, the **TStringProperty** defines its **AllEqual** method as follows:

```
function TStringProperty.AllEqual : Boolean;
var
  I : Integer;
  V : string;
begin
  Result := False;
  if PropCount > 1 then
  begin
    V := GetStrValue;                          { Get Current String Value }
    for I := 1 to PropCount - 1 do
    begin
      if GetStrValueAt( I ) <> V then          { Get Other String Values }
        Exit;
    end;
  end;
  Result := True;
end;
```

Registering a Property Editor

As with components, in order for the Delphi Object Inspector to use a new property editor, the new editor must be registered with Delphi. This is accomplished by using the **RegisterPropertyEditor** procedure. This procedure is defined in the DsgnIntf unit and its heading is shown below:

```
procedure RegisterPropertyEditor( PropertyType : PTypeInfo;
                                  ComponentClass : TClass;
                                  const PropertyName : string;
                                  EditorClass : TPropertyEditorClass );
```

The first parameter is a reference to information pertaining to the type of property being edited. This parameter is always set by calling the **TypeInfo** function, passing it the property type; for example, **TypeInfo(string)**. The second parameter is used to restrict a property editor's usage to only a particular component type. If this parameter is set to **nil**, the property editor is registered for *all* properties of the specified property type. The third parameter is used to specify the name of the property. This parameter is valid only if the second parameter is not **nil**. By specifying the name of the property, the property editor can be registered for a single property within a component, even though the component may contain additional properties of the same property type. The final parameter is the type of the property editor to be used for the specified property.

How these parameters are specified can have dramatic effects on how a property editor is registered. This is demonstrated in the following statements:

```
RegisterPropertyEditor( TypeInfo( TStrings ), nil, '', TRzStringListProperty );

RegisterPropertyEditor( TypeInfo( string ), TRzClockStatus, 'Format',
                        TRzClockFormatProperty );
```

The first statement is the most common and least restrictive form of property editor registration. In this statement, the **TRzStringListProperty** editor is registered for all properties of type **TStrings**. The editor is also registered for properties that are descendants of **TStrings** but do not have their own editors registered.

The second statement is the most restrictive form of property editor registration. In this example, the **TRzClockFormatProperty** editor is registered for *only* the **Format** property of the RzClockStatus component. Other string properties defined in the RzClockStatus component are unaffected by this property editor.

You may have noticed that the **RegisterPropertyEditor** procedure does support a third form of registration. Specifically, a component class may be specified while the property name is left blank. This form has the effect of registering the property editor for all properties defined in the specified component that are of the specified property type. This form of property editor registration is seldom used.

A final comment on registration: It's possible for multiple property editors to be assigned to the same property. For example, the following two registration statements would affect the **ActivePage** property:

```
RegisterPropertyEditor( TypeInfo( string ), nil, '', TStringProperty );
```

```
RegisterPropertyEditor( TypeInfo( string ), TNotebook, 'ActivePage',
                   TPageNameProperty );
```

Delphi resolves this conflict by always using the most *recently* registered property editor for a given property. In the above example, the **TPageNameProperty** editor overrides the default **TStringProperty** editor for **ActivePage**.

Organization

Where should property editor classes be placed? There are three possible locations for a property editor class. First, the property editor could reside in the same unit as the component that contains the property in question. However, this option makes sense only if no other components use the same property. In addition, this approach should only be used if the property editor does not display a dialog box.

As we will see, property editor dialog boxes are simply Delphi forms that are created dynamically by the property editor class. In order to create the correct dialog box, the property editor class must have access to the form unit corresponding to the desired form. This is easily handled by adding the form unit to the **uses** clause of the unit defining the property editor.

Unfortunately, this approach has an undesirable side effect. To illustrate this, consider the following scenario: UnitC contains the **TSampleComponent** class along with a property editor, called **TSampleProperty**. UnitF is a Delphi form unit that contains the **TSampleEditDlg** form. In order for the **TSampleProperty** class to have access to the form class, UnitF must be added to UnitC's **uses** clause. This arrangement is illustrated in Figure 14.2.

The problem with this arrangement stems from the fact that if a SampleComponent is dropped onto a form, the UnitC unit is added to the **uses** clause. This is also illustrated in Figure 14.2 where Unit1 represents a form in an application that uses the **TSampleComponent** class. Because UnitC is added to Unit1's **uses** clause, the code for the component is included in the application using **Form1**.

More significant, however, is that the form resource file is also linked into the resulting application. This is inappropriate because the property editor's form file is used only within the Delphi design environment. In fact, this form cannot be displayed by the application because Delphi's smart linker does not link in the property editor class. The property editor class that is used to invoke the form is not referenced by the application, and therefore gets removed from the application's code.

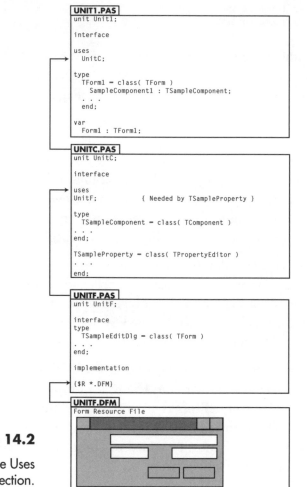

UNIT1.PAS
```
unit Unit1;

interface

uses
  UnitC;

type
  TForm1 = class( TForm )
    SampleComponent1 : TSampleComponent;
    . . .
  end;

var
  Form1 : TForm1;
```

UNITC.PAS
```
unit UnitC;

interface

uses
UnitF;            { Needed by TSampleProperty }

type
  TSampleComponent = class( TComponent )
. . .
end;

TSampleProperty = class( TPropertyEditor )
. . .
end;
```

UNITF.PAS
```
unit UnitF;

interface
type
  TSampleEditDlg = class( TForm )
. . .
end;

implementation

{$R *.DFM}
```

UNITF.DFM
```
Form Resource File
```

Figure 14.2

The Uses
Connection.

However, smart linking does not apply to resource files, and since UnitF is indirectly used by Unit1, the UNITF.DFM resource file is linked into the resulting EXE file. This has the adverse affect of increasing the size of the EXE file with useless data.

The second option (and the preferred option for dialog-driven property editors) is to place the property editor class inside the form unit. In the previous example, this means that the **TSampleProperty** class is moved to the UnitF unit. This in turn removes the UnitF unit from UnitC's **uses** clause. Therefore, any application using the **TSampleComponent** class will *not* include the UNITF.DFM resource file.

The third option is to place the property editor class in a *registration unit*. A registration unit is a Delphi unit that consolidates a number of **Register** procedures defined in separate units. It is common to place property editors inside these types of units when the property editor will be used for multiple components and properties. However, if the property editor displays a dialog box, the editor should be placed in the form file. Registering the editor for the appropriate components and properties is then handled by the **Register** procedure for that form unit.

Editing Properties within the Object Inspector

The first property editor that we will create demonstrates how to build a property editor that operates within the Object Inspector; that is, a property editor that does not display a dialog box. In our first example, a property editor will be created for the **Format** property of the RzClockStatus component.

Recall that this component is one of the status control descendants that were presented in Chapter 9. In particular, this control displays the current date and time. The format of the value displayed by the control is determined by the **Format** property. The format string stored in this property is passed to the **FormatDateTime** procedure whenever the control is updated.

There are two reasons for creating this **TRzClockFormatProperty**. First, by default, the format of the display is updated only after the user presses the Enter key. To provide better visual feedback, this new property editor will update the display after every keypress. The second reason for creating this editor is to provide a list of predefined formats to make it easier for the user to choose an appropriate **Format** value. The desired effect is illustrated in Figure 14.3.

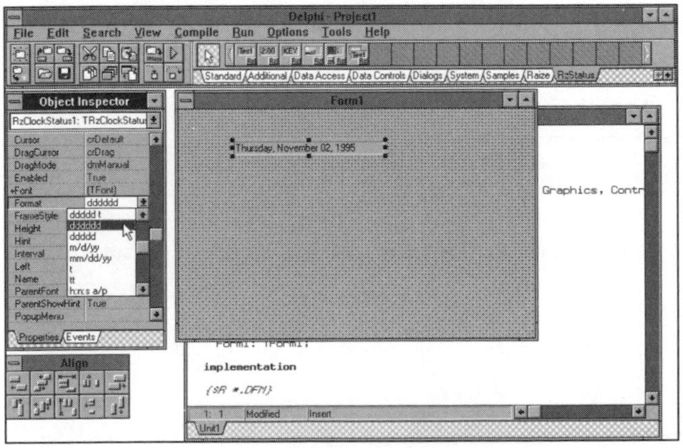

Figure 14.3

Selecting a Predefined Format.

The **TRzClockFormatProperty** class is a very simple property editor requiring only two methods. Listing 14.1 shows the source code for this class. Since this editor is designed only for the **Format** property of the RzClockStatus component and the editor does not display a dialog box, this class definition resides in the **RzStatus** unit along with the component.

Listing 14.1   RZSTATUS.PAS—The RzStatus Unit (Part 3)

```
{==========================================================================}
{= RzStatus Unit                                                          =}
{=                                                                        =}
{= This is a partial listing of the RzStatus unit.                        =}
{= Only the TRzClockFormatProperty class is listed.                       =}
{=                                                                        =}
{= Building Custom Delphi Components - Ray Konopka                         =}
{==========================================================================}

unit RzStatus;

interface

uses
  Messages, WinTypes, Controls, Classes, Graphics, ExtCtrls, Menus,
  RzCommon, Buttons, SysUtils, DBTables, DB, DsgnIntf;

type
  {= TRzClockFormatProperty                                               =}
  {=    Property editor for the Format Property. Updates the value of the =}
  {=    property after each keypress instead of waiting until the Enter key=}
  {=    is pressed.                                                       =}

  TRzClockFormatProperty = class( TStringProperty )
  public
    function GetAttributes : TPropertyAttributes; override;
    procedure GetValues( Proc : TGetStrProc ); override;
  end;

implementation


{===================================}
{== TRzClockFormatProperty Methods ==}
{===================================}

function TRzClockFormatProperty.GetAttributes : TPropertyAttributes;
begin
  Result := [ paValueList, paMultiSelect, paAutoUpdate ];
end;
```

```
procedure TRzClockFormatProperty.GetValues( Proc : TGetStrProc );
begin
  Proc( 'c' );
  Proc( 'dddddd tt' );
  Proc( 'ddddd t' );
  Proc( 'dddddd' );
  Proc( 'ddddd' );
  Proc( 'm/d/yy' );
  Proc( 'mm/dd/yy' );
  Proc( 't' );
  Proc( 'tt' );
  Proc( 'h:n:s a/p' );
  Proc( 'hh:nn:ss am/pm' );
  Proc( 'h:n:s' );
  Proc( 'hh:nn:ss' );
end;



{=======================}
{== Register Procedure ==}
{=======================}

procedure Register;
begin
  RegisterComponents( RaizeStatusPage,
                      [ TRzStatusControl, TRzClockStatus, TRzKeyStatus,
                        TRzGlyphStatus, TRzResourceStatus ] );

  RegisterComponents( RaizeStatusPage, [ TRzDBStatusControl ] );

  RegisterPropertyEditor( TypeInfo( string ), TRzClockStatus, 'Format',
                          TRzClockFormatProperty );
end;


end.
```

The first interesting aspect of this property editor is that it is derived from **TStringProperty**. This makes sense for this particular editor because the default processing of **TStringProperty** handles getting and setting the property value appropriately. Furthermore, **TStringProperty** already knows how to handle multiple selection, so the **paMultiSelect** attribute can be specified in the **GetAttributes** method.

By Convention

Property editor class names end with "Property." For example: **TCursorProperty**, **TFontNameProperty**, and **TComponentNameProperty**.

The **GetAttributes** method is overridden in this property editor so that it may specify two additional attributes. First, the **paAutoUpdate** attribute is included so that our first requirement can be satisfied. That is, this attribute causes the Object Inspector to call the **SetValue** method after every keypress. Therefore, as the user enters a format string, the component on the form will immediately display the date and time according to the new format. It is amazing how such a little enhancement makes a component so much easier to use.

The second attribute added to the set is **paValueList**. Recall from Table 14.2 that this attribute is required to instruct the Object Inspector to display a list of items in a combo box. The only task left for this property editor is to specify the list of items.

This is handled in the **GetValues** method. The **Proc** parameter references a procedure that adds items to the combo box created by the Object Inspector. Within the **GetValues** method, the **Proc** procedure is called for each format string to be added to the combo box.

Of course, we cannot forget about the **Register** procedure. For this particular editor, a new line is added to the **Register** procedure defined in the **RzStatus** unit. The entire procedure is also listed in Listing 14.1. Notice that this editor is only used by the **Format** property in the RzClockStatus component.

Editing Properties Using a Dialog Box

In our second property editor example, we add some complexity by having the editor edit an object type and display a dialog box. It requires a little extra work, but the payoff is tremendous. This example also demonstrates one of the major benefits of writing custom property editors: the ability to edit properties that were previously not editable.

In this section, a property editor will be created for the **TabStops** property of the RzTabbedListBox component. This component was introduced in Chapter 8 as a demonstration of how to enhance an existing component. Recall that the **TabStops** property was declared as a **TRzTabStopList**. You may also recall that this property was declared as a **public** property. This was necessary because, by default, the Object Inspector does not know how to edit a **TRzTabStopList** property.

This is the primary reason for creating the **TRzTabStopProperty** editor. Once the **TRzTabStopProperty** editor is registered, the Object Inspector will be able to edit the **TabStops** property. This is quite significant, because it means that this property can be moved to the **published** section of the component where it can then be modified at design-time.

Since the **TabStops** property represents a list of integer values, the default property editors cannot be used. None of the default editors is designed to handle a list of values. Therefore, to edit the values in this list, a special dialog box is created, which will be used to visually edit the values in the list. Figure 14.4 shows the property editor dialog box that will be displayed to edit the **TabStops**.

The TRzTabStopProperty Class

Surprisingly, the **TRzTabStopProperty** class definition is relatively small. Only three methods need to be overridden in this class. Listing 14.2 shows that the class starts off by overriding the **GetAttributes** method. The only attribute applicable for this type of editor is **paDialog**.

Listing 14.2   RZTABEDT.PAS—The TRzTabStopProperty Class

```
type
  TRzTabStopProperty = class( TPropertyEditor )
    function GetAttributes : TPropertyAttributes; override;
    function GetValue : string; override;
    procedure Edit; override;
  end;


{==========================}
{== TRzTabStopProperty ==}
{==========================}

function TRzTabStopProperty.GetAttributes : TPropertyAttributes;
begin
  Result := [ paDialog ];                    { Display Dialog when Invoked }
end;


function TRzTabStopProperty.GetValue : string;
begin                                  { Display Type Name in Object Inspector }
  Result := Format( '(%s)', [ GetPropType^.Name ] );
end;


procedure TRzTabStopProperty.Edit;
var
  Dialog : TRzTabStopEditDlg;
  I : Integer;
begin
```

```
Dialog := TRzTabStopEditDlg.Create( Application );
try
  Dialog.Caption := GetComponent(0).Owner.Name + '.' + GetComponent(0).Name +
                   '.' + GetName + ' - ' + Dialog.Caption;

  { Set Preview List Box strings and Font to be same as component's }
  Dialog.LstPreview.Items := TRzTabbedListBox( GetComponent( 0 ) ).Items;
  Dialog.LstPreview.Font := TRzTabbedListBox( GetComponent( 0 ) ).Font;

  Dialog.LstPreview.TabStops := TRzTabStopList( GetOrdValue );

                                  { Add preset tabs to the LstTabs list box }
  for I := 0 to Dialog.LstPreview.TabStops.Count - 1 do
    Dialog.LstTabs.Items.Add( IntToStr( Dialog.LstPreview.TabStops[ I ] ) );

  if Dialog.ShowModal = mrOK then                       { Display Dialog Box }
  begin             { If user presses OK, move TabList from Dlg to Property }
    SetOrdValue( Longint( Dialog.LstPreview.TabStops ) );
  end;
finally
  Dialog.Free;                               { Don't forget to free dialog box }
end;
end; {= TRzTabStopProperty.Edit =}
```

The **GetValue** method is overridden so that a string value can be displayed in the
value column of the Object Inspector. For object properties that cannot easily be
converted into a text string, it is common practice to simply display the property
type within parentheses.

Figure 14.4

Setting Tab
Stops at
Design-Time.

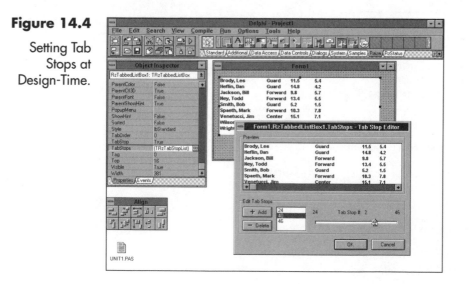

So how does one obtain the property type name? The **GetPropType** method returns a reference to a **TTypeInfo** record. One of the pieces of information stored in this record is the name of the type. The **GetValues** method calls the **GetPropType** method to retrieve the correct name and then uses the **Format** function to wrap the name in parentheses.

The third and final method defined in the **TRzTabStopProperty** class is the **Edit** method. This method actually looks more complicated than it is. This method starts off by creating an instance of the **TRzTabStopEditDlg** class. This is simply a Delphi form class that will be covered shortly.

Once the dialog is created, its **Caption** is set to reflect the current property being edited. Next, the preview list box of the dialog is updated to reflect the contents and font used by the underlying component. The **GetComponent** method inherited from **TPropertyEditor** is used to obtain a reference to the RzTabbedListBox component currently selected.

The **GetComponent** method is used primarily for handling situations where multiple components are selected. The **GetComponent** method takes a single parameter that represents the index of one of the selected components. However, passing a zero to this method is valid even if only one component is selected. Note that **GetComponent**'s return type is **TComponent**. Therefore, in order to reference individual properties of the component, the return value will need to be typecasted.

The next step performed by the **Edit** method is one of the most important. The **GetOrdValue** support method is called to obtain a pointer to the **TRzTabStopList** property value. Since a pointer is represented by four bytes, it is treated the same as a long integer. This assignment statement copies the tab stop values from the selected component's property to the **TabStops** property of the **LstPreview** list box. The **LstPreview** list box becomes the temporary workspace for editing the tab stops while the form is active.

After setting up the list boxes used in the form, the dialog is displayed. If the user presses the OK button in the dialog to accept the changes, the tab stops stored in the **LstPreview** list are copied back into the underlying property by calling the **SetOrdValue** method. The final step is to free the dialog object.

The TRzTabStopEditDlg Form

The actual editing performed by this property editor is not handled by the **TRzTabStopProperty** class. Instead, the real editing occurs in the

TRzTabStopEditDlg form class. Fortunately, building the editing dialog is no different from building a Delphi application. In fact, the usual process for building a dialog-driven property editor starts with creating a new form file. The form will become the editing dialog and the property editor class will be written in the same unit.

> **By Convention**
>
> Form classes that are used by property (and component) editors end with "EditDlg." Examples include: **TNotebookEditDlg**, **TStrEditDlg**, and **TRzTabStopEditDlg**.

Listing 14.3 also shows the **RzTabEdt** unit, but this time the **TRzTabStopEditDlg** class is listed. As mentioned before, the **LstPreview** list box is used to try out new tab stop settings. In the bottom portion of the dialog, the user can add or delete tab stops by pressing the Add and Delete buttons, respectively. The list box that appears next to both of these buttons displays the current values of all tab stops. This list is always synchronized with the **TabStops** property of the **LstPreview** component.

Yes, the **LstPreview** list box is an RzTabbedListBox component. It is necessary to use this component in order to provide visual feedback as tab stops values are modified using the track bar control. As the user moves the track bar, the selected tab stop is adjusted accordingly.

Listing 14.3   RZTABEDT.PAS—The TRzTabStopEditDlg Class

```
{===========================================================================}
{= RzTabEdt Unit                                                           =}
{=                                                                         =}
{= This unit implements a property editor for the TabStop property associated =}
{= with the TRzTabbedListBox component.  This unit defines the             =}
{= TRzTabStopProperty class and the TRzTabStopEditDlg class.  The property  =}
{= editor class displays the dialog in its Edit method.  The dialog allows  =}
{= the user to modify the TabStop property at design-time.                 =}
{=                                                                         =}
{= Building Custom Delphi Components - Ray Konopka                         =}
{===========================================================================}

unit RzTabEdt;

interface

uses
  SysUtils, WinTypes, WinProcs, Messages, Classes, Graphics, Controls,
  Forms, Dialogs, StdCtrls, Buttons, RzTabLst, Spin, DsgnIntf, RzTrkBar;
```

```
type
  TRzTabStopEditDlg = class(TForm)
    BtnOK: TButton;
    BtnCancel: TButton;
    GrpPreview: TGroupBox;
    GrpTabStops: TGroupBox;
    BtnAdd: TBitBtn;
    LstTabs: TListBox;
    BtnDelete: TBitBtn;
    LblMin: TLabel;
    LblMax: TLabel;
    Label3: TLabel;
    LblTabNum: TLabel;
    LstPreview: TRzTabbedListBox;
    TrkTabPos: TRzTrackBar;
    procedure BtnAddClick(Sender: TObject);
    procedure BtnDeleteClick(Sender: TObject);
    procedure LstTabsClick(Sender: TObject);
    procedure FormShow(Sender: TObject);
    procedure TrkTabPosChange(Sender: TObject);
    procedure FormCreate(Sender: TObject);
  private
    FUpdating : Boolean;
  end;


procedure Register;

implementation

{$R *.DFM}


{=================================}
{== TRzTabStopEditDlg Methods ==}
{=================================}

procedure TRzTabStopEditDlg.FormCreate(Sender: TObject);
begin
  FUpdating := False;
end;


procedure TRzTabStopEditDlg.BtnAddClick(Sender: TObject);
var
  NewTab : Word;
  Idx    : Integer;
begin
  NewTab := 8;
  if LstPreview.TabStops.Count > 0 then
  begin                 { Add a new tab stop 8 positions after the last tab stop }
    NewTab := LstPreview.TabStops[ LstPreview.TabStops.Count - 1 ] + 8;
  end;
```

```
    Idx := LstTabs.Items.Add( IntToStr( NewTab ) );{ Add TabStop to Editing List }
    LstPreview.TabStops.Add( NewTab );              { Add Tab stop to Preview list }

    LstTabs.ItemIndex := Idx;                    { Select the newly added tab stop }
    LstTabsClick( nil );                                    { Update Track Bar }
    BtnDelete.Enabled := True;
    TrkTabPos.Enabled := True;
  end;


procedure TRzTabStopEditDlg.BtnDeleteClick(Sender: TObject);
var
  Index : Integer;
begin
  Index := LstTabs.ItemIndex;
  LstPreview.TabStops.Delete( Index );               { Remove selected Tab Stop }
  LstTabs.Items.Delete( Index );

  if LstTabs.Items.Count > 0 then
  begin
    if Index = LstTabs.Items.Count then
      Dec( Index );
    LstTabs.ItemIndex := Index;
    LstTabsClick( nil );                                    { Update Track Bar }
  end
  else
  begin
    BtnDelete.Enabled := False;
    TrkTabPos.Enabled := False;
  end;
end;


{= TRzTabStopEditDlg.LstTabsClick                                              =}
{=   This method updates the Min and Max values of the track bar to reflect    =}
{=   the range a particular tab stop may move.  A tab stop may not move past   =}
{=   a tab stop that exists before or after it in the list.  Setting the       =}
{=   track bar range ensures that this cannot happen. The FUpdating flag is    =}
{=   set at the beginning of this method to prevent a change in the            =}
{=   TrackBar's Min or Max value from causing the TrkTabPosChange event from   =}
{=   altering the display.                                                     =}

procedure TRzTabStopEditDlg.LstTabsClick(Sender: TObject);
begin
  FUpdating := True;
  TrkTabPos.Min := 0;
  TrkTabPos.Max := 100;
  if LstTabs.ItemIndex > 0 then                 { Get Previous Tab Stop Value }
    TrkTabPos.Min := StrToInt( LstTabs.Items[ LstTabs.ItemIndex - 1 ] )
  else
    TrkTabPos.Min := 0;
  if LstTabs.ItemIndex < LstTabs.Items.Count - 1 then    { Get Next Tab Value }
    TrkTabPos.Max := StrToInt( LstTabs.Items[ LstTabs.ItemIndex + 1 ] )
```

```
    else
      TrkTabPos.Max := 100;

    { Update TrackBar position to reflect currently selected tab stop }
    TrkTabPos.Position := LstPreview.TabStops[ LstTabs.ItemIndex ];
    LblTabNum.Caption := IntToStr( LstTabs.ItemIndex + 1 );
    LblMin.Caption := IntToStr( TrkTabPos.Min );
    LblMax.Caption := IntToStr( TrkTabPos.Max );
    FUpdating := False;
  end;


procedure TRzTabStopEditDlg.FormShow(Sender: TObject);
begin
  if LstTabs.Items.Count > 0 then
  begin
    LstTabs.ItemIndex := 0;
    LstTabsClick( nil );
    BtnDelete.Enabled := True;
    TrkTabPos.Enabled := True;
  end;
end;


{= TRzTabStopEditDlg.TrkTabPosChange                                =}
{=   As the track bar is moved, the value of the selected tab stop is updated.=}
{=   The change is immediately reflected in the Tab and Preview List boxes.   =}

procedure TRzTabStopEditDlg.TrkTabPosChange(Sender: TObject);
var
  I : Integer;
begin
  if not FUpdating then
  begin
    I := LstTabs.ItemIndex;
    LstPreview.TabStops[ I ] := TrkTabPos.Position;
    LstTabs.Items[ I ] := IntToStr( TrkTabPos.Position );
    LstTabs.ItemIndex := I;
  end;
end;




{=======================}
{== Register Procedure ==}
{=======================}

procedure Register;
begin
  RegisterPropertyEditor( TypeInfo( TRzTabStopList ), TRzTabbedListBox,
                          'TabStops', TRzTabStopProperty );
end;


end.
```

As a final note, the **RzTabEdt** unit contains the **Register** procedure for this property editor. This prevents the form file from being inadvertently included in an application. The **RegisterPropertyEditor** call for the **TRzTabStopProperty** follows the same format used for the **TRzClockStatusProperty**. That is, the property editor is registered for a specific property; in this case, the **TabStops** property of the **TRzTabbedListBox** component.

Component Editors

There are two primary reasons for creating a component editor. The first reason is to add menu items to the context menu that is displayed by the Form Designer when the component is selected. An example of this is the **TNotebookEditor**, which provides two additional menu items for navigating through the various pages of the Notebook component. The second reason for creating a custom component editor is to change the action that is performed when the component is double-clicked. For example, the **TDatasetEditor** displays the Fields Editor when a user double clicks on a Dataset component.

All component editors in Delphi descend from the **TComponentEditor** class. This class provides the necessary methods that enable it to be manipulated by the Form Designer. Like property editors, creating a new custom component editor requires defining a new class and overriding some of its inherited methods.

> **By Convention**
>
> Component editor classes end with "Editor." For example, the following component editors are predefined in Delphi: **TDatasetEditor**, **TNotebookEditor**, and **TReportEditor**.

Building a Component Editor

Building a component editor is actually easier than building a property editor. This is because the Form Designer provides direct access to the component being edited through the **Component** property defined in the **TComponentEditor** class. Unlike property editors, component editors do not have to be concerned with providing a string representation of the property values of a component. However, to perform actual editing, component editors are similar to property editors in that this is accomplished by overriding certain methods.

When a component is selected and the user presses the right mouse button (or Alt+F10), the Form Designer displays the context menu. The Form Designer calls the **GetVerbCount** method to determine if there are any custom menu items that need to be added. A custom component editor overrides this method to return the number of items to be added. If this method returns a number greater than zero, the **GetVerb** method is called once for each item to be added.

The **GetVerb** method is responsible for specifying the strings to be used for the new menu items. When the **GetVerb** method is called, it is passed an index parameter that indicates which menu item is being added. This method is overridden to return a string value to the Form Designer based in the index parameter.

When the user selects one of the newly added menu items, the **ExecuteVerb** method of the component editor is called. This method receives as its only parameter the index of the menu item that was selected. Therefore, the **ExecuteVerb** method is responsible for dispatching the appropriate action based on the selected menu item. Since a component editor has direct access to the component, virtually any type of editing can be performed on the component.

When the component is double-clicked, the component editor's **Edit** method is called. This method provides another way of invoking some action. If the **Edit** method is not overridden in a descendent class, the inherited method of the **TComponentEditor** class will execute the first verb defined in the editor. Of course, this only occurs if the **GetVerbCount** method returns a value greater than zero.

Because of this default processing, it is more common to perform all editing through the **ExecuteVerb** method, and not bother overriding the **Edit** method. This approach is beneficial because it provides both keyboard and mouse support with no extra effort.

There is one final step that must be performed by all component editors. Whenever the editor modifies the selected component, the editor *must* inform the Form Designer that the component has been modified. This is accomplished by calling the **Modified** method of the inherited **Designer** property. Calling this method instructs the Form Designer to update the appearance of the component if necessary.

The Default Component Editor

The **TDefaultEditor** class is a direct descendant of the **TComponentEditor** class. By default, whenever a component is selected on a form, the Form Designer creates an instance of the **TDefaultEditor** unless a custom component editor has been registered for the selected component. The default component editor does not add any menu items to the context menu, but it does provide an **Edit** method.

When the component is double-clicked by the user, the **Edit** method searches through the component's events looking for the **OnCreate**, **OnChange**, or **OnClick** event, in this order. Whichever one it finds first, the **Edit** method generates the event handler for the appropriate event in the form file. If none of these events is present in the selected component, an event handler is generated for the first defined event.

Generally, the **TDefaultEditor** class is only used as an ancestor when a new component editor only adds menu items to the context menu. By descending from **TDefaultEditor**, the default double-click processing described above will continue to work. The first menu item will not be executed as it is in the **TComponentEditor.Edit** method.

Registering a Component Editor

Component editors are registered, oddly enough, using the **RegisterComponentEditor** procedure. The procedure is quite simple, requiring only two parameters. The first parameter is a reference to the component class with which the component editor will be associated. The second parameter specifies the new component editor. For example, the following statement registers the **TDatasetEditor** for the Dataset component:

```
RegisterComponentEditor( TDataset, TDatasetEditor );
```

Organization

The same basic principles that were presented for property editors also apply to component editors. If a component editor presents the user with a dialog box, it must not reside in the same unit as the component.

Editing a Label

Now that we have a basic understanding of how component editors work, let's apply this knowledge and build a component editor for the RzLabel component. The RzLabel component was introduced in Chapter 9 as an enhanced label component that provides additional properties that give the label a three-dimensional appearance.

The component editor that we'll be creating in this section demonstrates both aspects of component editors described earlier. That is, the **TRzLabelEditor** adds menu items to the component's context menu and displays a custom editing dialog.

Focusing on the context menu, this new component editor adds four new menu items. The first item displays the editing dialog box that will be described shortly. The next three menu items allow the user to quickly change the **TextStyle** property of the component. Figure 14.5 shows that the user can select the Raised, Recessed, or Shadow TextStyle directly from the context menu.

Figure 14.6 shows the editing dialog that is displayed whenever the user selects the first menu item of the context menu or double-clicks on the component. This

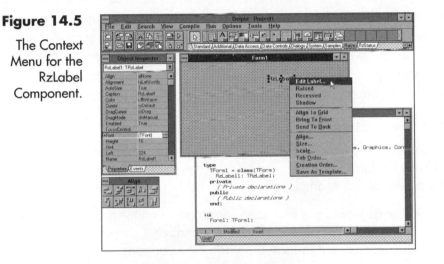

Figure 14.5

The Context Menu for the RzLabel Component.

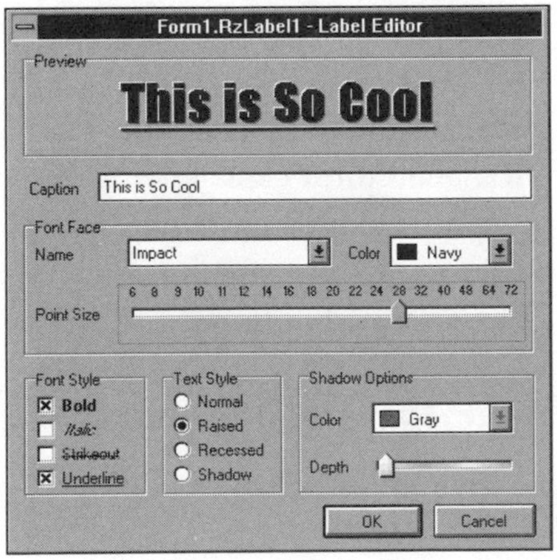

Figure 14.6

The RzLabel Component Editor.

dialog is designed to make it extremely easy for a user to customize the label. Many of the component's properties can be edited directly on this dialog without having to open up multiple dialog boxes or deal with multiple properties in the Object Inspector.

Notice that this dialog minimizes the number of actions a user must take to make a change in the label. For example, to change the **TextStyle** property of the label, radio buttons are displayed for each option. Likewise, a TrackBar component is used to select a point size without having to scroll through a combo box.

Yes, it is true that all of the changes that can be made using the editing dialog can also be made with the Object Inspector. However, there is one significant advantage to using the component editor: The component editor allows the user to try different combinations without affecting the current property values of the component. The user can always press the Cancel button to discard any modifications made in the dialog box. This is simply not possible with the Object Inspector, because only one property can be edited at a time. When a user moves to a different property, all changes made to the earlier property are recorded.

> **By Convention**
>
> The caption of the dialog that is displayed to edit a component should include the form name followed by the component name, separated by a period. For example, "Form1.RzLabel3 - Label Editor."
>
> A similar convention is also used for property editor dialogs. In this case, the form name, component name, and property name are all concatenated to form the start of the caption.

The TRzLabelEditor Class

Listing 14.4 shows a partial listing of the RzLblEdt unit. The source code shown in this listing describes the **TRzLabelEditor** class. Like the property editors covered in the earlier sections, this component editor requires very little code. In fact, component editors in general do not require much code at all. If any extensive editing is required, it is usually placed within the editing dialog.

Listing 14.4   RZLBLEDT.PAS—The TRzLabelEditor Class

```
type
  TRzLabelEditor = class( TComponentEditor )
    function GetVerbCount : Integer; override;
```

```
    function GetVerb( Index : Integer ) : string; override;
    procedure ExecuteVerb( Index : Integer ); override;
  end;


{=============================}
{== TRzLabelEditor Methods ==}
{=============================}

function TRzLabelEditor.GetVerbCount : Integer;
begin
  Result := 4;
end;


function TRzLabelEditor.GetVerb( Index : Integer ) : string;
begin
  case Index of
    0: Result := 'Edit &Label...';
    1: Result := 'Ra&ised';
    2: Result := '&Recessed';
    3: Result := 'Shado&w';
  end;
end;


procedure TRzLabelEditor.ExecuteVerb( Index : Integer );
var
  Dialog : TRzLabelEditDlg;

  procedure CopyLabel( Dest, Source : TRzLabel );
  begin
    Dest.Caption := Source.Caption;
    Dest.Font := Source.Font;
    Dest.TextStyle := Source.TextStyle;
    Dest.ShadowColor := Source.ShadowColor;
    Dest.ShadowDepth := Source.ShadowDepth;
  end;

begin
  case Index of
    0:                                                    { Edit Label... }
    begin
      Dialog := TRzLabelEditDlg.Create( Application );

      try
        { Copy Attributes to Dialog Box LblPreview Component }
        CopyLabel( Dialog.LblPreview, Component as TRzLabel );

        Dialog.Caption := Component.Owner.Name + '.' + Component.Name +
                          Dialog.Caption;
        Dialog.InitSettings;              { Update all controls on dialog box }
```

```
    if Dialog.ShowModal = mrOK then                    { Display Dialog Box }
    begin
      CopyLabel( Component as TRzLabel, Dialog.LblPreview );
      Designer.Modified;          { Tell Form Designer to Update Label on Form }
    end;
  finally
    Dialog.Free;                              { Don't forget to free dialog box }
  end;
end;

  1:                                          { Change TextStyle to tsRaised }
  begin
    TRzLabel( Component ).TextStyle := tsRaised;
    Designer.Modified;
  end;

  2:                                          { Change TextStyle to tsRecessed }
  begin
    TRzLabel( Component ).TextStyle := tsRecessed;
    Designer.Modified;
  end;

  3:                                          { Change TextStyle to tsShadow }
  begin
    TRzLabel( Component ).TextStyle := tsShadow;
    Designer.Modified;
  end;
  end; { case }
end; {= TRzLabelEditor.ExecuteVerb =}
```

Following the guidelines presented earlier, this component editor performs all of its editing within the **ExecuteVerb** method. Of course, in order to have the **ExecuteVerb** method called, the **GetVerbCount** and **GetVerb** methods must be overridden. The **GetVerbCount** method simply returns the value 4 to instruct the Form Designer that four additional menu items will be added to the context menu.

When the Form Designer needs to display the context menu, it calls the component editor's **GetVerb** method four times, once for each menu item. Each time the **GetVerb** method is called, an index representing the menu item is passed to the function. This index is used to determine which string value to return to the Form Designer.

 Don't forget keyboard access for the context menu. As with regular menus, the & symbol can be placed before a character to designate it as an access key. But, be careful! Do *not* use any of the following letters, because they have already been used for the default menu items: A, B, C, E, F, G, O, S, T.

The third and final method defined in the **TRzLabelEditor** class is the **ExecuteVerb** method. This method is responsible for providing the action to be executed when the user selects one of the menu items on the context menu. For the second through fourth menu items, the **ExecuteVerb** method simply sets the component's **TextStyle** property to the selected value. Notice that the component being edited is accessible through the **Component** property.

When the first menu item is chosen or the user double-clicks on the component, the **ExecuteVerb** method displays the Label Editor dialog. The code inside the **case** block for value 0 should look familiar. It has the same general structure as the **TRzTabStopProperty.Edit** method used to display the **TRzTabStopEditDlg** form.

The process is very similar. First, the appropriate dialog box is created; in this case, an instance of the **TRzLabelEditDlg** class. Next, the dialog is initialized by copying data from the underlying properties to temporary workspaces located on the dialog. For the **TRzLabelEditor**, all modifications affect the **LblPreview** component.

Once initialized, the dialog box is displayed to the user in a modal state. If the dialog is closed by the user pressing the OK button, the underlying component (or property) is updated to reflect the new value. And finally, if the component has been changed by the editor, the Form Designer is informed of the change by making a call to its **Modified** method.

As a final note regarding the **TRzLabelEditor** class, notice that this class descends from **TComponentEditor** rather than **TDefaultEditor**. This was done so that the **Edit** method defined in the **TComponentEditor** would be used. Recall that the **TComponentEditor.Edit** method executes the first menu item when the component is double-clicked. This feature eliminates the need to provide a custom **Edit** method in the **TRzLabelEditor** class.

The TRzLabelEditDlg Form

Listing 14.5 shows the source code for the **TRzLabelEditDlg** form class. With the associated RZLBLEDT.DFM file, this class defines the edit dialog for the **TRzLabelEditor** component editor. Most of the methods defined in this class are event handlers that are responsible for updating the preview label whenever a change is made to its attributes. There is also a significant amount of code used in setting up the dialog box.

Boolean variables can be assigned directly to a Boolean expression. For example, instead of writing the following code to set the Bold Check Box state,

```
if fsBold in LblPreview.Font.Style then
  ChkBold.Checked := True
else
  ChkBold.Checked := False;
```

use the following:

```
ChkBold.Checked := fsBold in LblPreview.Font.Style;
```

Listing 14.5   RZLBLEDT.PAS—The TRzLabelEditDlg Class

```
{=================================================================}
{= RzLblEdt Unit                                                 =}
{=                                                               =}
{= This unit implements a component editor for the RzLabel component. This  =}
{= unit defines the TRzLabelEditor class and the TRzLabelEditDlg class. The  =}
{= TRzLabelEditor displays the TRzLabelEditDlg form when the component is    =}
{= double-clicked or the first context menu item is chosen. The form provides =}
{= a more visual way of editing the properties of the RzLabel component with  =}
{= immediate visual feedback.                                    =}
{=                                                               =}
{= Building Custom Delphi Components - Ray Konopka               =}
{=================================================================}

unit RzLblEdt;

interface

uses
  SysUtils, WinTypes, WinProcs, Messages, Classes, Graphics, Controls,
  Forms, Dialogs, StdCtrls, Rzlabel, ExtCtrls, Spin, Buttons, RzTrkBar,
  DsgnIntf;

type
  TRzLabelEditDlg = class(TForm)
    GrpPreview: TGroupBox;
    GrpTextStyle: TRadioGroup;
    EdtCaption: TEdit;
    LblPreview: TRzLabel;
    GrpFontStyle: TGroupBox;
    ChkBold: TCheckBox;
    ChkItalic: TCheckBox;
    ChkStrikeout: TCheckBox;
    ChkUnderline: TCheckBox;
    Label1: TLabel;
    GrpShadow: TGroupBox;
```

```
    TrkShadow: TRzTrackBar;
    CbxShadowColor: TComboBox;
    Label4: TLabel;
    Label5: TLabel;
    BtnOK: TButton;
    BtnCancel: TButton;
    GrpFontFace: TGroupBox;
    TrkPointSize: TRzTrackBar;
    CbxFonts: TComboBox;
    CbxFontColor: TComboBox;
    Label2: TLabel;
    Label3: TLabel;
    Label6: TLabel;
    procedure EdtCaptionChange(Sender: TObject);
    procedure GrpTextStyleClick(Sender: TObject);
    procedure TrkPointSizeDrawTick( TrackBar: TRzTrackBar; Canvas: TCanvas;
                                    Location: TPoint; Index: Integer );
    procedure TrkPointSizeChange(Sender: TObject);
    procedure TrkShadowChange(Sender: TObject);
    procedure FormCreate(Sender: TObject);
    procedure CbxFontsChange(Sender: TObject);
    procedure ChkBoldClick(Sender: TObject);
    procedure ChkItalicClick(Sender: TObject);
    procedure ChkStrikeoutClick(Sender: TObject);
    procedure CbxColorDrawItem( Control: TWinControl; Index: Integer;
                                Rect: TRect; State: TOwnerDrawState );
    procedure ChkUnderlineClick(Sender: TObject);
    procedure CbxFontColorChange(Sender: TObject);
    procedure CbxShadowColorChange(Sender: TObject);
  public
    procedure InitSettings;
  end;


procedure Register;

implementation

{$R *.DFM}


{=====================================================}
{== Implementation Specific Types and Constants ==}
{=====================================================}

const                                      { Support Point Size Track Bar }
  PointSizes : array[ 0..17 ] of string[ 2 ] =
    ( '6', '8', '9', '10', '11', '12', '14', '16', '18', '20',
      '22', '24', '28', '32', '40', '48', '64', '72' );

type                                { Supports Owner Draw Color Combo Boxes }
  TColorRec = record
    Color : TColor;
```

```
    Name : string[ 7 ];
  end;

const
  Colors : array[ 0..15 ] of TColorRec = (
    ( Color : clBlack;   Name : 'Black' ),
    ( Color : clMaroon;  Name : 'Maroon' ),
    ( Color : clGreen;   Name : 'Green' ),
    ( Color : clOlive;   Name : 'Olive' ),
    ( Color : clNavy;    Name : 'Navy' ),
    ( Color : clPurple;  Name : 'Purple' ),
    ( Color : clTeal;    Name : 'Teal' ),
    ( Color : clGray;    Name : 'Gray' ),
    ( Color : clSilver;  Name : 'Silver' ),
    ( Color : clRed;     Name : 'Red' ),
    ( Color : clLime;    Name : 'Lime' ),
    ( Color : clYellow;  Name : 'Yellow' ),
    ( Color : clBlue;    Name : 'Blue' ),
    ( Color : clFuchsia; Name : 'Fuchsia' ),
    ( Color : clAqua;    Name : 'Aqua' ),
    ( Color : clWhite;   Name : 'White' ) );



{=============================}
{== TRzLabelEditDlg Methods ==}
{=============================}

{= NOTE:  All changes made through the control on this dialog box affect only =}
{=        the preview label (LblPreview).  Only if the OK button is pressed   =}
{=        are the changes reflected in the selected component.                =}


procedure TRzLabelEditDlg.FormCreate(Sender: TObject);
begin
  CbxFonts.Items := Screen.Fonts;
end;


procedure TRzLabelEditDlg.InitSettings;

  function PositionFromPointSize( P : Integer ) : Integer;
  var
    I : Integer;
  begin
    I := 0;
    while ( I < 18 ) and ( StrToInt( PointSizes[ I ] ) <> P ) do
      Inc( I );
    if I = 18 then
      Result := 2
    else
      Result := I;
  end;
```

```
    function IndexFromColor( C : TColor ) : Integer;
    var
      I : Integer;
    begin
      I := 0;
      while (I < 16) and ( ColorToRGB(Colors[ I ].Color) <> ColorToRGB(C) ) do
        Inc( I );
      if I = 16 then
        Result := 0
      else
        Result := I;
    end;

begin {= TRzLabelEditDlg.InitSettings =}
  EdtCaption.Text := LblPreview.Caption;
  CbxFonts.ItemIndex := CbxFonts.Items.IndexOf( LblPreview.Font.Name );
  CbxFontColor.ItemIndex := IndexFromColor( LblPreview.Font.Color );
  TrkPointSize.Position := PositionFromPointSize( LblPreview.Font.Size );

  { Font Styles }
  ChkBold.Checked := fsBold in LblPreview.Font.Style;
  ChkItalic.Checked := fsItalic in LblPreview.Font.Style;
  ChkStrikeout.Checked := fsStrikeout in LblPreview.Font.Style;
  ChkUnderline.Checked := fsUnderline in LblPreview.Font.Style;

  { Text Style }
  GrpTextStyle.ItemIndex := Ord( LblPreview.TextStyle );

  { Shadow Options }
  CbxShadowColor.ItemIndex := IndexFromColor( LblPreview.ShadowColor );
  TrkShadow.Position := LblPreview.ShadowDepth;
end; {= TRzLabelEditDlg.InitSettings =}


procedure TRzLabelEditDlg.EdtCaptionChange(Sender: TObject);
begin
  LblPreview.Caption := EdtCaption.Text;
end;


procedure TRzLabelEditDlg.CbxFontsChange(Sender: TObject);
begin
  LblPreview.Font.Name := CbxFonts.Text;
end;


{= TRzLabelEditDlg.TrkPointSizeDrawTick                           =}
{=   Owner draw method is used to display point values at each tick mark.   =}

procedure TRzLabelEditDlg.TrkPointSizeDrawTick(TrackBar: TRzTrackBar;
  Canvas: TCanvas; Location: TPoint; Index: Integer);
var
  S : string;
```

```
  W : Integer;
begin
  Canvas.Brush.Color := TrackBar.Color;
  Canvas.Font.Name := 'Small Fonts';
  Canvas.Font.Size := 7;
  Canvas.Font.Style := [];
  W := Canvas.TextWidth( PointSizes[ Index ] );
  Canvas.TextOut( Location.X - (W div 2), 1, PointSizes[ Index ] );
end;


procedure TRzLabelEditDlg.TrkPointSizeChange(Sender: TObject);
begin
  LblPreview.Font.Size := StrToInt( PointSizes[ TrkPointSize.Position ] );
end;


procedure TRzLabelEditDlg.ChkBoldClick(Sender: TObject);
begin
  if ChkBold.Checked then
    LblPreview.Font.Style := LblPreview.Font.Style + [ fsBold ]
  else
    LblPreview.Font.Style := LblPreview.Font.Style - [ fsBold ]
end;


procedure TRzLabelEditDlg.ChkItalicClick(Sender: TObject);
begin
  if ChkItalic.Checked then
    LblPreview.Font.Style := LblPreview.Font.Style + [ fsItalic ]
  else
    LblPreview.Font.Style := LblPreview.Font.Style - [ fsItalic ]
end;


procedure TRzLabelEditDlg.ChkStrikeoutClick(Sender: TObject);
begin
  if ChkStrikeout.Checked then
    LblPreview.Font.Style := LblPreview.Font.Style + [ fsStrikeout ]
  else
    LblPreview.Font.Style := LblPreview.Font.Style - [ fsStrikeout ]
end;


procedure TRzLabelEditDlg.ChkUnderlineClick(Sender: TObject);
begin
  if ChkUnderline.Checked then
    LblPreview.Font.Style := LblPreview.Font.Style + [ fsUnderline ]
  else
    LblPreview.Font.Style := LblPreview.Font.Style - [ fsUnderline ]
end;
```

```
procedure TRzLabelEditDlg.GrpTextStyleClick(Sender: TObject);
begin
  LblPreview.TextStyle := TTextStyle( GrpTextStyle.ItemIndex );

  TrkShadow.Enabled := LblPreview.TextStyle = tsShadow;
  CbxShadowColor.Enabled := LblPreview.TextStyle = tsShadow;
end;


procedure TRzLabelEditDlg.TrkShadowChange(Sender: TObject);
begin
  LblPreview.ShadowDepth := TrkShadow.Position;
end;


{= TRzLabelEditDlg.CbxColorDrawItem                                 =}
{=   This owner-draw method is used to draw color entries for both the Font  =}
{=   Color and Shadow Color Combo Boxes.                            =}

procedure TRzLabelEditDlg.CbxColorDrawItem( Control : TWinControl;
                                            Index : Integer; Rect : TRect;
                                            State : TOwnerDrawState );
var
  R : TRect;
begin
  R := Rect;
  InflateRect( R, -2, -2 );
  R.Right := 20;
  with ( Control as TComboBox ).Canvas do
  begin
    FillRect( Rect );                              { Clear list item rectangle }
    Brush.Color := Colors[ Index ].Color;          { Select correct color }
    Rectangle( R.Left, R.Top, R.Right, R.Bottom );     { Draw color rectangle }
    if odSelected in State then
      Brush.Color := clHighlight
    else
      Brush.Color := (Control as TComboBox).Color;
    TextOut( Rect.Left + 24, Rect.Top + 2, Colors[ Index ].Name );
  end;
end;


procedure TRzLabelEditDlg.CbxFontColorChange(Sender: TObject);
begin
  LblPreview.Font.Color := Colors[ CbxFontColor.ItemIndex ].Color;
end;


procedure TRzLabelEditDlg.CbxShadowColorChange(Sender: TObject);
begin
  LblPreview.ShadowColor := Colors[ CbxShadowColor.ItemIndex ].Color;
end;
```

```
{=========================}
{== Register Procedure ==}
{=========================}

procedure Register;
begin
  RegisterComponentEditor( TRzLabel, TRzLabelEditor );
end;

end.
```

The form that is used to edit RzLabel components is fairly straightforward. The preview area is occupied by an RzLabel component. Any change that is made using the controls in this dialog immediately update the label in the preview area. This allows the user to see exactly what the label will look like.

There are two features of this form that deserve attention. First, the RzTrackBar component that is used to select a point size has its **TickStyle** set to **tkOwnerDraw** so that it may display the point sizes at each tick location. The **OnDrawTick** event handler uses the **PointSizes** constant array to map the track bar's position values to the correct point size. (I knew that providing owner-draw support in the RzTrackBar component would come in handy.)

The second interesting feature of this editor involves the two combo boxes used to select colors. Both of these controls behave exactly as does the color combo box that is part of the common dialog box for selecting a font. This is illustrated in Figure 14.7. This effect is achieved by specifying each combo box to be owner-

Figure 14.7

Owner Draw
Combo Boxes.

draw, and then writing an **OnDrawItem** event handler to display the appropriate color in each line. Notice that Delphi's event architecture allows both color combo boxes to use the same **OnDrawItem** event handler.

Looking Ahead...

Providing custom property editors and component editors can dramatically change the way a component is used at design-time. Design-time editors can even give your components a professional quality. However, if your component does not work correctly, the effects of a custom editor are secondary. In the next chapter, we'll investigate several debugging techniques that can be used during the development of components.

Chapter 15

Testing and Debugging Components

Testing and Debugging Components

Delphi components present a unique debugging challenge—on which you can bring to bear some special debugging tools and techniques.

In discussing all of the components that have been presented in this book, there has been one assumption that has remained throughout. That is, all of the components do indeed work. This is an important assumption because it allowed us to focus on the techniques used in building the various types of components without having to worry about such issues as why the Zip code edit field didn't appear at first in the RzAddress component. I forgot to set its **Parent** property. Or why Delphi crashed when I deleted a Table component that was connected to an RzDBEmployee's **Dataset** property—forgot the **Notification** method on this one.

The point is, there were a number of grueling hours spent after each component was written just getting all the bugs out. In fact, it was the events that took place during debugging and testing that served as the source for many of the tips that appear throughout this book. Unfortunately, even with all of the tips, it's inevitable that you will run into a bug or two when developing components of your own. Hopefully, they won't be as nasty as the memory allocation issues I ran into in developing the RzMailMessage component.

That last sentence emphasizes an important point. Debugging and testing are very integral parts in *developing* a component. This is nothing new. The same principle holds true for application development. What makes things more complicated is that components can be used in two different contexts: runtime and design-time. This means more chances for bugs. Fortunately, there are number of tools that can be used to track down and eliminate bugs in your components.

In this chapter, I will present three tools that can be used to debug components. All three have their strengths and weaknesses. Each tool, however, is unique in that it excels at a particular aspect of the debugging process. There is no one perfect tool, and it is up to the component writer to determine which tool should be used for a particular bug.

Before we get started, it should also be noted that this chapter does not describe the art of debugging in broad terms. I believe it is safe to assume that people reading this book have had their share of experience in debugging applications, whether or not they were developed in Delphi. Fortunately, the same principles still apply when debugging components. However, because of the two ways in which components are used, no one debugging tool adequately handles all debugging problems.

Testing: Bug Detection

The first step in debugging a component is realizing you have a bug. Of course, this can only be achieved by testing the component. Therefore, before discussing the various tools available for locating bugs, a review of component testing is in order.

Once a component is ready for testing, it's very tempting to install the component, drop one on a form, and proceed to use it in an application. As tempting as this is, testing the component using the Delphi design environment should be deferred until after the component has been tested under a more controlled setting.

The Delphi design environment offers very little control over how a component is manipulated. For example, immediately after a component is dropped onto a form, the Object Inspector calls the read access methods for all published properties. There is no way to prevent this from happening. Unfortunately, the effects of this can be misleading. For instance, if there is a problem in one of these methods, it will appear as though there is a problem in the constructor. In general, it is very difficult to isolate a particular feature of a component within the design environment.

Testing under the Delphi design environment can also be more risky. In particular, when a component is installed and registered, its source code becomes linked into the current component library. The COMPLIB.DCL file represents the default component library. Recall from Chapter 7 that this file is actually a dynamic link library that is loaded into memory when Delphi starts. Since all of the components reside in the same DLL, one ill-behaved component can quite easily cause general protection faults and other errors within the component library. If the fault is significant enough, Delphi itself can crash.

Runtime Testing

A better approach is to test the component using a test application that dynamically creates the component. This process was introduced in Chapter 7. In this section, we revisit this topic so that it can be described more completely. In particular, we'll take a closer look at the advantages of this approach, as well as the different ways in which a component can be tested in this manner.

The test application is designed to test the runtime behavior of a component. There are several benefits to this approach. First, because the runtime and design-time features of most components overlap, testing the runtime features will also test many of the design-time features.

Second, runtime testing is much more controlled. Unlike the design environment, the runtime environment gives a developer much more control over how a component is manipulated. Specifically, only the methods that are called by the test application will be executed. This dramatically reduces the chances of searching down the wrong path for a bug.

Third, if an error does occur in the component, only the test application is affected, as opposed to Delphi itself. This is especially significant when dealing with memory errors and protection faults. Crashing the test application is much less of a problem than crashing Delphi. If you have ever crashed Delphi, you know what a pain this can be.

When Delphi terminates unexpectedly, several of the Delphi DLLs remain loaded in memory. Delphi cannot be restarted when these DLLs are already loaded. Therefore, the remaining DLLs must be removed from memory. The easiest way to do this is to restart Windows. Another method is to use a utility that allows you to selectively remove each module from memory. In either case, getting Delphi back up and running is a very time-consuming task.

A More Realistic Example

The test application presented in Chapter 7 was very simplistic. This is because the component that was being tested, RzButton, is very simple. In this section, a test application is built for the RzTrackBar component. This component was introduced in Chapter 10 and has several properties that must be tested, and some events to test as well.

The process of runtime testing is based on the ability to dynamically create the selected component. This is significant because it allows the developer to control how and when the component is created. There are five basic steps that must be performed to dynamically create a component in a test application:

1. Add the component unit to the main form's uses clause

2. Add a component reference to the form's class declaration

3. Create the component

4. Assign the component's **Parent** property

5. Set additional properties of the component

To be more complete, the last step usually involves more than just setting additional properties. A complex component, like RzTrackBar, requires additional methods and event handlers to be created in the test application. Listing 15.1 contains the source code for the **TTrkMain** unit, which is the main form for the **TstTrack** project.

Listing 15.1 TTRKMAIN.PAS—Testing the RzTrackBar

```
unit TTrkMain;

interface

uses
  SysUtils, WinTypes, WinProcs, Messages, Classes, Graphics, Controls,
  Forms, Dialogs, RzTrkBar, StdCtrls, Tabs, ExtCtrls;

type
  TForm1 = class(TForm)
    BtnMax: TButton;
    BtnEnable: TButton;
    LblPosition: TLabel;
    GrpThumbSize: TRadioGroup;
    BtnShowTicks: TButton;
    GrpThumbStyle: TRadioGroup;
    BtnTrackColor: TButton;
    BtnTrackWidth: TButton;
```

```
    BtnOwnerDraw: TButton;
    BtnCreate: TButton;
    BtnDestroy: TButton;
    GrpOrientation: TRadioGroup;
    procedure BtnEnableClick(Sender: TObject);
    procedure GrpThumbSizeClick(Sender: TObject);
    procedure BtnShowTicksClick(Sender: TObject);
    procedure GrpThumbStyleClick(Sender: TObject);
    procedure BtnTrackColorClick(Sender: TObject);
    procedure BtnTrackWidthClick(Sender: TObject);
    procedure BtnOwnerDrawClick(Sender: TObject);
    procedure BtnMaxClick(Sender: TObject);
    procedure BtnCreateClick(Sender: TObject);
    procedure BtnDestroyClick(Sender: TObject);
  private
    { Private declarations }
  public
    { Public declarations }
    TrkTest : TRzTrackBar;
    procedure DrawTheTick( TrackBar : TRzTrackBar; Canvas : TCanvas;
                           Location : TPoint; Index : Integer );
    procedure TrkChange( Sender : TObject );
  end;

var
  Form1: TForm1;

implementation

{$R *.DFM}


procedure TForm1.BtnCreateClick(Sender: TObject);
begin
  TrkTest := TRzTrackBar.Create( Self );
  TrkTest.Parent := Self;

  if GrpOrientation.ItemIndex = 0 then                { Horizontal TrackBar}
    TrkTest.SetBounds( 10, 100, 250, 50 )
  else                                                { Vertical TrackBar }
    TrkTest.SetBounds( 50, 20, 50, 250 );

  TrkTest.PageSize := 4;                       { Set Initial Property Values }

  TrkTest.OnChange := TrkChange;                   { Set up Event Handlers }
  TrkTest.TickStyle := tkOwnerDraw;
  TrkTest.OnDrawTick := DrawTheTick;
end;


procedure TForm1.BtnDestroyClick(Sender: TObject);
begin
```

```
    TrkTest.Free;
  end;


procedure TForm1.TrkChange( Sender : TObject );
begin
  LblPosition.Caption := 'Position = ' + IntToStr( TrkTest.Position );
end;


procedure TForm1.BtnMaxClick(Sender: TObject);
begin
  if TrkTest.Max = 10 then
    TrkTest.Max := 15
  else
    TrkTest.Max := 10;
end;


procedure TForm1.BtnEnableClick(Sender: TObject);
begin
  TrkTest.Enabled := not TrkTest.Enabled;
end;


procedure TForm1.BtnTrackColorClick(Sender: TObject);
begin
  TrkTest.TrackColor := clTeal;
end;


procedure TForm1.BtnTrackWidthClick(Sender: TObject);
begin
  TrkTest.TrackWidth := 12;
end;


procedure TForm1.GrpThumbSizeClick(Sender: TObject);
begin
  TrkTest.ThumbSize := TThumbSize( GrpThumbSize.ItemIndex );
end;


procedure TForm1.GrpThumbStyleClick(Sender: TObject);
begin
  TrkTest.ThumbStyle := TThumbStyle( GrpThumbStyle.ItemIndex );
end;


procedure TForm1.BtnOwnerDrawClick(Sender: TObject);
begin
  if TrkTest.TickStyle = tkOwnerDraw then
    TrkTest.TickStyle := tkStandard
```

```
    else
      TrkTest.TickStyle := tkOwnerDraw;
end;


procedure TForm1.DrawTheTick( TrackBar: TRzTrackBar; Canvas : TCanvas;
                              Location : TPoint; Index : Integer );
begin
  { Draw Gray Circles on Both Sides of Track at each Tick Mark Location }

  with Canvas, Location do
  begin
    Brush.Color := clGray;
    Brush.Style := bsSolid;
    if TrackBar.Orientation = toVertical then
    begin
      Ellipse( 2, Y - 4, 10, Y + 4 );
      Ellipse( TrackBar.Width - 10, Y - 4, TrackBar.Width - 2, Y + 4 );
    end
    else
    begin
      Ellipse( X - 4, 2, X + 4, 10 );
      Ellipse( X - 4, TrackBar.Height - 10, X + 4, TrackBar.Height - 2 );
    end;
  end; { with }
end;


procedure TForm1.BtnShowTicksClick(Sender: TObject);
begin
  TrkTest.ShowTicks := not TrkTest.ShowTicks;
end;


end.
```

First, the **RzTrkBar** unit is added to the **uses** clause because Delphi automatically adds component units only when they are dropped onto a form at design-time. Since we are creating the component at runtime, this must be done manually. Next, the **TrkTest** component is declared in the **public** section of the main form.

The test application in Chapter 7 dynamically created the component being tested in the **FormCreate** method. While this is the most common location for creating the test component, it is not the only one available. For instance, the TstTrack program creates the component in the **BtnCreateClick** event handler. By delaying the creation of the component, it is possible to create it differently without having to rewrite the program. In particular, the orientation of the track bar is selected by the tester before the component is created. The corresponding Delete button is used to destroy the test component so that another one can be created during the same program session.

Once the component is created, the golden rule of dynamically creating components applies. That is, do not forget to set the component's **Parent** property. Recall that setting the **Parent** property puts the component on its parent's **Controls** list, which ensures that the component gets painted. After the **Parent** property is set, it's usually necessary to modify some of the component's properties. From Listing 15.1, we see that the **PageSize** property is changed from its default value of 1 to 4. More interesting, however, are the assignments that follow.

Since the **TRzTrackBar** class defines two new events, **OnChange** and **OnDrawTick**, event handlers for each event are specified after the component is created. Again, since we do not have the luxury of manipulating the component in the design environment, each of the event handlers must be written manually.

In addition to the track bar event handlers, Listing 15.1 also shows a few event handlers for some buttons that have been dropped onto the main form. The buttons are used to change the values of various properties of the component while the program is running. For example, the Enable button that appears in Figure 15.1 is used to toggle the **Enabled** property of the track bar.

Testing properties like this is very important in determining if a component behaves correctly. In this program, the Enable button simulates the operation of the Object Inspector. That is, when the Enable button is pressed, the **Enabled** property of the **TrkTest** component toggles between **True** and **False**. This is exactly what happens when a component user double clicks the **Enabled** property in the Object Inspector.

Why is this important? Isn't it sufficient to just set the **Enabled** property to **True**, run the test program, then change the code to set the property to **False**, and rerun the program? This will be sufficient in most cases. However, the key is to test what happens when the property *changes*. Recall from Chapter 10 that when the track bar is in a disabled state, the track and the thumb are displayed using a dithered bitmap. If this bitmap is not correctly cleared when the track bar returns to an enabled state, the component will not be painted correctly.

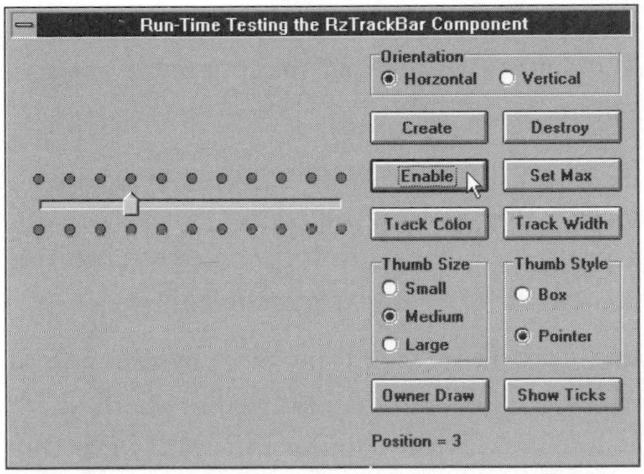

Figure 15.1

Testing the
RzTrackBar.

Use the RadioGroup component to test properties that hold enumerated values. Drop one on the testing form and set its **Items** string list to contain strings representing each of the enumerated values. Be sure to list them in order. Next, create an event handler for the **OnClick** event of the RadioGroup, and use group's **ItemIndex** to set the test component's property. Since enumerated values are actually integer values, the **ItemIndex** can be directly assigned to the new component's property by using a typecast. For example:

```
TrkTest.ThumbSize := TThumbSize( GrpThumbSize.ItemIndex );
```

Testing Guidelines

It is important not to make the test application overly complicated. The goal is to test the component, not to test the test *application*. The TstTrack project presented here is on the verge of being a bit too fancy for a test application, but for this chapter it was necessary to demonstrate the various ways a component can be tested. In practice, it is not necessary to test every feature of a component in a single testing run. In fact, it is often more manageable to test only a few features, then go back and modify the testing code to test another group of features.

Once the test application is created, the testing process begins. Unfortunately, there is no particular set of rules that describes how a component should be tested, but here are a few guidelines that can help.

First, concentrate on the new properties that were defined in the component. Initially, it is usually safe to assume that the inherited properties of the component will behave correctly.

Second, be sure to test any property interactions. For example, in the RzTrackBar component, if the **Max** property is changed to a value less than the current position, the **Position** property is changed to become equal to the new **Max** value. These types of interactions must always be tested.

Third, test paint methods. There is nothing more irritating than seeing a component not paint itself correctly when manipulated in the design environment. Ensuring correct visualization of your components starts with runtime testing.

Finally, do not forget to test any events defined in the component. There are a couple of things that need to be tested with respect to events. First of all, does the event get triggered when expected? And when it does get triggered, does the event handler receive the correct parameters?

It's important to realize that these guidelines only address features specific to components. Since a component is just a code module, the same principles that apply to testing applications also apply to testing components. For example, if a component allocates dynamic memory, it should be verified that the correct amount of memory is released when the component is destroyed.

Again, there is no magic formula that can be followed when it comes to testing components. The primary purpose of testing is to verify that a component functions properly. Unfortunately, verification is rarely a smooth process because problems surface as different aspects of the component are tested. When a problem does arise, testing is put on hold and the debugging process starts.

Using the Delphi Debugger

Delphi's integrated debugger is the debugging tool most familiar to Delphi developers. The Delphi debugger offers many features found in traditional stand-alone debuggers including breakpoints, program execution control, and the ability to watch variables. Of course, the major benefit of the Delphi debugger is that it is integrated into the Delphi development environment. This integration has a significant productivity advantage. Being integrated, the debugger is immediately available in the development environment. It is not necessary to switch to another tool to locate a bug, and once the bug is found, the source code can be immediately modified.

If a problem arises during the runtime testing of a component, the Delphi debugger can be used to locate the bug. Using the Delphi debugger to locate a bug in a component is no different from debugging a normal Delphi application. In fact, it is exactly the same process because the component unit is treated just like any other unit used by the main form of a Delphi program.

The only setup that is required to use the integrated debugger is that the testing application and the component unit must be compiled with debug information. This is accomplished by selecting the Options|Project menu item to display the Project Options dialog box and switching to the Compiler page as shown in Figure 15.2. To add debug information, make sure the options in the Debugging group box are checked.

If these options have to be changed, it's a good idea to rebuild the testing application by selecting the Compile|Build All menu item. This is usually necessary because changing the compiler options does *not* force units to be recompiled. For example, if the component unit has already been compiled and is up to date, changing the debug directives will not force the component unit to be recompiled. Rebuilding the application ensures that debug information is added to both the main form and component units. Once the application is compiled with debug information, the integrated debugger is invoked by running the program from within Delphi.

Integrated Debugging Features

As mentioned earlier, the Delphi integrated debugger has many of the same features found in stand-alone debuggers. There are three basic categories of debugging features available in the Delphi debugger:

Figure 15.2

Including Debug Information for Delphi's Integrated Debugger.

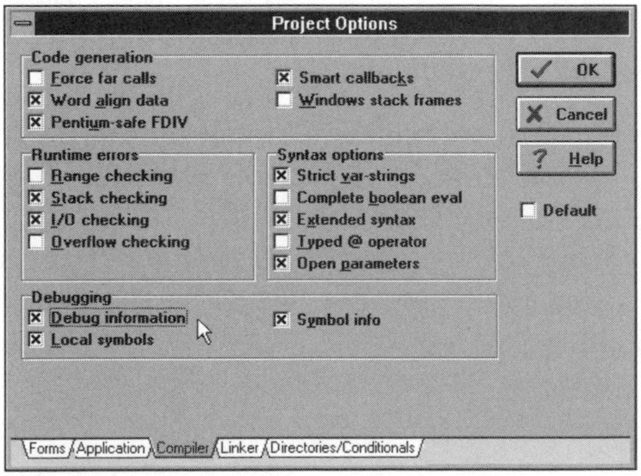

- Controlling program execution
- Setting breakpoints
- Examining data

The most important feature provided by any debugger is the ability to control which program statements get executed. The Delphi debugger provides all of the basic control operations. The first is the ability to run the program at normal speed. This is typically the first command that starts a debugging session. The Run To Cursor command can also be used to run the program at normal speed. This option, however, only runs the program until the line of code the cursor is on is reached. At this point, execution is paused, and the execution point is highlighted in the code editor window.

At this point, the Trace Into and Step Over commands become useful. Both commands allow only one line of code to be executed at a time. The difference between the two commands is only apparent when the source line contains a call to a procedure or function. In this case, the Trace Into command causes the debugger to step into the specified procedure or function. That is, the execution point is placed on the procedure's first executable statement. The Step Over command prevents the debugger from stepping into the specified procedure, and simply moves the execution point to the following statement.

Of course, in order for the Trace Into and Step Over functions to be of value, you must be able to pause execution at a particular point, a breakpoint. There are two different types of breakpoints that can be set in Delphi: *simple and conditional.* Simple breakpoints always pause the program's execution at the point they are encountered. Conditional breakpoints only pause execution when their associated expression evaluates to **True**. It is important to note that this expression is only evaluated when the breakpoint position is encountered. The Delphi debugger does not support global breakpoints.

Once execution is paused, it's helpful to be able to view the contents of variables to locate a bug. Delphi provides three tools for examining the values of data during a debugging session:

- Watch List window
- Evaluate/Modify dialog box
- Call Stack window

The Watch List window is basically an expression monitor, where an expression consists of variables, data structure elements, and constants, combined with the standard language operators. For example, Figure 15.3 shows five property values being displayed in the Watch List window. The contents of this window are updated during the course of the program so that the window always displays the current value of each expression.

The Evaluate/Modify dialog box is similar to the Watch List window in that it is used to display the current value of expressions. However, unlike the Watch List window, if the expression being evaluated is a variable or data structure, its contents can be modified. Modifying a variable or data structure in this fashion is generally done to test a possible solution before actually coding the change.

When debugging events and event handlers, it is often beneficial to determine which component method caused the event to be triggered. This information can be obtained using the Call Stack window. The Call Stack window displays the current sequence of function calls with the most recent call at the top of the list. In addition, Figure 15.3 shows that each function is displayed with the parameter values that were used when the function was called. The Call Stack window also serves as a navigational aid. When you double-click on one of the procedures or functions listed in the window, the code editor window highlights the source line that caused the function call.

Figure 15.3

Delphi's
Integrated
Debugger.

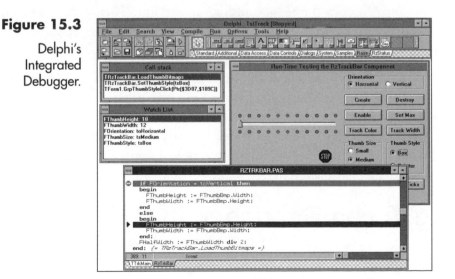

Strengths and Weaknesses

The strength of the Delphi debugger comes from its integration into the Delphi development environment. This provides component writers with an easily accessible and easy to use debugger. Through this integration, it is not necessary to leave the development environment to isolate bugs. This increases productivity because once a bug is found, it can be immediately corrected in the code editor. The Delphi debugger also provides a set of tools that are adequate for handling a wide variety of debugging tasks.

However, the integrated debugger is not without its problems. First and foremost, the Delphi debugger can only be used to debug a component at runtime. It is not possible to use the integrated debugger to debug a component at design-time. Therefore, if a bug occurs only while operating at design-time, the integrated debugger cannot be used to locate it.

Another limitation of the integrated debugger is in the way it handles debugging Paint methods. Since most components are highly visual, it is often necessary to locate a problem that affects the way in which a component is displayed. This can be quite a challenging task using the integrated debugger. That's because a breakpoint in the **Paint** method will cause the **Paint** method to be continually called in a never-ending loop. This loop is caused by the integrated debugger taking control from the testing form. When a program is allowed to continue running, the form regains the focus and forces a repaint. This causes the **Paint** method of the component to be executed again, which in turn causes the breakpoint to be fired again, and the loop starts over.

Furthermore, the Delphi debugger does not provide advanced debugging features found in stand-alone debuggers. For example, the integrated debugger does not provide a way to set global breakpoints, or view the CPU register values. These types of features are extremely helpful for very complex debugging problems. So, what should you do if a debugging problem exceeds the capabilities of the integrated debugger? Switch to a more powerful debugger, of course.

Using Turbo Debugger for Windows

Turbo Debugger for Windows (TDW) is just such a tool. TDW is Borland's stand-alone debugger, which indicates all of the features found in the integrated debugger, plus a whole lot more. TDW is included in the Borland RAD Pack for

Delphi and is also sold separately. It should be noted that only version 4.6 (or later) of TDW can be used to debug Delphi programs. Earlier versions of the debugger do not support properties and Object Pascal exceptions.

Debugging the Test Application

If a component does not operate correctly at runtime and experiences any of the types of problems described earlier that cannot be handled by the integrated debugger, you may decide to use TDW to debug the test application. However, before TDW can debug a Delphi program, the program must be recompiled with symbolic debug information added to the executable file. Including the extra information simply requires setting the Include TDW Debug Info check box that is located on the Linker page of the Options|Project dialog box. This dialog is shown in Figure 15.4.

After rebuilding the test application, the stand-alone debugger can be started. Next, the program to be debugged is loaded using the File|Open command. Selecting the name of the testing application's execute file (for example, TSTTRACK.EXE) causes the program to be loaded into TDW. After the program's symbol information is loaded by the debugger, the project source file (for example, TSTTRACK.DPR) is loaded into a module window. Module windows are equivalent to read-only code editor windows in Delphi.

At this point, the test application is not running. This allows you to set initial breakpoints before the program starts. Since it is rare to place a breakpoint in the main project source file, the View|Module command is used to display either the

Figure 15.4

Including TDW
Information.

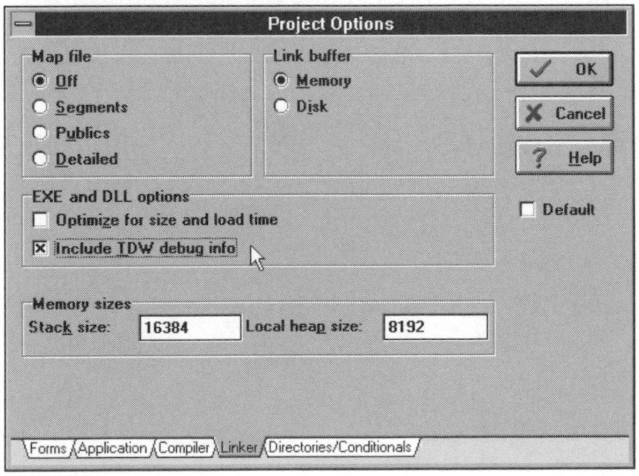

main form unit or the component unit. If the selected source does not reside in the same directory as the test program, it may be necessary to specify the path of the source file in the Options|Path for Source dialog box.

Once the initial set of breakpoints has been set, the test application can be executed by pressing the F9 key. Notice that this is the same keystroke used in Delphi to run the program. Actually, most of the keystroke commands for operating TDW are the same as those used in the integrated debugger. Table 15.1 summarizes the keystrokes used in both debuggers.

TDW Features

TDW is a full-featured debugging tool that provides enhanced tools in all three categories of debugging features. To start, TDW offers more options in controlling a program's execution than Delphi. Specifically, in addition to the Run, Trace Into, and Step Over commands available in Delphi, TDW offers an Until Return command and a Back Trace option.

The Until Return command instructs the debugger to continue executing the current procedure or function at normal speed until it is about to return to its caller. At this point the debugger interrupts and pauses execution. This is a great feature for those times when you accidentally press F7 instead of F8 and jump to a procedure you did not want to step into.

The Back Trace command allows you to reverse the execution of your program. It is similar to an undo operation. Being able to restore the computer to its state before the statement was executed, the developer is able to make modifications to the variables used in that statement, and then re-execute the statement using the modified values.

Table 15.1 Keystroke Differences Between Delphi and TDW

Debugging Operation	Delphi Keystroke	TDW Keystroke
Run	F9	F9
Trace	F7	F7
Step	F8	F8
Run to Cursor	F4	F4
Restart Program	Ctrl+F2	Ctrl+F2
Toggle Breakpoint	F5	F2
Evaluate/Modify	Ctrl+F7	Ctrl+F4
Add Watch	Ctrl+F5	Ctrl+F7

TDW also provides three more types of breakpoints. In addition to the simple and conditional breakpoints available in Delphi, TDW supports:

- Changed-memory breakpoints
- Global breakpoints
- Hardware breakpoints

Changed-memory breakpoints cause execution to be paused when the value stored at a specific memory location changes. When the breakpoint is first encountered, the breakpoint will fire if the specified memory location has been changed since the program started. After the initial encounter, each time the breakpoint is reached, it will fire only if the memory location has changed since the last time the breakpoint was encountered.

Global breakpoints are enhanced versions of conditional and changed-memory breakpoints. Global breakpoints differ from these earlier breakpoint types in two ways. First, they are monitored continuously as the program executes. That is, a global breakpoint is evaluated after each line of code is executed. Second, global breakpoints are not tied to a particular source code line. Whenever the condition evaluates to **True**, or the specified memory location changes, the breakpoint immediately pauses program execution. This makes global breakpoints very useful tools in tracking down code that corrupts data.

Hardware breakpoints are global, changed-memory breakpoints that rely on the debugging registers of the CPU to detect memory changes. Hardware breakpoints provide efficiency gains rather than added functionality. Instead of using software to monitor the breakpoints, this task is moved to the hardware level.

There are many more ways of examining data with TDW than with Delphi. In addition to the Watch List window, the Call Stack window, and the Evaluate/ Modify dialog box, TDW offers the following ways to view data:

- Variables window
- Inspector windows
- CPU window

The Variables window displays all of the variables that are accessible at the current execution point in the program. The window separates local and global variables into two panes. The Local pane displays the variables and typed constants that are

defined within the current module as well as those defined in the current procedure or function. Note that the Variables window is not just a display tool. Any of
the values displayed in this window can also be modified.

Inspector windows provide a very powerful and flexible way of viewing data during a debugging session. Specifically, an Inspector window is used to display the
current value of a variable. What makes the Inspector windows so powerful is that
the way the data is displayed is determined by the data type of the variable being
inspected. Inspector windows are especially useful during component debugging.
By inspecting the test component, all of the data fields defined in the component
are displayed. This gives a complete view of the current state of the component, as
illustrated in Figure 15.5.

The CPU window is a six-paned window that displays all of the information
describing the current state of the CPU. The Code pane displays each line of
source code followed by its corresponding disassembled assembly instructions.
The Registers pane displays the current contents of the CPU's registers, and the
Flags pane shows the states of the eight CPU flags. The Dump and Stack panes
display hex-dumps of any memory region accessible to the current program and
the contents of the current program stack, respectively. And finally, the Selector
pane displays all of the Windows 3.X selectors.

Debugging Challenges

Once your component is tested at runtime and found to behave appropriately, it
becomes time to install the component on the Component Palette and test the

Figure 15.5

Inspecting the
TrkTest
Component.

```
-[■]-Inspecting TrkTest                                1-[↑][↓]-
@4DBF:0FF8 : @4D6F:0DB8
FBORDERWIDTH                      4 ($4)
FMAX                              10 ($A)
FMIN                              0 ($0)
FORIENTATION                      TOHORIZONTAL (0)
FPAGESIZE                         4 ($4)
FPOSITION                         0 ($0)
FTICKSTYLE                        TKOWNERDRAW (1)
FSHOWTICKS                        True
FSLIDING                          False
FTHUMBHEIGHT                      18 ($12)
FTHUMBRCT                         (0,0,0,0,(0,0),(0,0))
FTHUMBSIZE                        TSMEDIUM (1)
FTHUMBSTYLE                       TSPOINTER (1)
FTHUMBWIDTH                       12 ($C)
FHALFWIDTH                        6 ($6)
FTRACKCOLOR                       16777215 ($FFFFFF)

TRZTRACKBAR
```

component at design-time. Although the runtime and design-time interfaces of a component do overlap significantly, there are still some differences that may cause the component to behave unexpectedly in the design-time environment alone.

A classic example of this occurs when the component being tested has a property that references another component and does not define a **Notification** method. We have already seen that if the other component is deleted, a GPF occurs within the design environment. However, if the other component is deleted at runtime, the error condition will only be evident if the other component is referenced using the property.

Another situation that only occurs at design-time is the storing of a component in the form file. For example, in creating the **TabStops** property for the **TRzTabbedListBox** component, it was necessary to test that the correct tab stop values were stored in the form file. This can only be accomplished by dropping the list box onto the form and specifying some tab stops, after which the form needs to be saved. Next, the form is loaded into Delphi as a *.DFM so that its text representation is displayed. Within the form description, the values of the tab stops can be verified. This situation presents a significant challenge when the component data is not stored correctly in the form file.

But perhaps the greatest debugging challenge occurs in components that utilize custom property editors or component editors. Both the editor form and the corresponding component can be tested in isolation using separate test applications. However, the interface between the two can only be tested when the editor is invoked within the design environment.

Because these situations only occur at design-time, any bugs resulting from them will only be evident at design-time. When a bug occurs during the design-time operation of a component, the debugger must be present at design-time to locate the bug. The debugger must be able to load the COMPLIB.DCL dynamic link library, because the COMPLIB.DCL file contains the program code for all of the components, property editors, and component editors. However, to get access to the COMPLIB.DCL file, the debugger must first be able to debug Delphi itself, because Delphi is responsible for loading the library.

Debugging Delphi

Fortunately, TDW can handle the job. Unfortunately, there are many steps that must be performed in order to do this. The following paragraphs outline the steps necessary to debug the Delphi design environment using Turbo Debugger.

To begin, before TDW is launched, the component library must be rebuilt so that it includes symbolic debug information. By default, the component library is built *without* debug information. So, it is necessary to invoke the Options|Environment dialog box. Figure 15.6 shows that the Compile with Debug Info check box is located on the Library page. Check this option to include debug information, and then rebuild the component library.

Next, shut down Delphi and start Turbo Debugger. Once TDW is running, load the DELPHI.EXE program. When you press the OK button in the Open Program dialog box, you will get a message that states that the program does not have a symbol table. This is OK, because the Delphi program doesn't have one. The symbol table was only added to the COMPLIB.DCL file. Therefore, press the OK button on the message box to continue.

Next, we want to load the source code for the component that is to be tested. The purpose of this is so that breakpoints can be set. However, in order to load the source file, the symbols stored in the COMPLIB.DCL file must be loaded first. This is accomplished by selecting the View|Module menu item, or by pressing F3 to display the Load Module Source or DLL Symbols dialog box.

In the DLL Name edit field, enter the name of the component library file, usually COMPLIB.DCL. Then press the Add DLL button. This adds the file to the DLLs & Programs list and sets the Debug Startup setting to Yes. This setting will force the debugger to pause the program just after the DLL is loaded. It is during this pause that the component unit will be loaded. Therefore, do not change this setting.

Figure 15.6

Setting Up
COMPLIB.DCL
for Debugging.

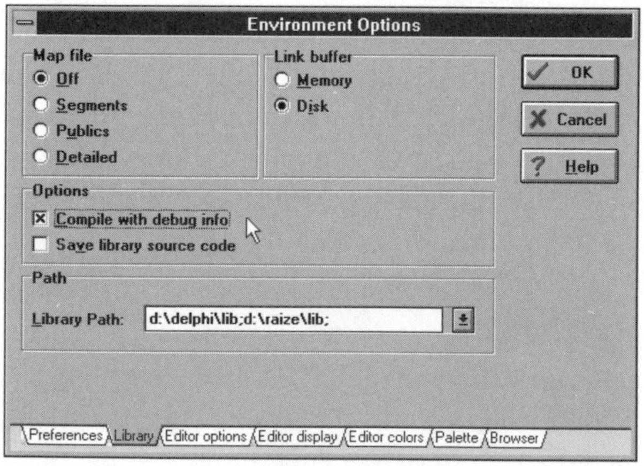

Next, close the dialog by pressing either the Load or Cancel button, and then press F9 to start Delphi. After Delphi loads the COMPLIB.DCL file, the debugger is activated. When the TDW window reappears, select the Options|Path for Source_ menu item to verify that the source file for your component is accessible.

At this point, display the Load Module dialog again by pressing F3. Now, the Source Modules list contains all of the modules that were compiled with debug information. Your component unit should be among this list. If not, you will need to shut TDW down and rebuild your component including debug information. From this list, select your component unit and press the Load button. The source code for your component (or property editor) will appear in a module window. From here all of the debugging features described earlier are available.

With the source code finally visible, set breakpoints at places of interest. You can place a breakpoint on any line that begins with a bullet (•). You can even place breakpoints in **Paint** methods without causing ill effects. TDW is smart enough to avoid the recursive problem experienced by Delphi's integrated debugger.

Once you have set some breakpoints, press F9 to finish loading Delphi. Once Delphi is completely loaded, you can proceed to test the design-time features of your component. When one of your breakpoints is reached, the debugger is once again activated. Now you can step through your code as it executes in the Delphi design environment. Pretty cool, huh?

Strengths and Weaknesses

Being a stand-alone tool, Turbo Debugger for Windows has only one purpose, debugging. With this single purpose, TDW offers a wide array of debugging features that are not available in the Delphi debugger. Furthermore, because it is not integrated into the Delphi environment, it is possible to debug components as they operate at design-time.

However, the added power of TDW does come at a cost, literally. Turbo Debugger must be purchased in addition to Delphi. Plus, the rapid nature of the Delphi development environment is sacrificed for more advanced debugging tools. Although TDW is an extremely valuable tool for design-time debugging, it is generally overkill to perform runtime testing under the stand-alone debugger. The integrated debugger provides sufficient tools to be effective and productive in this instance.

Tracking Debug Messages

What do you do if you don't have Turbo Debugger for Windows and you experience a design-time bug or need to debug a **Paint** method? There is an alternative to using TDW to determine the location of a bug. This third approach combines a small utility with an old-fashioned debugging approach.

Specifically, this approach relies on *debug messages* being generated by the component conveying status information to the developer. There are two parts to this process: First, the component must be modified so that it generates appropriate debug messages. Second, we need a tool that can monitor the messages that are generated.

The first part is the easier of the two. The Windows API includes the **OutputDebugString** function specifically designed for generating debug messages. This function sends a string parameter to the current debug message device. A debug message device is any program that monitors debug messages. For example, Turbo Debugger for Windows has a Log window that records debug messages that are generated by other programs.

Of course, the assumption is that we don't have TDW. In this case, we need another tool that is able to record debug messages. The Windows SDK comes with a sample program called DBWin, which is a small utility that does just this. The program was designed to be used with the debug version of Windows, but it useful even in the commercial release of Windows.

However, it is probably safe to assume that if you don't have TDW, you probably don't have the Windows SDK, either. This isn't a bad thing. With all of the visual programming tools available, the SDK is used more as a reference tool than as a development kit.

In light of this, I decided to build a small Delphi application that monitors debug messages. The resulting RzDBMsgs program is in included on the enclosed CD, along with the complete source code.

Sending Debug Messages

So how can **OutputDebugString** and **RzDBMsgs** be used to debug a Delphi component? As an example, consider the modified version of the **DrawTrack** method from the **TRzTrackBar** class that appears in Listing 15.2. **DrawTrack** is one of the methods that gets called when the component needs to be painted.

Listing 15.2   Using OutputDebugString

```
procedure TRzTrackBar.DrawTrack;

{—Debug Statements———————————————————}
var
  DbgMsg : array[ 0..255 ] of Char;
{—————————————————————————}

begin
  OutputDebugString( 'In DrawTrack'#13#10 );

  { Calculate the Size of the Track }
  if FOrientation = toVertical then
  begin
    FTrackRct.Top := FHalfWidth + FBorderWidth;
    FTrackRct.Bottom := Height - FBorderWidth - FHalfWidth;
    FTrackRct.Left := ( Width - FTrackWidth ) div 2;
    FTrackRct.Right := FTrackRct.Left + FTrackWidth;
  end
  else
  begin
    FTrackRct.Top := ( Height - FTrackWidth ) div 2;
    FTrackRct.Bottom := FTrackRct.Top + FTrackWidth;
    FTrackRct.Left := FHalfWidth + FBorderWidth;
    FTrackRct.Right := Width - FBorderWidth - FHalfWidth;
  end;

  {—Debug Statements————————————————}
  with FTrackRct do
  begin
    StrPCopy( DbgMsg, 'FTrackRct.left=' + IntToStr( Left ) + #13#10 );
    OutputDebugString( DbgMsg );
    StrPCopy( DbgMsg, 'FTrackRct.Top=' + IntToStr( Top ) + #13#10 );
    OutputDebugString( DbgMsg );
    StrPCopy( DbgMsg, 'FTrackRct.Right=' + IntToStr( Right ) + #13#10 );
    OutputDebugString( DbgMsg );
    StrPCopy( DbgMsg, 'FTrackRct.Bottom=' + IntToStr( Bottom ) + #13#10 );
    OutputDebugString( DbgMsg );
  end;
  {—————————————————————————}

  { Draw the Track }
  Canvas.Brush.Color := FTrackColor;

  if not Enabled then
    Canvas.Brush.Bitmap := FDitherBmp;

  Canvas.FillRect( FTrackRct );
  DrawCtl3DBorder( Canvas, FTrackRct );                    { From RzCommon unit }
end; {= TRzTrackBar.DrawTrack =}
```

As the component updates its display, the **OutputDebugString** calls send the size of the **FTrackRct** rectangle to the **RzDBMsgs** window. I added code like this during the testing phase to verify that the size of the track is adjusted accordingly when the size of the thumb is changed.

For example, consider a horizontally oriented track bar. The left and right edges of the track are positioned half the distance of the width of the thumb away from the edge of the component. Therefore, if the size of the thumb changes, the left and right sides of the track need to be adjusted accordingly. This is illustrated in Figure 15.7, which shows the debug messages generated as the size of the thumb is changed from **tsMedium** to **tsLarge**.

It's important to realize that obtaining this same information using the integrated debugger would be much more difficult, if not impossible, because of the recursive problem described earlier. But since the **OutputDebugString** function does not alter the focus when it sends a debug message, the recursive paint problem is avoided.

Strengths and Weaknesses

Although this approach does not provide the advanced debugging features found in TDW or even the integrated debugger, it does provide valuable feedback that can be used to locate a bug. This is, after all, the purpose of a debugger—to locate bugs. Furthermore, unlike the integrated debugger, this approach can be equally effective at design-time and runtime.

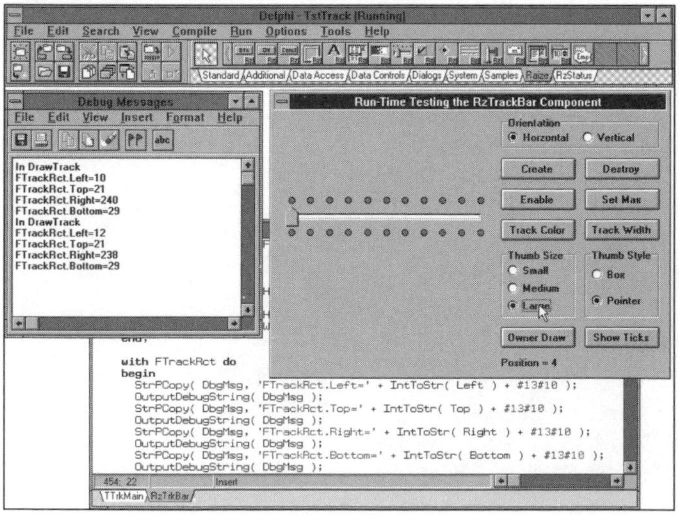

Figure 15.7

Catching Debug
Messages Using
RzDBMsgs.

An additional benefit of using the RzDBMsgs program is that it captures an execution trace of how your component is manipulated. Neither the Watch List window nor the Evaluate dialog box in the Delphi debugger is capable of providing this feature. And unlike the Log window in Turbo Debugger, the contents of the **RzDBMsgs** window can be saved to the Clipboard or sent to the printer.

This is not to say that this approach does not have its weaknesses. For instance, this approach is an "intrusive" approach. That is, the source code must be changed in order to generate debug messages. This is not necessary in either of the debuggers. In addition, if different information needs to be tracked, the program must be stopped, edited, and then recompiled.

However, the biggest disadvantage to this approach is caused by the **OutputDebugString** function. The fact that it requires a null-terminated string does not make this a very Delphi-friendly approach. Furthermore, if the message needs to display numeric data, the values must first be converted into strings. As you can see from Listing 15.2, all of this requires quite a bit of code, and even a local variable, simply to display some messages.

Using Writeln to Generate Debug Messages

Although it isn't possible to eliminate the intrusive nature of this approach, it is possible to eliminate the inadequacies of the **OutputDebugString** function. Before describing how this is accomplished, it's necessary to take a slight detour and review some of Delphi's history.

Delphi has a rich history in Object Pascal. Consider the **Write** and **Writeln** procedures. These two standard procedures are used by Delphi developers to write data to a disk file. But in the old days of character-based programming, the **Write** and **Writeln** procedures were also used to display information on the screen. In Object Pascal, the same input/output system is used for both file and display. To support displaying text on the screen, a text file called **Output** is automatically created, which directs all output to the screen. (A file called **Input** is also created, but it's connected to the keyboard.) If no file variable is specified in a **Writeln** call, the standard **Output** file is used.

Under Windows, displaying text is not as simple as writing to a standard output file. Well, actually it can be. Delphi provides the WinCrt unit, which allows a Windows program to use **Write** and **Writeln** to display information in a plain window. Many of the sample programs in Chapter 3 used the WinCrt unit.

The following steps demonstrate how to create a WinCrt application. First, select the File|Open Project menu item. Enter the file name to be used for the project. For example, enter TESTCRT.DPR. Pressing the OK button will create a file that looks like the following:

```
program Testcrt;

uses
  Forms;

{$R *.RES}

begin
  Application.Run;
end.
```

Next, replace the Forms unit with WinCrt, delete the *.RES line, and replace the **Application.Run** line with a **Writeln** statement. Your program should now look like this:

```
program Testcrt;

uses
  WinCrt;

begin
  Writeln( 'Delphi' );
end.
```

You can bypass these steps if you have the Gallery option selected for new projects. In this case, you can simply select the File|New Project menu item and select the CRT application template. Running this program creates a new window containing the string "Delphi."

If you've been using Pascal for a while, you are probably familiar with the **Writeln** procedure. In case you haven't had the opportunity to use this procedure, the sample program in Listing 15.3 illustrates many of the capabilities of **Write** and **Writeln**, and Figure 15.8 shows the output generated by this program.

Listing 15.3   TESTCRT.PAS—Demonstrating the Writeln Procedure

```pascal
program Testcrt;

uses
  WinCrt, SysUtils;

var
  Stz : array[ 0..255 ] of Char;                    { Null-Terminated String }
  N1, N2 : Integer;
  R1, R2 : Real;
  Flag : Boolean;

begin
  Writeln( 'DEMONSTRATION OF WRITE AND WRITELN PROCEDURES' );
  Writeln;                                            { Display a Blank Line }

  Writeln( '══STRINGS════════════════════════════════════════' );
  Writeln( 'Display simple string messages' );

  Write( 'Build Strings Using ' );
  Writeln( 'Write Procedure.' );

  StrCopy( Stz, 'This is a Null-Terminated String' );
  Writeln( 'PChar Support - ', Stz );
  Writeln;

  Writeln( '══NUMBERS═══════════════════════════════════════' );
  N1 := 23;
  N2 := 1534;
  R1 := 54.857;
  R2 := 192.7;
  Writeln( N1 );
  Writeln( 'Unformatted: ', R1 );
  Writeln( 'Formatted: ', R1:8:2 );        { 8 - Field Width, 2 - Decimal Places }
  Writeln;
  Writeln( 'Columns' );
  Writeln( 'Number: ', N1:5, '   Real: ', R1:8:2 );
  Writeln( 'Number: ', N2:5, '   Real: ', R2:8:2 );
  Writeln;

  Writeln( '══EXPRESSIONS═══════════════════════════════════' );
  Writeln( 'N1 * R1 + R2 = ', ( N1 * R1 + R2 ):8:2 );
  Writeln;

  Flag := True;
  Writeln( '══BOOLEAN VALUES════════════════════════════════' );
  Writeln( 'Flag = ', Flag, '  not Flag = ', not Flag );

end.
```

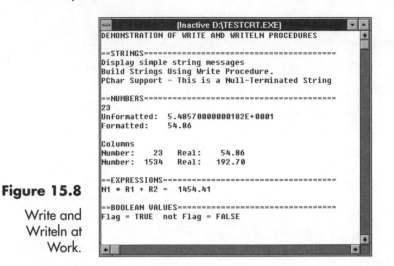

Figure 15.8

Write and
Writeln at
Work.

What's the Point?

Yes, that was a nice little history on **Write** and **Writeln**, but how does it help our problem with **OutputDebugString**? As it turns out, we can use the same technique used by the WinCrt unit to redirect the **Write** and **Writeln** procedures in a more appropriate way for debugging. Specifically, we can translate **Write** and **Writeln** procedure calls into **OutputDebugString** calls.

There are two major advantages to using this approach. First, since **Write** and **Writeln** can display Pascal string values, it is no longer necessary to deal with null-terminated strings. This makes it a more Delphi-friendly process. Second, the way in which **Write** and **Writeln** are used does not change. That is, any number of parameters may be passed to either of these two procedures. This also means that you do not have to spend time and effort building a null-terminated string containing all of the values to be displayed.

Text File Device Drivers

So how can we redirect where **Write** and **Writeln** send their output? This is accomplished by creating a *Text File Device Driver* (TFDD). Don't be alarmed. The term *device driver* sounds more complicated than it is. A Text File Device Driver is simply a set of functions that are used to define an interface between Object Pascal's file system and some other device.

The *device* used by the device driver can be virtually anything you want. For example, the WinCrt unit uses a TFDD that defines an interface between the file system and a plain window. Likewise, the Printers unit uses a TFDD to enable Delphi users to send output to the printer using **Write** and **Writeln** statements.

For this chapter, the device is any program that accepts debug messages generated by the **OutputDebugString** API call, in particular, **RzDBMsgs**. Listing 15.4 shows the source code for the RzDebug unit that defines this text file device driver.

Listing 15.4   RZDEBUG.PAS—The RzDebug Unit

```
{========================================================================}
{= RzDebug Unit                                                        =}
{=                                                                     =}
{= This unit defines a Text File Device Driver that defines an interface  =}
{= between the Object Pascal file system and any device than can accept debug =}
{= messages generated by the OutputDebugString API call.  For example, the  =}
{= RzDBMsgs program will display these messages in a window.            =}
{=                                                                     =}
{= Building Custom Delphi Components - Ray Konopka                      =}
{========================================================================}


unit RzDebug;

interface

procedure AssignDbg( var F : Text );


implementation

uses
  SysUtils, WinProcs;


{===============================}
{== Device Interface Functions ==}
{===============================}

function DbgClose( var F : TTextRec ) : Integer; far;
begin
  Result := 0;
end;


function DbgOutput( var F : TTextRec ) : Integer; far;
begin
  if F.BufPos <> 0 then
  begin
    F.Buffer[ F.BufPos ] := #0;
```

```
    OutputDebugString( PChar( F.BufPtr ) );
    F.BufPos := 0;
  end;
  Result := 0;
end;


function DbgOpen( var F : TTextRec ) : Integer; far;
begin
  F.Mode := fmOutput;                              { Always Open in Output Mode }
  F.InOutFunc := @DbgOutput;
  F.FlushFunc := @DbgOutput;
  F.CloseFunc := @DbgClose;
  Result := 0;
end;



{==============================}
{== Assign Device Procedure ==}
{==============================}

procedure AssignDbg( var F : Text );
begin
  with TTextRec( F ) do
  begin
    Handle := $FFFF;
    Mode := fmClosed;
    BufSize := SizeOf( Buffer );
    BufPtr := @Buffer;
    OpenFunc := @DbgOpen;
    Name[ 0 ] := #0;
  end;
end;


initialization
  AssignDbg( Output );
  Rewrite( Output );
end.
```

There are four operations associated with a text file: Open, Input/Output, Flush, and Close. A TFDD defines device-interface functions for each of these four operations. Each interface function has the same function header and must be declared using the far calling model. For example, the Open interface function in **RzDebug** is defined as:

```
function DbgOpen( var F : TTextRec ) : Integer; far;
```

The **TTextRec** record is defined in the SysUtils unit and contains the various attributes associated with a text file. The return value of each interface function is propagated to the standard **IOResult** variable, which can be queried by a developer after a file operation. If the interface function is successful, the return value should be set to zero. We'll come back to the **RzDebug** interface functions shortly. But first, let's take a look at how the interface is established.

In order to connect each interface function with a particular text file, a custom **Assign** procedure must be created. For example, the WinCrt and Printers units define the **AssignCrt** and **AssignPrn** procedures, respectively. The **RzDebug** unit defines the **AssignDbg** procedure. This procedure, like all **Assign** procedures, is responsible for specifying which interface function will be used when the text file is opened. Since the Object Pascal file system guarantees that the open operation will always occur first, it is not necessary to specify functions for the other operations. As we will soon see, this is done in the **DbgOpen** function.

The **AssignDbg** procedure is also responsible for setting the **Mode** field to **fmClosed**, setting **BufSize** to the size of the text file buffer, pointing the **BufPtr** field to the same buffer, and clearing the **Name** field. All assign procedures must perform these steps to establish the interface.

By Convention

Text file device drivers typically use a three-character identifier in the device-interface functions and the assign procedure. For example, the Printers unit defines the **AssignPrn** procedure and the **PrnOpen** function. Likewise, the RzDebug unit defines the **AssignDbg** procedure and the **DbgOpen** function.

Let's get back to the interface functions. The **AssignDbg** procedure only specifies a function for the Open operation. We have not yet assigned the function pointers for the remaining operations. The remaining connections are made in the **DbgOpen** function. This function is called when the file that has been assigned to this device is opened.

The **initialization** section of RzDebug shows where this occurs. First, the standard **Output** file is assigned to the debug device using **AssignDbg**, and then the file is opened by making a call to **Rewrite**. As a result, the **DbgOpen** function is called because the **AssignDbg** procedure set the file variable's **OpenFunc** field to point to the **DbgOpen** function.

The **DbgOpen** function then performs the remaining assignments. Typically, this function will query the value of the file variable's **Mode** field to determine how the file was opened. If the **Rewrite** procedure is called, **F.Mode** has an initial value of **fmOutput**. But if the **Reset** procedure is called, the **F.Mode** field enters the **DbgOpen** function with the value of **fmInput**. Regardless of how the file was opened, the **DbgOpen** function always resets the Mode to **fmOutput**.

Since there is no input interface defined for this device, the **DbgOpen** function assigns the **InOutFunc** pointer to the **DbgOutput** function. If the TFDD handled input, the **InOutFunc** pointer would be set to an input function if the file was opened for input. The **FlushFunc** is assigned to the same output function to ensure that anything written to the device is immediately sent out. And finally, the function sets the return value to zero.

The only other function of interest is the **DbgOutput** function, because the **DbgClose** simply returns a zero. The **DbgOutput** function first checks that the buffer contains data to be sent to the device by checking the **BufPos** value. **BufPos** indicates the number of characters in the buffer.

Because **OutputDebugString** expects a null-terminated string, before calling this API function the last position in the buffer is set to #0. Recall that **BufPtr** is set to point to the text file buffer in the **AssignDbg** procedure. The buffer is just an array of characters, and by typecasting the **BufPtr** field to a **PChar** we can call **OutputDebugString**. After that, the **BufPos** field is set to zero to indicate that all of the characters have been processed. Of course, don't forget to set the return value to zero.

 Text file device drivers are described in more detail in the *Object Pascal Language Guide.* But if you don't have Turbo Debugger, you probably don't have the language guide because it too is part of the RAD Pack. However, the language reference is available separately from Borland in hardcopy format. Plus, an Adobe Acrobat version is available in section 2 of the CompuServe Delphi forum (GO DELPHI) or via FTP at ftp.borland.com in the /pub/techinfo/techdocs/language/delphi/gen directory.

That's all it takes to create a Text File Device Driver. The result is that when the RzDebug unit is used in conjunction with the RzDBMsgs program, it becomes very easy to get information regarding how a component is behaving at runtime and design-time. Listing 15.5 shows the **DrawTrack** method again, but this time the **OutputDebugString** calls are replaced with a single **Writeln** call. In addition to a much simpler notation, there is no need to create a temporary local variable for converting the numeric data. The **Writeln** procedure takes care of this automatically. The only extra requirement needed by this new approach is that the RzDebug unit must be specified in the **uses** clause.

Listing 15.5   DrawTrack using Writeln

```
implementation

uses
  RzDebug;


procedure TRzTrackBar.DrawTrack;
begin
  { Calculate the Size of the Track }
  if FOrientation = toVertical then
  begin
    FTrackRct.Top := FHalfWidth + FBorderWidth;
    FTrackRct.Bottom := Height - FBorderWidth - FHalfWidth;
    FTrackRct.Left := ( Width - FTrackWidth ) div 2;
    FTrackRct.Right := FTrackRct.Left + FTrackWidth;
  end
  else
  begin
    FTrackRct.Top := ( Height - FTrackWidth ) div 2;
    FTrackRct.Bottom := FTrackRct.Top + FTrackWidth;
    FTrackRct.Left := FHalfWidth + FBorderWidth;
    FTrackRct.Right := Width - FBorderWidth - FHalfWidth;
  end;

  {—Debug Statements———————————————————————————————————}

  with FTrackRct do
    Writeln( 'FTrackRct: L=', Left, 'T=', Top, 'R=', Right, 'B=', Bottom );

  {————————————————————————————————————————————————————}

  { Draw the Track }
  Canvas.Brush.Color := FTrackColor;

  if not Enabled then
    Canvas.Brush.Bitmap := FDitherBmp;

  Canvas.FillRect( FTrackRct );
  DrawCtl3DBorder( Canvas, FTrackRct );                { From RzCommon unit }
end; {= TRzTrackBar.DrawTrack =}
```

Looking Ahead...

One more chapter to go! Chapter 16 closes the book by focusing on some of the finer details of creating professional quality components. Specifically, it illustrates the steps required to incorporate online help into your components. This is an absolute necessity for any component that is to be sold commercially.

Speaking of commercial components, the next chapter also discusses installation issues. This is an especially important topic when creating a library of components. You should not expect your component users to install each component separately. In the next and final chapter, we'll see how all of your components can be installed using a single registration unit.

Chapter 16

The Professional Touch

The
Professional
Touch

*Make your components stand out against the
others with those necessary final touches of
professionalism like online help.*

In the last chapter, we learned about testing components, along with the various
tools that can be used to locate the source of problems encountered along the
way. Once a component has passed testing, the component building process is
often seen as being complete, and the component is consequently distributed to
end users. Although this can be done (and all too often is) the results can be
detrimental to the overall success of the component. This is especially true if you
are writing components that will be used by other developers, or if you plan on
selling them commercially.

The simple truth is that the commercial component market just will not tolerate
unprofessional components, and releasing a component without professional features, such as online help, will not be accepted by this ever-growing market. This
chapter shows you how to add the professional features necessary to make your
components suitable for commercial release. Note that this does not mean that
these techniques should only be used if you are creating a third-party component
library. On the contrary, these same techniques are just as beneficial to in-house
software departments as to an individual developer.

So, what are these *professional* features? As mentioned above, a professional component must provide online help accessible through the Delphi environment.
Since Delphi provides an extensible help system, and providing online help support requires no changes to the component itself, there is no excuse not to provide this feature.

Another feature that should be considered is support for *internationalization*. This does not necessarily mean creating a component to be used globally. Instead, it means taking the necessary steps that make this task easier if it ever needs to be performed. Specifically, components that use a large number of literal strings should consider using a *string table* resource.

It has become common practice for third-party developers to include the source code for their components with the shipping library. I fully recommend this, by the way. However, doing so does present a potential problem. The problem arises when the user decides to recompile your source code—to include debug information, for example. Since you cannot be certain how Delphi will be configured for each user, you will need to take special precautions to ensure that your components compile correctly—or you'll suffer the headache of many support calls!

And let's not forget about installation. Although installing new components in Delphi is relatively easy, there are some techniques that can be used to make the installation process run more smoothly.

Online Help

There are two ways in which a user can request context-sensitive help on a component within the Delphi design environment. First, the user can press F1 while the Object Inspector has the focus. In this case, Delphi displays the help associated with the currently highlighted property or event. The second way occurs when the user presses the F1 key when a form has the focus. In this instance, Delphi displays the help screen associated with the currently selected component.

However, context-sensitive help is only available for components, properties, and events that Delphi knows about. For example, if we drop an RzLauncher component from Chapter 11 onto a from, select one of its properties in the Object Inspector, and then press F1, Delphi will display an error message stating that "There is no context-sensitive help registered for this topic." This occurs because we have not yet instructed Delphi on where to find help for the TRzLauncher component. In fact, we haven't even created a help file for this purpose.

If you have experience in creating online help, you may be wondering how creating a separate help file will allow Delphi to display component help information, since the WinHelp search engine does not allow searching across multiple help files. Delphi is able to do exactly this because it uses a new search engine called

MultiHelp in addition to the WinHelp engine. MultiHelp uses a master index to store keyword links to multiple help files. We will come back to this shortly, but first we must create the component help file.

Creating the Help Document

The first step in creating a component help file is to create a Rich Text Format (RTF) file that contains the help information to be displayed. This RTF file will be referred to as the help document for the component. I should point out that this section is not intended to describe the entire process of creating a Windows help file. Instead, it focuses on the issues specific to building a component help file.

 For a step-by-step guide through the process of creating a general help file, take a look at the *Creating Windows Help* file, CWH.HLP, located in the \DELPHI\BIN directory. It is very well organized, and demonstrates many online help features. Another worthwhile resource is the book *Developers' Guide to WINHELP.EXE* by Jim Mischel (John Wiley & Sons, 1994).

There are two basic ways of creating the help document. First, any word processor that can handle RTF files can be used. Microsoft Word and WordPerfect are examples. Second, a help authoring tool like ForeHelp or RoboHelp can be used to create the document. The example presented in this chapter uses the first approach to avoid describing product-specific features.

The help document is organized into a series of pages, with each page representing a help screen. For example, selecting the Help|Contents menu item in Delphi displays the Contents help screen. Each page specifies several footnotes. These footnotes convey information to the search engine and are not displayed in the resulting help file. Table 16.1 lists the common footnote types.

Table 16.1 Common Help Footnotes		
Footnote Symbol	**Identifies**	**Purpose**
#	Context String	Uniquely identifies the topic
$	Topic Title	Appears as the topic title in the list of topics displayed in the Search dialog box and in the History list
K	Keywords	These words or phrases appear in the keyword list displayed in the Search dialog box

Jumping to a different topic and displaying a popup window are two basic features used quite extensively in component help files. Each feature relies on a hotspot on which the user clicks to start the action. The two types of hotspots are distinguished by how they are formatted. In particular, to create a hotspot that jumps to another topic, apply double-underline formatting to the text. Immediately after the hotspot text, you must specify the context string of the topic to jump to. This context string must be formatted as hidden text. The same steps are used to create a hotspot that displays a popup window, but instead of using a double-underline, the hotspot text is formatted with a single underline.

Let's take a look at a real example. Figure 16.1 shows the first page of the RZLAUNCH.RTF file. This file contains the online help information for only the RzLauncher component. The figure has been annotated to indicate the various font styles and sizes used throughout the page. The layout shown matches the layout used for the standard Delphi components.

Also following the Delphi convention, located underneath the title are hotspots for the Properties, Methods, and Events popup windows. These are indeed popup hotspots because they are underlined with a single line, and are followed by a hidden context string. The hidden strings are displayed in Figure 16.2. Notice that **ProgramName** in the description body is specified as a topic jump to that property.

Figure 16.1

Conventional
Layout for
Component Help.

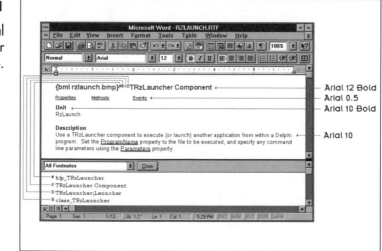

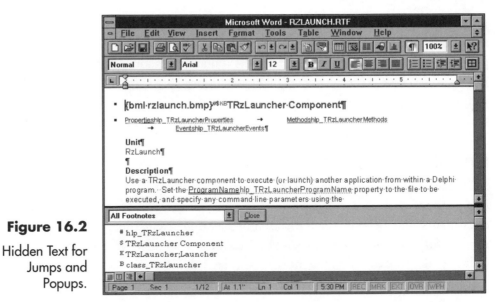

Figure 16.2

Hidden Text for
Jumps and
Popups.

Now let's take a closer look at the footnotes specified in Figure 16.1. The lines on the left map each footnote symbol in the body to its corresponding footnote string. The first three footnotes are the common footnotes described earlier. The "#" footnote specifies the context string for this screen (or topic) to be **hlp_TRzLauncher**. The "$" footnote specifies the title of the topic, and the "K" footnote specifies two search strings, "TRzLauncher" and "Launcher." The search strings will appear in the list of keywords displayed in the WinHelp Search dialog box. Therefore, the user can find help for this component by searching for "TRzLauncher" or just "Launcher."

The "B" Footnote

Notice the last footnote in Figure 16.1. The "B" footnote was not mentioned before because it is only used by Delphi for searching for component-related help. "B" footnotes must appear on the following types of screens in order for Delphi to be able to correctly find the topic:

- Main Component Screens
- Property Screens
- Event Screens

Notice that method screens do not have to specify a "B" footnote. The "B" footnote serves the same function as "K" footnotes, that is, to specify keywords. But, unlike "K" footnotes, "B" footnotes do not appear in the Search dialog box.

Furthermore, the "B" footnote keyword must be structured in a particular format. Table 16.2 describes the various formats. Notice that since Figure 16.1 displays the main component screen for the TRzLauncher component, the "B" footnote is set to **class_TRzLauncher**. Likewise, Figure 16.3 shows the **ProgramName** property screen with its "B" footnote set to **prop_TRzLauncherProgramName** because this property is specific to the **TRzLauncher** component.

Creating the Help File

After the help document is written, the help file (*.HLP) can be created. To do this we need to create a *help project* file that will be used to specify which help documents will be used in the file. Since a single help file can consist of any number of help documents, it's a good idea to create a separate help document (*.RTF) file for each component.

Table 16.2   "B" Footnote Formats

Screen Type	"B" Footnote Format	Example
Main Component Screen	"class_" + Component Class Name	class_TRzLauncher
Generic Property	"prop_" + Property Name	prop_Height
Generic Event	"event_" + Event Name	event_OnClick
Component Specific Property	"prop_" + Component Class Name + Property Name	prop_TRzLauncherStartDir
Component Specific Event	"event_" + Component Class Name + Event Name	event_TzLauncherOnFinished

---

Figure 16.3

Help Screen for a Property.

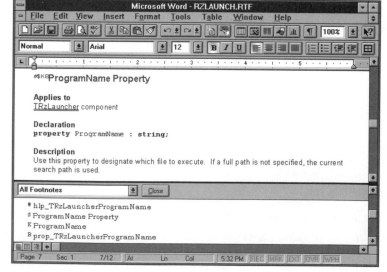

Listing 16.1 shows the contents of the RAIZEHLP.HPJ file. This file represents the help project file for all of the components that have been presented in this book. For clarity, however, only the RZLAUNCH.RTF file is listed in the Files section.

Listing 16.1 RAIZEHLP.HPJ—Help Project File

```
[OPTIONS]
TITLE=Raize Component Library Help
COMPRESS=TRUE

[FILES]
RzLaunch.rtf
```

The help project file is a plain ASCII file and, therefore, can be created using any text editor. Once the project file is created, it must be compiled to generate the RAIZEHLP.HLP file. Fortunately, the Windows 3.1 Help Compiler comes with Delphi. It can be found in the \DELPHI\BIN directory with the HC31.EXE file name. The RAIZEHLP.HLP project file is compiled at a DOS prompt using the following command:

```
C:\> HC31 RAIZEHLP
```

If everything is correct in the RZLAUNCH.RTF file, the RAIZEHLP.HLP file will be created.

Creating the Keyword File

At this point, we have a help file containing information pertaining to the **TRzLauncher** component. However, before Delphi can search this file, there are two more steps that must be performed. The first step involves creating a keyword file (*.KWF) that Delphi can merge into its master search index.

Creating a keyword file is accomplished by running the KWGEN program located in the \DELPHI\HELP directory. Figure 16.4 shows that the program operates off the help project file. After KWGEN is started, enter the appropriate help project file either manually or by using the Browse button. The output file name is automatically generated. After specifying the help project, press the OK button. The KWGEN program will then search all the RTF files used by the selected help project to build the resulting keyword file.

Figure 16.4

Generating a
Keyword File
with KWGEN.

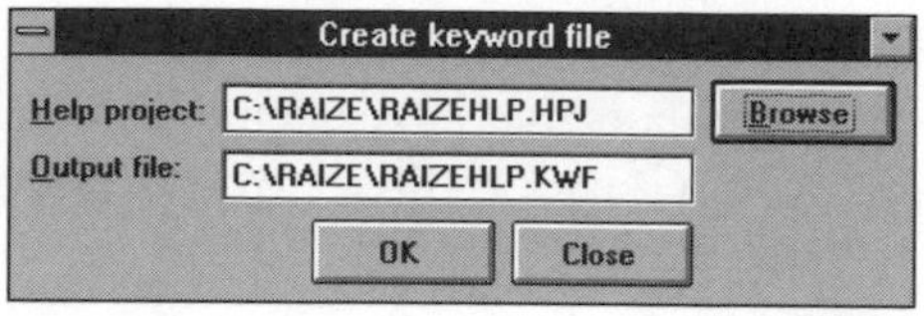

Create keyword file	
Help project:	C:\RAIZE\RAIZEHLP.HPJ	**Browse**
Output file:	C:\RAIZE\RAIZEHLP.KWF	
	OK	**Close**

Merging Keywords into the Master Index

The last step that needs to be performed is to merge the newly created keyword
file into Delphi's master help index file, DELPHI.HDX. By merging the keywords, Delphi will know to load the RAIZEHLP.HLP file if help for **TRzLauncher**
is requested.

To merge a keyword file into the Delphi master index, the HelpInst program, also
located in \DELPHI\HELP, is used. In order to run the HelpInst program, Delphi
must be shut down. It is also a good idea to make a backup of the DELPHI.HDX
file, which is located in the \DELPHI\BIN directory.

The main window for the HelpInst program is displayed in Figure 16.5. Initially,
the keyword file list is empty because the HelpInst program starts without an
index file loaded. Therefore, the first step is to load the DELPHI.HDX file. Next,
press the plus button to add the new keyword file, and then press the save button
to update the index file.

Due to a bug in the HelpInst program, the directories specified
in the Options|Search Paths dialog box are not saved when the
program terminates. Therefore, each time HelpInst is run, any
keyword file not residing in the \DELPHI\HELP directory will
not be found. You can avoid this problem by copying the keyword file to the \DELPHI\HELP directory.

Figure 16.5

Adding the
New Keyword
File with
HelpInst.

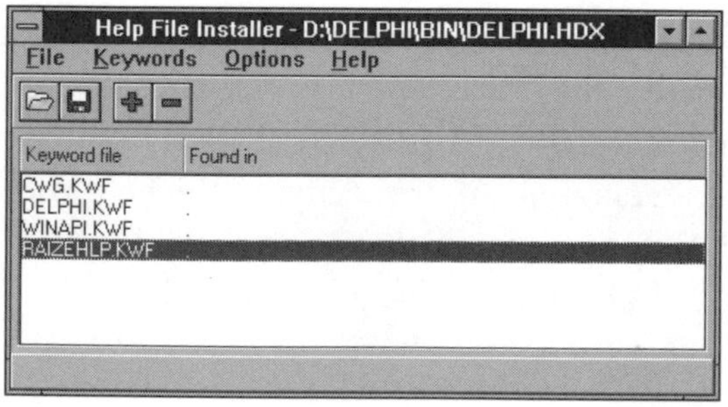

Help File Installer - D:\DELPHI\BIN\DELPHI.HDX	
File Keywords Options Help	
Keyword file	Found in
CWG.KWF	.
DELPHI.KWF	.
WINAPI.KWF	.
RAIZEHLP.KWF	

Once the keyword file has been merged into Delphi's master help index, Delphi will be able to search for help on your components. However, unless the new help file is on the current path, Delphi will not be able to load the help file. There are two options to resolve this. First, move the help file to a directory on the current path. A good place is the \DELPHI\BIN directory. The second option is to add a line to the Files section of the WINHELP.INI file located in the Windows directory. Each entry in this file specifies the location of a help file. For example, each entry has the following form:

```
<filename>.hlp=<fullpath>
```

where <filename> is the name of the help file and <fullpath> indicates where the file is located.

Once the RAIZEHLP.HLP file is made available using either of these methods, context-sensitive help can be requested from within the Delphi design environment for **TRzLauncher** and its properties and events. Figure 16.6 shows the main component screen being displayed for the **RzLauncher1** component on **Form1**.

String Tables

String tables are one of the least-used resource types, which is a shame because they are so easy to use in Delphi. String tables store strings that are used in an application. Because the strings are part of the resource file, they can be changed

Figure 16.6

Getting Online Help for Custom Components.

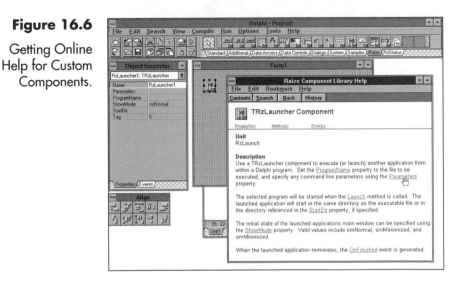

without having to recompile the source code. In addition, moving literal strings from code to a string table frees memory in the data segment.

It is highly recommended that error messages, prompts, and other text be stored in string tables. Besides the advantages given above, if you're considering distributing your components internationally, it is imperative that you utilize string tables to handle language differences.

To demonstrate how to incorporate a string table into a component, let's take another look at the RzMailMessage component from Chapter 11. In particular, consider the **CreateMapiError** function shown in Listing 16.2. Recall that this function was called if one of the Messaging API calls failed. The strings that make up the **MapiErrMsgs** constant array are good candidates to be moved into a string table.

Listing 16.2   RzMail Unit Using Hard-Coded String Literals

```
unit RzMail;
. . .
implementation

uses
  RzCommon, SmplMapi;

const
  MapiErrMsgs : array[ mapi_User_Abort..mapi_E_Not_Supported ] of string[ 24 ] =
    ( 'User Abort',
      'Failure',
      'Login Failure',
      'Disk Full',
      'Insufficient Memory',
      'Access Denied',
      '',
      'Too Many Sessions',
      'Too Many Files',
      'Too Many Recipients',
      'Attachment Not Found',
      'Attachment Open Failure',
      'Attachment Write Failure',
      'Unknown Recipient',
      'Bad RecipType',
      'No Messages',
      'Invalid Message',
      'Text Too Large',
      'Invalid Session',
      'Type Not Supported',
      'Ambiguous Recipient',
```

```
            'Message In Use',
            'Network Failure',
            'Invalid EditFields',
            'Invalid Recips',
            'Not Supported' );


function CreateMapiError( ErrCode : Integer ) : Exception;
begin
  if ErrCode = mapi_User_Abort then     { If user abort, raise silent exception }
  begin
    Result := EMapiUserAbort.Create( 'MAPI: Process Aborted by User' );
  end
  else
  begin
    Result := EMapiError.CreateFmt( 'MAPI: %s. ErrorCode = %d',
                                    [ MapiErrMsgs[ ErrCode ], ErrCode ] );
    EMapiError( Result ).ErrorCode := ErrCode;
  end;
end;
```

Creating the String Table

A string table can be created in one of two ways. First, a Windows resource editor, such as Resource Workshop, can be used to create the table. The second option is to create the string table manually. Because of the simple structure of the string table resource type, this is not an unreasonable alternative.

The format of a string table is quite simple. Each entry in the table consists of a numeric identifier and an associated string. The identifier is used to reference the particular string from within code. Because the integer identifiers have less meaning than their string counterparts, it is common to create a set of constants to represent each string resource identifier.

Listing 16.3 shows the source code for the MapiMsgs unit. This unit consists only of an **interface** section that declares constants for each of the strings to be placed in the string table. The starting value of 25100 is an arbitrary value chosen to avoid conflict with other string resource identifiers.

By Convention

Constants representing string resource identifiers start with the letter *S*.

Listing 16.3   MAPIMSGS.PAS—The MapiMsgs Unit

```
{=============================================================================}
{= MapiMsgs Unit                                                            =}
{=                                                                          =}
{= This unit defines several string resource constants used to retrieve the =}
{= corresponding string table entry for MAPI error messages.                =}
{=                                                                          =}
{= Building Custom Delphi Components - Ray Konopka                           =}
{=============================================================================}

unit MapiMsgs;

interface

{$R MAPIMSGS.RES}

const
  SMapiBase                   = 25100;
  SMapiUserAbort              = 25101;
  SMapiFailure                = 25102;
  SMapiLoginFailure           = 25103;
  SMapiDiskFull               = 25104;
  SMapiInsufficientMemory     = 25105;
  SMapiAccessDenied           = 25106;
  SMapiTooManySessions        = 25108;
  SMapiTooManyFiles           = 25109;
  SMapiTooManyRecipients      = 25110;
  SMapiAttachmentNotFound     = 25111;
  SMapiAttachmentOpenFailure  = 25112;
  SMapiAttachmentWriteFailure = 25113;
  SMapiUnknownRecipient       = 25114;
  SMapiBadRecipType           = 25115;
  SMapiNoMessages             = 25116;
  SMapiInvalidMessage         = 25117;
  SMapiTextTooLarge           = 25118;
  SMapiInvalidSession         = 25119;
  SMapiTypeNotSupported       = 25120;
  SMapiAmbiguousRecipient     = 25121;
  SMapiMessageInUse           = 25122;
  SMapiNetworkFailure         = 25123;
  SMapiInvalidEditFields      = 25124;
  SMapiInvalidRecips          = 25125;
  SMapiNotSupported           = 25126;

implementation

end.
```

Creating the MapiMsgs unit serves three purposes. First, it will be used by the code modules that need to reference these strings. In particular, the RzMail unit will use the MapiMsgs unit. Second, the MAPIMSGS.PAS file can be included into the MAPIMSGS.RC resource file shown in Listing 16.4. This allows the resource file to use the same constants, which ensures that the correct string is synchronized to a particular ID. Third, the MapiMsgs unit is responsible for including the MAPIMSGS.RES file into the current project. MAPIMSGS.RES is the compiled version of MAPIMSGS.RC.

Listing 16.4 MAPIMSGS.RC—MapiMsgs String Resource File

```
#include "mapimsgs.pas"

STRINGTABLE
{
 SMapiUserAbort, "User Abort"
 SMapiFailure, "General Failure"
 SMapiLoginFailure, "Login Failure"
 SMapiDiskFull, "Disk Full"
 SMapiInsufficientMemory, "Insufficient Memory"
 SMapiAccessDenied, "Access Denied"
 SMapiTooManySessions, "Too Many Sessions"
 SMapiTooManyFiles, "Too Many Files"
 SMapiTooManyRecipients, "Too Many Recipients"
 SMapiAttachmentNotFound, "Attachment Not Found"
 SMapiAttachmentOpenFailure, "Attachment Open Failure"
 SMapiAttachmentWriteFailure, "Attachment Write Failure"
 SMapiUnknownRecipient, "Unknown Recipient"
 SMapiBadRecipType, "Bad Recipient Type"
 SMapiNoMessages, "No Messages"
 SMapiInvalidMessage, "Invalid Message"
 SMapiTextTooLarge, "Text Too Large"
 SMapiInvalidSession, "Invalid Session"
 SMapiTypeNotSupported, "Type Not Supported"
 SMapiAmbiguousRecipient, "Ambiguous Recipient"
 SMapiMessageInUse, "Message In Use"
 SMapiNetworkFailure, "Network Failure"
 SMapiInvalidEditFields, "Invalid Edit Fields"
 SMapiInvalidRecips, "Invalid Recipients"
 SMapiNotSupported, "Feature Not Supported"
}
```

Once the resource file is created, it needs to be compiled into a binary .RES file so that it can be referenced by the MapiMsgs unit and thus be included into the current project using the RzMail component. If you are using Resource Workshop, the RES file can be created when the RC file is saved by making sure the .RES Multi-save option is checked in the Preferences dialog box.

If you created the .RC file manually, you will need to use the command line resource compiler to create the corresponding .RES file. For the MAPIMSGS.RC file the following command is entered at a DOS prompt:

```
C:\> BRC -R MAPIMSGS
```

BRC is the Borland Resource Compiler that comes with Delphi. It can be found
in the \DELPHI\BIN directory. The -R option simply indicates that the
MAPIMSGS.RC file should be compiled only. The BRC program is also capable
of binding a resource file to an existing executable file. For this example, we only
need to create the RES file because the binding will be handled by the Delphi
compiler.

Once the MAPIMSGS.RES file is created, we can rewrite the **CreateMapiError**
to get the strings it needs to display from the string table rather than the
MapiErrMsgs constant. To get a string stored in a string table, the **LoadStr** function is used. This function returns the string corresponding to the ID that is
passed in its only parameter. Listing 16.5 shows the new version of the RzMail
unit using the MapiMsgs unit.

Listing 16.5   RzMail Unit Using String Table Resource

```
unit RzMail;
. . .
implementation

uses
  RzCommon, SmplMapi, MapiMsgs;                           { New Unit - MapiMsgs }


function CreateMapiError( ErrCode : Integer ) : Exception;
begin
  if ErrCode = mapi_User_Abort then     { If user abort, raise silent exception }
  begin
    Result := EMapiUserAbort.Create( LoadStr( SMapiUserAbort ) );
  end
  else
  begin
    Result := EMapiError.CreateFmt( 'MAPI: %s. ErrorCode = %d',
                                    [ LoadStr( SMapiBase + ErrCode ), ErrCode]);
    EMapiError( Result ).ErrorCode := ErrCode;
  end;
end;
```

The Common Raize Include File

As mentioned at the beginning of this chapter, it has become common for vendors to include the source code for their components. If you plan on doing this,
you should seriously consider using a common include file in all of your compo-

nent units. The purpose of the include file is to set compiler directives and conditional defines that govern how the component is compiled.

This is especially important when distributing the source code along with the compiled versions of your components. If the user decides to recompile your code, you cannot assume that the compiler settings on that machine are the same as the ones you used to develop the component. Therefore, by creating a common include file, no matter what the current compiler settings are in the Delphi IDE, your component units will always be compiled with the correct settings.

For these same reasons, a common include file is essential for multi-person development teams. The include file guarantees that everyone builds the components using the same options.

As an example of a common include file, we need to look no further than the enclosed CD. On the CD there are two sets of source files for the components presented in this book. The first set is located in the BOOKSRC directory. Under this directory there are sub-directories for each chapter (for example, CH01). Each sub-directory contains all of the source code that is listed in that particular chapter. The BOOKSRC directory is designed to be an electronic reference that parallels the book chapters.

The second set of source files is located in the RAIZE\LIB directory. This directory contains the working set of components. That is, the components in this directory are the production versions, and they incorporate all of the features described in this chapter. In particular, all of the source files include the RAIZE.INC include file, which is shown in Listing 16.6

Listing 16.6 RAIZE.INC—Common Include File for Raize Components

```
{============================================================}
{= Raize Include File                                      =}
{=                                                         =}
{= This file is included in each component unit and serves as a common   =}
{= place to add conditional defines and compiler directives to be used by all =}
{= component units.                                        =}
{=                                                         =}
{= Building Custom Delphi Components - Ray Konopka          =}
{= Copyright © 1995 by Raize Software Solutions, Inc.      =}
{============================================================}
```

```
{== Code Generation Directives ==}

{$F-}     { Force Far Calls }
{$A+}     { Word Align Data }
{$U-}     { Pentium-Save FDIV }
{$K-}     { Smart Callbacks }
{$W-}     { Windows Stack Frame }


{== Runtime Errors ==}

{$IFOPT D+}
  {$R+}     { Range Checking - On - if compiled with Debug Information }
{$ELSE}
  {$R-}     { Range Checking - Off - if compiled without Debug Information }
{$ENDIF}

{$S+}     { Stack Checking }
{$I+}     { I/O Checking }
{$Q-}     { Overflow Checking }


{== Syntax Options ==}

{$V-}     { Strict Var-Strings }
{$B-}     { Complete Boolean Evaluation }
{$X+}     { Extended Syntax }
{$T-}     { Typed @ Operator }
{$P+}     { Open Parameters }


{== Miscellaneous Directives ==}

{$C MOVEABLE DEMANDLOAD DISCARDABLE}     { Code Segment Attribute }
{$G+}     { 286 Instructions }
{$N+}     { Numeric Coprocessor }
{$Z-}     { Word Size Enumerated Types }
```

An interesting aspect of this include file is that it does not specify any settings for the $D, $L, or $Y directives. This is because these directives are associated with including debug information into the compiled unit. Since these options have no impact on how the code is compiled, it is not necessary to specify these. Besides, when a library is built for distribution, debug information is usually turned off. However, the component user may opt to recompile the source code and include debug information. The point is that the common include file does not prevent the user from doing this.

Also notice that this is an include file and not a unit file. Therefore, the Object Pascal include file directive $I is used to effectively embed the contents of the

RAIZE.INC file into the current source file. As an example, the following code fragment shows the first few lines of the RzPrgres unit:

```
{=============================================================}
{= RzPrgres Unit                                            =}
{=                                                          =}
{= Building Custom Delphi Components - Ray Konopka          =}
{=============================================================}

{$I RAIZE.INC}

unit RzPrgres;

interface

uses
  WinTypes, Classes, Graphics, Controls, Menus, ExtCtrls, RzCommon;

type
  TProgressBorderStyle = ( bsFlat, bsCtl3D, bsStatusControl );
  TProgressOrientation = ( poHorizontal, poVertical );
  TPercentRange = 0..100;
  TProgressChangeEvent = procedure(Sender: TObject; Percent: Integer) of object;

  TRzProgressBar = class( TGraphicControl )
  private
```

What if you have a component unit that needs to use a different compiler directive? In situations like this, specify the new directive *after* the include file statement. This way, you can essentially override any of the common settings on a unit by unit basis.

Installation Issues

There are two issues with respect to installing Delphi components. The first one involves copying the component units from a distribution disk to a user's hard disk. The recommended method is to copy all of your component units to a single directory. This is important because the Delphi search path is limited to only 127 characters. Installing your components into more than one directory means taking up extra space on the search path.

The second install issue is with respect to installing the components in Delphi. Although each component unit provides a **Register** procedure, you should avoid having the user install each component unit individually. A better approach is to create a registration unit for your library of components. The purpose of the registration unit is to provide a way for the end user to install all of your components by installing just a single unit.

The Registration Unit

Listing 16.7 shows the source code for the RaizeReg unit. This registration unit is located in the RAIZE\LIB directory on the enclosed CD. This directory contains the production versions of all the components built in this book.

The RaizeReg unit simply includes each component unit on its **uses** clause, and then calls each component unit's **Register** procedure from within its own **Register** procedure. Therefore, when the user installs the RaizeReg unit, all of the components will be installed.

> **By Convention**
>
> The name of the registration unit ends with "Reg" and starts with an identifier representing the collection of components. The Reg suffix makes it easier for end users to find the registration unit during the install process.

Listing 16.7 RAIZEREG.PAS—Registration Unit for Raize Components

```
{===============================================================}
{= RaizeReg Unit                                              =}
{=                                                            =}
{= Registration Unit for all components from Raize Software Solutions, Inc.  =}
{= To install these components add this unit to the list      =}
{= of Installed Units in Delphi's Options|Install Components dialog.  =}
{=                                                            =}
{= Building Custom Delphi Components - Ray Konopka            =}
{===============================================================}

unit RaizeReg;

interface

procedure Register;

implementation

uses
```

```
Forms, Classes, Controls, SysUtils, RzAbout,
RzBtn, RzPanel, RzLabel, RzLblEdt, RzTabLst, RzTabEdt,
RzStatus, RzPrgres, RzTrkBar, RzBWCC, RzAddr, RzLaunch,
RzMail, RzLookup, RzDBSpin, RzDBEmp, RzStrEdt;


{============================}
{== Register Procedure ==}
{============================}

procedure Register;
begin
  RzBtn.Register;
  RzPanel.Register;
  RzLabel.Register;
  RzLblEdt.Register;
  RzTabLst.Register;
  RzTabEdt.Register;
  RzStatus.Register;
  RzPrgres.Register;
  RzTrkBar.Register;
  RzBWCC.Register;
  RzAddr.Register;
  RzLaunch.Register;
  RzMail.Register;
  RzLookup.Register;
  RzDBSpin.Register;
  RzDBEmp.Register;
  RzStrEdt.Register;
  RzAbout.Register;
end;


end.
```

If you look at some of the registration units that ship with Delphi (for example, StdReg) you'll see the registration unit's **Register** procedure has actual calls to **RegisterComponents, RegisterPropertyEditor,** and **RegisterComponentEditor.** The philosophy behind this approach is that the burden of registration is removed from each component unit and placed in a single file.

However, I find the approach demonstrated by the RaizeReg unit to be more flexible. In particular, the RaizeReg unit supports installing a subset of the components. That is, the user could opt to install just the RzMail and RzLabel units. Of course, each one would have to be installed separately, but this is not even possible if all the register procedures are placed in one file.

The Component Resource File

Back in Chapter 7, we talked about how to create the component resource file for a component. In that discussion, it was stated that a component resource file should be created for each component unit. This is sufficient when a single component is installed, but when a registration unit is installed, none of the component DCR files will be detected by Delphi. As the registration unit is being installed, Delphi searches for a DCR file using the name of the registration unit, and since it doesn't exist, none of the component bitmaps is installed.

Fortunately, this problem can be handled. Instead of creating separate DCR files for each component, create a single DCR file containing all of the bitmaps. Since DCR files are just Windows RES files in disguise, there is no problem storing any number of bitmaps in a DCR file. This is demonstrated in Figure 16.7, which shows the RAIZEREG.DCR file being edited by Resource Workshop.

 Do not underestimate the importance of well designed bitmaps to represent your components. The component bitmaps are the first impression users will have of your components. Unprofessional bitmaps give the impression of unprofessional components. If you are in the business of building components for the commercial market, you may want to get a professional graphics artist to design the bitmaps.

Figure 16.7

Editing the RaizeReg Component Resource File.

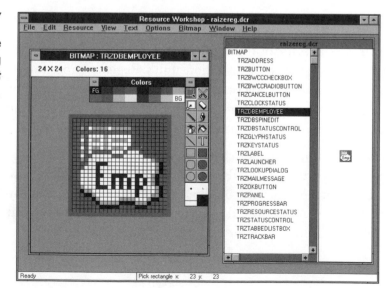

End of Construction

In the first fifteen chapters, this area was called *Looking Ahead*. The former title worked well because there was always some aspect of building custom Delphi components that still needed to be covered. Now, at the end of this chapter, the construction project that was started way back in Chapter 1 is complete. And what a project is was! Over twenty different custom components, three property editors, one component editor, some online help, and several supporting classes.

One of my primary goals in writing this book was to provide a wide variety of component examples that cover virtually every aspect of building custom Delphi components. The components also had to be more than just demonstrations. To be truly effective models, they needed to be capable of being sold as a commercial package. In fact, this was the driving force behind the creation of the Raize Component Library. The experience I gained in creating this library is expressed throughout this entire book, especially in the Tips and By Convention blocks.

Delphi is truly a remarkable tool. Delphi is the only development environment that encourages developers to create custom components. Hopefully, this book will do the same!

Best of Luck!

Appendices

Moving to Delphi32

With a new version of Delphi entering the marketplace, you may be wondering if the information in this book is still relevant. The simple answer to this is, *yes!* Even though the examples in this book are presented running under Windows 3.X, all of the material covered in this book is equally applicable to the 32-bit version of Delphi.

Now you may be wondering, how is this possible, considering the fundamental differences between Windows 3.X, Windows 95, and Windows NT? This level of support is possible because, from the beginning, the Visual Component Library (VCL) was designed to be fully compatible across all three platforms. In fact, during the development of Delphi for Windows (Delphi16), a 16-bit version and a 32-bit version of the VCL were being developed concurrently. And before Delphi16 was released, Borland had a working version of the VCL running under Windows NT and Windows 95.

The object-oriented nature of the VCL allows it to abstract many of the differences between these different operating systems and make them transparent to the developer. This greatly simplifies the migration path from Delphi16 to Delphi32. Actually, for most components, moving to 32 bits will simply require recompiling the component unit with Delphi32.

Notice that I said most components. As usual, there are always exceptions to deal with when moving from one operating system to another. But also note that the problems that do occur result from changes in the underlying operating system, and its application programming interface (API), rather than from some deficiency in the VCL. To be more specific, problems occur only when a developer writes code that relies on a feature available in 16-bit Windows but not Win32. For example, any code that relies on the segmented nature of Windows 3.X will not compile under Delphi32.

That's an easy one. However, there are more subtle issues that become evident when you begin to move to 32-bit Windows. This appendix highlights several of the portability problems that you may encounter when converting your components. There are four general areas that deserve attention:

- Unsupported Functions
- Calling Conventions
- Long Strings
- Resource File Format

Unsupported Functions

Because the segmented architecture of Windows 3.X is replaced with a flat 32-bit address space in Windows 95 and Windows NT, there are a number of features that are no longer supported. Table A.1 shows that the segment oriented run-time library functions of Delphi16 are no longer available in Delphi32. For this same reason, Table A.2 lists a number of exception classes that are no longer raised in 32-bit Windows.

Table A.1 Obsolete RTL Functions in Delphi32		
CSeg	PrefixSeg	Seg
DSeg	PtrRec	Ofs
SSeg	SPtr	Ptr

Table A.2 Unsupported Exception Classes in Delphi32	
EBreakpoint	EPageFault
EFault	EProcessorException
EGPFault	ESingleStep
EInavlidOpCode	EStatckFault

However, the number of RTL functions missing from Delphi32 is trivial compared to the differences between the Win16 API and the Win32 API. Table A.3 lists all 110 Win16 API functions that are either no longer supported or significantly different under Win32.

Table A.3 Windows API Functions that Have Changed in Win32

Function Name	Dropped	Enhanced	Comments
AccessResource	x		
AddFontResource		x	Must use string, not handle, for filename
AllocDSToCSAlias	x		
AllocResource	x		
AllocSelector	x		
ChangeSelector	x		
CloseComm	x		Use CloseFile instead
CloseSound	x		Use MMSystem sound functions instead
CountVoiceNotes	x		Use MMSystem sound functions instead
DefineHandleTable	x		
DeviceCapabilities	x		Use DeviceCapabilitiesEx instead
DeviceMode	x		Use DeviceModeEx instead
DlgDirSelect	x		Use DlgDirSelectEx instead
DlgDirSelectComboBox	x		Use DlgDirSelectComboBoxEx instead
DOS3Call	x		Use named, portable Win32 API instead
ExtDeviceMode	x		Use ExtDeviceModeEx instead
FlushComm	x		Use PurgeComm instead
FreeSelector	x		
GetAspectRatioFilter	x		Use GetAspectRatioFilterEx instead
GetBitmapDimension	x		Use GetBitmapDimensionEx instead
GetBrushOrg	x		Use GetBrushOrgEx instead
GetClassWord		x	Most GCW_* values are no longer 16-bit
GetCodeHandle	x		
GetCodeInfo	x		
GetCommError	x		Use GetCommState instead
GetCurrentPDB	x		
GetCurrentPosition	x		Use GetCurrentPositionEx instead
GetEnvironment	x		
GetFreeSpace	x		Use GlobalMemoryStatus instead

Table A.3 Windows API Functions that Have Changed in Win32 (continued)

Function Name	Dropped	Enhanced	Comments
GetFreeSystemResources	x		Use GlobalMemoryStatus instead
GetInstanceData	x		
GetKBCodePage	x		
GetMetaFileBits	x		Use GetMetaFileBitsEx instead
GetModuleUsage	x		
GetTempDrive	x		
GetTextExtent	x		Use GetTextExtentPoint instead
GetTextExtentEx	x		Use GetTextExtentExPoint instead
GetThresholdEvent	x		Use MMSystem sound functions instead
GetThresholdStatus	x		Use MMSystem sound functions instead
GetViewportExt	x		Use GetViewportExtEx instead
GetViewportOrg	x		Use GetViewportOrgEx instead
GetWindowExt	x		Use GetWindowExtEx instead
GetWindowOrg	x		Use GetWindowOrgEx instead
GetWindowWord		x	Window information now stored as 32-bits
GlobalCompact	x		
GlobalDosAlloc	x		
GlobalDosFree	x		
GlobalFix	x		
GlobalLRUNewest	x		
GlobalLRUOldest	x		
GlobalNotify	x		
GlobalPageLock	x		
GlobalPageUnlock	x		
GlobalUnfix	x		
GlobalUnwire	x		
GlobalWire	x		
LimitEMSPages	x		
LocalCompact	x		
LocalInit	x		
LocalNotify	x		
LocalShrink	x		
LockSegment	x		
MoveTo	x		Use MoveToEx instead
NetBIOSCall	x		

Table A.3   Windows API Functions that Have Changed in Win32 (continued)

Function Name	Dropped	Enhanced	Comments
OffsetViewportOrg	x		Use OffsetViewportOrgEx instead
OffsetWindowOrg	x		Use OffsetWindowOrgEx instead
OpenComm	x		Use OpenFile instead
OpenSound	x		Use MMSystem sound functions instead
ProfClear	x		
ProfFinish	x		
ProfFlush	x		
ProfInsChk	x		
ProfSampRate	x		
ProfSetup	x		
ProfStart	x		
ProfStop	x		
ReadComm	x		Use ReadFile instead
RemoveFontResource		x	Must use string, not handle, for filename
ScaleViewportExt	x		Use ScaleViewportExtEx instead
ScaleWindowExt	x		Use ScaleWindowExtEx instead
SetBitmapDimension	x		Use SetBitmapDimensionEx instead
SetClassWord		x	Most GCW_* values are no longer 16-bit
SetCommEventMask	x		Use SetCommMask instead
SetEnvironment	x		
SetMetaFileBits	x		Use SetMetaFileBitsEx instead
SetResourceHandler	x		
SetSoundNoise	x		Use MMSystem sound functions instead
SetSwapAreaSize	x		
SetViewportExt	x		Use SetViewportExtEx instead
SetViewportOrg	x		Use SetViewportOrgEx instead
SetVoiceAccent	x		Use MMSystem sound functions instead
SetVoiceEnvelope	x		Use MMSystem sound functions instead
SetVoiceNote	x		Use MMSystem sound functions instead
SetVoiceQueueSize	x		Use MMSystem sound functions instead
SetVoiceSound	x		Use MMSystem sound functions instead
SetVoiceThreshold	x		Use MMSystem sound functions instead
SetWindowExt	x		Use SetWindowExtEx instead
SetWindowOrg	x		Use SetWindowOrgEx instead
SetWindowWord		x	Window information now stored as 32-bits

Table A.3 Windows API Functions that Have Changed in Win32 (continued)

Function Name	Dropped	Enhanced	Comments
StartSound	x		Use MMSystem sound functions instead
StopSound	x		Use MMSystem sound functions instead
SwitchStackBack	x		
SwitchStackTo	x		
SyncAllVoices	x		Use MMSystem sound functions instead
UngetCommChar	x		
UnlockSegment	x		
ValidateCodeSegments	x		
ValidateFreeSpaces	x		
WaitSoundState	x		Use MMSystem sound functions instead
WriteComm	x		Use WriteFile instead

Notice that about half of the functions are replaced by some other Win32 specific function. That's the good news. The bad news is that the other half of the functions are not supported at all in Win32, which can create a serious problem when converting a component.

I ran into this exact problem when converting the **RzLauncher** component. Recall from Chapter 11 that the **RzLauncher** component provides an **OnFinished** event that gets generated when the application that was launched by the component terminates. Unfortunately, the **TRzLauncher** class utilized the **GetModuleUsage** function to determine if the launched application was still running. You will note that **GetModuleUsage** is one of the functions listed in Table A.3.

To provide this same functionality under Win32, I had to use a different method of determining whether or not an application was still active. This required switching from a task-oriented approach to a process-oriented approach. The key was to use the **GetProcessExitCode** Win32 API function to determine if the process was still active. However, in order to use the **GetProcessExitCode** function, you need the handle of the process to query. Fortunately, the extended version of **ShellExecute**, **ShellExecuteEx**, provides a simple way to get the process handle.

Listing A.1 shows the source code for the new and improved **RzLaunch** unit. Notice the use of conditional compilation. Delphi32 automatically defines the **WIN32** symbol—and Delphi16 does not. Therefore, by using the {$IFDEF} directive, the **RzLaunch** unit can be compiled under both Delphi16 and Delphi32.

Listing A.1   RZLAUNCH.PAS—Dual Platform RzLaunch Unit

```
{================================================================}
{= RzLaunch Unit                                                =}
{=                                                              =}
{= This unit implements the TRzLauncher component. This component is used to =}
{= launch an application from within a Delphi application. To actually run =}
{= the desired program, the ShellExecute function is used.      =}
{=                                                              =}
{= Building Custom Delphi Components - Ray Konopka              =}
{================================================================}

{$I RAIZE.INC}

unit RzLaunch;

interface

uses
  SysUtils, WinTypes, WinProcs, Messages, Classes, Graphics, Controls,
  Forms, Dialogs, ExtCtrls, RzCommon;

type
  ELaunchError = class( Exception )                { Custom Exception Class }
    ErrorCode : Integer;
  end;

  TShowMode = ( smNormal, smMaximized, smMinimized );

const
  ShowWindowModes : array[ TShowMode ] of Integer =
    ( sw_Normal, sw_ShowMaximized, sw_ShowMinimized );

type
  TRzLauncher = class(TComponent)
  private
    FHInstance : THandle;
    {$IFDEF WIN32}
    FProcessHnd : THandle;
    {$ENDIF}
    FProgramName : string;
    FParameters : string;
    FShowMode : TShowMode;
    FStartDir : string;
    FTimer : TTimer;
    FOnFinished : TNotifyEvent;
  protected
    procedure Finished; dynamic;
    {$IFDEF WIN32}
    function AppHasTerminated : Boolean;
    {$ENDIF}
    procedure TimerExpired( Sender : TObject );
  public
    constructor Create( AOwner : TComponent ); override;
```

```
    destructor Destroy; override;
    procedure Launch;

    property HInstance : THandle                          { Read Only Property }
      read FHInstance;
  published
    property ProgramName : string
      read FProgramName
      write FProgramName;

    property Parameters : string
      read FParameters
      write FParameters;

    property ShowMode : TShowMode
      read FShowMode
      write FShowMode
      default smNormal;

    property StartDir : string
      read FStartDir
      write FStartDir;

    property OnFinished : TNotifyEvent
      read FOnFinished
      write FOnFinished;
  end;

procedure Register;

implementation


uses
  ShellApi, LnchMsgs;


function CreateLaunchError( ErrCode : Integer ) : ELaunchError;
begin
  Result := ELaunchError.Create( LoadStr( SLaunchOutOfMemory + ErrCode ) );
  Result.ErrorCode := ErrCode;
end;




{==========================}
{== TRzLauncher Methods ==}
{==========================}

constructor TRzLauncher.Create( AOwner : TComponent );
begin
  inherited Create( AOwner );
```

```
    FShowMode := smNormal;
    FTimer := TTimer.Create( Self );
    FTimer.Enabled := False;
    FTimer.OnTimer := TimerExpired;
    FHInstance := 0;
  end;


destructor TRzLauncher.Destroy;
begin
  FTimer.Enabled := False;                                    { Turn Off Timer }
  inherited Destroy;
end;


procedure TRzLauncher.Finished;
begin
  if Assigned( FOnFinished ) then
    FOnFinished( Self );
end;


{$IFDEF WIN32}

function TRzLauncher.AppHasTerminated : Boolean;
var
  ExitCode : DWord;
begin
  GetExitCodeProcess( FProcessHnd, ExitCode );
  Result := ExitCode <> still_Active;
end;


procedure TRzLauncher.TimerExpired( Sender : TObject );
begin
  if AppHasTerminated then
  begin
    FHInstance := 0;
    FTimer.Enabled := False;
    Finished;
  end;
end;

{$ELSE}

procedure TRzLauncher.TimerExpired( Sender : TObject );
begin
  { This is not the most reliable way of determining if the app }
  { is still running, but it works under most circumstances. }
  if GetModuleUsage( FHInstance ) = 0 then
  begin
    FHInstance := 0;
```

```
    FTimer.Enabled := False;
    Finished;
  end;
end;

{$ENDIF}


procedure TRzLauncher.Launch;
var
  PgmStz : array[ 0..255 ] of Char;
  ParamStz : array[ 0..255 ] of Char;
  DirStz : array[ 0..255 ] of Char;
  {$IFDEF WIN32}
  ShellInfo : TShellExecuteInfo;
  {$ELSE}
  Hnd : THandle;
  {$ENDIF}
begin
  FHInstance := 0;
  StrPCopy( PgmStz, FProgramName );
  StrPCopy( ParamStz, FParameters );
  StrPCopy( DirStz, FStartDir );

  {$IFDEF WIN32}

  FillChar( ShellInfo, SizeOf( TShellExecuteInfo ), 0 );
  ShellInfo.cbSize := SizeOf( TShellExecuteInfo );
  ShellInfo.fMask := SEE_MASK_NOCLOSEPROCESS;
  ShellInfo.Wnd := HWnd_Desktop;
  ShellInfo.lpFile := PgmStz;
  ShellInfo.lpParameters := ParamStz;
  ShellInfo.lpDirectory := DirStz;
  ShellInfo.nShow := ShowWindowModes[ FShowMode ];

  if ShellExecuteEx( @ShellInfo ) then
  begin
    FHInstance := ShellInfo.hInstApp;
    FProcessHnd := ShellInfo.hProcess;                    { Get Process Handle }
    FTimer.Enabled := True;                                      { Start Timer }
  end
  else
    raise CreateLaunchError( ShellInfo.hInstApp )

  {$ELSE}

  Hnd := ShellExecute( HWnd_Desktop, 'open', PgmStz, ParamStz, DirStz,
                       ShowWindowModes[ FShowMode ] );
  if Hnd <= 32 then
    raise CreateLaunchError( Hnd )
  else
  begin
    FHInstance := Hnd;
```

```
    FTimer.Enabled := True;                                      { Start Timer }
  end;

  {$ENDIF}

end; {= TRzLauncher.Launch =}


{=========================}
{== Register Procedure ==}
{=========================}

procedure Register;
begin
  RegisterComponents( RaizePage, [ TRzLauncher ] );
end;

end.
```

Calling Conventions

Delphi32 introduces many new compiler optimizations that are automatically performed by the compiler. The optimizations involve increasing register utilization, eliminating call stack overhead, removing common subexpressions, and introducing loop induction variables. All of the optimizations are guaranteed to be correct and in no way change the meaning of the code.

To support many of these optimizations, a strong emphasis on register usage has been incorporated into Delphi32. For example, heavily used variables are automatically placed into registers, which reduces access time. This in turn allows the compiler to generate faster and more compact code, because it's not necessary to move variable contents from memory into registers.

Not only does the compiler use registers whenever possible, it uses them efficiently. That is, the compiler analyzes a variable's usage to determine if a register can be reused. For example, if two variables are used exclusively in different sections of code, the compiler is able to use a single register for both variables.

In addition to utilizing registers for variables, the compiler will also attempt to use registers when passing parameters to procedures and functions. Delphi32 introduces a new calling convention, dubbed fastcall, in which the first three parameters that will fit into a 32-bit register are placed in the EAX, EDX, and ECX registers, respectively. Any remaining parameters are passed using the stack-oriented Pascal calling convention.

For procedures and functions in which all of the parameters can be placed into registers, a stack frame is not needed to temporarily hold the values. By eliminating the need to generate extra code for creating and destroying the stack frame, procedure and function calls are more efficient.

This sounds great—so what's the problem? Under Windows 3.X, the default calling convention in Delphi is **pascal**, which is the same convention used by the virtually all Win16 API functions. However, when moving to Windows 95 or Windows NT, the default calling convention changes. Unfortunately, Delphi32 and Win32 use different default conventions. Specifically, Delphi32 uses **fastcall** while Win32 uses yet another calling convention called **stdcall**.

You need to be aware of this difference whenever you create a declaration for a procedure or function defined in a dynamic link library (DLL). In order for the function to work properly, the Delphi32 declaration of the function must specify the **stdcall** directive. This ensures that the parameters passed to the function are passed in the correct order, and in the correct manner.

I ran into this problem when converting the RzMailMessage component. Recall from Chapter 11 that this component utilizes the Simple MAPI functions. These functions are defined in MAPI.DLL and are accessible through the SmplMapi unit. Unfortunately, the SmplMapi unit from Chapter 11 will not work under Delphi32. First, MAPI.DLL is a 16-bit DLL. MAPI32.DLL must be used under Delphi32. Second, the Simple MAPI functions defined in MAPI32.DLL are declared using the **stdcall** calling convention.

Converting the SmplMapi unit to be used in both Delphi16 and Delphi32 is relatively simple. Listing A.2 shows that the 12 Simple MAPI functions are declared twice, with each set residing in a conditional block. The functions are identical in both conditional blocks except that the WIN32 versions are terminated with the **stdcall** directive.

Also note that the correct DLL is used by placing the **MAPI_DLL** constant declaration in a conditional block. The constant is then used in the external function declarations at the end of the unit.

 When creating a dual platform import unit, be careful when declaring the external function declarations. There are several ways in which the function can be mapped to the entry point in the DLL. If you opt to reference the external function using its index in the DLL, as was done in the version from Chapter 11, be sure that the index values used in both DLLs are the same. They are not always the same, as is the case with the MAPI and MAPI32 DLLs. Therefore, the new version of the SmplMapi unit references the external functions by name.

Listing A.2   SMPLMAPI.PAS - Delphi32 Compatible SmplMapi Unit

```
{================================================================}
{- SmplMapi Unit                                               -}
{-                                                             -}
{- This is an interface unit to the constants, types, procedures, and  -}
{- functions defined for the Simple Messaging API. (i.e. MAPI.DLL)     -}
{-                                                             -}
{- Building Custom Delphi Components - Ray Konopka             -}
{================================================================}

{$I RAIZE.INC}

unit SmplMapi;

interface

. . .                             { Types and Constants Removed for Readability }

{-- The 12 Simple MAPI Functions --}

{$IFDEF WIN32}
function MapiLogon( WndParent : Longint; Name, Password : PChar;
                    Flags, Reserved : Longint;
                    var Session : Longint ) : Longint; stdcall;

function MapiLogoff( Session, WndParent,
                     flFlags, ulReserved : Longint ) : Longint; stdcall;

function MapiSendMail( Session, WndParent : Longint;
                       var Msg : TMapiMessage;
                       Flags, Reserved : Longint ) : Longint; stdcall;

function MapiSendDocuments( WndParent : Longint;
                            DelimChar, FullPaths, FileNames : PChar;
                            Reserved : Longint ) : Longint; stdcall;

function MapiFindNext( Session, WndParent : Longint;
                       MessageType, SeedMessageID : PChar;
                       Flags, Reserved : Longint;
                       MessageID : PChar ) : Longint; stdcall;
```

```
function MapiReadMail( Session, WndParent : Longint;
                      MessageID : PChar; Flags, Reserved : Longint;
                      var MessageOut : PMapiMessage ) : Longint; stdcall;

function MapiSaveMail( Session, WndParent : Longint;
                       var Msg : TMapiMessage; Flags, Reserved : Longint;
                       MessageID : PChar ) : Longint; stdcall;

function MapiDeleteMail( Session, WndParent : Longint;
                         MessageID : PChar;
                         Flags, Reserved : Longint ) : Longint; stdcall;

function MapiFreeBuffer( Memory : Pointer ) : Longint; stdcall;

function MapiAddress( Session, WndParent : Longint;
                      Caption : PChar; EditFields : Longint;
                      Labels : PChar; RecipsCount : Longint;
                      var Recips : PMapiRecipDesc; Flags, Reserved : Longint;
                      NewRecipsCount : Pointer;
                      var NewRecips : PMapiRecipDesc ) : Longint; stdcall;

function MapiDetails( Session, WndParent : Longint;
                      var Recip : PMapiRecipDesc;
                      Flags, Reserved : Longint ) : Longint; stdcall;

function MapiResolveName( Session, WndParent : Longint;
                          Name : PChar; Flags, Reserved : Longint;
                          var Recip : PMapiRecipDesc ) : Longint; stdcall;

{$ELSE}

function MapiLogon( WndParent : Longint; Name, Password : PChar;
                    Flags, Reserved : Longint;
                    var Session : Longint ) : Longint;

function MapiLogoff( Session, WndParent,
                     flFlags, ulReserved : Longint ) : Longint;


function MapiSendMail( Session, WndParent : Longint;
                       var Msg : TMapiMessage;
                       Flags, Reserved : Longint ) : Longint;

function MapiSendDocuments( WndParent : Longint;
                            DelimChar, FullPaths, FileNames : PChar;
                            Reserved : Longint ) : Longint;

function MapiFindNext( Session, WndParent : Longint;
                       MessageType, SeedMessageID : PChar;
                       Flags, Reserved : Longint; MessageID : PChar ) : Longint;
```

```
function MapiReadMail( Session, WndParent : Longint;
                       MessageID : PChar; Flags, Reserved : Longint;
                       var MessageOut : PMapiMessage ) : Longint;

function MapiSaveMail( Session, WndParent : Longint;
                       var Msg : TMapiMessage; Flags, Reserved : Longint;
                       MessageID : PChar ) : Longint;

function MapiDeleteMail( Session, WndParent : Longint;
                         MessageID : PChar;
                         Flags, Reserved : Longint ) : Longint;

function MapiFreeBuffer( Memory : Pointer ) : Longint;

function MapiAddress( Session, WndParent : Longint;
                      Caption : PChar; EditFields : Longint;
                      Labels : PChar; RecipsCount : Longint;
                      var Recips : PMapiRecipDesc; Flags, Reserved : Longint;
                      NewRecipsCount : Pointer;
                      var NewRecips : PMapiRecipDesc ) : Longint;

function MapiDetails( Session, WndParent : Longint;
                      var Recip : PMapiRecipDesc;
                      Flags, Reserved : Longint ) : Longint;

function MapiResolveName( Session, WndParent : Longint;
                          Name : PChar; Flags, Reserved : Longint;
                          var Recip : PMapiRecipDesc ) : Longint;

{$ENDIF}

. . .

implementation

{$IFDEF WIN32}
const
  MAPI_DLL = 'MAPI32';
{$ELSE}
const
  MAPI_DLL = 'MAPI';
{$ENDIF}

function MapiLogon;          external MAPI_DLL name 'MAPILogon';
function MAPILogoff;         external MAPI_DLL name 'MAPILogoff';
function MAPISendMail;       external MAPI_DLL name 'MAPISendMail';
function MAPISendDocuments;  external MAPI_DLL name 'MAPISendDocuments';
function MAPIFindNext;       external MAPI_DLL name 'MAPIFindNext';
function MAPIReadMail;       external MAPI_DLL name 'MAPIReadMail';
function MAPISaveMail;       external MAPI_DLL name 'MAPISaveMail';
function MAPIDeleteMail;     external MAPI_DLL name 'MAPIDeleteMail';
```

```
function MAPIFreeBuffer;    external MAPI_DLL name 'MAPIFreeBuffer';
function MAPIAddress;       external MAPI_DLL name 'MAPIAddress';
function MAPIDetails;       external MAPI_DLL name 'MAPIDetails';
function MAPIResolveName;   external MAPI_DLL name 'MAPIResolveName';

end.
```

Long Strings

Delphi32 introduces several new language enhancements, but perhaps the most significant is the incorporation of long strings. Delphi32 now supports virtually unlimited length strings in addition to maintaining backward compatibility with traditional Pascal strings.

Delphi32 long strings combine the flexibility and ease-of-use of standard Pascal strings with the unlimited length capabilities of null-terminated strings. In fact, although long strings are terminated with a #0 character, they are compatible with both null-terminated strings *and* standard Pascal strings. And since long strings are automatically allocated from the heap, they do not require the overhead that is required with null-terminated strings.

Remarkably, no extra coding is needed to take advantage of this feature. By default, the **string** type automatically declares a long string. However, because long strings are allocated from the heap, it is not possible to directly modify the length of the string by altering the zero byte of the string. For example,

```
S[ 0 ] := L;
```

will have to be rewritten under Delphi32. The new **SetLength** and **SetString** functions must be used to allocate more memory to a string.

Resource File Format

Windows 95 and Windows NT do not use the same resource file format as Windows 3.X. This will cause a problem in any component that includes a resource file. For example, the RzTrackBar component stored all of the bitmaps used to represent the various thumbs in a resource file.

When moving this component to Delphi32, the code compiled without any problems. However, the component could not be linked into a test application or installed into Delphi because the RZTRKBAR.RES file was in the wrong format. The solution to this problem was to create the RZTBAR32.RES file. This file contains the same bitmaps that are stored in RZTRKBAR.RES, but in the Win32 format.

Listing A.3 shows how the RzTrkBar unit links in the appropriate resource file using conditional compilation. Notice that the **LoadThumbBitmaps** method has not been altered. This is because the bitmap names in both resource files are the same. From the component's perspective, it doesn't matter where it gets the bitmaps.

Listing A.3 RZTRKBAR.PAS—Delphi32 Compatible RzTrkBar Unit

```
{======================================================================}
{= RzTrkBar Unit                                                      =}
{=                                                                    =}
{= The TRzTrackBar component is a slider control that mimics the behavior of =}
{= the Windows 95 TrackBar control. This control works with mouse -and-  =}
{= keyboard input.                                                    =}
{=                                                                    =}
{= Building Custom Delphi Components - Ray Konopka                     =}
{======================================================================}


{$I RAIZE.INC}

unit RzTrkBar;

interface

uses
  Messages, WinTypes, WinProcs, Classes, Graphics, Controls, Menus,
  ExtCtrls, RzCommon;

type
  . . .

  TRzTrackBar = class( TCustomControl )
  private
    . . .
  protected
    . . .
  public
    . . .
  published
    . . .
  end;


procedure Register;
```

```
implementation

{$IFDEF WIN32}                              { Link in Bitmaps for Thumbs }
{$R RZTBAR32.RES}                                  { Win32 Resource File }
{$ELSE}
{$R RZTRKBAR.RES}                                  { Win16 Resource File }
{$ENDIF}


uses
  SysUtils;


{=========================}
{== TRzTrackBar Methods ==}
{=========================}


. . .


{ Array Constants hold all bitmap resource names for easy access }

const
  ThumbBitmapNames : array[ TTrackOrientation, TThumbSize ] of PChar =
    ( ( 'SmHorzThumb', 'MedHorzThumb', 'LgHorzThumb' ),
      ( 'SmVertThumb', 'MedVertThumb', 'LgVertThumb' ) );
  MaskBitmapNames : array[ TTrackOrientation, TThumbSize ] of PChar =
    ( ( 'SmHorzThumbMask', 'MedHorzThumbMask', 'LgHorzThumbMask' ),
      ( 'SmVertThumbMask', 'MedVertThumbMask', 'LgVertThumbMask' ) );
  BoxBitmapNames : array[ TTrackOrientation, TThumbSize ] of PChar =
    ( ( 'SmHorzBox', 'MedHorzBox', 'LgHorzBox' ),
      ( 'SmVertBox', 'MedVertBox', 'LgVertBox' ) );


procedure TRzTrackBar.LoadThumbBitmaps;
begin
  if FThumbStyle = tsPointer then
  begin
    FThumbBmp.Handle := LoadBitmap( HInstance,
                             ThumbBitmapNames[ FOrientation, FThumbSize ]);
    FMaskBmp.Handle := LoadBitmap( HInstance,
                            MaskBitmapNames[ FOrientation, FThumbSize ] );
  end
  else
  begin
    FThumbBmp.Handle := LoadBitmap( HInstance,
                             BoxBitmapNames[ FOrientation, FThumbSize ]);
  end;

  if FOrientation = toVertical then
  begin
    FThumbHeight := FThumbBmp.Width;
    FThumbWidth := FThumbBmp.Height;
  end
  else
```

```
  begin
    FThumbHeight := FThumbBmp.Height;
    FThumbWidth := FThumbBmp.Width;
  end;
  FHalfWidth := FThumbWidth div 2;
end; {= TRzTrackBar.LoadThumbBitmaps =}
```

Even if you do not create a component that requires a separate resource file, you will still run into the resource type conflict if you create a component resource file for your components. Recall that a Delphi Component Resource file (*.DCR) is simply a Windows RES file with a different extension. As such, DCR files that you create for Delphi16 are not compatible with Delphi32.

Unfortunately, there is no way to instruct Delphi to search for a different component resource file when it installs a component or registration unit. If you are using a registration unit, as recommended in Chapter 16, then you will need to create a separate version for installation under Delphi32.

Raize Component Library

All of the components presented in this book were initially built using Delphi 1.0 for Windows (Delphi16). And although this book was completed before Delphi32 was released, a pre-release version of Delphi32 was available for testing. Therefore, after each component was constructed in Delphi16, it was recompiled and tested under Delphi32. As a result, the source code for the Raize Component Library located in \RAIZE\LIB directory on the enclosed CD is compatible with both Delphi16 and Delphi32.

To install the components under Delphi32, you must use the RzReg32 registration unit also located in the \RAIZE\LIB directory. This unit must be used so that the corresponding RZREG32.DCR component resource file will be used by Delphi. The RZREG32.DCR file contains the same component bitmaps as RAIZEREG.DCR, but the former uses the Win32 resource file format.

Table A.4 summarizes the process of converting all of the components in the Raize Component Library. It took roughly a week to convert all of the components. Most of this however, was spent trying to figure out an alternative to **GetModuleUsage**. I also got hung up on trying to figure out why my mail component kept generating an access violation whenever I called a MAPI32 function. Of course, I did not have an appendix like this to help point me in the right direction. But, now you do!

Table A.4   Results from Moving Raize Component Library to Delphi32

Component	Installed by RzReg32	Changes Required	Comments
RzButton	Yes	No	
RzOKButton	Yes	No	
RzCancelButton	Yes	No	
RzPanel	Yes	No	
RzLabel	Yes	No	
RzTabbedListBox	No	N/A	No code changes. Compiles correctly. However, inherited Memo component does not handle tab stops correctly. Expected to operate correctly in released version.
RzProgressBar	Yes	No	
RzStatusControl	Yes	No	
RzGlyphStatus	No	N/A	Bug in field test prevents this component from compiling. Expected to work correctly in released version.
RzKeyStatus	Yes	No	
RzClockStatus	Yes	No	
RzDBStatusControl	Yes	No	
RzResourceStatus	Yes	Yes	GetFreeSystemResources API function no longer supported.
RzTrackBar	Yes	No	No code changes. Resource file needed to be updated.
RzBwccCheckBox	No	N/A	Did not port b/c only a 16-bit demonstration
RzBwccRadioButton	No	N/A	Did not port b/c only a 16-bit demonstration
RzAddress	Yes	No	
RzLauncher	Yes	Yes	GetModuleUsage no longer available. Resource file needed to be updated.
RzMailMessage	Yes	Yes	With long strings, GetText method of TStringList is no longer necessary, and not available in Delphi32. MapiMsgs resource files updated to Win32.
RzLookup	Yes	No	
RzDBSpinEdit	Yes	Yes	Custom painting updated to reflect Win95 controls
RzDBEmployee	Yes	No	

The Standard Exception Class Hierarchy

As we've discovered throughout the course of this book, it's often necessary to raise an exception within a custom component to indicate an error condition. The common approach is to create a new custom exception class specifically designed to classify the error condition. However, as more and more components are created, we may find that if a new exception class is created for each component, the object-oriented benefits of exception classification begin to deteriorate.

When you need to raise an exception in your components, it's a good idea to check to see if an existing exception class sufficiently classifies the error. If so, use it. If not, you might try descending from a class other than **Exception**. This gives component users the ability to classify types of errors in their exception handlers.

Of course, this is easier said than done. The standard exceptions are defined all throughout the VCL source files. Unfortunately, the Delphi *User's Guide* mentions only a few of the many classes that make up the hierarchy. The *VCL Reference* is a little better in providing descriptions for more of the exceptions, but some are still omitted. What's worse is that the hierarchy described in the *VCL Reference* is incorrect.

The following table displays all of the classes that make up the standard Delphi exception class hierarchy. Next to each class name is the unit in which its declaration can be found.

Table B.1 The Standard Exception Class Hierarchy

Exception Class	Unit
Exception	SysUtils
EAbort	SysUtils
EComponentError	Classes
EConvertError	SysUtils
EDatabaseError	DB
EDBEngineError	DB
EDBEditError	Mask
EDDEError	DDEMan
EInOutError	SysUtils
EIntError	SysUtils
EDivByZero	SysUtils
EIntOverflow	SysUtils
ERangeError	SysUtils
EInvalidCast	SysUtils
EInvalidGraphic	Graphics
EInvalidGraphicOperation	Graphics
EInvalidGridOperation	Grids
EInvalidOperation	Controls
EInvalidPointer	SysUtils
EListError	Classes
EMathError	SysUtils
EInvalidOp	SysUtils
EOverflow	SysUtils
EUnderflow	SysUtils
EZeroDivide	SysUtils
EMCIDeviceError	MPlayer
EMenuError	Menus

Exception Class	Unit
Table B.1 The Standard Exception Class Hierarchy (continued)	
EOutlineError	Outline
EOutOfMemory	SysUtils
EOutOfResources	Controls
EParserError	Classes
EPrinter	Printers
EProcessorException	SysUtils
EBreakpoint	SysUtils
EFault	SysUtils
EGPFault	SysUtils
EInvalidOpCode	SysUtils
EPageFault	SysUtils
EStackFault	SysUtils
ESingleStep	SysUtils
EPropertyError	DsgnIntf
EReportError	Report
EResNotFound	Classes
EStreamError	Classes
EFCreateError	Classes
EFilerError	Classes
EClassNotFound	Classes
EInvalidImage	Classes
EMethodNotFound	Classes
EReadError	Classes
EWriteError	Classes
EFOpenError	Classes
EStringListError	Classes

VCL Source Code Declaration Finder

Has this ever happened to you? You've purchased the Delphi VCL source code and you're working on a new component, and then you need to look up a class declaration or an enumerated type. The only problem is that you can't remember which source file contains the class declaration, so you spend several minutes scanning through the source files looking for the right one.

Tabel C.1 can help you quickly find the source file that contains a given type. The table lists all of the types that are declared in the interface sections of the Delphi VCL source files. All the types are listed alphabetically, so scanning for the desired type is a snap. Next to each type is the name of the unit that contains that type.

Table C.1 VCL Declarations

Type	Unit
TAlign	Controls
TAlignment	Classes
TApplication	Forms
TAttachMode	Outline
TAutoActivate	TOCtrl

Table C.1 VCL Declarations (continued)

Type	Unit
TBatchMode	DBTables
TBatchMove	DBTables
TBCDField	DBTables
TBevel	ExtCtrls
TBevelShape	ExtCtrls
TBevelStyle	ExtCtrls
TBevelWidth	ExtCtrls
TBitBtn	Buttons
TBitBtnKind	Buttons
TBitmap	Graphics
TBlobField	DBTables
TBlobStream	DBTables
TBlobStreamMode	DBTables
TBookmark	DB
TBooleanField	DBTables
TBorderIcons	Forms
TBorderStyle	Forms
TBorderWidth	ExtCtrls
TBrush	Graphics
TBrushStyle	Graphics
TButton	StdCtrls
TButtonLayout	Buttons
TButtonSet	MPlayer & DBCtrls
TButtonStyle	Buttons
TByteArray	SysUtils
TBytesField	DBTables
TCanvas	Graphics
TCaption	Controls
TCaptionProperty	DsgnIntf
TChangeRange	Outline
TCharProperty	DsgnIntf
TCheckBox	StdCtrls
TCheckBoxState	StdCtrls
TClassProperty	DsgnIntf

Table C.1 VCL Declarations (continued)

Type	Unit
TClipboard	Clipbrd
TCloseAction	Forms
TCloseEvent	Forms
TCloseQueryEvent	Forms
TColor	Graphics
TColorDialog	Dialogs
TColorDialogOptions	Dialogs
TColorProperty	DsgnIntf
TComboBox	StdCtrls
TComboBoxStyle	StdCtrls
TComponent	Classes
TComponentEditor	DsgnIntf
TComponentList	DsgnIntf
TComponentName	Classes
TComponentNameProperty	DsgnIntf
TComponentProperty	DsgnIntf
TControl	Controls
TControlCanvas	Controls
TControlScrollBar	Forms
TControlState	Controls
TControlStyle	Controls
TCopyMode	Graphics
TCreateModuleFlags	ToolIntf
TCurrencyField	DBTables
TCursor	Controls
TCursorProperty	DsgnIntf
TCustomCheckBox	StdCtrls
TCustomColors	Dialogs
TCustomComboBox	StdCtrls
TCustomControl	Controls
TCustomDBGrid	DBGrids
TCustomEdit	StdCtrls
TCustomGrid	Grids
TCustomGroupBox	StdCtrls

Table C.1	VCL Declarations (continued)
Type	**Unit**
TCustomLabel	StdCtrls
TCustomListBox	StdCtrls
TCustomMaskEdit	Mask
TCustomMemo	StdCtrls
TCustomOutline	Outline
TCustomPanel	ExtCtrls
TCustomRadioGroup	ExtCtrls
TDatabase	DB
TDataChangeEvent	DB
TDataMode	DDEMan
TDatasetNotifyEvent	DB
TDatasetState	DB
TDataSource	DB
TDateField	DBTables
TDateTime	System
TDateTimeField	DBTables
TDBCheckBox	DBCtrls
TDBComboBox	DBCtrls
TDBEdit	DBCtrls
TDBGrid	DBGrids
TDBGridOptions	DBGrids
TDBImage	DBCtrls
TDBListBox	DBCtrls
TDBLookupCombo	DBLookup
TDBLookupComboStyle	DBLookup
TDBLookupList	DBLookup
TDBLookupListOptions	DBLookup
TDBMemo	DBCtrls
TDBNavigator	DBCtrls
TDBRadioGroup	DBCtrls
TDBText	DBCtrls
TDDEClientConv	DDEMan
TDDEClientItem	DDEMan

Table C.1 VCL Declarations (continued)

Type	Unit
TDDEServerConv	DDEMan
TDDEServerItem	DDEMan
TDefaultEditor	DsgnIntf
TDesigner	Forms
TDirectoryListBox	FileCtrl
TDragDropEvent	Controls
TDragMode	Controls
TDragOverEvent	Controls
TDragState	Controls
TDrawCellEvent	Grids
TDrawDataCellEvent	DBGrids
TDrawGrid	Grids
TDrawItemEvent	StdCtrls
TDrawTabEvent	Tabs
TDriveComboBox	FileCtrl
TDuplicates	Classes
TEdit	StdCtrls
TEditCharCase	StdCtrls
TEndDragEvent	Controls
TEnumProperty	DsgnIntf
TExceptionEvent	Forms
TExpertState	ExptIntf
TExpertStyle	ExptIntf
TFDApplyEvent	Dialogs
TField	DB
TFieldGetTextEvent	DB
TFieldNotifyEvent	DB
TFieldSetTextEvent	DB
TFileEditStyle	Dialogs
TFileExt	Dialogs
TFileListBox	FileCtrl
TFieldClass	DB

Table C.1 VCL Declarations (continued)

Type	Unit
TFieldDef	DB
TFieldDefs	DB
TFieldType	DB
TFileName	SysUtils
TFiler	Classes
TFileRec	SysUtils
TFileStream	Classes
TFileType	FileCtrl
TFillStyle	Graphics
TFilterComboBox	FileCtrl
TFindDialog	Dialogs
TFindItemKind	Menus
TFindOptions	Dialogs
TFloatField	DBTables
TFloatFormat	SysUtils
TFloatProperty	DsgnIntf
TFloatRec	SysUtils
TFont	Graphics
TFontDialog	Dialogs
TFontDialogDevice	Dialogs
TFontDialogOptions	Dialogs
TFontName	Graphics
TFontNameProperty	DsgnIntf
TFontPitch	Graphics
TFontProperty	DsgnIntf
TFontStyles	Graphics
TForm	Forms
TFormBorderStyle	Forms
TFormDesigner	DsgnIntf
TFormState	Forms
TFormStyle	Forms
TGetEditEvent	Grids
TGraphic	Graphics

Table C.1 VCL Declarations (continued)	
Type	**Unit**
TGraphicControl	Controls
TGraphicField	DBTables
TGraphicsObject	Graphics
TGridDrawState	Grids
TGridOptions	Grids
TGridRect	Grids
TGroupBox	StdCtrls
THandleStream	Classes
THeader	ExtCtrls
THelpContent	Classes
THelpEvent	Classes
THintInfo	Forms
THintWindow	Controls
TIcon	Graphics
TIdleEvent	Forms
TIExpert	ExptIntf
TImage	ExtCtrls
TIndexDef	DBTables
TIndexDefs	DBTables
TIndexOptions	DB
TIniFile	IniFiles
TIntegerField	DBTables
TIntegerProperty	DsgnIntf
TInterface	VirtIntf
TIStream	VirtIntf
TIToolServices	ToolIntf
TKey	Controls
TKeyEvent	Controls
TKeyPressEvent	Controls
TLabel	StdCtrls
TLeftRight	Classes

Table C.1 VCL Declarations (continued)

Type	Unit
TList	Classes
TListBox	StdCtrls
TListBoxStyle	StdCtrls
TLocale	DB
TLoginEvent	DB
TMacroEvent	DDEMan
TMainMenu	Menus
TMaskEdit	Mask
TMeasureItemEvent	StdCtrls
TMeasureTabEvent	Tabs
TMediaPlayer	MPlayer
TMemo	StdCtrls
TMemoField	DBTables
TMemoryStream	Classes
TMenuBreak	Menus
TMenuItem	Menus
TMessageEvent	Forms
TMetafile	Graphics
TMethod	SysUtils
TMethodProperty	DsgnIntf
TModalResult	Forms
TModalResultProperty	DsgnIntf
TMouseButton	Controls
TMouseEvent	Controls
TMouseMoveEvent	Controls
TMovedEvent	Grids
TMPBtnType	MPlayer
TMPDevCapsSet	MPlayer
TMPDeviceTypes	MPlayer
TMPFilenameProperty	DsgnIntf
TMPModes	MPlayer
TMPNotifyValues	MPlayer
TMPTimeFormats	MPlayer
TMsgDlgButtons	Dialogs
TMsgDlgType	Dialogs

Table C.1 VCL Declarations (continued)

Type	Unit
TNavigateBtn	DBCtrls
TNotebook	ExtCtrls
TNotifyEvent	Classes
TNumGlyphs	Buttons
TOLEContainer	TOCtrl
TOLEDropNotify	TOCtrl
TOpenDialog	Dialogs
TOpenOptions	Dialogs
TOrdinalProperty	DsgnIntf
TOutline	Outline
TOutlineNode	Outline
TOutlineOptions	Outline
TOutlineStyle	Outline
TOutlineType	Outline
TOwnerDrawState	StdCtrls
TPaintBox	ExtCtrls
TPanel	ExtCtrls
TPanelBevel	ExtCtrls
TParam	DBTables
TParamBindMode	DBTables
TParams	DBTables
TParamType	DBTables
TPasswordEvent	DB
TPen	Graphics
TPenMode	Graphics
TPenStyle	Graphics
TPersistent	Classes
TPicture	Graphics
TPoint	WinTypes
TPopupAlignment	Menus
TPopupMenu	Menus
TPosition	Forms

Table C.1 VCL Declarations (continued)	
Type	**Unit**
TPrintDialog	Dialogs
TPrintDialogOptions	Dialogs
TPrinter	Printers
TPrinterOrientation	Printers
TPrinterSetupDialog	Dialogs
TPrintRange	Dialogs
TPrintScale	Forms
TPropertyAttribute	DsgnIntf
TPropertyAttributes	DsgnIntf
TPropertyEditor	DsgnIntf
TQuery	DBTables
TRadioButton	StdCtrls
TRadioGroup	ExtCtrls
TReader	Classes
TRect	WinTypes
TReplaceDialog	Dialogs
TReport	Report
TSaveDialog	Dialogs
TScreen	Forms
TScrollBar	StdCtrls
TScrollBarInc	Forms
TScrollBarKind	Forms
TScrollBox	Forms
TScrollCode	StdCtrls
TScrollEvent	StdCtrls
TScrollingWinControl	Forms
TScrollStyle	StdCtrls
TSearchRec	SysUtils
TSectionEvent	Headers
TSelectCellEvent	Grids
TSelectDirOpts	FileCtrl

Table C.1 VCL Declarations (continued)

Type	Unit
TSession	DB
TSetEditEvent	Grids
TSetElementProperty	DsgnIntf
TSetProperty	DsgnIntf
TShape	ExtCtrls
TShapeType	ExtCtrls
TShiftState	Classes
TShortCut	Menus
TShortCutProperty	DsgnIntf
TShowAction	Forms
TShowHintEvent	Forms
TSmallintField	DBTables
TSpeedButton	Buttons
TStatusLineEvent	TOCtrl
TStoredProc	DBTables
TStream	Classes
TStringField	DBTables
TStringGrid	Grids
TStringList	Classes
TStringProperty	DsgnIntf
TStrings	Classes
TSymbolStr	DB
TTabbedNotebook	TabNotBk
TTabChangeEvent	Tabs
TTable	DBTables
TTabOrder	Controls
TTabOrderProperty	DsgnIntf
TTabSet	Tabs
TTabStyle	Tabs
TTextCase	FileCtrl
TTextRec	SysUtils
TTileMode	Forms
TTimeField	DBTables

Table C.1 VCL Declarations (continued)	
Type	**Unit**
TTimer	ExtCtrls
TTranslation	DB
TVarBytesField	DBTables
TVarRec	System
TWinControl	Controls
TWindowState	Forms
TWinOleHelper	Forms
TWriter	Classes
TWordArray	SysUtils
TWordField	DBTables
TZoomFactor	TOCtrl

What's on the CD-ROM

The companion CD-ROM for this book contains all the source code from the book, as well as a huge assortment of freeware and shareware custom controls that have been created by other programmers.

Here is a breakdown of the directory structure of the CD-ROM:

\BOOKSRC   All the source code from the book, organized by chapter

\CONTROLS   A few files you may need to put into your WINDOWS \SYSTEM directory if you didn't perform a complete VB4 install

\RAIZE   A setup file that will install all the necessary files needed for the book's sample applications

The sample code listings in the \BOOKSRC directory are all explained in their respective chapters, so let me talk a little about the sample controls and demos I've included on the CD-ROM.

Keep in mind that all of the sample controls were written by someone else, and they most certainly want credit for their work. Often, the authors don't want money, but they would appreciate you sending them email describing the work you've done with (or on the) control. Check the ZIP files for a README file or some other form of documentation that will tell you what, if anything, the original author wants in return for use of the control.

The controls on the CD-ROM range from simple fixes to problems with Delphi's controls to complex image controls. Some controls have good documentation while others have none. It's up to you to experiment a little and explore the controls.

Many of these controls can be found online at the Coriolis Group's Delphi Explorer Web site (http://www.coriolis.com), so be sure to check this site for up-to-the-minute updates and for new controls. You can even upload your own controls if you want to share them with the world. Just send email to controls@coriolis.com) along with a short note explaining what you're sending, and then attach the controls and documentation.

Here are descriptions of a few of the more interesting custom controls that I've included on the CD-ROM.

Control: Button Page

Location: \CONTROLS\BTNPAGE.ZIP

Online: davidszk@ozemail.com.au

Description: Button Page stores a component or group of components, saves their properties, and offers the ability to recall them at any time when using a form. Button Page also has a built-in glyph manager that allows selection of any glyph and can automatically insert the glyph into a TBitBtn or TSpeedButton. Button Page can also keep track of projects (this utility has saved me hours in developing forms and managing projects). There are some quirky features that may not work properly, but overall I think you will find this utility to be useful.

Control: TCube

Location: \CONTROLS\SPINCUBE.ZIP

Description: This fun little control is great for adding a little graphics to your applications. I've used it many times as an icon or hourglass. All the control does is show a 2D representation of a 3D cube spinning. You can control the colors, shading, and rotation at design time and runtime. It's not extremely useful as it stands, but with a little work on your part, it can be customized for many different applications.

Control: TAlphaPanel

Location: \CONTROLS\ALPHABAR.ZIP

Online: 100116.3354@compuserve.com

Description: TAlphaPanel is a panel component that includes speedbuttons. TAlphaPanel was designed as an index panel that automatically moves users from place to place within an alphabetically sorted field of a database. It's a nice idea that may give you inspiration in developing your own database applications.

Control: Delphi Resource Editor

Location: \CONTROLS\DELPHRES.ZIP

Online: 100065.55@compuserve.com

Description: This is a very thoroughly tested and powerful resource editor for Delphi resource files. The resource editor can handle version information and string resources, process icon and bitmap resources, and perform may other helpful services. It does not take over all the functions of the resource editor that ships with Delphi; it is more of a complementary product, taking over where Delphi left off.

Control: Dtools Package

Location: \CONTROLS\DTOOLS10.ZIP

Online: 75212.664@compuserve.com

Description: This is a really cool package of freeware controls put together by Tim Noonan. He implemented several new types of buttons and knobs, and created a very cool LED display. If you want a non-standard look to your Windows applications, you have to check out these controls.

Control: TExecFile

Location: \CONTROLS\EXECFILE.ZIP

Online: 75024.2760@compuserve.com

Description: The TExecFile is a non-visual component that you place onto your form to allow easy execution of other Windows or DOS applications from within your own original Delphi application. Although running another application from within your own seems like no great task, I've had many programmers ask me how to do it. I think you will also find that use of this component beats fumbling around with code or special functions each time you wish to run an outside application. TExecFile may also be useful for chaining your Delphi application or executing multiple modules belonging to the same application.

Control: TBufferFile

Location: \CONTROLS\FILEBUFF.ZIP

Description: TBufferFile provides simple file buffering for Delphi. It works only with binary files and treats each file as a stream of bytes. Basically, it provides the same functionality as **BlockWrite**() and **BlockRead** on a Reset(f,1) untyped file. Also provided is a file called BUFFTEST.PAS, which is a visual test stub used to compare times between an unbuffered file and the current unit. Borland in its wisdom decided to remove TBufStream in this release; here's a suitable replacement.

Control: ImageLib VCL/DLL

Location: \CONTROLS\IMAGELIB.ZIP

Online: 74742,1444@compuserve.com

Description: The ImageLib VCLS\DLL is an inexpensive way to add JPEG, GIF, SCM, and PCX support to your applications. True, other image libraries support many more formats than ImageLib does, but those libraries are expensive and add a lot of overhead to your applications.

In addition, ImageLib adds DBMultiImage and DBMultiMedia controls to store and display JPEG, BMP, GIF, SCM, PCX, AVI, MOV, MID, WAV, and RMI multimedia files from a TBlobField in Paradox databases. Very powerful and very useful at a great price.

Control: TInstall

Location: \CONTROLS\INSTALL2.ZIP

Online: 73612.3477@compuserve.com

Description: The Install component provides generic installation services for applications written in Delphi. The TInstall component handles file copying, adding aliases to the BDE, and adding window groups and program items. The TInstall component also has events that allow you to override any or all of the default installation dialogs, at design time. And because the TInstall component is written in Delphi, you can create your own descendent types of the TInstall component. This is a great tool for creating fully customized installation routines. Install utilities are good, but don't always give you the level of control you need. So check this out.

Control: TOpenGrid

Location: \CONTROLS\MULTI.ZIP

Online: 76460.3450@compuserve.com

Description: Here's a handy little upgrade that fixes a shortcoming in one of Delphi's standard controls. The problem is that Delphi's DBGrid control does not wrap text when the contents of a text cell are too long to be fully displayed. TOpenGrid fixes this problem.

Control: TRotatel

Location: \CONTROLS\ROTATEL.ZIP

Online: 73730.2505@compuserve.com

Description: This control doesn't do much, but what it does do, it does well. Basically, what you get here is a rotating label control. The demo that's in the ZIP file shows you what the control can do. Very simple, but very useful.

Control: Screen Dream

Location: \CONTROLS\SCNDM10.ZIP

Description: The Screen Dream package was designed to assist you in developing Multimedia Packages. It is the first in a series called Coding Completely Optional. This first package contains three visual controls. It also contains source code to allow powerful, flexible and easy creation of toolbars.

- *TDevice_Independence*   The TDevice_Independence control allows you to create resolution-independent applications. You simply drop it on the form to create a full-screen application for any resolution.
- *TClientMove*   The TClientMove control lets you create captionless forms that can still be moved by the user. Its sole purpose is to allow the user to click in the client area of the form and drag it to another location on the screen.
- *TTileBgnd*   The TTileBgnd component lets you add tiled bitmap backgrounds to your forms. It gives you an easy way to add texture and style to your applications. It also allows you to put borders on these forms. The TTileBgnd component doesn't work on MDI forms, but does work on MDI child forms.

Control: TSmiley

Location: \CONTROLS\SMILEY.ZIP

Online: Just about everywhere!

Description: Some people have called this component a joke, while others have said it is the most revolutionary component ever dreamed up! You'll have to install this one and judge for yourself. Check out the README file in the ZIP file for more information.

Control: Winsock Connectivity

Location: \CONTROLS\SOCKET2.ZIP

Online: 71062,2754@compuserve.com

Description: The Sockets component provides Delphi with a component capable of performing TCP/IP sockets functions by interfacing with WINSOCK.DLL. To use this component you must have a Winsock 1.1 compatible TCP/IP stack. The control has been tested with Trumpet 2.1C, Chameleon 4.03, PC/TCP, and the native stacks in Windows NT and Windows 95. If you need to have low-level control of protocols like FTP, SMTP, and Finger, then this is a good place to start.

Control: TAutoBtn

Location: \CONTROLS\TAUTO13.ZIP

Online: http://widewest.com.au/aerosoft

Description: If you need a button component with a little more firepower than the standard Delphi button, TAutoBtn is the ticket. TAutoBtn includes many cool functions like masking, blinking, and alternative images. Very useful and very robust. Check out the component's Web site for the latest and greatest information and updates.

Control: TLHA

Location: \CONTROLS\TLHA.ZIP

Online: ian@adone.com

Description: If you don't know what LHA is, then you should. It's a compression method used quite extensively for many different functions. This control makes it easy to compress and decompress files and information using the LHA method. The control is actually just a wrapper for the LHA.DLL file that ships with the package. Make sure you look at all the README files for licensing information.

Control: TWebGif

Location: \CONTROLS\WEB.ZIP

Online: leviathan@dlep1.itg.ti.com

Description: The TWebGif component can retrieve and display GIF files retrieved from a given URL. You could use this control as part of your own custom Web browser or find a new use for it. Source code is included for your customization needs.

Control: Word API Wrapper

Location: \CONTROLS\WORDAPI.ZIP

Online: 100116.3455@compuscrve.com

Description: This is a translation of the Word API for Borland Pascal 7. It works with Borland's Delphi as well, and allows you to use some of the Word-specific functions within your own programs. It's pretty low-level stuff, but if you need word-processing power, it's a real time saver.

Control: TZoomDBDemo

Location: \CONTROLS\ZMEMO.ZIP

Online: Huw@cix.compulink.co.uk

Description: TZoomDbMemo is a descendent of the standard Delphi TDbMemo. It adds the ability to produce a zoomed Modal edit screen for viewing or changing the contents of the memo field—rather like that used by Microsoft Access. TZoomDbMemo also has properties for setting the Title text displayed on the zoomed edit window and optionally a status word (Edit, View, Insert) alongside the window title.

This is just a small sampling of all the components and modules provided for you. You will soon find that many of these controls are real time savers and you may wonder how you got by without them. Don't be afraid to experiment with the controls and even play with the source code to customize them even more.

INDEX